OLD FLEET STREET

THE
'VILLAGE LONDON'
SERIES
from
THE ALDERMAN PRESS

OLD FLEET STREET

by

WALTER THORNBURY

THE ALDERMAN PRESS

British Library Cataloguing in Publication Data.

Thornbury, Walter
    [Old and new London. Vol 1-2] Old Fleet Street.
    1. Fleet Street (London, England) ——— History
    I. [Old & new London. Vol 1-2] II. Title
    942. 1'2   DA685. F5

ISBN 0 946619 22 0

This edition published 1986
The Alderman Press, 1/7 Church Street,
Edmonton, London N9 9DR

Printed and bound in Great Britain
by The Camelot Press Ltd., Southampton.

CONTENTS.

———◆———

CONTENTS.

LIST OF ILLUSTRATIONS.

————•⋈•————

LONDON AS IT WAS AND AS IT IS.

WRITING the history of a vast city like London is like writing a history of the ocean—the area is so vast, its inhabitants are so multifarious, the treasures that lie in its depths so countless. What aspect of the great chameleon city shall one select? for, as Boswell, with more than his usual sense, once remarked, "London is to the politician merely a seat of government, to the grazier a cattle market, to the merchant a huge exchange, to the dramatic enthusiast a congeries of theatres, to the man of pleasure an assemblage of taverns." If we follow one path alone, we must neglect other roads equally important; let us, then, consider the metropolis as a whole, for, as Johnson's friend well says, "the intellectual man is struck with London as comprehending the whole of human life in all its variety, the contemplation of which is inexhaustible." In histories, in biographies, in scientific records, and in chronicles of the past, however humble, let us gather materials for a record of the great and the wise, the base and the noble, the odd and the witty, who have inhabited London and left their names upon its walls. Wherever the glimmer of the cross of St. Paul's can be seen, we shall wander from street to alley, from alley to street, noting almost every event of interest that has taken place there since London became a city.

Had it been our lot to write of London before the Great Fire, we should have only had to visit 65,000 houses. If in Dr. Johnson's time, we might have done like energetic Dr. Birch, and have perambulated the twenty-mile circuit of London in six hours' hard walking; but who now could put a girdle round the metropolis in less than double that time? The houses now grow by streets at a time, and the nearly four million inhabitants would take a lifetime to study. Addison probably knew something of London when he called it "an aggregate of various nations, distinguished from each other by their respective customs, manners, and interests—the St. James's courtiers from the Cheapside citizens, the Temple lawyers from the Smithfield drovers;" but what would the *Spectator* say now to the 157,600 domestic servants, the 33,600 commercial clerks, the 31,600 carpenters, the 81,900 dressmakers, the 31,000 shoemakers, the 23,500 tailors, the 12,000 butchers, the 7,100 publicans, &c., to which the population returns of 1871 depose, all of whom he would have to observe and visit before he could say he knew all the ways, oddities, humours—the joys and sorrows, in fact— of this great centre of civilisation?

The houses of old London are incrusted as thick with anecdotes, legends, and traditions as an old ship is with barnacles. Strange stories about strange men grow like moss in every crevice of its bricks. Let us, then, roll together like a great snowball the mass of information that time and our predecessors have accumulated, and reduce it to some shape and form. Old London is passing away even as we dip our pen in the ink, and we would fain erect quickly our itinerant photographic machine, and secure some views of it before it is gone. Roman London, Saxon London, Norman London, Elizabethan London, Stuart London, Queen Anne's London, we shall in turn rifle to fill our museum, on whose shelves the Roman lamp and the vessel full of tears will stand side by side with Vanessa's fan; the sword-knot of Rochester by the note-book of Goldsmith. The history of London is an epitome of the history of England. Few great men indeed that England has produced but have some associations that connect them with London. To be able to recall these associations in a London walk is a pleasure perpetually renewing, and to all intents inexhaustible.

Let us, then, at once, without longer halting at the gate, seize the pilgrim staff and start upon our voyage of discovery, through a dreamland that will be now Goldsmith's, now Gower's, now Shakespeare's, now Pope's London. In Cannon Street, by the old central milestone of London, grave Romans will meet us and talk of Cæsar and his legions. In Fleet Street we shall come upon Chaucer beating the malapert Franciscan friar; at Temple Bar, stare upwards at the ghastly Jacobite heads. In Smithfield we shall meet Froissart's knights riding to the tournament; in the Strand see the misguided Earl of Essex defending his house against Queen Elizabeth's troops, who are turning towards him the cannon on the roof of St. Clement's church.

But let us first, rather than glance at scattered pictures in a gallery which is so full of them, measure out, as it were, our future walks, briefly glancing at the special doors where we shall billet our readers. This brief summary will serve to broadly epitomise the subject, and will prove the ceaseless variety of interest which it involves.

We have selected Temple Bar, that old gateway, as a point of departure, because it is the centre, as near as can be, of historical London. It is in itself full of interest. We begin with it as a rude wooden building, which, after the Great Fire, Wren turned into an arch of stone, with a room above, where Messrs. Childs, the bankers, used to store their books and archives. The heads of some of the Rye House conspirators, in Charles II.'s time, first adorned the Bar; and after that, one after the other, many rash Jacobite heads, in 1715 and 1745, arrived at the same bad eminence. In many a royal procession and many a City riot, this gate has figured as a halting-place and a point of defence. The last rebel's head was blown down in 1772; and the last spike was not removed till the beginning of the present century. In the Popish Plot days of Charles II. vast processions used to come to Temple Bar to illuminate the supposed statue of Queen Elizabeth, in the south-east niche (though it probably really represented Anne of Denmark); and at great bonfires at the Temple gate the frenzied people burned effigies of the Pope, while thousands of squibs were discharged, with shouts that frightened the Popish Portuguese Queen, at that time living at Somerset House, forsaken by her dissolute scapegrace of a husband.

Turning our faces now towards the black dome that rises like a half-eclipsed planet over Ludgate Hill, we first pass along Fleet Street, a locality full to overflowing with ancient memorials, and in its modern aspect not less interesting. This street has been from time immemorial the high road for royal processions. Richard II. has passed along here to St. Paul's, his parti-coloured robes jingling with golden bells; and Queen Elizabeth, be-ruffled and be-fardingaled, has glanced at those gable-ends east of St. Dunstan's, as she rode in her cumbrous plumed coach to thank God at St. Paul's for the scattering and shattering of the Armada. Here Cromwell, a king in all but name and twice a king by nature, received the keys of the City, as he rode to Guildhall to preside at the banquet of the obsequious Mayor. William of Orange and Queen Anne both clattered over these stones to return thanks for victories over the French; so did George III., when he came to thank God for his partial restoration from insanity; and so did Queen Victoria in 1872, to give thanks for the recovery of the Prince of Wales from grievous sickness.

We recall many odd figures in this street: the old printers who succeeded Caxton, who published for Shakespeare or who timidly speculated in Milton's epic, that great product of a sorry age; next, the old bankers, who, at Child's and Hoare's, laid the foundations of permanent wealth, and from simple City goldsmiths were gradually transformed to great capitalists. Izaak Walton, honest shopkeeper and patient angler, eyes us from his latticed window near Chancery Lane; and close by we see the child Cowley reading the "Fairy Queen" in a window-seat, and already feeling in himself the inspiration of his later years. The lesser celebrities of later times call to us as we pass. Garrick's friend Hardham, of the snuff-shop; and that busy, vain demagogue, Alderman Waithman, whom Cobbett abused because he was not zealous enough for poor hunted Queen Caroline. Then there are the shop where barometers were first sold, the great watchmakers, Tompion and Pinchbeck, to chronicle, and the two churches to notice. St. Dunstan's is interesting for its early preachers, the good Romaine and the pious Baxter; and St. Bride's has anecdotes and legends of its own, and a peal of bells which have in their time excited as much admiration as those giant hammermen at the old St. Dunstan's clock, which are now in Regent's Park. The newspaper offices, too, furnish many curious illustrations of the progress of that great organ of modern civilisation, the press. At the "Devil" we meet Ben Jonson and his club; and at John Murray's old shop we stop to see Byron lunging with his stick at favourite volumes on the shelves, to the bookseller's great but concealed annoyance. Nor do we forget to sketch Dr. Johnson at Temple Bar, bantering his fellow Jacobite, Goldsmith, about the warning heads upon the gate; at Child's bank pausing to observe the dinnerless authors returning downcast at the rejection of brilliant but fruitless proposals; or stopping with Boswell, one hand upon a street post, to shake the night air with his Cyclopean laughter. Varied as the

colours in a kaleidoscope are the figures that will meet us in these perambulations; mutable as an opal are the feelings they arouse. To the man of facts they furnish facts; to the man of imagination, quick-changing fancies; to the man of science, curious memoranda; to the historian, bright-worded details, that vivify old pictures now often dim in tone; to the man of the world, traits of manners; to the general thinker, aspects of feelings and of passions which expand the knowledge of human nature; for all these many-coloured stones are joined by the one golden string of London's history.

But if Fleet Street itself is rich in associations, its side streets, north and south, are yet richer. Here anecdote and story are clustered in even closer compass. In these side binns lies hid the choicest wine; for when Fleet Street had long since become two vast rows of shops, authors, wits, poets, and memorable persons of all kinds, still inhabited the "closes" and alleys that branch from the main thoroughfare. Nobles and lawyers long dwelt round St. Dunstan's and St. Bride's. Scholars, poets, and literati of all kind, long sought refuge from the grind and busy roar of commerce in the quiet inns and "closes," north and south. In what was Shire Lane we come upon the great Kit-Kat Club, where Addison, Garth, Steele, and Congreve disported; and we look in on that very evening when the Duke of Kingston, with fatherly pride, brought his little daughter, afterwards Lady Mary Wortley Montagu, and, setting her on the table, proposed her as a toast. Following the lane down till it becomes a nest of coiners, thieves, and bullies, we pass on to Bell Yard, to call on Pope's lawyer friend, Fortescue; and in Chancery Lane we are deep among the lawyers again. Ghosts of Jarndyces v. Jarndyces, from the Middle Ages downwards, haunt this thoroughfare, where Wolsey once lived in his pride and state. Izaak Walton dwelt in this lane once upon a time; and that mischievous adviser of Charles I., the Earl of Strafford, was born here. Hazlitt resided in Southampton Buildings when he fell in love with the tailor's daughter and wrote that most stultifying confession of his vanity and weakness, "The New Pygmalion." Fetter Lane brings us fresh stores of subjects, all essentially connected with the place, deriving an interest from and imparting a new interest to it. Praise-God-Barebones, Dryden, Otway, Baxter, and Mrs. Brownrigg form truly a strange bouquet. By mutual contrast the incongruous group serves, however, to illustrate various epochs of London life, and the background serves to explain the actions and the social position of each and all these motley beings.

In Crane Court, the early home of the Royal Society, Newton is the central personage; and we tarry to sketch the progress of science and to smile at the crudity of its early experiments and theories. In Bolt Court we pause to see a great man die. Here especially Dr. Johnson's figure ever stands like a statue, and we shall find his black servant at the door and his dependents wrangling in the front parlour. Burke and Boswell are on their way to call, and Reynolds is taking coach in the adjoining street. Nor is even Shoe Lane without its associations, for at the north-east end the corpse of poor, dishonoured Chatterton lies still under some neglected rubbish heap; and close by the brilliant Cavalier poet, Lovelace, pined and perished, almost in beggary.

The southern side of Fleet Street is somewhat less noticeable. Still, in Salisbury Square the worthy old printer Richardson, amid the din of a noisy office, wrote his great and pathetic novels; while in Mitre Buildings Charles Lamb held those delightful conversations, so full of quaint and kindly thoughts, which were shared in by Hazlitt and all the people whom Lamb has immortalised in "Elia"—bibulous Burney, George Dyer, Holcroft, Coleridge, Hone, Godwin, and Leigh Hunt.

Whitefriars and Blackfriars are our next places of pilgrimage, and they open up quite new lines of reading and of thought. Though the Great Fire swept them bare, no district of London has preserved its old lines so closely; and, walking in Whitefriars, we can still stare through the gate that once barred off the brawling Copper Captains of Charles II.'s Alsatia from the contemptuous Templars of King's Bench Walk. Whitefriars was at first a Carmelite convent, founded, before Blackfriars, on land given by Edward I.; the chapter-house was given by Henry VII. to his physician, Dr. Butts (a man mentioned by Shakespeare), and in the reign of Edward VI. the church was demolished. Whitefriars then, though still partially inhabited by great people, soon sank into a sanctuary for runaway bankrupts, cheats, and gamblers. The hall of the monastery was turned into a theatre, where many of Dryden's plays first appeared. The players favoured this quarter, where, in the reign of James I., two henchmen of Lord Sanquhar, a revengeful young Scottish nobleman, shot at his own door a poor fencing-master, who had accidentally put out their master's eye several years before in a contest of skill. The two men were hung opposite the White-friars gate in Fleet Street. This disreputable and lawless nest of river-side alleys was called Alsatia, from its resemblance to the seat of the war then raging on the frontiers of France, in the dominions

of King James's son-in-law, the Prince Palatine. Its roystering bullies and shifty money-lenders are admirably sketched by Shadwell in his *Squire of Alsatia*, an excellent comedy freely used by Sir Walter Scott in his "Fortunes of Nigel," who has laid several of his strongest scenes in this once scampish region. That great scholar Selden lived in Whitefriars with the Countess Dowager of Kent, whom he was supposed to have married; and, singularly enough, the best edition of his works was printed in Dogwell Court, Whitefriars, by those eminent printers, Bowyer & Son. At the back of Whitefriars we come upon Bridewell, the site of a palace of the Norman kings. Cardinal Wolsey afterwards owned the house, which Henry VIII. reclaimed in his rough and not very scrupulous manner. It was the old palace to which Henry summoned all the priors and abbots of England, and where he first announced his intention of divorcing Katherine of Arragon. After this it fell into decay. The good Ridley, the martyr, begged it of Edward VI. for a workhouse and a school. Hogarth painted the female prisoners here beating hemp under the lash of a cruel turnkey; and Pennant has left a curious sketch of the herd of girls whom he saw run like hounds to be fed when a gaoler entered.

If Whitefriars was inhabited by actors, Blackfriars was equally favoured by players and by painters. The old convent, removed from Holborn, was often used for Parliaments. Charles V. lodged here when he came over to win Henry against Francis; and Burbage, the great player of "Richard the Third," built a theatre in Blackfriars, because the Precinct was out of the jurisdiction of the City, then ill-disposed to the players. Shakespeare had a house here, which he left to his favourite daughter, the deed of conveyance of which sold, in 1841, for £165 15s. He must have thought of his well-known neighbourhood when he wrote the scenes of Henry VIII., where Katherine was divorced and Wolsey fell, for both events were decided in Blackfriars Parliaments. Oliver, the great miniature painter, and Jansen, a favourite portrait painter of James I., lived in Blackfriars, where we shall call upon them; and Vandyke spent nine happy years here by the river side. The most remarkable event connected with Blackfriars is the falling in of the floor of a Roman Catholic private chapel in 1623, by which fifty-nine persons perished, including the priest, to the exultation of the Puritans, who pronounced the event a visitation of Heaven on Popish superstition. Pamphlets of the time, well rummaged by us, describe the scene with curious exactness, and mention the singular escapes of several persons on the "Fatal Vespers," as they were afterwards called.

Leaving the racket of Alsatia and its wild doings behind us, we come next to that great monastery of lawyers, the Temple—like Whitefriars and Blackfriars, also the site of a bygone convent. The warlike Templars came here in their white cloaks and red crosses from their first establishment in Southampton Buildings, and they held it during all the Crusades, in which they fought so valorously against the Paynim, till they grew proud and corrupt, and were suspected of worshipping idols and ridiculing Christianity. Their work done, they perished, and the Knights of St. John took possession of their halls, church, and cloisters. The incoming lawyers became tenants of the Crown, and the parade-ground of the Templars and the river-side terrace and gardens were tenanted by more peaceful occupants. The manners and customs of the lawyers of various ages, their quaint revels, fox-huntings in hall, and dances round the coal fire, deserve special notice; and swarms of anecdotes and odd sayings and doings buzz round us as we write of the various denizens of the Temple—Dr. Johnson, Goldsmith, Lamb, Coke, Plowden, Jefferies, Cowper, Butler, Parsons, Sheridan, and Tom Moore; and we linger at the pretty little fountain and think of those who have celebrated its praise. Every binn of this cellar of lawyers has its story, and a volume might well be written in recording the toils and struggles, successes and failures, of the illustrious owners of Temple chambers.

Thence we pass to Ludgate, where that old London inn, the "Belle Sauvage," calls up associations of the early days of theatres, especially of Banks and his wonderful performing horse, that walked up one of the towers of Old St. Paul's. Hone's shop will remind us of the delightful books he published, aided by Lamb and Leigh Hunt. The ancient entrance of the city, Ludgate, has quite a history of its own. It was a debtors' prison, rebuilt in the time of King John from the remains of demolished Jewish houses, and was enlarged by the widow of Stephen Forster, Lord Mayor in the reign of Henry VI., who, tradition says, had been himself a prisoner in Ludgate, till released by a rich widow, who saw his handsome face through the grate, and married him. St. Martin's Church, Ludgate, is one of Wren's churches, and is chiefly remarkable for its stolid conceit in always getting in the way of the west front of St. Paul's.

The great Cathedral has been the scene of events that illustrate almost every age of English history. This is the third St. Paul's. The first, often supposed to have been built on the site of a Roman temple of Diana, was burnt down in the last year of William the Conqueror. Innumerable events connected with the history of the City happened here, from the killing a bishop at the north door, in the reign of Edward II., to the public exposure of Richard II.'s body after his murder; while at the Cross in the churchyard the authorities of the City, and even our kings, often attended the public sermons, and in the same place the citizens once held their Folkmotes, riotous enough on many an occasion. Great men's tombs abounded in Old St. Paul's—John of Gaunt, Lord Bacon's father, Sir Philip Sydney, Donne, the poet, and Vandyke being very prominent among them. Fired by lightning in Elizabeth's reign, when the Cathedral had become a resort of newsmongers and a thoroughfare for porters and carriers, it was partly rebuilt in Charles I.'s reign by Inigo Jones. The repairs were stopped by the civil wars, when the Puritans seized the funds, pulled down the scaffolding, and turned the church into a cavalry barrack. The Great Fire swept all clear for Wren, who now found a fine field for his genius; but vexatious difficulties embarrassed him at the very outset. His first great plan was rejected, and the Duke of York (afterwards James II.) is said to have insisted on side recesses, that might serve as chantry chapels when the church became Roman Catholic. Wren was accused of delays and chidden for the faults of petty workmen, and, as the Duchess of Marlborough laughingly remarked, was dragged up and down in a basket two or three times a week for a paltry £200 a year. The narrow escape of Sir James Thornhill from falling from a scaffold while painting the dome is a tradition of St. Paul's, matched by the terrible adventure of Mr. Gwyn, who when measuring the dome slid down the convex surface till his foot was stayed by a small projecting lump of lead. This leads us naturally on to the curious monomaniac who believed himself the slave of a demon who lived in the bell of the Cathedral, and whose case is singularly deserving of analysis. We shall give a short sketch of the heroes whose tombs have been admitted into St. Paul's, and having come to those of the great demi-gods of the old wars, Nelson and Wellington, pass to anecdotes about the clock and bells, and arrive at the singular story of the soldier whose life was saved by his proving that he had heard St. Paul's clock strike thirteen. Queen Anne's statue in the churchyard, too, has given rise to epigrams worthy of preservation, and the progress of the restoration of the Cathedral will be carefully detailed.

Cheapside, famous from the Saxon days, next invites our wandering feet. The north side remained a field as late as the reign of Edward III., and tournaments were held there. The knights, whose deeds Froissart has immortalised, broke spears there, in the presence of the Queen and her ladies, who smiled on their champions from a wooden tower erected across the street. Afterwards a stone shed was raised for the same sights, and rising, who was besieged there, and eventually burned out and put to death. The great Cross of Cheapside recalls many interesting associations, for it was one of the nine Eleanor crosses. Regilt for many coronations, it was eventually pulled down by the Puritans during the civil wars. Then

THE OLD WOODEN TEMPLE BAR (*see page* 2).
As Erected in the Reign of James I.

there Henry VIII., disguised as a yeoman, with a halbert on his shoulder, came on one occasion to see the great City procession of the night watch by torchlight on St. John's Eve. Wren afterwards, when he rebuilt Bow Church, provided a balcony in the tower for the Royal Family to witness similar pageants. Old Bow Church, we must not forget to record, was seized in the reign of Richard I. by Longbeard, the desperate ringleader of a Saxon there was the Standard, near Bow Church, where Wat Tyler and Jack Cade beheaded several objectionable nobles and citizens; and the great Conduit at the east end—each with its memorable history. But the great feature of Cheapside is, after all, Guildhall. This is the hall which Whittington paved and where Walworth once ruled. In Guildhall Lady Jane Grey and her husband were tried; here the Jesuit Garnet was arraigned

SOUTH-EAST VIEW OF LONDON IN 1550.
From an Engraving by Wood, in Mr. Crace's Collection.

for his share in the Gunpowder Plot; here also Charles I. appealed to the Common Council to arrest Hampden and the other patriots who had fled from his eager claws into the friendly City; and here, in the spot still sacred to liberty, the Lords and Parliament declared for the Prince of Orange. To pass this spot without some salient anecdotes of the various Lord Mayors would be a disgrace; and the banquets themselves, from that of Whittington, when he threw Henry V.'s bonds for £60,000 into a spice bonfire, to those in the present reign, deserve some notice and comment. The curiosities of Guildhall in themselves are not to be lightly passed over, for they record many vicissitudes of the great City; and Gog and Magog are personages of importance secondary only to that of Lord Mayor.

Then the Mansion House, built in 1789, leads us to much chat about "gold chains, warm furs, broad banners and broad faces;" for a folio might be well filled with curious anecdotes of the Lord Mayors of various ages—from Sir John Norman, who first went in procession to Westminster by water, to Sir John Shorter (James II.), who was killed by a fall from his horse as he stopped at Newgate, according to custom, to take a tankard of wine, nutmeg, and sugar. There is a word to say of many a celebrity in the long roll of Mayors— more especially of Beckford, who is said to have startled George III. by a violent patriotic remon- strance, and of the notorious John Wilkes, that ugly demagogue, who led the City in many an attack on the King and his unwise Ministers.

The tributaries of Cheapside also abound in interest, and mark various stages in the history of the great City. Bread Street was the bread market of the time of Edward I., and is especially honoured for being the birthplace of Milton; and in Milk Street (the old milk market) Sir Thomas More was born. Gutter Lane reminds us of its first Danish owner; and many other turnings have their memorable legends and traditions.

The Halls of the City Companies, the great hos- pitals, and Gothic schools, will each by turn detain us; and we shall not forget to call at the Bank, the South-Sea House, and other great proofs of past commercial folly and present wealth. The Bank, projected by a Scotch theorist in 1691 (William III.), after many migrations, settled down in Threadneedle Street in 1734. It has a his- tory of its own, and we shall see during the Gordon Riots the old pewter inkstands melted down for bullets, and, prodigy of prodigies! Wilkes himself rushing out to seize the cowardly ring- leaders!

By many old houses of good pedigree and by several City churches worthy a visit, we come at last to the Monument, which Wren erected and which Cibber decorated. This pillar, which Pope compared to "a tall bully," once bore an inscrip- tion that greatly offended the Court. It attributed the Great Fire of London, which began close by there, to the Popish faction; but the words were erased in 1831. Littleton, who compiled the Dic- tionary, once wrote a Latin inscription for the Monument, which contained the names of seven Lord Mayors in one word :—

"Fordo-Watermanno-Harrisono-Hookero-Vinero-
Sheldono-Davisonam."

But the learned production was, singularly enough, never used. The word, which Littleton called "an heptastic vocable," comprehended the names of the seven Lord Mayors in whose mayoralties the Monument was begun, continued, and completed.

On London Bridge we might linger for many chapters. The first bridge thrown over the Thames was a wooden one, erected by the nuns of St. Mary's Monastery, a convent of sisters endowed by the daughter of a rich Thames ferryman. The bridge figures as a fortified place in the early Danish invasions, and the Norwegian Prince Olaf nearly dragged it to pieces in trying to dispossess the Danes, who held it in 1008. It was swept away in a flood, and its successor was burnt. In the reign of Henry II., Pious Peter, a chaplain of St. Mary Colechurch, in the Poultry, built a stone bridge a little further west, and the king helped him with the proceeds of a tax on wool, which gave rise to the old saying that "London Bridge was built upon woolpacks." Peter's bridge was a curious structure, with nineteen pointed arches and a drawbridge. There was a fortified gate- house at each end, and a gothic chapel towards the centre, dedicated to St. Thomas à Becket, the murdered Archbishop of Canterbury. In Queen Elizabeth's reign there were shops on either side, with flat roofs, arbours, and gardens, and at the south end rose a great four-storey wooden house, brought from Holland, which was covered with carving and gilding. In the Middle Ages, London Bridge was the scene of affrays of all kinds. Soon after it was built, the houses upon it caught fire at both ends, and 3,000 persons perished, wedged in among the flames. Henry III. was driven back here by the rebellious De Montfort, Earl of Leicester. Wat Tyler entered the City by London Bridge; and, later, Richard II. was received here with gorgeous ceremonies. It was the scene of one of Henry V.'s greatest triumphs, and also of his stately funeral procession. Jack Cade seized London Bridge, and as he passed slashed in two the ropes of the drawbridge, though soon after his head was stuck on the gate-house. From this bridge the rebel Wyatt was driven by the guns of the Tower; and in Elizabeth's reign water-works were erected on the bridge. There was a great conflagration on the bridge in 1632, and eventually the Great Fire almost destroyed it. In the Middle Ages countless rebels' heads were stuck on the gate-houses of London Bridge. Brave Wallace's was placed there; and so were the heads of Henry VIII.'s victims—Fisher, Bishop of Rochester and Sir Thomas More, the latter trophy being carried off by the stratagem of his brave daughter. Garnet, the Gunpowder-Plot Jesuit, also contributed to the ghastly triumphs of justice. Several celebrated painters, including Hogarth, lived at one time or another on the bridge; and Swift and Pope used to frequent the shop of a witty bookseller, who lived under the northern gate. One or two celebrated suicides have taken place at London Bridge, and among these we may mention that of Sir William Temple's son, who was Secretary of War, and Eustace Budgell, a broken-down author, who left behind him as an apology the following sophism :—

"What Cato did and Addison approved, cannot be wrong."

Pleasanter is it to remember the anecdote of the brave apprentice, who leaped into the Thames from the window of a house on the bridge to save his master's infant daughter, whom a care-less nurse had dropped into the river. When the girl grew up, many noble suitors came, but the generous father was obdurate. " No," said the honest citizen; "Osborne saved her, and Osborne shall have her." And so he had; and Osborne's great grandson throve and became the first Duke of Leeds. The frequent loss of lives in shooting the arches of the old bridge, where the fall was at times five feet, led at last to a cry for a new bridge, and one was commenced in 1824. Rennie designed it, and in 1831 William IV. and Queen Adelaide opened it. One hundred and twenty thousand tons of stone went to its forma-tion. The old bridge was not entirely removed till 1832, when the bones of the builder, Pious Peter of Colechurch, were found in the crypt of the central chapel, where tradition had de-clared they lay. The iron of the piles of the old bridge was bought by a cutler in the Strand, and produced steel of the highest quality. Part of the old stone was purchased by Alderman

Harmer, to build his house, Ingress Abbey, near Greenhithe.

Southwark, a Roman station and cemetery, is by no means without a history. It was burned by William the Conqueror, and had been the scene of battles against the Danes. It possessed palaces, monasteries, a mint, and fortifications. The Bishops of Winchester and Rochester once lived here in splendour; and the locality boasted its four Elizabethan theatres. The Globe was Shake-speare's summer theatre, and here it was that his greatest triumphs were attained. What was acted there is best told by making Shakespeare's share in the management distinctly understood; nor can we leave Southwark without visiting the " Tabard Inn," from whence Chaucer's nine-and-twenty jovial pilgrims set out for Canterbury.

The Tower rises next before our eyes; and as we pass under its battlements the grimmest and most tragic scenes of English history seem again rising before us. Whether Cæsar first built a tower here or William the Conqueror, may never be decided; but one thing is certain, that more tears have been shed within these walls than anywhere else in London. Every stone has its story. Here Wallace, in chains, thought of Scotland; here Queen Anne Boleyn placed her white hands round her slender neck, and said the headsman would have little trouble. Here Catharine Howard, Sir Thomas More, Cranmer, Northumberland, Lady Jane Grey, Wyatt, and the Earl of Essex all perished. Here, Clarence was drowned in a butt of wine and the two boy princes were murdered. Many victims of kings, many kingly victims, have here perished. Many patriots have here sighed for liberty. The poisoning of Overbury is a mystery of the Tower, the perusal of which never wearies though the dark secret be unsolvable; and we can never cease to sympathise with that brave woman, the Countess of Nithsdale, who risked her life to save her husband's. From Laud and Strafford we turn to Eliot and Hutchinson—for Cavaliers and Puritans were both by turns prisoners in the Tower. From Lord William Russell and Algernon Sydney we come down in the chronicle of suffering to the Jacobites of 1715 and 1745; from them to Wilkes, Lord George Gordon, Burdett, and, last of all the Tower pri-soners, to the infamous Thistlewood.

Leaving the crimson scaffold on Tower Hill, we return as sightseers to glance over the armoury and to catch the sparkle of the Royal jewels. Here is the identical crown which the daring villain, Blood, stole, and the heart-shaped ruby that the Black Prince once wore; here we see the swords, sceptres, and diadems of many of our monarchs. In the armoury are suits on which many lances have splintered and swords struck; the imperishable steel clothes of many a dead king are here, unchanged since the owners doffed them. This suit was the Earl of Leicester's—the "Kenilworth" earl, for see his cognizance of the bear and ragged staff on the horse's chanfron. This richly-gilt suit was worn by the ill-starred son of James II., Prince Henry, who, as many thought, was poisoned by Buckingham; and this quaint mask, with ram's horns and spectacles, belonged to Will Somers, Henry VIII.'s jester.

From the Tower we break away into the far east, among the old clothes shops, the bird markets, the costermongers, and the weavers of Whitechapel and Spitalfields. We are far from jewels here and Court splendour, and we come to plain working people and their homely ways. Spitalfields was the site of a priory of Augustine canons, however, and has ancient traditions of its own. The weavers, of French origin, are an interesting race—we shall have to sketch their sayings and doings; and we shall search Whitechapel diligently for old houses and odd people. The district may not furnish so many interesting scenes and anecdotes as the West End, but it is well worthy of study from many modern points of view.

Smithfield and Holborn are regions fertile in associations. Smithfield, that broad plain, the scene of so many martyrdoms, tournaments, and executions, forms an interesting subject for a diversified chapter. In this market-place the ruffians of Henry VIII.'s time met to fight out their quarrels with sword and buckler. Here the brave Wallace was executed like a common robber; and here "the gentle Mortimer" was led to a shameful death. The spot was the scene of great jousts in Edward III.'s chivalrous reign, when, after the battle of Poictiers, the Kings of France and Scotland came seven days running to see spears shivered and "the Lady of the Sun" bestow the prizes of valour. In this same field Walworth slew the rebel Wat Tyler, who had treated Richard II. with insolence, and by this prompt blow dispersed the insurgents, who had grown so dangerously strong. In Henry VIII.'s reign poisoners were boiled to death in Smithfield; and in cruel Mary's reign the Protestant martyrs were burned in the same place. "Of the two hundred and seventy-seven persons burnt for heresy in Mary's reign," says a modern antiquary, "the greater number perished in Smithfield; and ashes and charred bodies have been dug up opposite to the gateway of Bartholomew's Church and at the west end of Long Lane." After the Great Fire the houseless citizens were sheltered here in tents. Over against the corner where the Great Fire abated is Cock Lane, the scene of the rapping ghost, in which Dr. Johnson believed and concerning which Goldsmith wrote a catchpenny pamphlet.

Holborn and its tributaries come next, and are by no means deficient in legends and matter of general interest. "The original name of the street was the Hollow Bourne," says a modern etymologist, "not the Old Bourne;" it was not paved till the reign of Henry V. The ride up "the Heavy Hill" from Newgate to Tyburn has been sketched by Hogarth and sung by Swift. In Ely Place once lived the Bishop of Ely; and in Hatton Garden resided Queen Elizabeth's favourite, the dancing chancellor, Sir Christopher Hatton. In Furnival's Inn Dickens wrote "Pickwick." In Barnard's Inn died the last of the alchemists. In Staple's Inn Dr. Johnson wrote "Rasselas," to pay the expenses of his mother's funeral. In Brooke Street, where Chatterton poisoned himself, lived Lord Brooke, a poet and statesman, who was a patron of Ben Jonson and Shakespeare, and who was assassinated by a servant whose name he had omitted in his will. Milton lived for some time in a house in Holborn that opened at the back on Lincoln's Inn Fields. Fox Court leads us to the curious inquiry whether Savage, the poet, was a conscious or an unconscious impostor; and at the Blue Boar Inn Cromwell and Ireton discovered by stratagem the treacherous letter of King Charles to his queen, that rendered Cromwell for ever the King's enemy. These are only a few of the countless associations of Holborn.

Newgate is a gloomy but an interesting subject for us. Many wild faces have stared through its bars since, in King John's time, it became a City prison. We shall look in on Sarah Malcolm, Mrs. Brownrigg, Jack Sheppard, Governor Wall, and other interesting criminals; we shall stand at Wren's elbow when he designs the new prison, and follow the Gordon Rioters when they storm in over the burning walls.

The Strand stands next to Fleet Street as a central point of old memories. It is not merely full, it positively teems. For centuries it was a fashionable street, and noblemen inhabited the south side especially, for the sake of the river. In Essex Street, on a part of the Temple, Queen Elizabeth's rash favourite (the Earl of Essex) was besieged, after his hopeless foray into the City. In Arundel Street lived the Earls of Arundel; in Buckingham Street Charles I.'s greedy favourite began a palace. There were royal palaces, too, in the Strand, for at the Savoy lived John of Gaunt; old Somerset House was built by the Protector Somerset with the stones of the churches he had pulled down. Henrietta Maria (Charles I.'s Queen) and poor neglected Catherine of Braganza dwelt at Somerset House; and it was here that Sir Edmondbury Godfrey, the zealous Protestant magistrate, was supposed to have been murdered. There is, too, the history of Lord Burleigh's house (in Cecil Street) to record; and of Northumberland House, with the recollections of its many noble inmates. On the other side of the Strand we have to note Butcher Row (now pulled down), where the Gunpowder Plot conspirators met; Exeter House, where Lord Burleigh's wily son lived; and, finally, Exeter 'Change, where the poet Gay lay in state. Nor shall we forget Cross's menagerie and the elephant Chunee; nor omit mention of many of the eccentric old shopkeepers who once inhabited the 'Change. At Charing Cross we shall stop to see the old Cromwellians die bravely, and to stare at the pillory, where in their time many incomparable scoundrels ignominiously stood. The Nelson Column and the surrounding statues have stories of their own; and St. Martin's Lane is specially interesting as the haunt of half the painters of the early Georgian era. There are anecdotes of Hogarth and his friends to be picked up here in abundance, and the locality generally deserves exploration, from the quaintness and cleverness of its former inhabitants.

In Covent Garden we break fresh ground. We found St. Martin's Lane full of artists, Guildhall full of aldermen, the Strand full of noblemen—the old monastic garden will prove to be crowded with actors. We shall trace the market from the first few sheds under the wall of Bedford House to the present grand temple of Flora and Pomona. We shall see Evans's a new mansion, inhabited by Ben Jonson's friend and patron, Sir Kenelm Digby, alternately tenanted by Sir Harry Vane, Denzil Holles (one of the five refractory members whom Charles I. went to the House of Commons so imprudently to seize), and Admiral Russell, who defeated the French at La Hogue. The ghost of Parson Ford, in which Johnson believed, awaits us at the doorway of the Hummums. There are several duels to witness in the Piazza; Dryden to call upon as he sits, the arbiter of wits, by the fireside at Will's Coffee House; Addison is to be found at Button's; at the "Bedford" we shall meet Garrick and Quin, and stop a moment at Tom King's, close to St. Paul's portico, to watch Hogarth's revellers fight with swords and shovels, that frosty morning when the painter sketched the prim old maid going to early service. We shall look in at the Tavistock, to see Sir Peter Lely and Sir Godfrey Kneller at work on portraits of

beauties of the Carolean and Jacobean Courts; remembering that in the same rooms Sir James Thornhill afterwards painted, and poor Richard Wilson produced those fine landscapes which so few had the taste to buy. The old hustings deserve a word; and we shall have to record the lamentable murder of Miss Ray by her lover, at the north-east angle of the square. The neighbourhood of Covent Garden, too, is rife with stories of great actors and painters, and nearly every house furnishes its quota of anecdote.

The history of Drury Lane and Covent Garden theatres supplies us with endless anecdotes of actors, and with humorous and pathetic narratives that embrace the whole region both of tragedy and comedy. Quin's jokes, Garrick's weaknesses, the celebrated O. P. riots, contrast with the miserable end of some popular favourites and the caprices of genius. The oddities of Munden, the humour of Liston, only serve to render the gloom of Kean's downfall more terrible, and to show the wreck and ruin of many unhappy men, equally wilful though less gifted. There is a perennial charm about theatrical stories, and the history of these theatres must be illustrated by many a sketch of the loves and rivalries of actors, their fantastic tricks, their practical jokes, their gay progress to success or ruin. Changes of popular taste are marked by the changes of character in the pieces that have been performed in various ages; and the history of the two theatres will include various illustrative sketches of dramatic writers, as well as actors. There was a vast interval in literature between the tragedies of Addison and Murphy and the comedies of Holcroft, O'Keefe, and Morton; the descent to modern melodrama and burlesque must be traced through various gradations, and the reasons shown for the many modifications both classes of entertainments have undergone.

Westminster, from the night St. Peter came over from Lambeth in the fisherman's boat, and chose a site for the Abbey in the midst of Thorney Island, to the present day, has been a spot where the pilgrim to historic shrines loves to linger. Need we remind our readers that Edward the Confessor built the Abbey, or that William the Conqueror was crowned here, the ceremony ending in tumult and blood? How vast the store of facts from which we have to cull! We see the Jews being beaten nearly to death for daring to attend the coronation of Richard I.; we observe Edward I. watching the sacred stone of Scotland being placed beneath his coronation chair; we behold for the first time, at Richard II.'s coronation, the champion riding into the Hall, to challenge all who refuse

allegiance; we see, at the funeral of Anne of Bo-
hemia, Richard beating the Earl of Arundel for
wishing to leave before the service is over. We hear
the *Te Deum* that is sung for the victory of Agincourt, and watch Henry VI. selecting a site for a
resting-place; we hear for the last time, at the
coronation of Henry VIII., the sanction of the
Pope bestowed upon an English monarch; we pity
poor Queen Caroline attempting to enter the Abbey
to see her worthless husband crowned; and we view
through them: in St. James's seeing Charles II. feeding his ducks or playing "pall-mall;" in Hyde Park
observing the fashions and extravagancies of many
generations. "Romeo" Coates will whisk past us in
his fantastic chariot, and the beaus and oddities of
many generations will pace past us in review.
There will be celebrated duels to describe, and
various strange follies to deride. We shall see
Cromwell thrown from his coach, and shall witness
the foot-races that Pepys describes. Dryden's

BRIDEWELL IN 1666 (*see page* 4).

the last coronation, and draw auguries of a purer if
not a happier age. The old Hall, too; could we
neglect that ancient chamber, where Charles I. was
sentenced to death, and where Cromwell was
throned in almost regal splendour? We must see
it in all its special moments; when the seven
bishops were acquitted, and the shout of joy shook
London as with an earthquake; and when the rebel
lords were tried. We must hear Lord Byron tried
for his duel with Mr. Chaworth, and mad Lord
Ferrers condemned for shooting his steward. We
shall get a side-view of the shameless Duchess of
Kingston, and hear Burke and Sheridan grow
eloquent over the misdeeds of Warren Hastings.
The parks now draw us westward, and we wander
gallants and masked ladies will receive some mention; and we shall tell of bygone encampments
and of many events now almost forgotten.

Kensington will recall many anecdotes of William
of Orange, his beloved Queen, stupid Prince George
of Denmark, and George II., who all died at the
palace, the old seat of the Finches. We are sure
to find good company in the gardens. Still as
when Tickell sang, every walk

"Seems from afar a moving tulip bed,
　Where rich brocades and glossy damasks glow,
　And chintz, the rival of the showery bow."

There is Newton's house at South Kensington
to visit, and Wilkie's and Mrs. Inchbald's; and,

above all, there is Holland House, the scene of the delightful Whig coteries of Tom Moore's time. Here Addison lived to regret his marriage with a lady of rank, and here he died. At Kensington Charles James Fox spent his youth.

And now Chelsea brings us pleasant recollections of Sir Thomas More, Swift, Sir Robert Walpole, and Atterbury. "Chelsith," Sir Thomas More used to call it when Holbein was lodging in his house and King Henry, who afterwards

fiddle. Saltero was a barber, who drew teeth, drew customers, wrote verses, and collected curiosities.

"Some relics of the Sheban queen
And fragments of the famed Bob Crusoe."

Swift lodged at Chelsea, over against the Jacobite Bishop Atterbury, who so nearly lost his head. In one of his delightful letters to Stella Swift describes "the Old Original Chelsea Bun House," and the r-r-r-rare Chelsea buns. He used to leave his best gown and perriwig at Mrs. Vanhomrig's, in

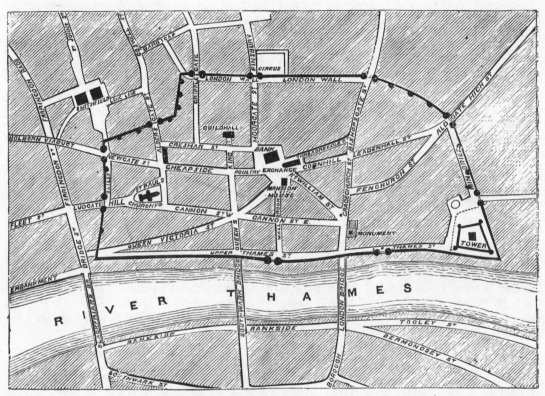

PART OF MODERN LONDON, SHOWING THE ANCIENT WALL (see page 20).

beheaded his old friend, used to come to dinner, and after dinner walk round the fair garden with his arm round his host's neck. More was fond of walking on the flat roof of his gate-house, which commanded a pleasant prospect of the Thames and the fields beyond. Let us hope the tradition is not true that he used to bind heretics to a tree in his garden. In 1717 Chelsea contained only 350 houses, and these in 1725 had grown to 1,350. There is Cheyne Walk, so called from the Lords Cheyne, owners of the manor; and we must not forget Don Saltero and his famous coffee-house, the oddities of which Steele pleasantly sketched in the *Tatler*. The Don was famous for his skill in brewing punch and for his excellent playing on the

Suffolk Street, then walk up Pall Mall, through the park, out at Buckingham House, and on to Chelsea, a little beyond the church (5,748 steps), he says, in less than an hour, which was leisurely walking even for the contemplative and observant dean. Smollet laid a scene of his "Humphrey Clinker" in Chelsea, where he lived for some time.

The Princess Elizabeth, when a girl, lived at Chelsea, with that dangerous man, with whom she is said to have fallen in love, the Lord Admiral, Seymour, afterwards beheaded. He was the second husband of Katherine Parr, one of the many wives of Elizabeth's father. Cremorne was, in Walpole's days, the villa of Lord Cremorne, an Irish nobleman; and near here, at a river-side cottage died, in miserly and cynical obscurity, the greatest of our modern landscape painters, Turner. Then there is Chelsea Hospital to visit. This hospital was built by Wren; Charles II., it is said at Nell Gwynn's suggestion, originated the good work, which was finished by William and Mary. Dr. Arbuthnot, that good man so beloved by the Pope set, was physician here, and the Rev. Philip Francis, who translated Horace, was chaplain. Nor can we leave Chelsea without remembering Sir Hans Sloane, whose collection of antiquities, sold for £20,000, formed the first nucleus of the British Museum, and who resided at Chelsea; nor shall we forget the Chelsea china manufactory, one of the earliest porcelain manufactories in England, patronized by George II., who brought over German artificers from Brunswick and Saxony. In the reign of Louis XV. the French manufacturers began to regard it with jealousy and petitioned their king for special privileges. Ranelagh, too, that old pleasure-garden which Dr. Johnson declared was "the finest thing he had ever seen," deserves a word; Horace Walpole was constantly there, though at first, he owns, he preferred Vauxhall; and Lord Chesterfield was so fond of it that he used to say he should order all his letters to be directed there.

The West End squares are pleasant spots for our purpose, and at many doors we shall have to make a call. In Landsdowne House (in Berkeley Square) it is supposed by many that Lord Shelburne, Colonel Barre, and Dunning wrote "Junius"; certain it is that the Marquis of Landsdowne, in 1809, acknowledged the possession of the secret, but died the following week, before he could disclose it. Here, in 1774, that persecuted philosopher, Dr. Priestley, the librarian to Lord Shelburne, discovered oxygen. In this square Horace Walpole (that delightful letter-writer) died, and Lord Clive destroyed himself. Then there is Grosvenor Square, where that fat, easy-going Minister, Lord North, lived, where Wilkes the notorious resided, and where the Cato-Street conspirators planned to kill all the Cabinet Ministers, who had been invited to dinner by the Earl of Harrowby. In Hanover Square we visit Lord Rodney, &c. In St. James's Square we recall William III. coming to the Earl of Romney's to see fireworks let off and, later, the Prince Regent, from a balcony, displaying to the people the Eagles captured at Waterloo. Queen Caroline resided here during her trial, and many of Charles II.'s frail beauties also resided in the same spot. In Cavendish Square we stop to describe the splendid projects of that great Duke of Chandos whom

Pope ridiculed. Nor are the lesser squares by any means devoid of interest.

In Pall Mall the laziest gleaner of London traditions might find a harvest. On the site of Carlton House—the Prince Regent's palace—were, in the reign of Henry VI., monastic buildings, in which (under Henry VIII.) Erasmus afterwards resided. They were pulled down at the Reformation. Nell Gwynn lived here, and so did Sir William Temple, Swift's early patron, the pious Boyle, and that poor puff-ball of vanity and pretence—Bubb Doddington. Here we have to record the unhappy duel at the "Star and Garter" tavern between Lord Byron and Mr. Chaworth, and the murder of Mr. Thynne by his rival, Count Köningsmark. There is Boydell's Shakespeare Gallery to notice, and Dodsley's shop, which Burke, Johnson, and Garrick so often visited. There is also the origin of the Royal Academy, at a house opposite Market Lane, to chronicle, many club-houses to visit, and curious memorabilia of all kinds to be sifted, selected, contrasted, mounted, and placed in sequence for view.

Then comes Marylebone, formerly a suburb, famous only for its hunting park (now Regent's Park), its gardens, and its bowling-greens. In Queen Elizabeth's time the Russian ambassadors were sent to hunt in Marylebone Park; Cromwell sold it—deer, timber, and all—for £13,000. The Marylebone Bowling Greens, which preceded the gardens, were at first the resort of noblemen and gentlemen, but eventually highwaymen began to frequent them. The Duke of Buckingham (whom Lady Mary Wortley Montagu glances at in the line,

"Some dukes at Marybone bowl time away")

used, at an annual dinner to the frequenters of the gardens, to give the agreeable toast,—"May as many of us as remain unhanged next spring meet here again." Eventually burlettas were produced—one written by Chatterton; and Dr. Arne conducted Handel's music. Marylebone, in the time of Hogarth, was a favourite place for prize fights and back-sword combats, the great champion being Figg, that bullet-headed man with the bald, plaistered head, whom Hogarth has represented mounting grim sentry in his "Southwark Fair." The great building at Marylebone began between 1718 and 1729. In 1739 there were only 577 houses in the parish; in 1851 there were 16,669. In many of the nooks and corners of Marylebone we shall find curious facts and stories worth the unravelling.

The eastern squares, in Bloomsbury and St. Pancras, are regions not by any means to be lightly passed by. Bloomsbury Square was built by the Earl of Southampton, about the time of the Restoration, and was thought one of the wonders of England. Baxter lived here when he was tormented by Judge Jefferies ; Sir Hans Sloane was one of its inhabitants ; so was that great physician, Dr. Radcliffe. The burning of Mansfield House by Lord George Gordon's rioters has to be minutely described. In Russell Square we visit the houses of Sir Thomas Lawrence and of Judge Talfourd, and search for

Sir Cloudesley Shovel, Sir Joseph Banks, and Burnet, the historian, were all inhabitants of this locality.

Islington brings us back to days when Henry VIII. came there to hawk the partridge and the heron, and when the London citizens wandered out across the northern fields to drink milk and eat cheesecakes. The old houses abound in legends of Sir Walter Raleigh, Topham, the strong man, George Morland, the artist, and Henderson, the actor. At Canonbury, the old tower of the country house of

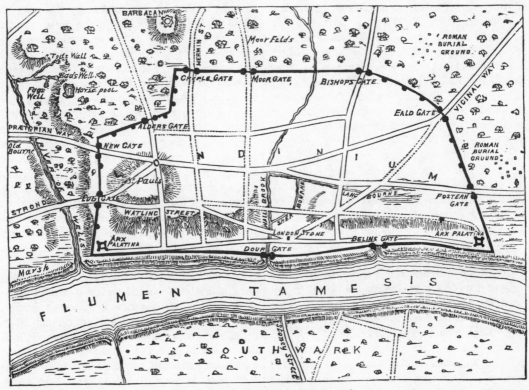

PLAN OF ROMAN LONDON (*see page* 20).

that celebrated spot in London legend, "The Field of the Forty Footsteps," where two brothers, it is said, killed each other in a duel for a lady, who sat by watching the fight. Then there is Red Lion Square, where tradition says some faithful adherents, at the Restoration, buried the body of Cromwell, to prevent its desecration at Tyburn ; and we have to cull some stories of a good old inhabitant, Jonas Hanway, the great promoter of many of the London charities, the first man who habitually used an umbrella and Dr. Johnson's spirited opponent on the important question of tea. Soho Square, too, has many a tradition, for the Duke of Monmouth lived there in great splendour ; and in Hogarth's time Mrs. Cornelys made the square celebrated by her masquerades, which in time became disreputable.

the Prior of St. Bartholomew recalls to us Goldsmith, who used to come there to hide from his creditors, go to bed early, and write steadily.

At Highgate and Hampstead we shall scour the northern uplands of London by no means in vain, as we shall find Belsize House, in Charles II.'s time, openly besieged by robbers and, long afterwards, highwaymen swarming in the same locality. The chalybeate wells of Hampstead lead us on to the Heath, where wolves were to be found in the twelfth century and highwaymen as late as 1803. Good company awaits us at pleasant Hampstead —Lord Erskine, Lord Chatham, Keats, Akenside, Leigh Hunt, and Sir T. Fowell Buxton ; Booth, Wilkes, and Colley Cibber ; Mrs. Barbauld, honest Dick Steele, and Joanna Baillie. As for Highgate, for ages a mere hamlet, a forest, it once boasted a bishop's palace, and there we gather, with free hand, memories of Sacheverell, Rowe, Dr. Watts, Hogarth, Coleridge, and Lord Mansfield; Ireton, Marvell, and Dick Whittington, the worthy demi-god of London apprentices to the end of time.

Lambeth, where Harold was crowned, can hold its own in interest with any part of London—for it once possessed two ecclesiastical palaces and many places of amusement. Lambeth Palace itself is a spot of extreme interest. Here Wat Tyler's men dragged off Archbishop Sudbury to execution; here, when Laud was seized, the Parliamentary soldiers turned the palace into a prison for Royalists and demolished the great hall. Outside the walls of the church James II.'s Queen cowered in the December rain with her child, till a coach could be brought from the neighbouring inn to convey her to Gravesend to take ship for France. The Gordon rioters attacked the palace in 1780, but were driven off by a detachment of Guards. The Lollards' Tower has to be visited, and the sayings and doings of a long line of prelates to be reviewed. Vauxhall brings us back to the days when Walpole went there with Lady Caroline Petersham and helped to stew chickens in a china dish over a lamp; or we go further back and accompany Addison and the worthy Sir Roger de Coverley, and join them over a glass of good ale and a slice of hung beef.

Astley's Amphitheatre recalls to us many amusing stories of that old soldier, Ducrow, and of his friends and rivals, which join on very naturally to those other theatrical traditions to which Drury Lane and Covent Garden have already led us.

So we mean to roam from flower to flower, over as varied a garden as the imagination can well conceive. There have been brave workers before us in the field, and we shall build upon good foundations. We hope to be catholic in our selections; we shall prune away only the superfluous; we shall condense anecdotes only where we think we can

make them pithier and racier. We will neglect no fact that is interesting, and blend together all that old Time can give us bearing upon London. Street by street we shall delve and rake for illustrative story, despising no book, however humble, no pamphlet, however obscure, if it only throws some light on the celebrities of London, its topographical history, its manners and customs. Such is a brief summary of our plan.

St. Paul's rises before us with its great black dome and stately row of sable columns; the Tower, with its central citadel, flanked by the spear-like masts of the river shipping; the great world of roofs spreads below us as we launch upon our venturous voyage of discovery. From Boadicea leading on her scythed chariots at Battle Bridge to Queen Victoria in the Thanksgiving procession of yesterday is a long period over which to range. We have whole generations of Londoners to defile before us—painted Britons, hooded Saxons, mailed Crusaders, Chaucer's men in hoods, friars, citizens, warriors, Shakespeare's friends, Johnson's companions, Goldsmith's jovial "Bohemians," Hogarth's fellow-painters, soldiers, lawyers, statesmen, merchants. Nevertheless, at our spells they will gather from the four winds, and at our command march off to their old billets in their old houses, where we may best cross-examine them and collect their impressions of the life of their times.

The subject is as entertaining as any dream Imagination ever evoked and as varied as human nature. Its classification is a certain bond of union, and will act as an excellent cement for the multiform stones with which we shall rear our building. Lists of names, dry pedigrees, rows of dates, we leave to the herald and the topographer; but we shall pass by little that can throw light on the history of London in any generation, and we shall dwell more especially on the events of the later centuries, because they are more akin to us and are bound to us by closer sympathies.

CHAPTER I.
ROMAN LONDON.

Buried London—Our Early Relations—The Founder of London—A distinguished Visitor at Romney Marsh—Cæsar re-visits the "Town on the Lake"—The Borders of Old London—Cæsar fails to make much out of the Britons—King *Brown*—The Derivation of the name of London—The Queen of the Iceni—London Stone and London Roads—London's Earlier and Newer Walls—The Site of St. Paul's—Fabulous Claims to Idolatrous Renown—Existing Relics of Roman London—Treasures from the Bed of the Thames—What we Tread underfoot in London—A vast Field of Story.

EIGHTEEN feet below the level of Cheapside lies hidden Roman London, and deeper even than that is buried the earlier London of those savage charioteers who, long ages ago, bravely confronted the legions of Rome. In nearly all parts of the

City there have been discovered tesselated pavements, Roman tombs, lamps, vases, sandals, keys, ornaments, weapons, coins, and statues of the ancient Roman gods. So the present has grown up upon the ashes of the past.

Trees that are to live long grow slowly. Slow and stately as an oak London grew and grew, till now nearly four million souls represent its leaves. Our London is very old. Centuries before Christ there probably came the first few half-naked fishermen and hunters, who reared, with flint axes and such rude tools, some miserable huts on the rising ground that, forming the north bank of the Thames, slopes to the river some sixty miles from where it joins the sea. According to some, the river spread out like a vast lake between the Surrey and the Essex hills in those times when the first half-savage settlers found the low slopes of the future London places of health and defence amid a vast and dismal region of fen, swamp, and forest. The heroism and the cruelties, the hopes and fears of those poor barbarians, darkness never to be removed has hidden from us for ever. In later days monkish historians, whom Milton afterwards followed, ignored these poor early relations of ours, and invented, as a more fitting ancestor of Englishmen, Brute, a fugitive nephew of Æneas of Troy. But, stroll on where we will, the pertinacious savage, with his limbs stained blue and his flint axe red with blood, is a ghost not easily to be exorcised from the banks of the Thames, and in some Welsh veins his blood no doubt flows at this very day. The founder of London had no historian to record his hopes : a place where big salmon were to be found, and plenty of wild boars were to be met with, was probably his highest ambition. How he bartered with Phœnicians or Gauls for amber or iron no Druid has recorded. How he slew the foraging Belgæ, or was slain by them and dispossessed, no bard has sung. Whether he was generous and heroic as the New Zealander, or ape-like and thievish as the Bushman, no ethnologist has yet proved. The very ashes of the founder of London have long since turned to earth, air, and water.

No doubt the few huts that formed early London were fought for over and over again, as wolves wrangle round a carcass. On Cornhill there probably dwelt petty kings who warred with the kings of Ludgate ; and in Southwark there lurked or burrowed other chiefs who, perhaps by intrigue or force, struggled for centuries to get a foothold in Thames Street. But to such infusoria History (glorying only in offenders, criminals, and robbers on the largest scale) justly pays no heed. This alone we know, that the early rulers of London before the Christian era passed away like the wild beasts they fought and slew, and their very names have perished. One line of an old blind Greek poet might have immortalised them among the motley nations that crowded into Troy or swarmed under its walls ; but, alas for them, that line was never written ! No, Founder of London ! thy name was written on fluid ooze of the marsh, and the first tide that washed over it from the Nore obliterated it for ever. Yet, perhaps even now thou sleepest as quietly fathoms deep in soft mud, in some still nook of Barking Creek, as if all the world were ringing with thy glory.

But descending quick to the lower but safer and firmer ground of fact, let us cautiously drive our first pile into the shaky morass of early London history.

A learned modern antiquary, Thomas Lewin, has proved, as nearly as any such things can be proved, that Julius Cæsar and 8,000 men, who had sailed from Boulogne, landed near Romney Marsh about half-past five o'clock on Sunday the 27th of August, 55 years before the birth of our Saviour. Centuries before that very remarkable August day on which the brave standard-bearer of Cæsar's Tenth Legion sprang from his gilt galley into the sea and, eagle in hand, advanced against the javelins of the painted Britons who lined the shore, there is now no doubt London was already existing as a British town of some importance, and known to the fishermen and merchants of the Gauls and Belgians. Strabo, a Greek geographer who flourished in the reign of Augustus, speaks of British merchants as bringing to the Seine and the Rhine shiploads of corn, cattle, iron, hides, slaves, and dogs, and taking back brass, ivory, amber ornaments, and vessels of glass. By these merchants the desirability of such a depôt as London, with its great and always navigable river, could not have been long overlooked.

In Cæsar's second and longer invasion in the next year (54 B.C.), when his 28 many-oared triremes and 560 transports, &c., in all 800, poured on the same Kentish coast 21,000 legionaries and 2,000 cavalry, there is little doubt that his strong foot left its imprint near that cluster of stockaded huts (more resembling a New Zealand pah than a modern English town) perhaps already called London—Llyn-don, the "town on the lake." After a battle at Challock Wood, Cæsar and his men crossed the Thames, as is supposed, at Coway Stakes, an ancient ford a little above Walton and below Weybridge. Cassivellaunus, King of Hertfordshire and Middlesex, had just slain in war Immanuent, King of Essex, and had driven out his son Mandubert. The Trinobantes, Mandubert's subjects, joined the Roman spearmen against the 4,000 scythed chariots of Cassivellaunus and the Catyeuchlani. Straight as the flight of an arrow was Cæsar's march upon the capital of Cassivellaunus, a city the barbaric name of which he either forgot or disregarded, but which he merely says was " protected by woods and marshes." This place north of the Thames has usually been thought to be Verulamium (St. Alban's); but it was far more likely London, as the Cassii, whose capital was Verulamium, were among the traitorous tribes who joined Cæsar against their oppressor Cassivellaunus. Moreover, Cæsar's brief description of the spot perfectly applies to Roman London, for

least is certain, that the legionaries carried their eagles swiftly over his stockades of earth and fallen trees, drove away the blue-stained warriors, and swept off the half-wild cattle stored up by the Britons. Shortly after, Cæsar returned to Gaul, having heard while in Britain of the death of his favourite daughter Julia, the wife of Pompey, his great rival. His camp at Richborough or Rutupiæ was far distant; the dreaded equinoctial gales were at hand; and Gaul, he knew, might at any moment of his absence start into a flame. His inglorious

ANCIENT ROMAN PAVEMENT FOUND IN THREADNEEDLE STREET, 1841 (*see page* 21).

ages protected on the north by a vast forest, full of deer and wild boars, and which, even as late as the reign of Henry II., covered a great region, but has now shrunk into the not .very wild districts of St. John's Wood and Caen Wood. On the north the town found a natural moat in the broad fens of Moorfields, Finsbury, and Houndsditch, while on the south ran the Fleet and the Old Bourne. Indeed, according to that credulous enthusiast, Stukeley, Cæsar, marching from Staines to London, encamped on the site of Old St. Pancras Church, round which edifice Stukeley found evident traces of a great Prætorian camp. However, whether Cassivellaunus, the King of Middlesex and Hertfordshire, had his capital at London or St. Alban's, this much at

campaign had lasted just four months and a half— his first had been far shorter. As Cæsar himself wrote to Cicero, our rude island was defended by stupendous rocks, there was not a scrap of the gold that had been reported, and the only prospect of booty was in slaves, from whom there could be expected neither " skill in letters nor in music." In sober truth, all Cæsar had won from the people of Kent and Hertfordshire had been blows and buffets, for there were *men* in Britain even then. The prowess of the British charioteers became a standing joke in Rome against the soldiers of Cæsar. Horace and Tibullus both speak of the Briton as unconquered. The bow which the strong Roman hand had for a moment bent quickly relapsed to its old shape the moment Cæsar, mounting his tall galley, turned his eyes towards Gaul.

The Mandubert who sought Cæsar's help is by some thought to be the son of the semi-fabulous King Lud (King *Brown*), the mythical founder of London, and, according to Milton, who, as we have said, follows the old historians, a descendant

conjecture is, however, now the most generally received, as it at once gives the modern pronunciation, to which Llyn-don would never have assimilated. The first British town was indeed a simple Celtic hill fortress, formed first on Tower Hill, and afterwards continued to Cornhill and Ludgate. It was moated on the south by the river, which it controlled;

PART OF OLD LONDON WALL, NEAR FALCON SQUARE (*see page* 21).

of Brute of Troy. The successor of the warlike Cassivellaunus had his capital at St. Alban's; his son Cunobelin (Shakespeare's Cymbeline)—a name which seems to glow with perpetual sunshine as we write it—had a palace at Colchester; and the son of Cunobelin was the famed Caradoc, or Caractacus, that hero of the Silures, who struggled bravely for nine long years against the generals of Rome.

Celtic etymologists differ, as etymologists usually do, about the derivation of the name of London. Lon, or Long, meant, they say, either a lake, a wood, a populous place, a plain, or a ship-town. This last

by fens on the north; and on the east by the marshy low ground of Wapping. It was a high, dry, and fortified point of communication between the river and the inland country of Essex and Hertfordshire, a safe sixty miles from the sea, and central as a depôt and meeting-place for the tribes of Kent and Middlesex.

Hitherto the London about which we have been conjecturing has been a mere cloud city. The first mention of real London is by Tacitus, who, writing in the reign of Nero (A.D. 62, more than a century after the landing of Cæsar), in that style of his so full of vigour and so sharp in outline, that it seems fit rather to be engraved on steel than written on perishable paper, says that Londinium, though not, indeed, dignified with the name of colony, was a place highly celebrated for the number of its merchants and the confluence of traffic. In the year 62 London was probably still without walls, and its inhabitants were not Roman citizens, like those of Verulamium (St. Alban's). When the Britons, roused by the wrongs of the fierce Boadicea (Queen of the Iceni, the people of Norfolk and Suffolk), bore down on London, her back still "bleeding from the Roman rods," she slew in London and Verulamium alone 70,000 citizens and allies of Rome; impaling many beautiful and well-born women, amid revelling sacrifices, in the grove of Andate, the British Goddess of Victory. It is supposed that after this reckless slaughter the tigress and her savage followers burned the cluster of wooden houses that then formed London to the ground. Certain it is, that when deep sections were made for a sewer in Lombard Street in 1786, the lowest stratum consisted of tesselated Roman pavements, their coloured dice laying scattered like flower leaves, and above that of a thick layer of wood ashes, as of the *débris* of charred wooden buildings. This ruin the Romans avenged by the slaughter of 80,000 Britons in a butchering fight, generally believed to have taken place at King's Cross (otherwise Battle Bridge), after which the fugitive Boadicea, in rage and despair, took poison and perished.

London probably soon sprang, phœnix-like, from the fire, though history leaves it in darkness to enjoy a lull of 200 years. In the early part of the second century Ptolemy, the geographer, speaks of it as a city of the Kentish people; but Mr. Craik very ingeniously conjectures that the Greek writer took his information from Phœnician works descriptive of Britain, written before even the invasion of Cæsar. Theodosius, a general of the Emperor Valentinian, who saved London from gathered hordes of Scots, Picts, Franks, and Saxons, is supposed to have repaired the walls of London, which had been first built by the Emperor Constantine early in the fourth century. In the reign of Theodosius, London, now called Augusta, became one of the chief, if not the chief, of the seventy Roman cities in Britain. In the famous "Itinerary" of Antoninus (about the end of the third century) London stands as the goal or starting-point of seven out of the fifteen great central Roman roads in England. Camden considers the London Stone, now enshrined in the south wall of St. Swithin's Church, Cannon Street, to have been the central milestone of Roman England, from which all the chief roads radiated, and by which the distances were reckoned. Wren supposed that Watling Street, of which Cannon Street is a part, was the High Street of Roman London. Another street ran west along Holborn from Cheapside, and from Cheapside probably north. A northern road ran by Aldgate, and probably Bishopsgate. The road from Dover came either over a ferry near the site of the present London Bridge or higher up at Dowgate, from Stoney Street on the Surrey side.

Early Roman London was scarcely larger than Hyde Park. Mr. Roach Smith, the best of all authorities on the subject, gives its length from the Tower to Ludgate, east and west, at about a mile; and north and south, that is from London Wall to the Thames, at about half a mile. The earliest Roman city was even smaller, for Roman sepulchres have been found in Bow Lane, Moorgate Street, Bishopsgate Within, which must at that time have been beyond the walls. The Roman cemeteries of Smithfield, St. Paul's, Whitechapel, the Minories, and Spitalfields, are of later dates, and are in all cases beyond the old line of circumvallation, according to the sound Roman custom fixed by law. The earlier London Mr. Roach Smith describes as an irregular space, the five main gates corresponding with Bridgegate, Ludgate, Bishopsgate, Aldersgate, and Aldgate. The north wall followed for some part the course of Cornhill and Leadenhall Street; the eastern Billiter Street and Mark Lane; the southern Thames Street; and the western the east side of Walbrook. Of the larger Roman wall, there were within the memory of man huge, shapeless masses, with trees growing upon them, opposite what is now Finsbury Circus. In 1852 a piece of Roman wall on Tower Hill was rescued from the improvers, and built into some stables and outhouses; but not before a careful sketch had been effected by the late Mr. Fairholt, one of the best of our antiquarian draughtsmen. The later Roman London was in general outline the same in shape and size as the London of the Saxons and Normans. The newer walls Pennant calculates at 3 miles 165 feet in circumference, they were 22 feet high, and guarded with forty lofty towers. At the end of the last century large portions of the old Roman wall were traceable in many places, but time has devoured almost the last morsels of that great *pièce de résistance*. In 1763 Mr. Gough made a drawing of a square Roman tower (one of three) then standing in Houndsditch. It was built in alternate layers of massive square stones and red tiles. The old loophole for the sentinel had been enlarged into a square latticed window. In 1857, while digging foundations for houses on the northeast side of Aldermanbury Postern, the workmen came on a portion of the Roman wall strengthened by blind arches. All that now substantially remains of the old fortification is a bastion in St. Giles's Church, Cripplegate; a fragment in St. Martin's Court, off Ludgate Hill; another portion exists in the Old Bailey, concealed behind houses; and a fourth, near George Street, Tower Hill. Portions of the wall have, however, been also broached in Falcon Square (one of which we have engraved), Bush Lane, Scott's Yard, and Cornhill, and others built in cellars and warehouses from opposite the Tower and Cripplegate.

The line of the Roman walls ran from the Tower straight to Aldgate; there making an angle, it continued to Bishopsgate. From there it turned westward to St. Giles's Churchyard, where it veered south to Falcon Square. At this point it continued west to Aldersgate, running under Christ's Hospital, and onward to Giltspur Street. There forming an angle, it proceeded directly to Ludgate towards the Thames, passing to the south of St. Andrew's Church. The wall then crossed Addle Street, and took a course along Upper and Lower Thames Street towards the Tower. In Thames Street the wall has been found built on oaken piles; on these was laid a stratum of chalk and stones, and over this a course of large, hewn sandstones, cemented with quicklime, sand, and pounded tile. The body of the wall was constructed of ragstone, flint, and lime, bonded at intervals with courses of plain and curve-edged tiles.

That Roman London grew slowly there is abundant proof. In building the new Exchange, the workmen came on a gravel-pit full of oyster-shells, cattle bones, old sandals, and shattered pottery. No coin found there being later than Severus indicates that this ground was bare waste outside the original city until at least the latter part of the third century. How far Roman London eventually spread its advancing waves of houses may be seen from the fact that Roman wall-paintings, indicating villas of men of wealth and position, have been found on both sides of High Street, Southwark, almost up to St. George's Church; while one of the outlying Roman cemeteries bordered the Kent Road.

From the horns of cattle having been dug up in St. Paul's Churchyard, the monks, ever eager to discover traces of that Paganism on which they engrafted Christianity, conjectured that a temple of Diana once stood on the site of St. Paul's. A stone altar, with a rude figure of the amazon goddess sculptured upon it, was indeed discovered in making the foundations for Goldsmiths' Hall, Cheapside; but this was a mere votive or private

altar, and proves nothing; and the ox bones, if any, found at St. Paul's, were perhaps refuse thrown into a rubbish-heap outside the old walls. As to the Temple of Apollo, supposed to have been replaced by Westminster Abbey, that is merely an invention of rival monks to glorify Thorney Island, and to render its antiquity equal to the fabulous claims of St. Paul's. Nor is there any positive proof that shrines to British gods ever stood on either place, though that they may have done so is not at all improbable.

The existing relics of Roman London are far more valuable and more numerous than is generally supposed. Innumerable tesselated pavements, masterpieces of artistic industry and taste, have been found in the City. A few of these should be noted. In 1854 part of the pavement of a room, twenty-eight feet square, was discovered, when the Excise Office was pulled down, between Bishopsgate Street and Broad Street. The central subject was supposed to be the Rape of Europa. A few years before another pavement was met with near the same spot. In 1841 two pavements were dug up under the French Protestant Church in Threadneedle Street. The best of these we have engraved. In 1792 a circular pavement was found in the same locality; and there has also been dug up in the same street a curious female head, the size of life, formed of coloured stones and glass. In 1805 a beautiful Roman pavement was disinterred on the north-east angle of the Bank of England, near the gate opening into Lothbury, and is now in the British Museum. In 1803 a fine specimen of pavement was found in front of the East-India House, Leadenhall Street, the central design being Bacchus reclining on a panther. In this pavement twenty distinct tints had been successfully used. Other pavements have been cut through in Crosby Square, Bartholemew Lane, Fenchurch Street, and College Street. The soil, according to Mr. Roach Smith, seems to have risen over them at the rate of nearly a foot in a century.

The statuary found in London should also not be forgotten. One of the most remarkable pieces was a colossal bronze head of the Emperor Hadrian, dredged up from the Thames a little below London Bridge. It is now in the British Museum. A colossal bronze hand, thirteen inches long, was also found in Thames Street, near the Tower. In 1857, near London Bridge, the dredgers found a beautiful bronze Apollino, a Mercury of exquisite design, a priest of Cybele, and a figure supposed to be Jupiter. The Apollino and Mercury are masterpieces of ideal beauty and grace. In 1842 a *chef d'œuvre* was dug out near the old Roman wall in Queen Street, Cheapside. It was the bronze stooping figure of an archer. It has silver eyes; and the perfect expression and anatomy display the highest art.

In 1825 a graceful little silver figure of the child Harpocrates, the God of Silence, looped with a gold chain, was found in the Thames, and is now in the British Museum. In 1839 a pair of gold armlets were dug up in Queen Street, Cheapside. In a kiln in St. Paul's Churchyard, in 1677, there were found lamps, bottles, urns, and dishes. Among other relics of Roman London drifted down by time we may instance articles of red glazed pottery, tiles, glass cups, window glass, bath scrapers, gold hair-pins, enamelled clasps, sandals, writing tablets, bronze spoons, forks, distaffs, bells, dice, and mill-stones. As for coins, which the Romans seem to have hid in every conceivable nook, Mr. Roach Smith says that within twenty years upwards of 2,000 were, to his own knowledge, found in London, chiefly in the bed of the Thames. Only one Greek coin, as far as we know, has ever been met with in London excavations.

The Romans left deep footprints wherever they trod. Many of our London streets still follow the lines they first laid down. The river bank still heaves beneath the ruins of their palaces. London Stone, as we have already shown, still stands to mark the starting-point of the great roads that they designed. In a lane out of the Strand there still exists a bath where their sinewy youth laved their limbs, dusty from the chariot races at the Campus Martius at Finsbury. The pavements trodden by the feet of Hadrian and Constantine still lie buried under the restless wheels that roll over our City streets. The ramparts which the legionaries guarded have not yet crumbled to dust, though the rude people they conquered have themselves long since grown into conquerors. Roman London now exists only in fragments, invisible save to the prying antiquary. As the seed is to be found hanging to the root of the ripe wheat, so some filaments of the first germ of London, of the British hut and the Roman villa, still exist hidden under the foundations of the busy city that now teems with thousands of inhabitants. We tread under foot daily the pride of our old oppressors.

CHAPTER II.

TEMPLE BAR.

Temple Bar—The Golgotha of English Traitors—When Temple Bar was made of Wood—Historical Pageants at Temple Bar—The Associations of Temple Bar—Mischievous Processions through Temple Bar—The First grim Trophy—Rye-House Plot Conspirators.

TEMPLE BAR was rebuilt by Sir Christopher Wren, in 1670-72, soon after the Great Fire had swept away eighty-nine London churches, four out of the seven City gates, 460 streets, and 13,200 houses, and had destroyed fifteen of the twenty-six wards, and laid waste 436 acres of buildings, from the Tower east-ward to the Inner Temple westward.

The old black gateway, once the dreaded Gol-gotha of English traitors, separated, it should be remembered, the Strand from Fleet Street, the city from the shire, and the Freedom of the City of London from the Liberty of the City of Westminster. As Hatton (1708—Queen Anne) says,—" This gate opens not immediately into the City itself, but into the Liberty or Freedom thereof." We need hardly say that nothing can be more erroneous than the ordinary London supposition that Temple Bar ever formed part of the City fortifications. Mr. Gilbert à Beckett, laughing at this tradition, once said in *Punch:* "Temple Bar has always seemed to me a weak point in the fortifications of London. Bless you, the besieging army would never stay to bom-bard it—they would dash through the barber's."

The Bar, after having been for many years a great obstruction to the traffic, was removed in the winter of 1877–8, whilst the New Law Courts were in process of erection. The Bar was of Portland stone, which London smoke alternately blackens and calcines ; and each façade had four Corinthian pilasters, an entablature, and an arched pediment. On the west (Strand) side, in two niches, stood, as eternal sentries, Charles I. and Charles II., in Roman costume. Charles I. long ago lost his bâton, as he once deliberately lost his head. Over the keystone of the central arch there used to be the royal arms. On the east side were James I. and Elizabeth (by many able writers supposed to be Anne of Denmark, the queen of James I.). She was pointing her white finger at Child's ; while he, looking down on the passing cabs, seemed to say, " I am nearly tired of standing ; suppose we go to Whitehall, and sit down a bit ? "

These affected, mean statues, with their crinkly drapery, were the work of a vain, half-crazed sculptor, named John Bushnell, who died mad in 1701. Bushnell, who had visited Rome and

Venice, executed Cowley's monument in Westminster Abbey, and the statues of Charles I., Charles II., and Gresham, in the old Exchange.

The slab over the eastern side of the arch bore the following inscription, which was all but obliterated by time :—

"Erected in the year 1670, Sir Samuel Starling, Mayor; continued in the year 1671, Sir Richard Ford, Lord Mayor; and finished in the year 1672, Sir George Waterman, Lord Mayor."

All these persons were friends of Pepys.

The upper part of the Bar was flanked by scrolls, but the fruit and flowers once sculptured on the pediment, and the supporters of the royal arms over the posterns, had crumbled away. In the centre of each façade was a semi-circular-headed, ecclesiastical-looking window, that cast a dim horny light into a room above the gate, held of the City, at an annual rent of some £50, by Messrs. Childs, the bankers, as a sort of muniment-room for their old account-books. There was here preserved, among other costlier treasures of Mammon, the private account-book of Charles II. The original Child was a friend of Pepys, and is mentioned by him as quarrelling with the Duke of York on Admiralty matters. The Child who succeeded him was a friend of Pope, and all but led him into the South-Sea-Bubble speculation.

There is no extant historical account of Temple Bar in which the following passage from Strype (George I.) is not to be found embedded like a fossil; it is, in fact, nearly all we London topographers know of the early history of the Bar :— "Anciently," says Strype, "there were only posts, rails, and a chain, such as are now in Holborn, Smithfield, and Whitechapel bars. Afterwards there was a house of timber erected across the street, with a narrow gateway and an entry on the south side of it under the house." This structure is to be seen in the view of London in the British Museum, 1620 (James I.), and in Hollar's seven-sheet map of London (Charles II.).

The date of the erection of the "wooden house" is not to be ascertained; but there is the house plain enough in a view of London to which Maitland affixes the date about 1560 (the second year of Elizabeth); so we may perhaps safely put it down as early as Edward VI. or Henry VIII. Indeed, if a certain scrap of history is correct—i.e., that bluff King Hal once threatened, if a certain Bill did not pass the Commons a little quicker, to fix the heads of several refractory M.P.s on the top of Temple Bar—we must suppose the old City toll-gate to be as old as the early Tudors.

After Simon de Montfort's death, at the battle of Evesham, 1265, Prince Edward, afterwards Edward I., punished the rebellious Londoners, who had befriended Montfort, by taking away all their street chains and bars, and locking them up in the Tower.

The earliest known documentary and historical notice of Temple Bar is in 1327, the first year of Edward III. ; and in the thirty-fourth year of the same reign we find, at an inquisition before the mayor, twelve witnesses deposing that the commonalty of the City had, time out of mind, had free ingress and egress from the City to Thames and from Thames to the City, through the great gate of the Templars situate within Temple Bar. This referred to some dispute about the right of way through the Temple, built in the reign of Henry I. In 1384 Richard II. granted a licence for paving Strand Street from Temple Bar to the Savoy, and collecting tolls to cover such charges.

The historical pageants that have taken place at Temple Bar deserve a notice, however short. On the 5th of November, 1422, the corpse of that brave and chivalrous king, the hero of Agincourt, Henry V., was borne to its rest at Westminster Abbey by the chief citizens and nobles, and every doorway from Southwark to Temple Bar had its mournful torch-bearer. In 1502-3 the hearse of Elizabeth of York, queen of Henry VII., halted at Temple Bar, on its way from the Tower to Westminster, and at the Bar the Abbots of Westminster and Bermondsey blessed the corpse, and the Earl of Derby and a large company of nobles joined the sable funeral throng. After sorrow came joy, and after joy sorrow—*Ita vita*. In the next reign poor Anne Boleyn, radiant with happiness and triumph, came through the Bar (May 31, 1534), on her way to the Tower, to be welcomed by the clamorous citizens, the day before her ill-starred coronation. Temple Bar on that occasion was new painted and repaired, and near it stood singing men and children—the Fleet Street conduit all the time running claret. The old gate figured more conspicuously the day before the coronation of that wondrous child, Edward VI. Two hogsheads of wine were then ladled out to the thirsty mob, and the gate at Temple Bar was painted with battlements and buttresses, richly hung with cloth of Arras, and all in a flutter with "fourteen standard flags." There were eight French trumpeters blowing their best, besides "a pair of regals," with children singing to the same. In September, 1553, when Edward's cold-hearted half-sister, Mary Tudor, came through the City, according to ancient English custom, the day

THE LAST OF TEMPLE BAR, 1877. (*From a Contemporary Drawing.*)

before her coronation, she did not ride on horse-back, as Edward had done, but sat in a chariot covered with cloth of tissue and drawn by six horses draped with the same. Minstrels piped and trumpeted at Ludgate, and Temple Bar was newly painted and hung.

Old Temple Bar, the background to many historical scenes, figures in the rash rebellion of Sir Thomas Wyatt. When he had fought his way down Piccadilly to the Strand, Temple Bar was thrown open to him, or forced open by him;

God solemnly at St. Paul's. The City waits stood in triumph on the roof of the gate. The Lord Mayor and Aldermen, in scarlet gowns, welcomed the queen and delivered up the City sword, then on her return they took horse and rode before her. The City Companies lined the north side of the street, the lawyers and gentlemen of the Inns of Court the south. Among the latter stood a person afterwards not altogether unknown, one Francis Bacon, who displayed his wit by saying to a friend, "Mark the courtiers! Those who

TEMPLE BAR, WEST FRONT, IN 1710. (*From Mr. Crace's Collection*).

but when he had been repulsed at Ludgate he was hemmed in by cavalry at Temple Bar, where he surrendered. This foolish revolt led to the death of innocent Lady Jane Grey, and brought sixty brave gentlemen to the scaffold and the gallows.

On Elizabeth's procession from the Tower before her coronation, January, 1559, Gogmagog the Albion, and Corineus the Briton, the two Guildhall giants, stood on the Bar; and on the south side there were chorister lads, one of whom, richly attired as a page, bade the queen farewell in the name of the whole City. In 1588, the glorious year in which the Armada was defeated, Elizabeth passed through the Bar on her way to return thanks to

bow first to the citizens are in debt; those who bow first to us are at law!"

In 1601, when the Earl of Essex made his insane attempt to rouse the City to rebellion, Temple Bar, we are told, was thrown open to him; but Ludgate being closed against him on his retreat from Cheap-side, he came back by boat to Essex House, where he surrendered after a short and useless resistance.

King James made his first public entry into his royal City of London, with his consort and son Henry, upon the 15th of March, 1603-4. The king was mounted upon a white genet, ambling through the crowded streets under a canopy held by eight gentlemen of the Privy Chamber, as representatives of the Barons of the Cinque Ports, and passed under six arches of triumph, to take his leave at the Temple of Janus, erected for the occasion at Temple Bar. This edifice was fifty-seven feet high, proportioned in every respect like a temple.

In June, 1649 (the year of the execution of Charles), Cromwell and the Parliament dined at Guildhall in state, and the mayor, says Whitelocke, delivered up the sword to the Speaker, at Temple Bar, as he had before done to King Charles.

Philips, Milton's nephew, who wrote the continuation of Baker's Chronicle, describes the ceremony at Temple Bar on the proclamation of Charles II. The old oak gates being shut, the king-at-arms, with tabard on and trumpet before him, knocked and gravely demanded entrance. The Lord Mayor appointed some one to ask who knocked. The king-at-arms replied, that if they would open the wicket, and let the Lord Mayor come thither, he would to him deliver his message. The Lord Mayor then appeared, tremendous in crimson velvet gown, and on horse-back, of all things in the world, the trumpets sounding as the gallant knight pricked forth to demand of the herald, who he was and what was his message. The bold herald, with his hat on, answered, regardless of Lindley Murray, who was yet unknown, "We are the herald-at-arms appointed and commanded by the Lords and Commons assembled in Parliament, and demand an entrance into the famous City of London, to proclaim Charles II. King of England, Scotland, France, and Ireland, and we expect your speedy answer to our demand." An alderman then replied, "The message is accepted," and the gates were thrown open.

When William III. came to see the City and the Lord Mayor's Show in 1689, the City militia, holding lighted flambeaux, lined Fleet Street as far as Temple Bar.

The shadow of every monarch and popular hero since Charles II.'s time has rested for at least a passing moment at the old gateway. Queen Anne passed here to return thanks at St. Paul's for the victory of Blenheim. Here Marlborough's coach ominously broke down in 1714, when he returned in triumph from his voluntary exile.

George III. passed through Temple Bar, young and happy, the year after his coronation, and again when, old and almost broken-hearted, he returned thanks for his partial recovery from insanity; and in our time that graceless son of his, the Prince Regent, came through the Bar in 1814, to thank God at St. Paul's for the downfall of Bonaparte.

On the 9th November, 1837, the accession of Queen Victoria, Sir Peter Laurie, picturesque in scarlet gown, Spanish hat, and black feathers, presented the City sword to the Queen at Temple Bar; Sir Peter was again ready with the same weapon in 1844, when the Queen opened the new Royal Exchange; but in 1851, when her Majesty once more visited the City, the old ceremony was (wrongly, we think) dispensed with.

At the funeral of Lord Nelson, the honoured corpse, followed by downcast old sailors, was met at the Bar by the Lord Mayor and the Corporation; and the Great Duke's funeral car, and the long train of representative soldiers, rested at the Bar, which was hung with black velvet.

A few earlier associations connected with the present Bar deserve a moment or two's recollection. On February 12th, when General Monk—"Honest George," as his old Cromwellian soldiers used to call him—entered London, dislodged the "Rump" Parliament, and prepared for the Restoration of Charles II., bonfires were lit, the City bells rung, and London broke into a sudden flame of joy. Pepys, walking homeward about ten o'clock, says: — "The common joy was everywhere to be seen. The number of bonfires—there being fourteen between St. Dunstan's and Temple Bar, and at Strand Bridge, east of Catherine Street, I could at one time tell thirty-one fires."

On November 17, 1679, the year after the sham Popish Plot concocted by those matchless scoundrels, Titus Oates, an expelled naval chaplain, and Bedloe, a swindler and thief, Temple Bar was made the spot for a great mob pilgrimage, on the anniversary of the accession of Queen Elizabeth. The ceremonial is supposed to have been organised by that restless plotter against a Popish succession, Lord Shaftesbury, and the gentlemen of the Green Ribbon Club, whose tavern, the "King's Head," was at the corner of Chancery Lane, opposite the Inner Temple gate. To scare and vex the Papists, the church bells began to ring out as early as three o'clock on the morning of that dangerous day. At dusk the procession of several thousand half-crazed torch-bearers started from Moorgate, along Bishopsgate Street, and down Houndsditch and Aldgate (passing Shaftesbury's house imagine the roar of the monster mob, the wave of torches, and the fiery fountains of squibs at that point!), then through Leadenhall Street and Cornhill, by the Royal Exchange, along Cheapside and on to Temple Bar, where the bonfire awaited the puppets. In a torrent of fire the noisy Protestants passed through the exulting City, making the Papists cower and shudder in their garrets and cellars, and before the flaming deluge opened a storm of shouting people.

This procession consisted of fifteen groups of priests, Jesuits, and friars, two following a man on a horse, holding up before him a dummy, dressed to represent Sir Edmondbury Godfrey, a Protestant justice and wood merchant, supposed to have been murdered by Roman Catholics at Somerset House. It was attended by a body-guard of 150 sword-bearers and a man roaring a political cry of the time through a brazen speaking-trumpet. The great bonfire was built up mountain high opposite the Inner Temple gate. Some zealous Protestants, by pre-arrangement, had crowned the prim and meagre statue of Elizabeth, upon the east side of the Bar, with a wreath of gilt laurel, and placed under her hand, which pointed to Child's Bank, a golden glistening shield, with the motto, "The Protestant Religion and Magna Charta," inscribed upon it. Several lighted torches were stuck before her niche. Lastly, amidst a fiery shower of squibs from every door and window, the Pope and his companions were toppled into the huge bonfire, with shouts that reached almost to Charing Cross.

These mischievous processions were continued till the reign of George I. There was to have been a magnificent display in November, 1711, when the Whigs were dreading the contemplated peace with the French and the return of Marlborough. But the Tories, declaring that the Kit-Cat Club was urging the mob to destroy the house of Harley, the Minister, and to tear him to pieces, seized on the wax figures in Drury Lane, and forbade the ceremony.

As early as two years after the Restoration, Sir Balthazar Gerbier, a restless architectural quack and adventurer of those days, wrote a pamphlet proposing a sumptuous gate at Temple Bar, and the levelling of the Fleet Valley. After the Great Fire Charles II. himself hurried the erection of the Bar, and promised money to carry out the work. During the Great Fire, Temple Bar was one of the stations for constables, 100 firemen, and 30 soldiers.

The Rye-House Plot brought the first trophy to the Golgotha of the Bar, in 1684, twelve years after its erection. Sir Thomas Armstrong was deep in the scheme. If the discreditable witnesses examined against Lord William Russell are to be believed, a plot had been concocted by a few desperate men to assassinate "the Blackbird and the Gold-finch"—as the conspirators called the King and the Duke of York—as they were in their coach on their way from Newmarket to London. This plan seems to have been the suggestion of Rumbold, a maltster, who lived in a lonely moated farm-house, called Rye House, about eighteen miles from London, near the river Ware, close to a by-road that leads from Bishop Stortford to Hoddesdon.

Charles II. had a violent hatred to Armstrong, who had been his Gentleman of the Horse, and was supposed to have incited his illegitimate son, the Duke of Monmouth, to rebellion. Sir Thomas was hanged at Tyburn. After the body had hung half an hour, the hangman cut it down, stripped it, lopped off the head, threw the heart into a fire, and divided the body into four parts. The fore-quarter (after being boiled in pitch at Newgate) was set on Temple Bar, the head was placed on Westminster Hall, and the rest of the body was sent to Stafford, which town Sir Thomas represented in Parliament.

Eleven years after, the heads of two more traitors —this time conspirators against William III.— joined the relic of Armstrong. Sir John Friend was a rich brewer at Aldgate. Parkyns was an old Warwickshire county gentleman. The plotters had several plans. One was to attack Kensington Palace at night, scale the outer wall, and storm or fire the building; another was to kill William on a Sunday, as he drove from Kensington to the chapel at St. James's Palace. The murderers agreed to assemble near where Apsley House now stands. Just as the royal coach passed from Hyde Park across to the Green Park, thirty conspirators agreed to fall on the twenty-five guards, and butcher the king before he could leap out of his carriage. These two Jacobite gentlemen died bravely, pro-claiming their entire loyalty to King James and the "Prince of Wales."

The unfortunate gentlemen who took a moody pleasure in drinking "the squeezing of the rotten Orange" had long passed on their doleful journey from Newgate to Tyburn before the ghastly pro-cession of the brave and unlucky men of the rising in 1715 began its mournful march.*

Sir Bernard Burke mentions a tradition that the head of the young Earl of Derwentwater was exposed on Temple Bar in 1716, and that his wife drove in a cart under the arch while a man hired for the purpose threw down to her the beloved head from the parapet above. But the story is entirely untrue, and is only a version of the way in which the head of Sir Thomas More was re-moved by his son-in-law and daughter from London Bridge, where that cruel tyrant Henry VIII. had placed it. Some years ago, when the Earl of

---

* Amongst these we must not forget Joseph Sullivan, who was executed at Tyburn for high treason, for enlisting men in the service of the Pretender. In the collection of broad-sides belonging to the Society of Antiquaries there is one of great interest, entitled "Perkins against Perkin, a dialogue between Sir William Perkins and Major Sulliviane, the two loggerheads upon Temple Bar, concerning the present junc-ture of affaires." Date uncertain.

Derwentwater's coffin was found in the family vault, the head was lying safe with the body. In 1716 there was, however, a traitor's head spiked on the Bar—that of Colonel John Oxburgh, the victim of mistaken fidelity to a bad cause. He was a brave Lancashire gentleman, who had surrendered with his forces at Preston. He displayed signal courage and resignation in prison, forgetting himself to comfort others.

The next victim was Mr. Christopher Layer, a young Norfolk man and a Jacobite barrister, living in Southampton Buildings, Chancery Lane. He plunged deeply into the Atterbury Plot of 1722, and, with Lords North and Grey, enlisted men, hired officers, and, taking advantage of the universal misery caused by the bursting of the South Sea Bubble, planned a general rising against George I. The scheme was, with four distinct bodies of Jacobites, to seize the Tower and the Bank, to arrest the king and the prince, and capture or kill Lord Cadogan, one of the Ministers. At the trial it was proved that Layer had been over to Rome, and had seen the Pretender, who, by proxy, had stood godfather to his child. Troops were to be sent from France ; barricades were to be thrown up all over London. The Jacobites had calculated that the Government had only 14,000 men to meet them— 3,000 of these would be wanted to guard London, 3,000 for Scotland, and 2,000 for the garrisons. The original design had been to take advantage of the king's departure for Hanover, and, in the words of one of the conspirators, the Jacobites were fully convinced that "they should walk King George out before Lady-day." Layer was hanged at Tyburn, and his head fixed upon Temple Bar.

Years after, one stormy night in 1753, the rebel's skull blew down, and was picked up by a non-juring attorney, named Pierce, who preserved it as a relic of the Jacobite martyr. It is said that Dr. Richard Rawlinson, an eminent antiquary, obtained what he thought was Layer's head, and desired in his will that it should be placed in his right hand when he was buried. Another version of the story is, that a spurious skull was foisted upon Rawlinson, who died happy in the possession of the doubtful treasure. Rawlinson was bantered by Addison for his pedantry, in one of the *Tatlers*, and was praised by Dr. Johnson for his learning.

The 1745 rebellion brought the heads of fresh victims to the Bar, and this was the last triumph of barbarous justice. Colonel Francis Towneley's was the sixth ; that of Fletcher (his fellow-officer), the seventh and last. The Earls of Kilmarnock and Cromarty, Lord Balmerino, and thirty-seven other rebels (thirty-six of them having been captured in Carlisle) were tried the same session. Towneley was a man of about fifty-four years of age, nephew of Mr. Towneley of Towneley Hall, Lancashire (of the "Towneley Marbles" family), who had been tried and acquitted in 1715, though many of his men were found guilty and executed. The nephew had gone over to France in 1727, and obtained a commission from the French king, whom he served for fifteen years, being at the siege of Philipsburg, and close to the Duke of Berwick when that general's head was shot off. About 1740, Towneley stole over to England to see his friends and to plot against the Hanover family ; and as soon as the rebels came into England, he met them between Lancaster and Preston, and came with them to Manchester. At the trial Roger M'Donald, an officer's servant, deposed to seeing Towneley on the retreat from Derby, and between Lancaster and Preston riding at the head of the Manchester regiment on a bay horse. He had a white cockade in his hat and wore a plaid sash.

George Fletcher, who was tried at the same time as Towneley, was a rash young chapman, who managed his widowed mother's provision shop "at Salford, just over the bridge in Manchester." His mother had begged him on her knees to keep out of the rebellion, even offering him a thousand pounds for his own pocket, if he would stay at home. He bought a captain's commission of Murray, the Pretender's secretary, for fifty pounds ; wore the smart white cockade and a Highland plaid sash lined with white silk; and headed the very first captain's guard mounted for the Pretender at Carlisle. A Manchester man deposed to seeing at the Exchange a sergeant, with a drum, beating up for volunteers for the Manchester regiment.

Fletcher, Towneley, and seven other unfortunate Jacobites were hanged on Kennington Common. Before the carts drove away, the men flung their prayer-books, written speeches, and gold-laced hats gaily to the crowd. Mr. James (Jemmy) Dawson, the hero of Shenstone's touching ballad, was one of the nine. As soon as they were dead the hangman cut down the bodies, disembowelled, beheaded, and quartered them, throwing the hearts into the fire. A monster—a fighting-man of the day, named Buckhorse—is said to have actually eaten a piece of Towneley's flesh, to show his loyalty. Before the ghastly scene was over, the heart of one unhappy spectator had already broken. The lady to whom James Dawson was engaged to be married followed the rebels to the common, and even came near enough to see, with pallid face, the fire kindling, the axe, the coffins, and all the other dreadful preparations. She bore up bravely, until she heard her lover was no more. Then she drew her head back into the coach, and crying out, " My dear, I follow thee—I follow thee ! Lord God, receive our souls, I pray Thee!" fell on the neck of a companion and expired. Mr. Dawson had behaved gallantly in prison, saying, " He did not care if they put a ton weight of iron upon him, it would not daunt him."

A curious old print of 1746, full of vulgar triumph, reproduces a " Temple Bar, the City Golgotha," representing the Bar with three heads on the top of it, spiked on long iron rods. The devil looks down in ribald triumph from above, and waves a rebel banner, on which, besides three coffins and a crown, is the motto, " A crown or a grave." Underneath are written these patriotic but doggrel lines :—

"Observe the banner which would all enslave,
  Which misled traytors did so proudly wave :
The devil seems the project to surprise ;
  A fiend confused from off the trophy flies.

While trembling rebels at the fabric gaze,
  And dread their fate with horror and amaze,
Let Britain's sons the emblematic view,
  And plainly see what is rebellion's due."

The heads of Fletcher and Townley were put on the Bar August 12, 1746. On August 15th Horace Walpole, writing to a friend, says he had just been roaming in the City, and "passed under the new heads on Temple Bar, where people make a trade of letting spy-glasses at a halfpenny a look." According to Mr. J. T. Smith, an old man living in 1825 remembered the last heads on Temple Bar being visible through a telescope across the space between the Bar and Leicester Fields.

Between two and three A.M., on the morning of January 20, 1766, a mysterious man was arrested by the watch as he was discharging, by the dim light, musket bullets at the two heads then remaining upon Temple Bar. On being questioned by the puzzled magistrate, he affected a disorder in his senses, and craftily declared that the patriotic reason for his eccentric conduct was his strong attachment to the present Government, and that he thought it not sufficient that a traitor should merely suffer death ; that this provoked his indignation, and it had been his constant practice for three nights past to amuse himself in the same manner. " And it is much to be feared," says the past record of the event, "that the man is a near relation to one of the unhappy sufferers." Upon searching this very suspicious marksman, about fifty musket bullets were found on him, wrapped up in a paper on which was written the motto, " Eripuit ille vitam."

After this, history leaves the heads of the unhappy Jacobites—those lips that love had kissed, those cheeks children had patted—to moulder on in the sun and in the rain, till the last day of March, 1772, when one of them (Towneley or Fletcher) fell. The last stormy gust of March threw it down, and a short time after a strong wind blew down the other ; and against the sky no more relics remained of a barbarous and unchristian revenge. In April, 1773, Boswell, whom we all despise and all like, dined at courtly Mr. Beauclerk's with Dr. Johnson, Lord Charlemont (Hogarth's friend), Sir Joshua Reynolds, and other members of the literary club, in Gerrard Street, Soho, it being the awful evening when Boswell was to be balloted for. The conversation turned on the new and commendable practice of erecting monuments to great men in St. Paul's. The Doctor observed : " I remember once being with Goldsmith in Westminster Abbey. Whilst we stood at Poet's Corner, I said to him,—

" Forsitan et nostrum nomen miscebitur illis."—OVID.

When we got to Temple Bar he stopped me, and pointing to the heads upon it, slily whispered,—

" Forsitan et nostrum nomen miscebitur *istis*."

This anecdote, so full of clever, arch wit, is sufficient to endear the old gateway to all lovers of Johnson and of Goldsmith.

According to Mr. Timbs, in his " London and Westminster," Mrs. Black, the wife of the editor of the *Morning Chronicle*, when asked if she remembered any heads on Temple Bar, used to reply, in her brusque, hearty way, " *Boys, I recollect the scene well!* I have seen on that Temple Bar, about which you ask, two human heads—real heads— traitors' heads—spiked on iron poles. There were two ; I saw one fall (March 31, 1772). Women shrieked as it fell ; men, as I have heard, shrieked. One woman near me fainted. Yes, boys, I recollect seeing human heads upon Temple Bar."

The cruel-looking spikes were removed early in the present century. The panelled oak gates were often renewed, though certainly shutting them too often never wore them out.

As early as 1790 Alderman Pickett (who built the St. Clement's arch), with other subversive reformers, tried to pull down Temple Bar. It was pronounced unworthy of form, of no antiquity, an ambuscade for pickpockets, and a record of only the dark and crimson pages of history.

A writer in the *Gentleman's Magazine*, in 1813 chronicling the clearance away of some hovels encroaching upon the building, says : " It will not be surprising if certain amateurs, busy in improving the architectural concerns of the City, should at length request of their brethren to allow the Bar or grand gate of entrance into the City of London to stand, after they have so repeatedly sought to obtain its destruction." In 1852 a proposal for its repair and restoration was defeated in the Common Council; and twelve months later, a number of bankers, merchants, and traders set their hands to a petition for its removal altogether, as serving no practical purpose, as it impeded ventilation and

of this sum £480 for his four stone monarchs. The mason was John Marshall, who carved the pedestal of the statue of Charles I. at Charing Cross and worked on the Monument in Fish Street Hill. In 1636 Inigo Jones had designed a new arch, the plan of which still exists. Wren, it is said, took his design of the Bar from an old temple at Rome.

The old Bar, once a protection, then an ornament, became an obstruction—the too narrow neck of a large decanter—a bone in the throat of Fleet

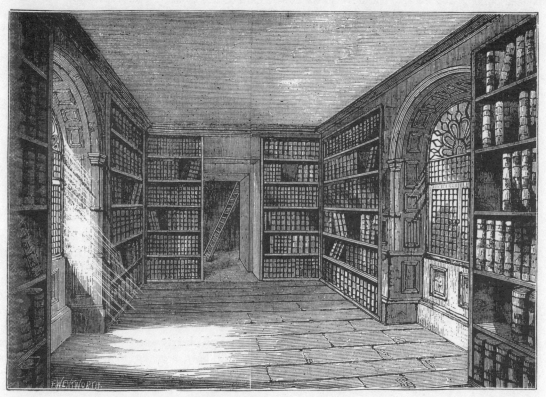

THE ROOM OVER TEMPLE BAR, 1876 (*see page* 37).

retarded improvements. Since then Mr. Heywood has proposed to make a circus at Temple Bar, leaving the archway in the centre; and Mr. W. Burges, the architect, suggested a new arch in keeping with the new Law Courts opposite.

It is a singular fact that the " Parentalia," a chronicle of Wren's works written by Wren's clever son, contains hardly anything about Temple Bar. According to Mr Noble, the Wren manuscripts in the British Museum, Wren's ledger in the Bodleian, and the Record Office documents, are equally silent; but from a folio at the Guildhall, entitled " Expenses of Public Buildings after the Great Fire," it would appear that the Bar cost altogether £1,397 10s.; Bushnell, the sculptor, receiving out

Street. It also became dilapidated and dangerous, and was eventually removed, as already stated, in 1877-8. Yet to the last we felt a lingering fondness for the old barrier that we had seen draped in black for a dead hero and glittering with gold in honour of a young bride. We had shared the sunshine that brightened it and the gloom that has darkened it, and we felt for it a species of friendship, in which it mutely shared. It is worthy of notice here that the visit of Her Majesty and the Prince of Wales to St. Paul's Cathedral, in the month of February, 1872, mentioned by us in a previous chapter, was the very last occasion on which Royalty passed in state through the gates of Temple Bar.

TITUS OATES IN THE PILLORY (*see page 33*).

CHAPTER III.

FLEET STREET—GENERAL INTRODUCTION.

Frays in Fleet Street—Chaucer and the Friar—The Duchess of Gloucester doing Penance for Witchcraft—Riots between Law Students and Citizens—'Prentice Riots—Oates in the Pillory—Entertainments in Fleet Street—Shop Signs—Burning the Boot—Trial of Hardy—Queen Caroline's Funeral.

ALAS, for the changes of time! The Fleet, that little, quick-flowing stream, once so bright and clear, is now a sewer! but its name remains immortalised by the street called after it.

Although, according to a modern antiquary, a Roman amphitheatre once stood on the site of the Fleet Prison, and Roman citizens were probably interred outside Ludgate, we know but little whether Roman buildings ever stood on the west side of the City gates. Stow, however, describes a stone pavement supported on piles being found, in 1595, near the Fleet Street end of Chancery Lane; so that we may presume the soil of the neighbourhood was originally marshy. The first British settlers there must probably have been restless spirits, impatient of the high rents and insufficient room inside the City walls, and willing, for economy, to risk the forays of any Saxon pirates who chose to steal up the river on a dusky night and sack the outlying cabins of London.

There were certainly rough doings in Fleet Street in the Middle Ages, for the City chronicles tell us of much blood spilt there and of many deeds of violence. In 1228 (Henry III.) we find, for instance, one Henry de Buke slaying a man named Le Ireis, or Le Tylor, of Fleet Bridge, then fleeing to the church of St. Mary, Southwark, and there claiming sanctuary. In 1311 (Edward II.) five of the king's not very respectable or law-fearing household were arrested in Fleet Street for a burglary; and though the weak king demanded them (they were perhaps servants of his Gascon favourite, Piers Gaveston, whom the barons afterwards killed), the City refused to give them up, and they probably had short shrive. In the same reign, when the Strand was full of bushes and thickets, Fleet Street could hardly have been continuous. Still, some shops in Fleet Street were, no doubt, even in Edward II.'s reign, of importance, for we find, in 1321, a Fleet Street bootmaker supplying the luxurious king with "six pairs of boots, with tassels of silk and drops of silver-gilt, the price of each pair being 5s." In Richard II.'s reign it is especially mentioned that Wat Tyler's fierce Kentish men sacked the Savoy church, and part of the Temple, and destroyed two forges which had been originally erected on each side of St. Dunstan's Church by the Knight Templars. The Priory of St. John of Jerusalem had paid a rent of

15s. for these forges, which same rent was given for more than a century after their destruction.

The poet Chaucer is said to have beaten a saucy Franciscan friar in Fleet Street, and to have been fined 2s. for the offence by the Honourable Society of the Inner Temple; so Speight had heard from one who had seen the entry in the records of the Inner Temple.

In King Henry IV.'s reign another crime disturbed Fleet Street. A Fleet Street goldsmith was murdered by ruffians in the Strand, and his body thrown under the Temple Stairs.

In 1440 (Henry VI.) a strange procession startled London citizens. Eleanor Cobham, Duchess of Gloucester, did penance through Fleet Street for witchcraft practised against the king. She and certain priests and necromancers had, it was said, melted a wax figure of young King Henry before a slow fire, praying that as that figure melted his life might melt also. Of the duchess's confederates, the Witch of Ely was burned at Smithfield, a canon of Westminster died in the Tower, and a third culprit was hung, drawn, and quartered at Tyburn. The duchess was brought from Westminster, and landed at the Temple Stairs, from whence, with a tall wax taper in her hand, she walked bareheaded to St. Paul's, where she offered at the high altar. Another day she did penance at Christ Church, Aldgate; a third day at St. Michael's, Cornhill, the Lord Mayor, sheriffs, and most of the Corporation following. She was then banished to the Isle of Man, and her ghost, they say, still haunts Peel Castle.

And now, in the long panorama of years, there rises in Fleet Street a clash of swords and a clatter of bucklers. In 1441 (Henry VI.) the general effervescence of the times spread beyond Ludgate, and there was a great affray in Fleet Street between the hot-blooded youths of the Inns of Court and the citizens, which lasted two days; the chief man in the riot was one of Clifford's Inn, named Harbottle; and this irrepressible Harbottle and his fellows only the appearance of the mayor and sheriffs could quiet. In 1458 (in the same reign) there was a more serious riot of the same kind; the students were then driven back by archers from the Conduit near Shoe Lane to their several inns, and some slain, including "the Queen's attornie," who certainly ought to have known better and kept closer to his parchments. Even the king's meek nature was roused at this; he committed the principal governors of Furnival's, Clifford's, and Barnard's inns to the castle of Hertford, and sent for several aldermen to Windsor Castle, where he either rated or imprisoned them, or both.

Fleet Street often figures in the chronicles of Elizabeth's reign. On one visit it is particularly said that she often graciously stopped her coach to speak to the poor; and a green branch of rosemary given to her by a poor woman near Fleet Bridge was seen, not without marvellous wonder of such as knew the presenter, when her Majesty reached Westminster. In the same reign we are told that the young Earl of Oxford, after attending his father's funeral in Essex, rode through Fleet Street to Westminster, attended by seven score horsemen, all in black. Such was the splendid and proud profusion of Elizabeth's nobles.

James's reign was a stormy one for Fleet Street. Many a time the ready 'prentices snatched their clubs (as we read in "The Fortunes of Nigel"), and, vaulting over their counters, joined in the fray that surged past their shops. In 1621 particularly, three 'prentices having abused Gondomar, the Spanish ambassador, as he passed their master's door in Fenchurch Street, the king ordered the riotous youths to be whipped from Aldgate to Temple Bar. In Fleet Street, however, the apprentices rose in force, and shouting "Rescue!" quickly released the lads and beat the marshalmen. If there had been any resistance, another thousand sturdy 'prentices would soon have carried on the war.

Nor did Charles's reign bring any quiet to Fleet Street, for then the Templars began to draw out their swords. On the 12th of January, 1627, the Templars, having chosen a Mr. Palmer as their Lord of Misrule, went out late at night into Fleet Street to collect his rents. At every door the jovial collectors winded the Temple horn, and if at the second blast the door was not courteously opened, my lord cried majestically, "Give fire, gunner!" and a sturdy smith burst the panels open with a huge sledge-hammer. The horrified Lord Mayor being appealed to soon arrived, attended by the watch of the ward and men armed with halberts. At eleven o'clock on the Sunday night the two monarchs came into collision in Hare Alley (now Hare Court). The Lord of Misrule bade my Lord Mayor come to him; but Palmer omitting to take off his hat, the halberts flew sharply round him, his subjects were soundly beaten, and he was dragged off to the Compter. There, with soiled finery, the new year's king was kept two days in durance, the attorney-general at last fetching the fallen monarch away in his own coach. At a court masque soon afterwards the king made the two rival potentates join hands; but the King of Misrule had, nevertheless, to refund all the five shillings' he had exacted, and repair all the Fleet Street doors his too handy gunner had destroyed. The very next year the quarrelsome street broke again into a rage, and four persons lost their lives. Of the rioters, two were executed within the week. One of these was John Stanford, of the duke's chamber, and the other Captain Nicholas Ashurst. The quarrel was about politics, and the courtiers seem to have been the offenders.

In Charles II.'s time the pillory was sometimes set up at the Temple gate; and here the wretch Titus Oates stood, amidst showers of unsavoury eggs and the curses of those who had learnt to see the horror of his crimes. Well said Judge Withers to this man, "I never pronounce criminal sentence but with some compassion; but you are such a villain and hardened sinner, that I can find no sentiment of compassion for you." The pillory had no fixed place, for in 1670 we find a Scotchman suffering at the Chancery Lane end for telling a victualler that his house would be fired by the Papists; and the next year a man stood upon the pillory at the end of Shoe Lane for insulting Lord Coventry, as he was starting as ambassador for Sweden.

In the reign of Queen Anne those pests of the London streets, the "Mohocks," seem to have infested Fleet Street. These drunken desperadoes—the predecessors of the roysterers who, in the times of the Regency, "boxed the Charlies," broke windows, and stole knockers—used to find a cruel pleasure in surrounding a quiet homeward-bound citizen and pricking him with their swords. Addison makes worthy Sir Roger de Coverley as much afraid of these night-birds as Swift himself; and the old baronet congratulates himself on escaping from the clutches of "the emperor and his black men," who had followed him half-way down Fleet Street. He, however, boasts that he threw them out at the end of Norfolk Street, where he doubled the corner, and scuttled safely into his quiet lodgings.

From Elizabethan times downwards, Fleet Street was a favourite haunt of showmen. Concerning these popular exhibitions Mr. Noble has, with great industry, collected the following curious enumeration:—

"Ben Jonson," says our trusty authority, "in *Every Man in his Humour*, speaks of 'a new motion of the city of Nineveh, with Jonas and the whale, at Fleet Bridge.' In 1611 'the Fleet Street mandrakes' were to be seen for a penny; and years later the giants of St. Dunstan's clock caused the street to be blocked up, and people to lose their time, their temper, and their money. During Queen Anne's reign, however, the wonders of Fleet Street were at their height. In 1702 a model of Amsterdam, thirty feet long by twenty feet wide, which had taken twelve years in making, was exhibited in Bell Yard; a child, fourteen years old, without thighs or legs, and eighteen inches high, was to be seen 'at the "Eagle and Child," a grocer's shop, near Shoe Lane;' a great Lincoln-shire ox, nineteen hands high, four yards long, as lately shown at Cambridge, was on view 'at the "White Horse," where the great elephant was seen;' and 'between the "Queen's Head" and "Crooked Billet," near Fleet Bridge,' were exhibited daily 'two strange, wonderful, and remarkable monstrous creatures—an old she-dromedary, seven feet high and ten feet long, lately arrived from Tartary, and her young one; being the greatest rarity and novelty that ever was seen in the three kingdomes before.' In 1710, at the 'Duke of Marlborough's Head,' in Fleet Street (by Shoe Lane), was exhibited the 'moving picture' mentioned in the *Tatler;* and here, in 1711, 'the great posture-master of Europe,' eclipsing the deceased Clarke and Higgins, greatly startled sight-seeing London. ' He extends his body into all deformed shapes; makes his hip and shoulder-bones meet together; lays his head upon the ground, and turns his body round twice or thrice, without stirring his face from the spot; stands upon one leg, and extends the other in a perpendicular line half a yard above his head; and extends his body from a table with his head a foot below his heels, having nothing to balance his body but his feet; with several other postures too tedious to mention.'

"And here, in 1718, De Hightrehight, the fire-eater, ate burning coals, swallowed flaming brimstone, and sucked a red-hot poker, five times a day!

"What will my billiard-loving friends say to the St. Dunstan's Inquest of the year 1720? 'Item, we present Thomas Bruce, for suffering a gaming-table (called a billiard-table, where people commonly frequent and game) to be kept in his house.' A score of years later, at the end of Wine Office Court, was exhibited an automaton clock, with three figures or statues, which at the word of command poured out red or white wine, represented a grocer shutting up his shop and a blackamoor who struck upon a bell the number of times asked. Giants and dwarfs were special features in Fleet Street. At the 'Rummer,' in Three Kings' Court, was to be seen an Essex woman. named Gordon,

not nineteen years old, though seven feet high, who died in 1737. At the 'Blew Boar and Green Tree' was on view an Italian giantess, above seven feet, weighing 425 lbs., who had been seen by ten reigning sovereigns. In 1768 died, in Shire Lane, Edward Bamford, another giant, seven feet four inches in height, who was buried in St. Dunstan's, though £200 was offered for his body for dissection. At the 'Globe,' in 1717, was shown Matthew Buchinger, a German dwarf, born in 1674, without hands, legs, feet, or thighs, twenty-nine inches high; yet can write, thread a needle, shuffle a pack of cards, play skittles, &c. A facsimile of his writing is among the Harleian MSS. And in 1712 appeared the Black Prince and his wife, each three feet high; and a Turkey horse, two feet odd high and twelve years old, in a box. Modern times have seen giants and dwarfs, but have they really equalled these? In 1822 the exhibition of a mermaid here was put a stop to by the Lord Chamberlain."

In old times Fleet Street was rendered picturesque, not only by its many gable-ended houses adorned with quaint carvings and plaster stamped in patterns, but also by the countless signs, gay with gilding and painted with strange devices, which hung above the shop-fronts. Heraldry exhausted all its stores to furnish emblems for different trades. Lions blue and red, falcons, and dragons of all colours, alternated with heads of John the Baptist, flying pigs, and hogs in armour. On a windy day these huge masses of painted timber creaked and waved overhead, to the terror of nervous pedestrians, nor were accidents by any means rare. On the 2nd of December, 1718 (Queen Anne), a signboard opposite Bride Lane, Fleet Street, having loosened the brickwork by its weight and movement, suddenly gave way, fell, and brought the house down with it, killing four persons, one of whom was the queen's jeweller. It was not, however, till 1761 (George II.) that these dangerous signboards were ordered to be placed flat against the walls of the houses.

When Dr. Johnson said, "Come and let us take a walk down Fleet Street," he proposed no very easy task. The streets in his early days, in London, had no side-pavements, and were roughly paved, with detestable gutters running down the centre. From these gutters the jumbling coaches of those days liberally scattered the mud on the unoffending pedestrians who happened to be crossing at the time. The sedan-chairs, too, were awkward impediments, and choleric people were disposed to fight for the wall. In 1766, when Lord Eldon came to London as a schoolboy, and put up at that humble hostelry the "White Horse," in Fetter Lane, he describes coming home from Drury Lane with his brother in a sedan. Turning out of Fleet Street into Fetter Lane, some rough fellows pushed against the chair at the corner and upset it, in their eagerness to pass first. Dr. Johnson's curious nervous habit of touching every street-post he passed was cured in 1766, by the laying down of side-pavements. On that occasion it is said two English paviours in Fleet Street bet that they would pave more in a day than four Scotchmen could. By three o'clock the Englishmen had got so much ahead that they went into a public-house for refreshment, and, afterwards returning to their work, won the wager.

In the Wilkes' riot of 1763, the mob burnt a large jack-boot in the centre of Fleet Street, in ridicule of Lord Bute; but a more serious affray took place in this street in 1769, when the noisy Wilkites closed the Bar, to stop a procession of 600 loyal citizens *en route* for St. James's, to present an address denouncing all attempts to spread sedition and uproot the constitution. The carriages were pelted with stones, and the City marshal, who tried to open the gates, was bedaubed with mud. Mr. Boehm and other loyalists took shelter in "Nando's Coffee House." About 150 of the frightened citizens, passing up Chancery Lane, got to the palace by a devious way, a hearse with two white horses and two black following them to St. James's Palace. Even there the Riot Act had to be read and the Guards sent for. When Mr. Boehm fled into "Nando's," in his alarm, he sent home his carriage containing the address. The mob searched the vehicle, but could not find the paper, upon

which Mr. Boehm hastened to the Court, and arrived just in time with the important document.

The treason trials of 1794 brought more noise and trouble to Fleet Street. Hardy, the secretary to the London Corresponding Society, was a shoemaker at No. 161; and during the trial of this approver of the French Revolution, Mr. John Scott (afterwards Lord Eldon) was in great danger from a Fleet Street crowd. "The mob," he says, "kept thickening round me till I came to Fleet Street, one of the worst parts that I had to pass through, and the cries began to be rather threatening. 'Down with him!' 'Now is the time, lads; do for him!' and various others, horrible enough; but I stood up, and spoke as loud as I could: 'You may do for me, if you like; but, remember, there will be another Attorney-General before eight o'clock to-morrow morning, and the king will not allow the trials to be stopped.' Upon this one man shouted out, 'Say you so? you are right to tell us. Let us give him three cheers, my lads!' So they actually cheered me, and I got safe to my own door."

There was great consternation in Fleet Street in November, 1820, when Queen Caroline, attended by 700 persons on horseback, passed publicly through it to return thanks at St. Paul's. Many persons in alarm barricaded their doors and windows. Still greater was the alarm in August, 1821, when the queen's funeral procession went by, after the deplorable fight with the Horse Guards at Cumberland Gate, when two of the rioters were killed.

With this rapid sketch of a few of the events in the history of Fleet Street, we begin our patient peregrination from house to house.

CHAPTER IV.

FLEET STREET (*continued*).

Dr. Johnson in Ambuscade at Temple Bar—The First Child—Dryden and Black Will—Rupert's Jewels—Telson's Bank—The Apollo Club at the "Devil"—"Old Sir Simon the King"—"Mull Sack"—Dr. Johnson's Supper to Mrs. Lennox—Will Waterproof at the "Cock"—The Duel at "Dick's Coffee House"—Lintot's Shop—Pope and Warburton—Lamb and the *Albion*—The Palace of Cardinal Wolsey—Mrs. Salmon's Waxwork—Isaak Walton—Praed's Bank—Murray and Byron—St. Dunstan's—Fleet Street Printers—Hoare's Bank and the "Golden Bottle"—The Real and Spurious "Mitre"—Hone's Trial—Cobbett's Shop—"Peele's Coffee House."

THERE is, in an almost unknown essay by Dr. Johnson, a delightful passage that connects him indissolubly with the neighbourhood of Temple Bar. The essay, written in 1756 for the *Universal Visitor*, is entitled "A Project for the Employment of Authors," and is full of humour, which, indeed, those who knew him best considered the chief feature of Johnson's genius. We rather pride ourselves on the discovery of this pleasant bit of autobiography :—"It is my practice," says Johnson,

"when I am in want of amusement, to place myself for an hour at Temple Bar, or any other narrow pass much frequented, and examine one by one the looks of the passengers, and I have commonly found that between the hours of eleven and four every sixth man is an author. They are seldom to be seen very early in the morning or late in the evening, but about dinner-time they are all in motion, and have one uniform eagerness in their faces, which gives little opportunity of discerning their hopes or fears, their pleasures or their pains. But in the afternoon, when they have all dined, or composed themselves to pass the day without a dinner, their passions have full play, and I can perceive one man wondering at the stupidity of the public, by which his new book has been totally neglected ; another cursing the French, who fright away literary curiosity by their threat of an invasion ;

No. 1—formerly a quiet, grave-looking house, next to Temple Bar, but now being replaced by a building more worthy of the site—is the oldest banking-house in London except one. For two centuries gold has here been shovelled about, and reams of bank-notes have been shuffled over by practised thumbs. Private banks originated in the stormy days before the Civil War, when wealthy

DR. TITUS OATES.

another swearing at his bookseller, who will advance no money without copy ; another perusing as he walks his publisher's bill ; another murmuring at an unanswerable criticism ; another determining to write no more to a generation of barbarians ; and another wishing to try once again whether he cannot awaken the drowsy world to a sense of his merit." This extract seems to us to form an admirable companion picture to that in which we have already shown Goldsmith bantering his brother Jacobite, Johnson, as they looked up together at the grim heads on Temple Bar.

citizens, afraid of what might happen, entrusted their money to their goldsmiths to take care of till the troubles had blown over. In the time of the Stuarts, Francis Child, an industrious apprentice of the old school, married the daughter of his master, William Wheeler, a goldsmith, who lived one door west of Temple Bar, and in due time succeeded to his estate and business. In the first London Directory (1677), among the fifty-eight goldsmiths, thirty-eight of whom lived in Lombard Street, "Blanchard & Child," at the "Marygold." Fleet Street, figure conspicuously as " keeping running cashes." The original Marygold (sometimes mistaken for a rising sun), with the motto, "Ainsi mon ame," gilt upon a green ground, elegantly designed in the French manner, is still to be seen in the bank "shop," and a marigold in full bloom still blossoms on the bank cheques. In the year 1678 it was at Mr. Blanchard's, the goldsmith's, next door to Temple Bar, that Dryden the poet, bruised and angry, deposited £50 as a reward for any one who would discover the bullies

the firm long preserved the dusty books of the unfortunate alderman, who fled to Holland. On the sallow leaves over which the poor alderman once groaned, you can read the items of our sale of Dunkirk to the French, the dishonourable surrender of which drove the nation almost to madness, and hastened the downfall of Lord Clarendon, who was supposed to have built a magnificent house (on the site of Albemarle Street, Piccadilly) with some of the very money. Charles II. himself banked here,

TEMPLE BAR AND THE "DEVIL TAVERN" (*see page* 38).

of Lord Rochester who had beaten him in Rose Alley for some scurrilous verses really written by the Earl of Dorset. The advertisement promises, if the discoverer be himself one of the actors, he shall still have the £50, without letting his name be known or receiving the least trouble by any prosecution. Black Will's cudgel was, after all, a clumsy way of making a repartee. In the course of the eighteenth century, the firm was joined by the descendants of Alderman Backwell, who had been nearly ruined by the iniquitous and arbitrary closing of the Exchequer in 1672 by order of Charles II., that needy and unprincipled king; but the worthy alderman lived to retrieve his position.

In a quaint oak-panelled room over Temple Bar

and drew his thousands with all the careless nonchalance of his nature. Nell Gwynne, Pepys, of the "Diary," and Prince Rupert also had accounts at Child's, and some of these ledgers were hoarded over Temple Bar in that Venetian-looking room, approached by strange prison-like passages, for which chamber Messrs. Child paid the City a rent of £21 a year.

When Prince Rupert died at his house in the Barbican, the valuable jewels of the old cavalry soldier, valued at £20,000, were disposed of in a lottery, managed by Mr. Francis Child, the goldsmith; the king himself, who took a half-business-like, half-boyish interest in the matter, counting the tickets among all the lords and ladies at Whitehall.

In North's "Life of Lord Keeper Guildford," the courtier and lawyer of the reign of Charles II., there is an anecdote that pleasantly connects Child's bank with the fees of the great lawyers who in that evil reign ruled in Chancery Lane :—

"The Lord Keeper Guildford's business increased," says his biographer, "even while he was solicitor, to be so much as to have overwhelmed one less dexterous ; but when he was made Attorney-General, though his gains by his office were great, they were much greater by his practice, for that flowed in upon him like an orage, enough to overset one that had not an extraordinary readiness in business. His skull-caps, which he wore when he had leisure to observe his constitution, as I touched before, were now destined to lie in a drawer, to receive the money that came in by fees. One had the gold, another the crowns and half-crowns, and another the smaller money. When these vessels were full, they were committed to his friend (the Hon. Roger North), who was constantly near him, to tell out the cash and put it into the bags according to the contents ; and so they went to his treasurers, Blanchard & Child, goldsmiths, Temple Bar."

Year by year Sir Francis Child grew in fame and honour. He was alderman, sheriff, Lord Mayor, President of Christ's Hospital, and M.P. for the City, and finally, dying in 1713, full of years, was buried under a grand black marble tomb in Fulham churchyard, and his account closed for ever. The family went on living in the sunshine. Sir Robert, the son of the Sir Francis, was also alderman of his ward ; and, on his death, his brother, Sir Francis, succeeded to all his father's dignities, became an East Indian director, and in 1725 received the special thanks of the citizens for promoting a special act for regulating City elections. Another member of this family (Sir Josiah Child) deserves special mention as one of the earliest writers on political economy and a man much in advance of his time. He saw through the old fallacy about the balance of trade, and explained clearly the true causes of the commercial prosperity of the Dutch. He also condemned the practice of each parish paying for its own poor, an evil which all Poor-law reformers have endeavoured to alter. Sir Josiah was at the head of the East India Company, already feeling its way towards the gold and diamonds of India. His brother was Governor of Bombay, and by the marriage of his numerous daughters the rich merchant became allied to several peers and peeresses of England. The grandson of Alderman Backwell married a daughter of the second Sir

Francis Child, and his daughter married William Praed, the Truro banker, who early in the present century opened a bank at 189, Fleet Street. So, like three strands of a gold chain, the three banking families were welded together. In 1689 Child's bank seems to have for a moment tottered, but was saved by the timely loan of £1,400 proffered by that overbearing woman, the Duchess of Marlborough. Hogarth is said to have made an oil sketch of the scene, which was sold at Hodgson's sale-room in 1834, and has since disappeared.

In Pennant's time (1793) the original goldsmith's shop seems to have still existed in Fleet Street, in connection with this bank. The principal of the firm was the celebrated Countess of Jersey, a former earl having assumed the name of Child on the countess inheriting the estates of her maternal grandfather, Robert Child, Esq., of Osterly Park, Middlesex. A small full-length portrait of this great beauty of George IV.'s court, painted by Lawrence in his elegant but meretricious manner, hung in the first-floor room of the old bank. The last Child died early in this century. In Chapter I., Book I., of his "Tale of Two Cities," Dickens has sketched Child's bank with quite an Hogarthian force and colour. He has playfully exaggerated the smallness, darkness, and ugliness of the building, of which he describes the partners as so proud ; but there is all his usual delightful humour in the description, occasionally passing into caricature :—

"Thus it had come to pass that Telson's was the triumphant perfection of inconvenience. After bursting open a door of idiotic obstinacy with a weak rattle in its throat, you fell into Telson's down two steps, and came to your senses in a miserable little shop with two little counters, where the oldest of men made your cheque shake as if the wind rustled it, while they examined the signature by the dingiest of windows, which were always under a shower-bath of mud from Fleet Street, and which were made the dingier by their own iron bars and the heavy shadow of Temple Bar. If your business necessitated your seeing 'the House,' you were put into a species of Condemned Hold at the back, where you meditated on a mis-spent life, until the House came with its hands in its pockets, and you could hardly blink at it in the dismal twilight."

In 1788 (George III.) the firm purchased the renowned "Devil Tavern," next door eastward, and upon the site erected a row of houses up a dim court called Child's Place, under which, on its demolition in 1879, some twenty feet below the level of the street, were found a series of stone arches, which had probably once formed part of an ancient chapel.

The noisy "Devil Tavern" (No. 2, Fleet Street) had stood next the quiet goldsmith's shop ever since the time of James I. Shakespeare himself must, day after day, have looked up at the old sign of St. Dunstan tweaking the Devil by the nose, that flaunted in the wind near the Bar. Perhaps the sign was originally a compliment to the goldsmith's men who frequented it, for St. Dunstan was, like St. Eloy, a patron saint of goldsmiths, and himself worked at the forge as an amateur artificer of church plate. It may, however, have only been a mark of respect to the saint, whose church stood hard by, to the east of Chancery Lane. At the "Devil" the Apollo Club, almost the first institution of the kind in London, held its merry meetings, presided over by that grim yet jovial despot, Ben Jonson. The bust of Apollo, skilfully modelled from the head of the Apollo Belvidere, that once kept watch over the door, and heard in its time millions of witty things and scores of fond recollections of Shakespeare by those who personally knew and loved him, is still preserved at Child's bank. They also show there among their heirlooms "The Welcome," probably written by immortal Ben himself, which is full of a jovial inspiration that speaks well for the canary at the "Devil." It used to stand over the chimney-piece, written in gilt letters on a black board, and some of the wittiest and wisest men of the reigns of James and Charles must have read it over their cups. The verses run,—

> " Welcome all who lead or follow
>   To the oracle of Apollo," &c.

Beneath these verses some enthusiastic disciple of the author has added the brief epitaph inscribed by an admirer on the crabbed old poet's tombstone in Westminster Abbey,—

> "O, rare Ben Jonson."

The rules of the club (said to have been originally cut on a slab of black marble) were placed above the fireplace. They were devised by Ben Jonson, in imitation of the rules of the Roman entertainments, collected by the learned Lipsius; and, as Leigh Hunt says, they display the author's usual style of elaborate and compiled learning, not without a taste of that dictatorial self-sufficiency that made him so many enemies. They were translated by Alexander Brome, a poetical attorney of the day, who was one of Ben Jonson's twelve adopted poetical sons. We have room only for the first few, to show the poetical character of the club :—

> " Let none but guests or clubbers hither come ;
>   Let dunces, fools, and sordid men keep home ;
>   Let learned, civil, merry men b' invited,
>   And modest, too ; nor be choice liquor slighted.
>   Let nothing in the treat offend the guest :
>   More for delight than cost prepare the feast."

The later rules forbid the discussion of serious and sacred subjects. No itinerant fiddlers (who then, as now, frequented taverns) were to be allowed to obtrude themselves. The feasts were to be celebrated with laughing, leaping, dancing, jests, and songs, and the jests were to be " without reflection." No man (and this smacks of Ben's arrogance) was to recite "insipid" poems, and no person was to be pressed to write verse. There were to be in this little Elysium of an evening no vain disputes, and no lovers were to mope about unsocially in corners. No fighting or brawling was to be tolerated, and no glasses or windows broken, nor was tapestry to be torn down in wantonness. The rooms were to be kept warm ; and, above all, any one who betrayed what the club chose to do or say was to be, *nolens volens*, banished. Over the clock in the kitchen some wit had inscribed in neat Latin the merry motto, " If the wine of last night hurts you, drink more to-day, and it will cure you "—a happy version of the dangerous axiom of " Take a hair of the dog that bit you."

At these club feasts the old poet with "the mountain belly and the rocky face," as he has painted himself, presided, ready to enter the ring against all comers. By degrees the stern man with the worn features, darkened by prison cell and hardened by battle-fields, had mellowed into a Falstaff. Long struggles with poverty had made Ben arrogant, for he had worked as a bricklayer in early life and had served in Flanders as a common soldier ; he had killed a rival actor in a duel, and had been in danger of having his nose slit in the pillory for a libel against King James's Scotch courtiers. Intellectually, too, Ben had reason to claim a sort of sovereignty over the minor poets. His *Every Man in his Humour* had been a great success ; Shakespeare had helped him forward, and been his bosom friend. Parts of his *Sejanus*, such as the speech of Envy, beginning,—

> " Light, I salute thee, but with wounded nerves,
>   Wishing thy golden splendour pitchy darkness,"

are as sublime as his songs, such as

> " Drink to me only with thine eyes,"

are graceful, serious, and lyrical. The great compass of his power and the command he had of the lyre no one could deny ; his learning Donne and Camden could vouch for. He had written the most beautiful of court masques ; his Bobadil some men preferred to Falstaff. Alas ! no Pepys or Boswell has noted the talk of those evenings.

A few glimpses of the meetings we have, and but a few. One night at the "Devil" a country gentleman was boastful of his property. It was all he had to boast about among the poets; Ben, chafed out of all decency and patience, at last roared, "What signify to us your dirt and your clods? Where you have an acre of land I have ten acres of wit!" "Have you so, good Mr. Wise-acre," retorted Master Shallow. "Why, now, Ben," cried out a laughing friend, "you seem to be quite stung." "I' faith, I never was so pricked by a hobnail before," growled Ben, with a surly smile.

Another story records the first visit to the "Devil" of Randolph, a clever poet and dramatist, who became a clergyman, and died young. The young poet, who had squandered all his money away in London pleasures, on a certain night, before he returned to Cambridge, resolved to go and see Ben and his associates at the "Devil," cost what it might. But there were two great obstacles—he was poor, and he was not invited. Nevertheless, drawn magnetically by the voices of the illustrious men in the Apollo, Randolph at last peeped in at the door among the waiters. Ben's quick eye soon detected the eager, pale face and the scholar's threadbare habit. "John Bo-peep," he shouted, "come in!" a summons Randolph gladly obeyed. The club-men instantly began rhyming on the meanness of the intruder's dress, and told him if he could not at once make a verse he must call for a quart of sack. There being four of his tormentors, Randolph, ready enough at such work, replied as quick as lightning:—

> "I, John Bo-peep, and you four sheep,
>   With each one his good fleece;
> If that you are willing to give me your shilling,
>   'Tis fifteen pence apiece."

"By the Lord!" roared the giant president, "I believe this is my son Randolph!" and on his owning himself, the young poet was kindly entertained, spent a glorious evening, was soaked in sack, "sealed of the tribe of Ben," and became one of the old poet's twelve adopted sons.

Shakerley Marmion, a contemporary dramatist of the day, has left a glowing Rubenesque picture of the Apollo evenings, evidently coloured from life. Careless, one of his characters, tells his friends he is full of oracles, for he has just come from Apollo. "From Apollo?" says his wondering friend. Then Careless replies, with an inspired fervour worthy of a Cavalier poet who fought bravely for King Charles:—

> "From the heaven
> Of my delight, where the boon Delphic god
> Drinks sack and keep his bacchanalia,
> And has his incense and his altars smoking,

> And speaks in sparkling prophecies; thence I come,
> My brains perfumed with the rich Indian vapour,
> And heightened with conceits. . . . .
> And from a mighty continent of pleasure
> Sails thy brave Careless."

Simon Wadloe, the host of the "Devil," who died in 1627, seems to have been a witty butt of a man, much such another as honest Jack Falstaff; a merry boon companion, not only witty himself, but the occasion of wit in others, quick at repartee, fond of proverbial sayings, curious in his wines. A good old song, set to a fine old tune, was written about him, and called "Old Sir Simon the King." This was the favourite old-fashioned ditty in which Fielding's rough and jovial Squire Western afterwards delighted.

Old Simon's successor, John Wadloe (probably his son), made a great figure at the Restoration procession by heading a band of young men all dressed in white. After the Great Fire John rebuilt the "Sun Tavern," behind the Royal Exchange, and was loyal, wealthy, and foolish enough to lend King Charles certain considerable sums, duly recorded in Exchequer documents, but not so duly paid.

In the troublous times of the Commonwealth the "Devil" was the favourite haunt of John Cottington, generally known as "Mull Sack," from his favourite beverage of spiced sherry negus. This impudent rascal, a sweep who had turned highwayman, with the most perfect impartiality rifled the pockets alternately of Cavaliers and Roundheads. Gold is of no religion; and your true cut-purse is of the broadest and most sceptical Church. He emptied the pockets of Lord Protector Cromwell one day, and another he stripped Charles II., then a Bohemian exile at Cologne, of plate valued at £1,500. One of his most impudent exploits was stealing a watch from Lady Fairfax, that brave woman who had the courage to denounce, from the gallery at Westminster Hall, the persons who, she considered, were about to become the murderers of Charles I. "This lady" (and a portly handsome woman she was, to judge by the old portraits), says a pamphlet-writer of the day, "used to go to a lecture on a week-day to Ludgate Church, where one Mr. Jacomb preached, being much followed by the Puritans. Mull Sack, observing this, and that she constantly wore her watch hanging by a chain from her waist, against the next time she came there dressed himself like an officer in the army; and having his comrades attending him like troopers, one of them takes off the pin of a coach-wheel that was going upwards through the gate, by which means it falling off, the passage was obstructed, so that the lady could not alight at the church door, but was forced to leave her coach without. Mull Sack, taking advantage of this, readily presented himself to her ladyship, and having the impudence to take her from her gentleman usher who attended her alighting, led her by the arm into the church; and by the way, with a pair of keen sharp scissors for the purpose, cut the chain in two, and got the watch clear away, she not missing it till the sermon was done, when she was going to see the time of the day."

The portrait of Mull Sack has the following verses beneath :—

" I walk the Strand and Westminster, and scorn
  To march i' the City, though I bear the horn.
My feather and my yellow band accord,
To prove me courtier ; my boot, spur, and sword,
My smoking-pipe, scarf, garter, rose on shoe,
Show my brave mind t' affect what gallants do.
I sing, dance, drink, and merrily pass the day,
And, like a chimney, sweep all care away."

In Charles II.'s time the "Devil" became frequented by lawyers and physicians. The talk now was about drugs and latitats, jalap and the law of escheats. Yet, still good company frequented it, for Steele describes Bickerstaff's sister Jenny's wedding entertainment there in October, 1709; and in 1710 (Queen Anne) Swift writes one of those charming letters to Stella to tell her that he had dined on October 12th at the "Devil," with Addison and Dr. Garth, when the good-natured doctor, whom every one loved, stood treat, and there must have been talk worth hearing. In the Apollo chamber the intolerable court odes of Colley Cibber, the poet laureate, used to be solemnly rehearsed with fitting music; and Pope, in "The Dunciad," says, scornfully :—

" Back to the 'Devil' the loud echoes roll,
  And 'Coll' each butcher roars in Hockly Hole."

But Colley had talent and he had brass, and it took many such lines to put him down. A good epigram on these public recitations runs thus :—

"When laureates make odes, do you ask of what sort?
  Do you ask if they're good or are evil?
You may judge : from the 'Devil' they come to the Court,
  And go from the Court to the 'Devil.'"

Dr. Kenrick afterwards gave lectures on Shakespeare at the Apollo. This Kenrick, originally a rule-maker, and the malicious assailant of Johnson and Garrick, was the Croker of his day. He originated the *London Review*, and when he assailed Johnson's "Shakespeare," Johnson laughingly replied, " That he was not going to be bound by Kenrick's rules."

In 1746 the Royal Society held its annual dinner in the old consecrated room, and in the year 1752 concerts of vocal and instrumental music were given in the same place. It was an upstairs chamber probably detached from the tavern, and lay up a "close," or court. A bottle of wine found in the vaults here in 1879, probably was as old as this dinner.

The last ray of light that fell on the "Devil" was in 1751. Dr. Johnson, then busy all day with his six amanuenses in a garret in Gough Square compiling his Dictionary, at night enjoyed his elephantine mirth at a club in Ivy Lane, Paternoster Row. One night at the club, Johnson proposed to celebrate the appearance of Mrs. Lennox's first novel, "The Life of Harriet Stuart," by a supper at the "Devil Tavern." Mrs. Lennox was a lady for whom Johnson had the greatest esteem, ranking her afterwards above Mrs. Carter, Mrs. Hannah More, or even his favourite, Miss Burney. Sir John Hawkins, that somewhat malign rival of Boswell, describes the night in a manner, for him, unusually genial. "Johnson," says Hawkins (and his words are too pleasant to condense), "proposed to us the celebrating the birth of Mrs. Lennox's first literary child, as he called her book, by a whole night spent in festivity. Upon his mentioning it to me, I told him I had never sat up a night in my life ; but he continuing to press me, and saying that I should find great delight in it, I, as did all the rest of the company, consented." (The club consisted of Hawkins, an attorney ; Dr. Salter, father of a master of the Charter House ; Dr. Hawkesworth, a popular author of the day ; Mr. Ryland, a merchant ; Mr. John Payne, a bookseller ; Mr. Samuel Dyer, a young man training for a Dissenting minister ; Dr. William M'Ghie, a Scotch physician ; Dr. Barker and Dr. Bathurst, young physicians.) "The place appointed was the 'Devil Tavern ;' and there, about the hour of eight, Mrs. Lennox and her husband (a tide-waiter in the Customs), a lady of her acquaintance, with the club and friends, to the number of twenty, assembled. The supper was elegant ; Johnson had directed that a magnificent hot apple-pie should make a part of it, and this he would have stuck with bay leaves, because, forsooth, Mrs. Lennox was an authoress and had written verses ; and, further, he had prepared for her a crown of laurel, with which, but not till he had invoked the Muses by some ceremonies of his own invention, he encircled her brows. The night passed, as must be imagined, in pleasant conversation and harmless mirth, intermingled at different periods with the refreshment of coffee and tea. About five a.m., Johnson's face shone with meridian splendour, though his drink had been only lemonade; but the far greater part of the company had deserted the colours of Bacchus, and were with difficulty rallied to partake of a second refreshment of coffee, which was scarcely ended when the day began to dawn.

opposite side of Fleet Street, still preserves the memory of the great club-room at the "Devil."

In 1764, on an Act passing for the removal of the dangerous projecting signs, the weather-beaten picture of the saint, with the Devil gibbering over his shoulder, was nailed up flat to the front of the

TEMPLE BAR IN DR. JOHNSON'S TIME (*see page* 41).

This phenomenon began to put us in mind of our reckoning; but the waiters were all so overcome with sleep that it was two hours before a bill could be had, and it was not till near eight that the creaking of the street-door gave the signal of our departure." How one longs to dredge up some notes of such a night's conversation from the cruel river of oblivion! The Apollo Court, on the

old gable-ended house. In 1775, Collins, a public lecturer and mimic, gave a satirical lecture at the "Devil" on modern oratory. In 1776 some young lawyers founded there a Pandemonium Club; and after that there is no further record of the "Devil" till it was pulled down and annexed by the neighbouring bankers. In Steele's time there was a "Devil Tavern" at Charing Cross, and a

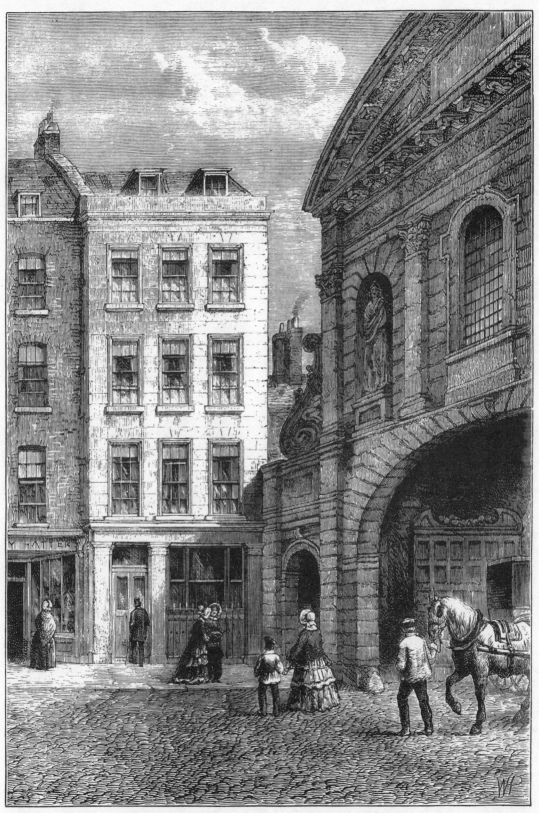

CHILD'S BANKING-HOUSE, FLEET STREET, NEXT TEMPLE BAR.
From a Drawing by Findley, 1855, in Mr. Crace's Collection (see page 36).

rival "Devil Tavern" near St. Dunstan's; but these competitors made no mark.

The "Cock Tavern" (201), opposite the Temple, has been immortalised by Tennyson as thoroughly as the "Devil" was by Ben Jonson. The playful verses inspired by a pint of generous port have made

"The violet of a legend blow
Among the chops and steaks"

for ever, though old Will Waterproof has long since descended for the last time the well-known cellar-stairs. The poem which has embalmed his name was, we believe, written when Mr. Tennyson had chambers in Lincoln's Inn Fields. At that time the room was lined with wainscoting, and the silver tankards of special customers hung in glittering rows in the bar. This tavern was shut up at the time of the Plague, and the advertisement announcing such closing is still extant. Pepys, in his "Diary," mentions bringing hither Mrs. Knipp, an actress, of whom his wife was very jealous; and here the gay couple "drank, eat a lobster, and sang, and mighty merry till almost midnight." On his way home to Seething Lane, the amorous Navy Office clerk with difficulty avoided two thieves with clubs, who met him at the entrance into the ruins of the Great Fire near St. Dunstan's. These dangerous meetings with Mrs. Knipp went on till one night Mrs. Pepys came to his bedside and threatened to pinch him with the red-hot tongs. The waiters at the "Cock" are fond of showing visitors one of the old tokens of the house in the time of Charles II. The old carved chimney-piece is of the age of James I.; and there is a doubtful tradition that the gilt bird that struts with such self-serene importance over the portal was the work of that great carver, Grinling Gibbons.

"Dick's Coffee House" (No. 8, south) was kept in George II.'s time by a Mrs. Yarrow and her daughter, who were much admired by the young Templars who patronised the place. The Rev. James Miller, reviving an old French comedietta by Rousseau, called "The Coffee House," and introducing malicious allusions to the landlady and her fair daughter, so exasperated the young barristers who frequented "Dick's," that they went in a body and hissed the piece from the boards. The author then wrote an apology, and published the play; but unluckily the artist who illustrated it took the Bar at "Dick's" as the background of his sketch. The Templars grew madder than ever at this, and Mr. Miller, who translated Voltaire's "Mahomet" for Garrick, never came up to the surface again. It was at "Dick's" that Cowper the poet showed the first symptoms of derangement.

When his mind was off its balance he read a letter in a newspaper at "Dick's," which he believed had been written to drive him to suicide. He went away and tried to hang himself; the garter breaking, he then resolved to drown himself; but, being hindered by some occurrence, repented for the moment. He was soon after sent to an asylum in Huntingdon.

In 1681 a quarrel arose between two hot-headed gallants in "Dick's" about the size of two dishes they had both seen at the "St. John's Head" in Chancery Lane. The matter eventually was roughly ended at the "Three Cranes" in the Vintry—a tavern mentioned by Ben Jonson—by one of them, Rowland St. John, running his companion, John Stiles, of Lincoln's Inn, through the body. The old coffee-house was demolished about 1875.

The "Rainbow Tavern" (No. 15, south) was the second coffee-house started in London. Four years before the Restoration, Mr. Farr, a barber, began the trade here, trusting probably to the young Temple barristers for support. The vintners grew jealous, and the neighbours, disliking the smell of the roasting coffee, indicted Farr as a nuisance. But he persevered, and the Arabian drink became popular. A satirist had soon to write regretfully,—

"And now, alas! the drink has credit got,
And he's no gentleman that drinks it not."

About 1780, according to Mr. Timbs, the "Rainbow" was kept by Alexander Moncrieff, grandfather of the dramatist who wrote *Tom and Jerry*.

Bernard Lintot, the bookseller, who published Pope's "Homer," lived in a shop between the two Temple gates (No. 16). In an inimitable letter to the Earl of Burlington, Pope has described how Lintot (Tonson's rival) overtook him once in Windsor Forest, as he was riding down to Oxford. When they were resting under a tree in the forest, Lintot, with a keen eye to business, pulled out "a mighty pretty 'Horace,'" and said to Pope, "What if you amused yourself in turning an ode till we mount again?" The poet smiled, but said nothing. Presently they remounted, and as they rode on Lintot stopped short, and broke out, after a long silence: "Well, sir, how far have we got?" "Seven miles," replied Pope, naïvely. He told Pope that by giving the hungry critics a dinner of a piece of beef and a pudding, he could make them see beauties in any author he chose. After all, Pope did well with Lintot, for he gained £5,320 by his "Homer." Dr. Young, the poet, once unfortunately sent to Lintot a letter meant for Tonson, and the first words that Lintot read were : ",That Bernard Lintot is so great a scoundrel." In the same shop, which was then occupied by Jacob Robinson, the publisher, Pope first met Warburton. An interesting account of this meeting is given by Sir John Hawkins, which it may not be out of place to quote here. " The friendship of Pope and Warburton," he says, "had its commencement in that bookseller's shop which is situate on the west side of the gateway leading down the Inner Temple Lane. Warburton had some dealings with Jacob Robinson, the publisher, to whom the shop belonged, and may be supposed to have been drawn there on business ; Pope might have made a call of the like kind. However that may be, there they met, and entering into conversation, which was not soon ended, conceived a mutual liking, and, as we may suppose, plighted their faith to each other. The fruit of this interview and of the subsequent communications of the parties was the publication, in November, 1739, of a pamphlet with this title, ' A Vindication of Mr. Pope's " Essay on Man," by the Author of " The Divine Legation of Moses." Printed for J. Robinson.' " At the Middle Temple Gate, Benjamin Motte, successor to Ben Tooke, published Swift's " Gulliver's Travels," for which he had grudgingly given only £200.

The third door from Chancery Lane (No. 197, north side), Mr. Timbs points out, was in Charles II.'s time a tombstone-cutter's ; and here, in 1684, Howel, whose " Letters" give us many curious pictures of his time, saw a huge monument to four of the Oxenham family, at the death of each of whom a white bird appeared fluttering about their bed. These miraculous occurrences had taken place at a town near Exeter, and the witnesses' names duly appeared below the epitaph. No. 197 was afterwards Rackstrow's museum of natural curiosities and anatomical figures ; and the proprietor put Sir Isaac Newton's head over the door for a sign. Among other prodigies was the skeleton of a whale more than seventy feet long. Donovan, a naturalist, succeded Rackstrow (who died in 1772) with his London museum. Then, by a harlequin change, No. 197 became the office of the *Albion* newspaper. Charles Lamb was turned over to this journal from the *Morning Post*. The editor, John Fenwick, the " Bigot" of Lamb's " Essay," was a needy, sanguine man, who had purchased the paper of a person named Lovell, who had stood in the pillory for a libel against the Prince of Wales. For a long time Fenwick contrived to pay the Stamp Office dues by money borrowed from compliant friends; "We,"

says Lamb, in his delightful way, " attached our small talents to the forlorn fortunes of our friend. Our occupation was now to write treason." Lamb hinted at possible abdications. Blocks, axes, and Whitehall tribunals were covered with flowers of so cunning a periphrasis—as, Mr. Bayes says, never naming the *thing* directly—that the keen eye of an Attorney-General was insufficient to detect the lurking snake among them.

At the south-west corner of Chancery Lane (No. 193) once stood an old house said to have been the residence of that unfortunate reformer, Sir John Oldcastle, Lord Cobham, who was burnt in St. Giles's Fields in 1417 (Henry V.) In Charles II.'s reign the celebrated Whig Green Ribbon Club used to meet here, and from the balcony flourish their periwigs, discharge squibs, and wave torches, when a great Protestant procession passed by, to burn the effigy of the Pope at the Temple Gate. The house, five stories high and covered with carvings, was pulled down for City improvements in 1799.

Upon the site of No. 192 (east corner of Chancery Lane) the father of Cowley, that fantastic poet of Charles II.'s time, it is said carried on the trade of a grocer. In 1740 a later grocer there sold the finest caper tea for 24s. per lb., his fine green for 18s. per lb., hyson at 16s. per lb., and bohea at 7s. per lb.

No house in Fleet Street has a more curious pedigree than that gilt and painted shop opposite Chancery Lane (No. 17, south side), falsely called " the palace of Henry VIII. and Cardinal Wolsey." It was originally the office of the Duchy of Cornwall, in the reign of James I. It is just possible that it was the house originally built by Sir Amyas Paulet, at Wolsey's command, in resentment for Sir Amyas having set Wolsey, when a mere parish priest, in the stocks for a brawl. Wolsey, at the time of the ignominious punishment, was schoolmaster to the children of the Marquis of Dorset. Paulet was confined to this house for five or six years, to appease the proud cardinal, who lived in Chancery Lane. Sir Amyas rebuilt his prison, covering the front with badges of the cardinal. It was afterwards " Nando's," a famous coffee-house, where Thurlow picked up his first great brief. One night Thurlow, arguing here keenly about the celebrated Douglas case, was heard by some lawyers with delight, and the next day, to his astonishment, was appointed junior counsel. This cause won him a silk gown, and so his fortune was made by that one lucky night at " Nando's." No. 17 was afterwards the place where Mrs. Salmon (the Madame Tussaud of early times) exhibited her waxwork kings and queens. There was a figure on crutches at the door; and Old Mother Shipton, the witch, kicked the astonished visitor as he left. Mrs. Salmon died in 1812. The exhibition was then sold for £500, and removed to Water Lane. When Mrs. Salmon first removed from St. Martin's-le-Grand to near St. Dunstan's Church, she announced, with true professional dignity, that the new locality "was more convenient for the quality's coaches to stand unmolested." Her "Royal Court of England" included 150 figures. When the exhibition removed to Water Lane, some thieves one night got in, stripped the effigies of their finery, and broke half of them, throwing them into a heap that almost touched the ceiling.

Tonson, Dryden's publisher, commenced business at the "Judge's Head," near the Inner Temple gate, so that when at the Kit-Kat Club he was not far from his own shop. One day Dryden, in a rage, drew the greedy bookseller with terrible force:—

"With leering looks, bull-faced, and speckled fair,
With two left legs and Judas-coloured hair,
And frowzy pores that taint the ambient air."

The poet promised a fuller portrait if the "dog" tormented him further.

Opposite Mrs. Salmon's, two doors west of old Chancery Lane, till 1799, when the lawyer's lane was widened, stood an old, picturesque, gabled house, which was once the milliner's shop kept, in 1624, by that good old soul, Isaak Walton. He was on the Vestry Board of St. Dunstan's, and was constable and overseer for the precinct next Temple Bar; and on pleasant summer evenings he used to stroll out to the Tottenham fields, rod in hand, to enjoy the gentle sport which he so much loved. He afterwards (1632) lived seven doors up Chancery Lane, west side, and there married the sister of that good Christian, Bishop Ken, who wrote the "Evening Hymn," one of the most simply beautiful religious poems ever written. It is pleasant in busy Fleet Street to think of the good old citizen on his guileless way to the river Lea, conning his verses on the delights of angling.

Praed's Bank (No. 189, north side) was founded early in this century by Mr. William Praed, a banker of Truro. The house had been originally the shop of Mrs. Salmon, till she moved to opposite Chancery Lane, and her wax kings and frail queens were replaced by piles of strong boxes and chests of gold. The house was rebuilt in 1802, from the designs of Sir John Soane, whose curious museum still exists in Lincoln's Inn Fields. Praed, that delightful poet of society, was of the banker's

family, and in him the poetry of refined wealth found a fitting exponent. Fleet Street, indeed, is rich in associations connected with bankers and booksellers; for at No. 19 (south side) we come to Messrs. Gosling's. This bank was founded in 1650 by Henry Pinckney, a goldsmith, at the sign of the "Three Squirrels"—a sign still to be seen in the ironwork over the centre window. The original sign of solid silver, about two feet in height, made to lock and unlock, was discovered in the house in 1858. It had probably been taken down on the general removal of out-door signs and forgotten. In a secret service-money account of the time of Charles II., there is an entry of a sum of £646 8s. 6d. for several parcels of gold and silver lace bought of William Gosling and partners by the fair Duchess of Cleveland, for the wedding clothes of the Ladies Sussex and Lichfield.

No. 32 (south side), still a publisher's, was originally kept for forty years by William Sandby, one of the partners of Snow's bank in the Strand. He sold the business and goodwill in 1762 for £400, to a lieutenant of the Royal Navy, named John M'Murray, who, dropping the Mac, became the well-known Tory publisher. Murray tried in vain to induce Falconer, the author of "The Shipwreck," to join him as a partner. The first Murray died in 1793. In 1812 John Murray, the son of the founder, removed to 50, Albemarle Street. In the *Athenæum* of 1843 a writer describes how Byron used to stroll in here fresh from his fencing-lessons at Angelo's or his sparring-bouts with Jackson. He was wont to make cruel lunges with his stick at what he called "the spruce books" on Murray's shelves, generally striking the doomed volume, and by no means improving the bindings. "I was sometimes, as you will guess," Murray used to say with a laugh, "glad to get rid of him." Here, in 1807, was published "Mrs. Rundell's Domestic Cookery;" in 1809, the *Quarterly Review;* and, in 1811, Byron's "Childe Harold."

The original Columbarian Society, long since extinct, was born at offices in Fleet Street, near St. Dunstan's. This society was replaced by the Pholoperisteron, dear to all pigeon-fanciers, which held its meetings at "Freemasons' Tavern," and eventually amalgamated with its rival, the National Columbarian, the fruitful union producing the National Peristeronic Society, now a flourishing institution, meeting periodically at "Evans's," and holding a great fluttering and most pleasant annual show at the Crystal Palace. It is on these occasions that clouds of carrier-pigeons are let off, to decide the speed with which the swiftest and best-trained bird can reach a certain spot (a flight, of course, previously known to the bird), generally in Belgium.

The first St. Dunstan's Church—"in the West," as it is now called, to distinguish it from one near Tower Street—was built prior to 1237. The present building was erected in 1831. The older church stood thirty feet forward, blocking the carriage-way, and shops with projecting signs were built against the east and west walls. The churchyard was a favourite locality for booksellers. One of the most interesting stories connected with the old building relates to Felton, the fanatical assassin of the Duke of Buckingham, the favourite of Charles I. The murderer's mother and sisters lodged at a haberdasher's in Fleet Street, and were attending service in St. Dunstan's Church when the news arrived from Portsmouth; they swooned away when they heard the name of the assassin. Many of the clergy of St. Dunstan's have been eminent men. Tyndale, the translator of the New Testament, did duty here. The poet Donne was another of the St. Dunstan's worthies; and Sherlock and Romaine both lectured at this church. The rectory house, sold in 1693, was No. 183. The clock of old St. Dunstan's was one of the great London sights in the last century. The giants that struck the hours had been set up in 1671, and were made by Thomas Harrys, of Water Lane, for £35 and the old clock. Lord Hertford purchased them, in 1830, for £210, and set them up at his villa in Regent's Park. When a child he was often taken to see them; and he then used to say that some day he would buy "those giants." Hatton, writing in 1708, says that these figures were more admired on Sundays by the populace than the most eloquent preacher in the pulpit within; and Cowper, in his " Table Talk," cleverly compares dull poets to the St. Dunstan's giants :—

> " When labour and when dulness, club in hand,
> Like the two figures at St. Dunstan stand,
> Beating alternately, in measured time,
> The clock-work tintinnabulum of rhyme."

The most interesting relic of modern St. Dunstan's is that unobtrusive figure of Queen Elizabeth at the east end. This figure first came to the old church from Ludgate when the City gates were destroyed in 1786. It was bought for £16 10s. when the old church came to the ground, and was re-erected over the vestry entrance. The companion statues of King Lud and his two sons were deposited in the parish bone-house. On one occasion when Baxter was preaching in the old church of St. Dunstan's, there arose a panic among the audience from two alarms of the building falling. Every face turned pale ; but the preacher, full of faith, sat calmly down in the pulpit till the panic subsided, then, resuming his sermon, said reprovingly, " We are in the service of God, to prepare ourselves that we may be fearless at the great noise of the dissolving world when the heavens shall pass away and the elements melt with fervent heat."

Mr. Noble, in his record of this parish, has remarked on the extraordinary longevity attained by the incumbents of St. Dunstan's. Dr. White held the living for forty-nine years ; Dr. Grant, for fifty-nine ; the Rev. Joseph Williamson (Wilkes's chaplain) for forty-one years ; while the Rev. William Romaine continued lecturer for forty-six years. The solution of the problem probably is that a good and secure income is the best promoter of longevity. Several members of the great banking family of Hoare are buried in St. Dunstan's ; but by far the most remarkable monument in the church bears the following inscription :—

" HOBSON JUDKINS, ESQ., late of Clifford's Inn, the Honest Solicitor, who departed this life June 30, 1812. This tablet was erected by his clients, as a token of gratitude and respect for his honest, faithful, and friendly conduct to them throughout life. Go, reader, and imitate Hobson Judkins."

Among the burials at St. Dunstan's noted in the registers, the following are the most remarkable :—1559-60, Doctor Oglethorpe, the Bishop of Carlisle, who crowned Queen Elizabeth ; 1664, Dame Bridgett Browne, wife of Sir Richard Browne, major-general of the City forces, who offered £1,000 reward for the capture of Oliver Cromwell ; 1732, Christopher Pinchbeck, the inventor of the metal named after him and a maker of musical clocks. The Plague seems to have made great havoc in St. Dunstan's, for in 1665, out of 856 burials, 568 in only three months are marked " P.," for Plague. The present church, built in 1830–3, was designed by John Shaw, who died on the twelfth day after the completion of the outer shell, leaving his son to finish his work. The church is of a flimsy Gothic, the true revival having hardly then commenced. The eight bells are from the old church. The two heads over the chief entrance are portraits of Tyndale and Dr. Donne ; and the painted window is the gift of the Hoare family.

According to Aubrey, Drayton, the great topographical poet, lived at " the bay-window house next the east end of St. Dunstan's Church." Now it is a clearly proved fact that the Great Fire stopped just three doors east of St. Dunstan's, as did also, Mr. Timbs says, another remarkable fire in 1730; so it is not impossible that the author of "The Polyolbion," that good epic poem, once lived at the present No. 180, though the next house eastward is certainly older than its neighbour. We have given a drawing of the house.

That shameless rogue, Edmund Curll, lived at translators lay three in a bed at the "Pewter Platter Inn" at Holborn. He published the most disgraceful books and forged letters. Curll, in his revengeful spite, accused Pope of pouring an emetic into his half-pint of canary when he and Curll and Lintot met by appointment at the "Swan Tavern."

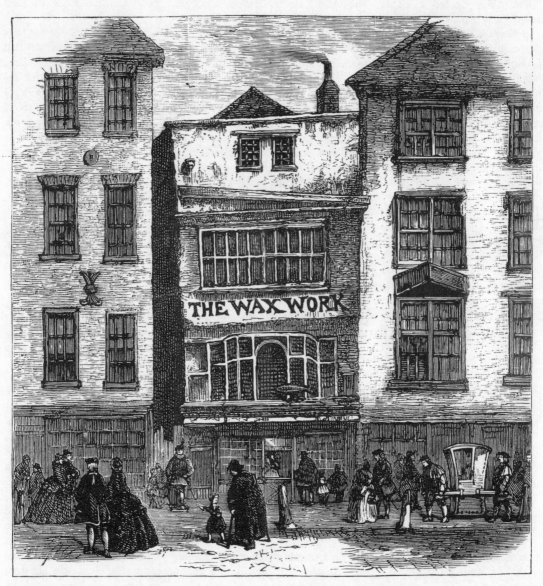

MRS. SALMON'S WAXWORK, FLEET STREET—"PALACE OF HENRY VIII. AND CARDINAL WOLSEY" (see page 45).

the "Dial and Bible," against St. Dunstan's Church. When this clever rascal was put in the pillory at Charing Cross, he persuaded the mob he was in for a political offence, and so secured the pity of the crowd. The author of "John Buncle" describes Curll as a tall, thin, awkward man, with goggle eyes, splay feet, and knock-knees. His Fleet Street. By St. Dunstan's, at the "Homer's Head," also lived the publisher of the first correct edition of "The Dunciad."

Among the booksellers who crowded round old St. Dunstan's were Thomas Marsh, of the "Prince's Arms," who printed Stow's "Chronicles;" and William Griffith, of the "Falcon," in St. Dunstan's

Churchyard, who, in the year 1565, issued, without the authors' consent, *Gorboduc*, written by Thomas Norton and Lord Buckhurst, the first real English tragedy and the first play written in English blank verse. John Smethwicke, a still more honoured name, "under the diall" of St. Dunstan's Church,

the three timid publishers who ventured on a certain poem, called "The Paradise Lost," giving John Milton, the blind poet, the enormous sum of £5 down, £5 on the sale of 1,300 copies of the first, second, and third impressions, in all the munificent recompense of £20; the agreement

ST. DUNSTAN'S CLOCK (*see page* 47).

published "Hamlet" and "Romeo and Juliet." Richard Marriot, another St. Dunstan's bookseller, published Quarles' "Emblems," Dr. Donne's "Sermons," that delightful, simple-hearted book, Isaak Walton's "Complete Angler," and Butler's "Hudibras," that wonderful mass of puns and quibbles, pressed close as potted meat. Matthias Walker, a St. Dunstan's bookseller, was one of

was given to the British Museum in 1852, by Samuel Rogers, the banker poet.

Nor in this list of Fleet Street printers must we forget to insert Richard Pynson, from Normandy, who had worked at Caxton's press, and was a contemporary of De Worde. According to Mr. T. C. Noble, to whose work we are deeply indebted, Pynson printed, at his office, the "George" (first in the Strand, and afterwards beside St. Dunstan's Church, in Fleet Street), no less than 215 works. The first of these, completed in the year 1483, was probably the first book printed in Fleet Street, afterwards a gathering-place for the ink-stained craft. A copy of this book, "Dives and Pauper," was sold a few years since for no less than £49. In 1497 the same busy Frenchman published an edition of "Terence," the first Latin classic printed in England. In 1508 he became printer to King Henry VII., and after this produced editions of Fabyan's and Froissart's "Chronicles." He seems to have had a bitter feud with a rival printer, named Robert Rudman, who pirated his trade-mark. In one of his books he thus quaintly falls foul of the enemy: "But truly Rudeman, because he is the rudest out of a thousand men. . . . . Truly I wonder now at last that he hath confessed it in his own typography, unless it chanced that even as the devil made a cobbler a mariner, he made him a printer. Formerly this scoundrel did prefer himself a bookseller, as well skilled as if he had started forth from Utopia. He knows well that he is free who pretendeth to books, although it be nothing more."

To this brief chronicle of early Fleet Street printers let us add Richard Bancks, who, in 1600, at his office, "the sign of the White Hart," printed that exquisite fairy poem, Shakespeare's "Midsummer Night's Dream." How one envies the "reader" of that office, the compositors—nay, even the sable imp who pulled the proof, and snatched a passage or two about Mustard and Pease Blossom in a surreptitious glance! Another great Fleet Street printer was Richard Grafton, the printer, as Mr. Noble says, of the first correct folio English translation of the Bible, by permission of Henry VIII. When in Paris, Grafton had to fly with his books from the Inquisition. After his patron Cromwell's execution, in 1540, Grafton was sent to the Fleet for printing Bibles; but in the happier times of Edward VI. he became king's printer at the Grey Friars, now Christ's Hospital. His former fellow-worker in Paris, Edward Whitchurch, set up his press at De Worde's old house, the "Sun," near the Fleet Street conduit. He published the "Paraphrase of Erasmus," a copy of which, Mr. Noble says, existed, with its desk-chains, in the vestry of St. Benet's, Gracechurch Street. Whitchurch married the widow of Archbishop Cranmer.

The "Hercules Pillars" (now No. 27, Fleet Street, south) was a celebrated tavern as early as the reign of James I., and in the now nameless alley by its side several houses of entertainment nestled themselves. The tavern is interesting to us chiefly because it was a favourite resort of Pepys, who frequently mentions it in his quaint and graphic way.

No. 37 (Hoare's Bank), south, is well known by the golden bottle that still hangs, exciting curiosity, over the fanlight of the entrance. Popular legend has it that this gilt case contains the original leather bottle carried by the founder when he came up to London, with the usual half-crown in his pocket, to seek his fortune. Sir Richard Colt Hoare, however, in his family history, destroys this romance. The bottle is merely a sign adopted by James Hoare, the founder of the bank, from his father having been a citizen and cooper of the city of London. James Hoare was a goldsmith who kept "running cash" at the "Golden Bottle" in Cheapside in 1677. The bank was removed to Fleet Street between 1687 and 1692. The original bank, described by Mr. Timbs as "a low-browed building with a narrow entrance," was pulled down about fifty years since. In the records of the debts of Lord Clarendon is the item, "To Mr. Hoare, for plate, £27 10s. 3d.;" and, by the secret service expenses of James II., "Charles Duncombe and James Hoare, Esqrs." appear to have executed for a time the office of master-workers at the Mint. A Sir Richard Hoare was Lord Mayor in 1713; and another of the same family, sheriff in 1740–41 and Lord Mayor in 1745, distinguished himself by his preparations to defend London against the "Pretender." In an autobiographical record still extant of the shrievalty of the first of these gentlemen, the writer says:—"After being regaled with sack and walnuts, I returned to my own house in Fleet Street, in my private capacity, to my great consolation and comfort." This Richard Hoare, with Beau Nash, Lady Hastings, &c., founded, in 1716, the Bath General Hospital, to which charity the firm still continue treasurers; and to this same philanthropic gentleman, Robert Nelson, who wrote the well-known book on "Fasts and Festivals," gave £100 in trust as the first legacy to the Society for Promoting Christian Knowledge. Mr. Noble quotes a curious broadside still extant in which the second Sir Richard Hoare, who died in 1754, denies a false and malicious report that he had attempted to cause a run on the Bank of England, and to occasion a disturbance in the City, by sending persons to the Bank with ten notes of £10 each. What a state of commercial wealth, to be shaken by the sudden demand of a mere £100!

Next to Hoare's once stood the "Mitre Tavern," where some of the most interesting of the meetings between Dr. Johnson and Boswell took place.

The old tavern was pulled down, in 1829, by the Messrs. Hoare, to extend their banking-house. The original "Mitre" was of Shakespeare's time. In some MS. poems by Richard Jackson, a contemporary of the great poet, are some verses beginning, "From the rich Lavinian shore," inscribed as "Shakespeare's rime, which he made at ye 'Mitre,' in Fleet Street." The balcony was partly burnt during the Great Fire, and had to be pulled down. Here, in June, 1763, Boswell came by solemn appointment to meet Johnson, so long the god of his idolatry. They had first met at the shop of Davis, the actor and bookseller, and afterwards near an eating-house in Butcher Row. Boswell describes his feelings with delightful sincerity and self-complacency. "We had," he says, "a good supper and port wine, of which Johnson then sometimes drank a bottle. The orthodox High Church sound of the Mitre, the figure and manner of the celebrated Samuel Johnson, the extraordinary power of his conversation, and the pride arising from finding myself admitted as his companion, produced a variety of sensations and a pleasing elevation of mind beyond what I had ever before experienced." That memorable evening Johnson ridiculed Colley Cibber's birthday odes and Paul Whitehead's "grand nonsense," and ran down Gray, who had declined his acquaintance. He talked of other poets, and praised poor Goldsmith as a worthy man and excellent author. Boswell fairly won the great man by his frank avowals and his adroit flattery. "Give me your hand," at last cried the great man to the small man: "I have taken a liking to you." They then finished a bottle of port each, and parted between one and two in the morning. As they shook hands, on their way to No. 1, Inner Temple Lane, where Johnson then lived, Johnson said, "Sir, I am glad we have met. I hope we shall pass many evenings, and mornings too, together." A few weeks after the Doctor and his young disciple met again at the "Mitre," and Goldsmith was present. The poet was full of love for Dr. Johnson, and speaking of some scapegrace, said tenderly, "He is now become miserable, and that insures the protection of Johnson." At another "Mitre" meeting, on a Scotch gentleman present praising Scotch scenery, Johnson uttered his bitter gibe, "Sir, let me tell you that the noblest prospect which a Scotchman ever sees is the high road that leads him to England." In the same month Johnson and Boswell met again at the "Mitre." The latter confessed his nerves were much shaken by the old port and the late tavern hours; and Johnson laughed at people who had accepted a pension

from the house of Hanover abusing him as a Jacobite. It was at the "Mitre" that Johnson urged Boswell to publish his "Travels in Corsica;" and at the "Mitre" he said finely of London, "Sir, the happiness of London is not to be conceived but by those who have been in it. I will venture to say there is more learning and science within the circumference of ten miles from where we sit than in all the rest of the kingdom." It was here the famous "Tour to the Hebrides" was planned and laid out. Another time we find Goldsmith and Boswell going arm-in-arm to Bolt Court, to prevail on Johnson to go and sup at the "Mitre;" but he was indisposed. Goldsmith, since "the big man" could not go, would not venture at the "Mitre" with Boswell alone. At Boswell's last "Mitre" evening with Johnson, May, 1778, Johnson would not leave Mrs. Williams, the blind old lady who lived with him, till he had promised to send her over some little dainty from the tavern. This was very kindly and worthy of the man who "had the coat but not the heart of a bear." From 1728 to 1753 the Society of Antiquaries met at the "Mitre," and discussed subjects then wrongly considered frivolous. The Royal Society held also conclaves at the same celebrated tavern; and here, in 1733, Thomas Topham, the strongest man of his day, in the presence of eight persons, rolled up with his iron fingers a large pewter dish. In 1788 the "Mitre" ceased to be a tavern, and became, first Macklin's Poet's Gallery, and then an auction-room. The present spurious "Mitre Tavern," in Mitre Court, was originally known as "Joe's Coffee-House."

It was at No. 56 (south side) that Lamb's friend, William Hone, the publisher of the delightful "Table Book" and "Every-day Book," commenced business about 1812. In 1815 he was brought before the Wardmote Inquest of St. Dunstan's for placarding his shop on Sundays, and for carrying on a retail trade as bookseller and stationer, not being a freeman. The Government had no doubt suggested the persecution of so troublesome an opponent, whose defence of himself is said to have all but killed Lord Ellenborough, the judge who tried him for publishing blasphemous parodies. In 1815 Hone took great interest in the case of Eliza Fenning, a poor innocent servant girl, who was hung for a supposed attempt to poison her master, a law stationer in Chancery Lane. It was afterwards believed that a nephew of Mr. Turner really put the poison in the dough of some dumplings, in revenge at being kept short of money. Mr. Cyrus Jay, a shrewd observer, was present at Hone's trial, and has described it with vividness :—

" Hone defended himself firmly and well, but he had no spark of eloquence about him. For years afterwards I was often with him, and he was made a great deal of in society. He became very religious, and died a member of Mr. Clayton's Independent chapel, worshipping at the Weigh House. The last important incident of Lord Ellenborough's political life was the part he took as presiding judge in Hone's trials for the publication of certain blasphemous parodies. At this time he was suffering from the most intense exhaustion, and his constitution was sinking under the fatigues of a long and sedulous discharge of his important duties. This did not deter him from taking his seat upon the bench on this occasion. When he entered the court, previous to the trial, Hone shouted out, 'I am glad to see you, Lord Ellenborough. I know what you are come here for; I know what you want.' 'I am come to do justice,' replied his lordship. 'My wish is to see justice done.' 'Is it not rather, my lord,' retorted Hone, 'to send a poor devil of a bookseller to rot in a dungeon?' In the course of the proceedings Lord Ellenborough more than once interfered. Hone, it must be acknowledged, with less vehemence than might have been expected, requested him to forbear. The next time his lordship made an observation, in answer to something the defendant urged in the course of his speech, Hone exclaimed, in a voice of thunder, 'I do not speak to you, my lord; you are not my judge; these,' pointing to the jury, 'these are my judges, and it is to them that I address myself.' Hone avenged himself on what he called the Chief Justice's partiality; he wounded him where he could not defend himself. Arguing that Athanasius was not the author of the creed that bears his name, he cited, by way of authority, passages from the writings of Gibbon and Warburton to establish his position. Fixing his eyes on Lord Ellenborough, he then said, 'And, further, your lordship's father, the late worthy Bishop of Carlisle, has taken a similar view of the same creed.' Lord Ellenborough could not endure this allusion to his father's heterodoxy. In a broken voice he exclaimed, 'For the sake of decency, forbear!' The *request* was immediately complied with. The jury acquitted Hone, a result which is said to have killed the Chief Justice; but this is probably not true. That he suffered in consequence of the trial is certain. After he entered his private room, when the trial was over, his strength had so far deserted him that his son was obliged to put his hat on for him. But he quickly recovered his spirits; and on his way home, in passing through Charing Cross, he pulled the check-string, and said, 'It just occurs to me that they sell here the best herrings in London; buy six.' Indeed Dr. Turner, afterwards Bishop of Calcutta, who accompanied him in his carriage, said that so far from his nerves being shaken by the hootings of the mob, Lord Ellenborough only observed that their saliva was worse than their bite. . . . .

"When Hone was tried before him for blasphemy, Lord Tenterden treated him with great forbearance; but Hone, not content with the indulgence, took to vilifying the judge. 'Even in a Turkish court I should not have met with the treatment I have experienced here,' he exclaimed. 'Certainly,' replied Lord Tenterden; 'the bowstring would have been round your neck an hour ago.'"

That sturdy political writer, William Cobbett, lived at No. 183 (north), and there published his *Political Register*. In 1819 he wrote from America, declaring that if Sir Robert Peel's Bank Bill passed, he would give Castlereagh leave to lay him on a gridiron and broil him alive, while Sidmouth stirred the coals, and Canning stood by and laughed at his groans. In 1827 he announced in his *Register* that he would place a gridiron on the front of his shop whenever Peel's Bill was repealed. The "Small Note Bill" was repealed, when there was a reduction of the interest of the National Debt. The gridiron so often threatened never actually went up, but it was to be seen a few years ago nailed on the gable end of a candle manufacturer's at Kensington. The two houses next to Cobbett's (184 and 185) are the oldest houses standing in Fleet Street.

"Peele's Coffee-House (Nos. 177 and 178, north side) once boasted a portrait of Dr. Johnson, said to be by Sir Joshua Reynolds, on the keystone of the mantelpiece. This coffee-house is of antiquity, but is chiefly memorable for its useful files of newspapers and for its having been the central committee-room of the Society for Repealing the Paper Duty. The struggle began in 1858, and eventually triumphed, thanks to the president, the Right Hon. T. Milner-Gibson, and the chairman, the late Mr. John Cassell. The house within the last few years has been entirely rebuilt. In former times "Peele's Coffee-House" was quite a house of call and post-office for money-lenders and bill-discounters; though crowds of barristers and solicitors also frequented it, in order to consult the files of London and country newspapers which were hoarded there for more than a century. Mr. Jay has left us an amusing sketch of one of the former frequenters of "Peele's"—the late Sir William Owen Barlow, a bencher of the Middle Temple. This methodical old gentleman had never travelled in a stage-coach or railway-carriage in his life, and had not for years read a book. He came in for dinner at the same hour every day, except in Term-time, and was very angry if any loud talkers disturbed him at his evening paper. He once requested the instant discharge of a waiter at " Peele's," because the civil but ungrammatical man had said, " There are a leg of mutton, and there is chops."

CHAPTER V.

FLEET STREET (continued).

The " Green Dragon "—The " Bolt-in-Tun "—Tompion and Pinchbeck—The *Record*—St. Bride's and its Memories—*Punch* and his Contributors —The *Dispatch*—The *Daily Telegraph*—The " Globe Tavern " and Goldsmith—The *Morning Advertiser*—The *Standard*—The *London Magazine*—A Strange Story—Alderman Waithman—Brutus Billy—Hardham and his " 37."

THE original " Green Dragon " (No. 56, south) was destroyed by the Great Fire, and the new building set six feet backward. During the Popish Plot several anti-papal clubs met here ; and from the windows Roger North stood to see the shouting, torch-waving procession pass along, to burn the Pope's effigy at Temple Bar. In the " Discussion Forum " many barristers of note, many judges, and Lord Chancellors of the future have tried their eloquence when young men.

No. 64 (south) was long a well-known coaching house, the " Bolt-in-Tun." In a grant to the White Friars, in the fifteenth century, it is spoken of as " Hospitium vocatum Le Boltenton." The old inn was demolished a few years ago, but its name is preserved in Bolt-in-Tun Yard, and the railway booking-office which partly occupies its site.

At No. 67 (corner of Whitefriars Street) once lived that famous watchmaker of Queen Anne's reign, Thomas Tompion, who is said, in 1700, to have begun a clock for St. Paul's Cathedral which was to go for a hundred years without winding up. He died in 1713. His apprentice, George Graham, invented, as Mr. Noble tells us, the horizontal escapement, in 1724. He was succeeded by Mudge and Dutton, who in 1768, made Dr. Johnson his first watch. The old shop was (1850) one of the last in Fleet Street to be modernised.

Between Bolt and Johnson's Courts (152–166, north)—say near " Anderton's Hotel "—there lived, in the reign of George II., at the sign of the " Astronomer's Musical Clock," Christopher Pinchbeck, an ingenious musical-clockmaker, who invented the "cheap and useful imitation of gold" which still bears his name. Pinchbeck often exhibited his musical automata in a booth at Bartholomew Fair and in conjunction with Fawkes the Conjuror, at Southwark Fair. He made, according to Mr. Edward T. Wood, the author of " Curiosities of Clocks and Watches,"

an exquisite musical clock, worth about £500, for Louis XIV., and a fine organ for the Great Mogul, valued at £300. He died in 1732. He removed to Fleet Street from Clerkenwell in 1721. His clocks played tunes and imitated the notes of birds. In 1765 he set up, at the Queen's House, a clock with four faces, showing the age of the moon, the day of the week and month, the time of sun rising, &c.

No. 161 (north) was the shop of Thomas Hardy, that agitating bootmaker, secretary to the London Corresponding Society, who was implicated in the John Horne Tooke trials of 1794 ; and next door, years after (No. 162), Richard Carlisle, a "freethinker," opened a lecturing, conversation, and discussion establishment, preached the " only true gospel," hung effigies of bishops outside his shop, and was eventually quieted by nine years' imprisonment, a punishment by no means undeserved. No. 76 (south) was once the entrance to the printing-office of Samuel Richardson, the author of " Clarissa," who afterwards lived in Salisbury Square, and there held levees of his admirers, to whom he read his works with an innocent vanity which occasionally met with disagreeable rebuffs.

"Anderton's Hotel " (No. 164, north side) occupies the site of a house given, as Mr. Noble says, in 1405, to the Goldsmiths' Company, under the singular title of " The Horn in the Hoop," probably at that time a tavern. In the register of St. Dunstan's is an entry (1597), " Ralph slaine at the Horne, buryed," but no further record exists of this hot-headed royster. In the reign of King James I. the " Horn " is described as " between the ' Red Lion,' over against Serjeants' Inn, and Three-legged Alley."

The *Record* (No. 169, north) was started in 1828 as an organ of the extreme Evangelical party. The first promoters were the late Mr. James Evans, a brother of Sir Andrew Agnew, and Mr. Andrew

HOARE'S OLD BANKING HOUSE, FROM A DRAWING BY SHEPHERD, 1838, IN MR. CRACE'S COLLECTION (*see page* 50).

Hamilton, of West Ham Common, the first secretary of the Alliance Insurance Company. Among their supporters were Henry Law, Dean of Gloucester, and Francis Close, afterwards Dean of Carlisle. Amongst its earliest writers was Dr. (now Cardinal) John Henry Newman, of Oxford. The paper was all but dying when a new "whip"

became celebrated for its uncompromising religious tone, and, as Mr. James Grant truly says, for the earliness and accuracy of its politico-ecclesiastical information.

The old church of St. Bride (Bridget) was of great antiquity. As early as 1235 we find a turbulent foreigner, named Henry de Battle, after slaying

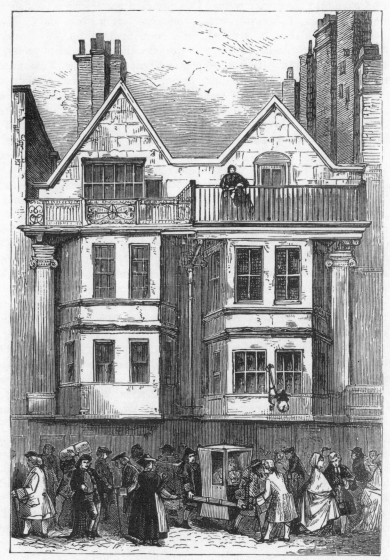

OLD HOUSES IN FLEET STREET, NEAR ST. DUNSTAN'S CHURCH (*see page* 52).

was made for money, and the Rev. Henry Blunt, of Chelsea, became for a short time its editor. The *Record* at last began to flourish and to assume a bolder and a more independent tone. Dean Milman's neology, the peculiarities of the Irvingites, and the dangerous Oxford Tracts, were alternately denounced in it. In due course the *Record* began to appear three times a week, and

one Thomas de Hall on the king's highway, flying for sanctuary to St. Bride's, where he was guarded by the aldermen and sheriffs, and examined in the church by the Constable of the Tower. The murderer, after confessing his crime, abjured the realm. In 1413 a priest of St. Bride's was hung for an intrigue in which he had been detected. William Venor, a warden of the Fleet Prison, added a body and side-aisles in 1480 (Edward IV.) At the Reformation there were orchards between the parsonage gardens and the Thames. In 1637, a document in the Record Office, quoted by Mr. Noble, mentions that Mr. Palmer, vicar of St. Bride's, at the service at seven a.m., sometimes omitted the prayer for the bishop, and, being generally lax as to forms, often read the service without surplice, gown, or even his cloak. This worthy man, whose living was sequestered in 1642, is recorded, in order to save money for the poor, to have lived in a bed-chamber in St. Bride's steeple. He founded an almshouse in Westminster, upon which Fuller remarks, in his quaint way, " It giveth the best light when one carrieth his lantern before him." The brother of Pepys was buried here in 1664 under his mother's pew. The old church was swallowed up by the Great Fire, and the present building erected in 1680, at a cost of £11,430 5s. 11d. The tower and spire were considered master-pieces of Wren. The spire, originally 234 feet high, was struck by lightning in 1754, and it is now only 226 feet high. It was again struck in 1803. The illuminated dial (the second erected in London) was set up permanently in 1827. The Spital sermons, now preached in Christ Church, Newgate Street, were preached in St. Bride's from the Restoration till 1797. They were originally all preached in the yard of the hospital of St. Mary Spital, Bishopsgate. Mr. Noble has ransacked the records relating to St. Bride's with the patience of old Stow. St. Bride's, he says, was renowned for its tithe-rate contests ; but after many lawsuits and great expense, a final settlement of the question was come to in the years 1705–6. An Act was passed in 1706, by which Thomas Townley, who had rented the tithes for twenty-one years, was to be paid £1,200 within two years, by quarterly payments and £400 a year afterwards. In 1869 the impropriate rectory of St. Bridget and the tithes thereof, except the advowson, the parsonage house, and Easter-dues offerings, were sold by auction for £2,700. It may be here worthy to note, says Mr. Noble, that in 1705 the number of rateable houses in the parish of St. Bride was 1,016, and the rental £18,374; in 1868 the rental was £205,407 gross, £168,996 rateable.

Mr. Noble also records pleasantly sundry musical feats accomplished on the bells of St. Bride's. In 1710 ten bells were cast for this church by Abraham Rudhall, of Gloucester, and on the 11th of January, 1717, it is recorded that the first complete peal of 5,040 grandsire caters ever rung was effected by the " London scholars." In 1718 two treble bells were added : and on the 9th of January,

1724, the first peal ever completed in this kingdom upon twelve bells was rung by the college youths ; and in 1726 the first peal of Bob Maximus, one of the ringers being Mr. Francis (afterwards Admiral) Geary. It was reported by the ancient ringers, says our trustworthy authority, that every one who rang in the last-mentioned peal left the church in his own carriage. Such was the dignity of the " campanularian ". art in those days. When St. Bride's bells were first put up, Fleet Street used to be thronged with carriages full of gentry, who had come far and near to hear the pleasant music float aloft. During the terrible Gordon Riots, in 1780, Brasbridge, the silversmith, who wrote an autobiography, says he went up to the top of St. Bride's steeple to see the awful spectacle of the conflagration of the Fleet Prison, but the flakes of fire, even at that great height, fell so thickly as to render the situation untenable.

Many great people lie in and around St. Bride's ; and Mr. Noble gives several curious extracts from the registers. Among the names we find Wynkyn de Worde, the second printer in London ; Baker, the chronicler ; Lovelace, the Cavalier poet, who died of want in Gunpowder Alley, Shoe Lane ; Ogilby, the translator of Homer ; the Countess of Orrery (1710) ; Elizabeth Thomas, a lady immortalised by Pope ; and John Hardham, the Fleet Street tobacconist. The entrance to the vault of Mr. Holden (a friend of Pepys), on the north side of the church, is a relic of the older building. Inside St. Bride's are monuments to Richardson, the novelist ; Nichols, the historian of Leicestershire ; and Alderman Waithman. Among the clergy of St. Bride's Mr. Noble notes John Cardmaker, who was burnt at Smithfield for heresy, in 1555 ; Fuller, the Church historian and author of the "Worthies," who was lecturer here ; Dr. Isaac Madox, originally an apprentice to a pastrycook, and who died Bishop of Winchester in 1759 ; and Dr. John Thomas, vicar, who died in 1793. There were two John Thomases among the City clergy of that time. They were both chaplains to the king, both good preachers, both squinted, and both died bishops !

The present approach to St. Bride's, designed by J. P. Papworth, in 1824, cost £10,000, and was urged forward by Mr. Blades, a Tory tradesman of Ludgate Hill, and a great opponent of Alderman Waithman. A fire that had destroyed some ricketty old houses gave the requisite opportunity for letting air and light round poor, smothered-up St. Bride's.

The office of *Punch* (No. 85, south side) is said to occupy the site of the small school, in the house of a tailor, in which Milton once earned a precarious living. Here, ever since 1841, the pleasant jester of Fleet Street has scared folly by the jangle of his bells and the blows of his staff. The best and most authentic account of the origin of *Punch* is to be found in the following communication to *Notes and Queries*, September 30, 1870. Mr. W. H. Wills, who was one of the earliest contributors to *Punch*, says :—

"The idea of converting *Punch* from a strolling to a literary laughing philosopher belongs to Mr. Henry Mayhew, former editor (with his schoolfellow Mr. Gilbert à Beckett) of *Figaro in London*. The first three numbers, issued in July and August, 1841, were composed almost entirely by that gentleman, Mr. Mark Lemon, Mr. Henry Plunkett ('Fusbos'), Mr. Stirling Coyne, and the writer of these lines. Messrs. Mayhew and Lemon put the numbers together, but did not formally dub themselves editors until the appearance of their 'Shilling's Worth of Nonsense.' The cartoons, then 'Punch's Pencillings,' and the smaller cuts, were drawn by Mr. A. S. Henning, Mr. Newman, and Mr. Alfred Forester ('Crowquill'); later, by Mr. Hablot Browne and Mr. Kenny Meadows. The designs were engraved by Mr. Ebenezer Landells, who occupied also the important position of 'capitalist.' Mr. Gilbert à Beckett's first contribution to *Punch*, 'The Abovebridge Navy,' appeared in No. 4, with Mr. John Leech's earliest cartoon, 'Foreign Affairs.' It was not till Mr. Leech's strong objection to treat political subjects was overcome, that, long after, he began to illustrate *Punch's* pages regularly. This he did, with the brilliant results that made his name famous, down to his untimely death. The letterpress description of 'Foreign Affairs' was written by Mr. Percival Leigh, who—also after an interval—steadily contributed. Mr. Douglas Jerrold began to wield *Punch's* baton in No. 9. His 'Peel Regularly Called in' was the first of those withering political satires, signed with a 'J' in the corner of each page opposite to the cartoon, that conferred on *Punch* a wholesome influence in politics. Mr. Albert Smith made his *début* in this wise :—At the birth of *Punch* had just died a periodical called (I think) the *Cosmorama*. When moribund, Mr. Henry Mayhew was called in to resuscitate it. This periodical bequeathed a comic census-paper filled up, in the character of a showman, so cleverly that the author was eagerly sought at the starting of *Punch*. He proved to be a medical student hailing from Chertsey, and signing the initials A. S.—'only,' remarked Jerrold, 'two-thirds of the truth, perhaps.' This pleasant supposition was, however, reversed at the very first introduction. On that occasion Mr. Albert Smith left the 'copy' of the opening of 'The Physiology of the London Medical Student.' The writers already named, with a few volunteers selected from the editor's box, filled the first volume, and belonged to the ante-'B. & E.' era of *Punch's* history. The proprietary had hitherto consisted of Messrs. Henry Mayhew, Lemon, Coyne, and Landells. The printer and publisher also held shares, and were treasurers. Although the popularity of *Punch* exceeded all expectation, the first volume ended in difficulties. From these storm-tossed seas *Punch* was rescued and brought into smooth water by Messrs. Bradbury & Evans, who acquired the copyright and organised the staff. Then it was that Mr. Mark Lemon was appointed sole editor, a new office having been created for Mr. Henry Mayhew—that of Suggestor-in-Chief; Mr. Mayhew's contributions, and his felicity in inventing pictorial and in 'putting' verbal witticisms, having already set a deep mark upon *Punch's* success. The second volume started merrily. Mr. John Oxenford contributed his first *jeu d'esprit* in its final number on 'Herr Döbler and the Candle-Counter.' Mr. Thackeray commenced his connection in the beginning of the third volume with 'Miss Tickletoby's Lectures on English History,' illustrated by himself. A few weeks later a handsome young student returned from Germany. He was heartily welcomed by his brother, Mr. Henry Mayhew, and then by the rest of the fraternity. Mr. Horace Mayhew's diploma joke consisted, I believe, of 'Questions addressées au Grand Concours aux Elèves d'Anglais du Collége St. Badaud, dans le Département de la Haute Cockaigne' (vol. iii., p. 89). Mr. Richard Doyle, Mr. Tenniel, Mr. Shirley Brooks, Mr. Tom Taylor, and the younger celebrities who now keep *Mr. Punch* in vigorous and jovial vitality, joined his establishment after some of the birth-mates had been drafted off to graver literary and other tasks."

Mr. Mark Lemon remained editor of *Punch* from 1841 till 1870, when he died. His successor was Shirley Brooks, whose reign lasted till his death in 1876. Mr. Gilbert à Beckett, who died at Boulogne in 1856, succeeded in the more varied kinds of composition, turning with extraordinary rapidity from a *Times* leader to a *Punch* epigram.

A pamphlet attributed to Mr. Blanchard conveys, after all, the most minute account of the origin of *Punch*. A favourite story of the literary gossipers who have made *Mr. Punch* their subject from time to time, says the writer, is that he was born in a tavern parlour. The idea usually presented to the public is, that a little society of great men used to meet together in a private room in a tavern close to Drury Lane Theatre. The truth is this :—

In the year 1841 there was a printing-office in a court running out of Fleet Street—No. 3, Crane Court—wherein was carried on the business of Mr. Joseph William Last. It was here that *Punch* first saw the light. The house, by the way, enjoys besides a distinction of a different kind—that of being the birthplace of "Parr's Life Pills;" for Mr. Herbert Ingram, who had not at that time launched the *Illustrated London News*, nor become a member of Parliament, was then introducing that since celebrated medicine to the public, and for that purpose had rented some rooms on the premises of his friend Mr. Last.

The circumstance which led to *Punch's* birth was simple enough. In June, 1841, Mr. Last called upon Mr. Alfred Mayhew, then in the office of his father, Mr. Joshua Mayhew, the well-known solicitor, of Carey Street, Lincoln's Inn Fields. Mr. Mayhew was Mr. Last's legal adviser, and Mr. Last was well acquainted with several of his sons. Upon the occasion in question Mr. Last made some inquiries of Mr. Alfred Mayhew concerning his brother Henry, and his occupation at the time. Mr. Henry Mayhew had, even at his then early age, a reputation for the high abilities which he afterwards developed, had already experience in various departments of literature, and had exercised his projective and inventive faculties in various ways. If his friends had heard nothing of him for a few months, they usually found that he had a new design in hand, which was, however, in many cases, of a more original than practical character. Mr. Henry Mayhew, as it appeared from his brother Alfred's reply, was not at that time engaged in any new effort of his creative genius, and would be open to a proposal for active service.

Having obtained Mr. Henry Mayhew's address, which was in Clement's Inn, Mr. Last called upon that gentleman on the following morning, and opened to him a proposal for a comic and satirical journal. Henry Mayhew readily entertained the idea; and the next question was, "Can you get up a staff?" Henry Mayhew mentioned his friend Mark Lemon as a good commencement; and the pair proceeded to call upon that gentleman, who was living, not far off, in Newcastle Street, Strand. The almost immediate result was the starting of *Punch*.

At a meeting at the "Edinburgh Castle" Mr. Mark Lemon drew up the original prospectus. It was at first intended to call the new publication "The Funny Dog," or "Funny Dog, with Comic Tales," and from the first the subsidiary title of the "London Charivari" was agreed upon. At a subsequent meeting at the printing-office, some one made some allusion to the "Punch," and some

joke about the "Lemon" in it. Henry Mayhew, with his usual electric quickness, at once flew at the idea, and cried out, "A good thought; we'll call it *Punch*." It was then remembered that, years before, Douglas Jerrold had edited a *Penny Punch* for Mr. Duncombe, of Middle Row, Holborn, but this was thought no objection, and the new name was carried by acclamation. It was agreed that there should be four proprietors—Messrs. Last, Landells, Lemon, and Mayhew. Last was to supply the printing, Landells the engraving, and Lemon and Mayhew were to be co-editors. George Hodder, with his usual good-nature, at once secured Mr. Percival Leigh as a contributor, and Leigh brought in his friend Mr. John Leech, and Leech brought in Albert Smith. Mr. Henning designed the cover. When Last had sunk £600, he sold his share to Messrs. Bradbury and Evans, on receiving the amount of his then outstanding liabilities. At the transfer, Henning and Newman both retired, Mr. Coyne and Mr. Grattan seldom contributed, and Messrs. Mayhew and Landells also seceded.

Mr. Hine, the artist, remained with *Punch* for many years; and among other artistic contributors who "came and went," to use Mr. Blanchard's own words, we must mention Birket Foster, Alfred Crowquill, Lee, Hamerton, John Gilbert, William Harvey, and Kenny Meadows, the last of whom illustrated one of Jerrold's earliest series, "Punch's Letters to His Son." *Punch's Almanac* for 1841 was concocted for the greater part by Dr. Maginn, who was then in the Fleet Prison, where Thackeray has drawn him, in the character of Captain Shandon, writing the famous prospectus for the *Pall Mall Gazette*. The earliest hits of *Punch* were Douglas Jerrold's articles signed " J." and Gilbert à Beckett's "Adventures of Mr. Briefless." In October, 1841, Mr. W. H. Wills, afterwards working editor of *Household Words* and *All the Year Round*, commenced " Punch's Guide to the Watering-Places." In January, 1842, Albert Smith commenced his lively " Physiology of London Evening Parties," which were illustrated by Newman; and he wrote the " Physiology of the London Idler," which Leech illustrated. In the third volume, Jerrold commenced " Punch's Letters to His Son;" and in the fourth volume, his "Story of a Feather;" Albert Smith's "Side-Scenes of Society" carried on the social dissections of the comic physiologist, and à Beckett began his " Heathen Mythology," and created the character of "Jenkins," the supposed fashionable correspondent of the *Morning Post*. *Punch* had begun his career by ridiculing Lord Melbourne; he now attacked Brougham, for his temporary subservience to Wellington; and Sir

James Graham came also in for a share of the rod; and the *Morning Herald* and *Standard* were christened "Mrs. Gamp" and "Mrs. Harris," as old-fogyish opponents of Peel and the Free-Traders. À Beckett's "Comic Blackstone" proved a great hit, from its daring originality; and incessant jokes were squibbed off on Lord John Russell, Prince Albert (for his military tailoring), Mr. Silk Buckingham and Lord William Lennox, Mr. Samuel Carter Hall and Mr. Harrison Ainsworth. Tennyson once, and once only, wrote for *Punch*, a reply to Lord Lytton (then Mr. Bulwer), who had coarsely attacked him in his "New Timon," where he had spoken flippantly of

> "A quaint farrago of absurd conceits,
> Out-babying Wordsworth and out-glittering Keats."

The epigram ended with these bitter and contemptuous lines,—

> "A Timon you? Nay, nay, for shame!
> It looks too arrogant a jest—
> That fierce old man—to take his name,
> You bandbox! Off, and let him rest."

Albert Smith left *Punch* many years before his death. In 1845, on his return from the East, Mr. Thackeray began his "Jeames's Diary," and became a regular contributor. Gilbert à Beckett was now beginning his "Comic History of England" and Douglas Jerrold his inimitable "Caudle Lectures." Thomas Hood occasionally contributed, but his immortal "Song of the Shirt" was his *chef-d'œuvre*. Coventry Patmore contributed once to *Punch;* his verses denounced General Pellisier and his cruelty at the caves of Dahra. Laman Blanchard occasionally wrote; his best poem was one on the marriage and temporary retirement of charming Mrs. Nisbett. In 1846 Thackeray's "Snobs of England" was highly successful. Richard Doyle's "Manners and Customs of ye English" brought *Punch* much increase. The present cover of *Punch* was designed by Doyle, who, being a zealous Roman Catholic, left Punch when it began to ridicule the Pope and condemn "Papal Aggression." *Punch* in his time has had his raps, but not many and not hard ones. Poor Angus B. Reach (whose mind went early in life), with Albert Smith and Shirley Brooks, ridiculed *Punch* in the *Man in the Moon;* and in 1847 the Poet Bunn—"Hot, cross Bunn"—provoked at incessant attacks on his operatic verses, hired a man of letters to write "A Word with *Punch*," and a few smart personalities soon silenced the jester. "Towards 1848," says Mr. Blanchard, "Douglas Jerrold, then writing plays and editing a magazine, began to write less for *Punch*." In 1857 he died. Among the later additions to the staff were Mr. Shirley Brooks and Mr. Tom Taylor, now its editor.

The *Dispatch* (No. 139, north) was established by Mr. Bell, in 1801. Moving from Bride Lane to Newcastle Street, and thence to Wine Office Court, it settled down in the present locality in 1824. Mr. Bell was an energetic man, and the paper succeeded in obtaining a good position; but he was not a man of large capital, and other persons had shares in the property. In consequence of difficulties between the proprietors there were at one time three *Dispatches* in the field— Bell's, Kent's, and Duckett's; but the two last-mentioned were short-lived, and Mr. Bell maintained his position. Bell's was a sporting paper, with many columns devoted to pugilism, and a woodcut exhibiting two boxers ready for an encounter. But the editor (says a story more or less authentic), Mr. Samuel Smith, who had obtained his post by cleverly reporting a fight near Canterbury, one day received a severe thrashing from a famous member of the ring. This changed the editor's opinions as to the propriety of boxing—at any-rate pugilism was repudiated by the *Dispatch* about 1829; and boxing, from the *Dispatch* point of view, was henceforward treated as a degrading and brutal amusement, unworthy of our civilisation.

Mr. Harmer (afterwards Alderman), a solicitor in extensive practice in Old Bailey cases, became connected with the paper about the time when the Fleet Street office was established, and contributed capital, which soon bore fruit. The success was so great, that for many years the *Dispatch* as a property was inferior only to the *Times*. It became famous for its letters on political subjects. The original "Publicola" was Mr. Williams, a violent and coarse but very vigorous and popular writer. He wrote weekly for about sixteen or seventeen years, and after his death the signature was assumed by Mr. Fox, the famous orator and member for Oldham. Other writers also borrowed the well-known signature. Eliza Cook wrote in the *Dispatch* in 1836, at first signing her poems "E." and "E.C."; but in the course of the following year her name appeared in full. She contributed a poem weekly for several years, relinquishing her connection with the paper in 1850. Afterwards, in 1869, when the property changed hands, she wrote two or three poems. Under the signature "Caustic," Mr. Serle, the dramatic author and editor, contributed a weekly letter for about twenty-seven years; and from 1856 till 1869 was editor-in-chief. In 1841–42 the *Dispatch* had a hard-fought duel with the *Times*. "Publicola" wrote a series of letters, which had the effect of preventing the election of Mr. Walter for Southwark. The *Times* retaliated when the time came for Alderman Harmer to succeed to the lord mayoralty. Day after day the *Times* returned to the attack, denouncing the *Dispatch* as an infidel paper; and Alderman Harmer, rejected by the City, resigned in conse-

Telegraph was started on June 29, 1855, by the late Colonel Sleigh. It was a single sheet, and the price twopence. Colonel Sleigh failing to make it a success, Mr. Lawson, the present chief proprietor of the paper, took the copyright as part security for money owed him as a printer by Colonel Sleigh.

ST. BRIDE'S CHURCH, FLEET STREET, AFTER THE FIRE, 1824 (*see page* 56).

quence his aldermanic gown. In 1857 the *Dispatch* commenced the publication of its famous "Atlas," giving away a good map weekly for about five years. The price was reduced from fivepence to twopence, at the beginning of 1869, and to a penny in 1870.

The *Daily Telegraph* office is No. 136 (north). Mr. Ingram, of the *Illustrated London News*, originated a paper called the *Telegraph*, which lasted only seven or eight weeks. The present *Daily*

In Mr. Lawson's hands the paper, reduced to a penny, became a great success. "It was," says Mr. Grant, in his "History of the Newspaper Press," "the first of the penny papers, while a single sheet, and as such was regarded as a newspaper marvel; but when it came out—which it did soon after the *Standard*—as a double sheet the size of the *Times*, published at fourpence, and for a penny, it created a sensation. Here was a penny paper, containing not only the same amount of telegraphic and general information as the other high-priced papers—their price being then fourpence — but also evidently written, in its leading article department, with an ability which could only be surpassed by that of the leading articles of the *Times* itself. This was indeed a new era in the morning journalism of the metropolis." When Mr. Lawson bought the *Telegraph*, the sum which he received for advertisements in the first number was

The "Globe Tavern" (No. 134, north), though now only a memory, abounds with traditions of Goldsmith and his motley friends. The house, in 1649, was leased to one Henry Hottersall for forty-one years, at the yearly rent of £75, ten gallons of Canary sack, and £400 fine. Mr. John Forster gives a delightful sketch of Goldsmith's Wednesday evening club at the "Globe," in 1767. When not at Johnson's great club, Oliver beguiled his cares at a shilling rubber club at the "Devil Tavern," or at a

WAITHMAN'S SHOP (*see page* 66).

exactly 7s. 6d. The daily receipts for advertisements are now said to exceed £1,000. Mr. Grant says that the remission of the tax on paper brought £12,000 a year extra to the *Telegraph*. Twelve pages for a penny is no uncommon thing with the *Telegraph* during the Parliamentary session. The returns of sales given by the *Telegraph* for the half-year ending 1870 showed an average daily sale of 190,885; and a competent authority estimates the average daily sale at the present time at over 200,000 copies. One of the printing-machines recently set up by the proprietors of the *Telegraph* throws off upwards of 200 copies per minute, or 12,000 an hour.

humble gathering in the parlour of the "Bedford," Covent Garden. A hanger-on of the theatres, who frequented the "Globe," has left notes which Mr. Forster has admirably used, and which we now abridge without further apology. Grim old Macklin belonged to the club it is certain; and among the less obscure members was King, the comedian, the celebrated impersonator of Lord Ogleby. Hugh Kelly, another member, was a clever young Irishman, who had chambers near Goldsmith in the Temple. He had been a stay-maker's apprentice, who, turning law writer, and soon landing as a hack for the magazines, set up as a satirist for the stage, and eventually, through Garrick's patronage, succeeded in sentimental comedy. It was of him Johnson said, "Sir, I never desire to converse with a man who has written more than he has read." Poor Kelly afterwards went to the Bar, and died of disappointment and over-work. A third member was Captain Thompson, a friend of Garrick, who wrote some good sea songs and edited "Andrew Marvell;" but foremost among all the boon companions was a needy Irish doctor named Glover, who had appeared on the stage, and who was said to have restored to life a man who had been hung; this Glover, who was famous for his songs and imitations, once had the impudence, like Theodore Hook, to introduce Goldsmith, during a summer ramble in Hampstead, to a party where he was an entire stranger, and to pass himself off as a friend of the host. "Our Dr. Glover," says Goldsmith, "had a constant levee of his distressed countrymen, whose wants, as far as he was able, he always relieved." Gordon, the fattest man in the club, was renowned for his jovial song of "Nottingham Ale;" and on special occasions Goldsmith himself would sing his favourite nonsense about the little old woman who was tossed seventeen times higher than the moon. A fat pork-butcher at the "Globe" used to offend Goldsmith by constantly shouting out, "Come, Noll, here's my service to you, old boy." After the success of *The Good-natured Man*, this coarse familiarity was more than Goldsmith's vanity could bear, so one special night he addressed the butcher with grave reproof. The stolid man, taking no notice, replied briskly, "Thankee, Mister Noll." "Well, where is the advantage of your reproof?" asked Glover. "In truth," said Goldsmith, good-naturedly, "I give it up; I ought to have known before that there is no putting a pig in the right way." Sometimes rather cruel tricks were played on the credulous poet. One evening Goldsmith came in clamorous for his supper, and ordered chops. Directly the supper came in, the wags, by pre-agreement, began to sniff and swear. Some pushed the plate away; others declared the rascal who had dared set such chops before a gentleman should be made to swallow them himself. The waiter was savagely rung up, and forced to eat the supper, to which he consented with well-feigned reluctance, the poet calmly ordering a fresh supper and a dram for the poor waiter, "who otherwise might get sick from so nauseating a meal." Poor Goldy! kindly even at his most foolish moments. A sadder story still connects Goldsmith with the "Globe." Ned Purdon, a worn-out booksellers' hack and a *protégé* of Goldsmith, dropped down dead in Smithfield. Goldsmith

wrote his epitaph as he came from his chambers in the Temple to the "Globe." The lines are :—

"Here lies poor Ned Purdon, from misery freed,
  Who long was a booksellers' hack ;
He led such a miserable life in this world,
  I don't think he'll wish to come back."

Goldsmith sat next Glover that night at the club, and Glover heard the poet repeat, *sotto voce*, with a mournful intonation, the words,—

"I don't think he'll wish to come back."

Oliver was musing over his own life, and Mr. Forster says touchingly, "It is not without a certain pathos to me, indeed, that he should have so repeated it."

Among other frequenters of the "Globe" were Boswell's friend Akerman, the keeper of Newgate, who thought it prudent never to return home till daybreak; and William Woodfall, the celebrated Parliamentary reporter. In later times Brasbridge, the sporting silversmith of Fleet Street, was a frequenter of the club. He tells us that among his associates was a surgeon, who, living on the Surrey side of the Thames, had to take a boat every night, Blackfriars Bridge not being then built. This nightly navigation cost him three or four shillings a time, yet, when the bridge came, he grumbled at having to pay a penny toll. Among other frequenters of the "Globe," Mr. Timbs enumerates "Archibald Hamilton, whose mind was 'fit for a lord chancellor;' Dunstall, the comedian; Carnan, the bookseller, who defeated the Stationers' Company in the almanack trial; and, later still, the eccentric Hugh Evelyn, who set up a claim upon the great Surrey estate of Sir Frederic Evelyn."

The *Standard* (in Shoe Lane), "the largest daily paper," was originally an evening paper alone. In 1826 a deputation of the leading men opposed to Catholic Emancipation waited on Mr. Charles Baldwin, proprietor of the *St. James's Chronicle*, and begged him to start an anti-Catholic evening paper, but Mr. Baldwin refused unless a preliminary sum of £15,000 was lodged at the banker's. A year later this sum was deposited, and in 1827 the *Evening Standard*, edited by Dr. Giffard, ex-editor of the *St. James's Chronicle*, appeared. Mr. Alaric Watts, the poet, was the first sub-editor; he was soon succeeded by the celebrated Dr. Maginn. The daily circulation soon rose from 700 or 800 copies to 3,000 and over. The profits Mr. Grant calculates at £7,000 to £8,000 a year. On the bankruptcy of Mr. Charles Baldwin, Mr. James Johnson bought the *Morning Herald* and *Standard*, plant and all, for £16,500. The new proprietor reduced the *Standard* from fourpence to twopence, and made it a morning as well as an evening paper. In 1858 he reduced it to a penny only. The result was a great success. The annual income of the *Standard* is now, Mr. Grant says, "much exceeding yearly the annual incomes of most of the ducal dignities of the land." The legend of the Duke of Newcastle presenting Dr. Giffard, in 1827, with £1,200 for a violent article against Roman Catholic claims, has been denied by Dr. Giffard's son in the *Times*. The Duke of Wellington once wrote to Dr. Giffard to dictate the line which the *Standard* and *Morning Herald* were to adopt on a certain question during the agitation on the Maynooth Bill; and Dr. Giffard withdrew his opposition to please Sir Robert Peel—a concession which injured the *Standard*. Yet in the following year, when Sir Robert Peel brought in his Bill for the abolition of the corn laws, he did not even pay Dr. Giffard the compliment of apprising him of his intention. Such is official gratitude when a tool is done with.

Near Shoe Lane lived one of Caxton's disciples. Wynkyn de Worde, who is supposed to have been one of Caxton's assistants or workmen, was a native of Lorraine. He carried on a prosperous career, says Dibdin, from 1502 to 1534, at the sign of the "Sun," in the parish of St. Bride's, Fleet Street. In upwards of four hundred works published by this industrious man he displayed unprecedented skill, elegance, and care, and his Gothic type was considered a pattern for his successors. The books that came from his press were chiefly grammars, romances, legends of the saints, and fugitive poems; he never ventured on an English New Testament, nor was any drama published bearing his name. His great patroness, Margaret, the mother of Henry VII., seems to have had little taste to guide De Worde in his selection, for he never reprinted the works of Chaucer or of Gower; nor did his humble patron, Robert Thorney, the mercer, lead him in a better direction. De Worde filled his black-letter books with rude engravings, which he used so indiscriminately that the same cut often served for books of a totally opposite character. By some writers De Worde is considered to be the first introducer of Roman letters into this country; but the honour of that mode of printing is now generally claimed by Pynson, a contemporary. Among other works published by De Worde were "The Ship of Fools," that great satire that was so long popular in England; Mandeville's lying "Travels;" "La Morte d'Arthur" (from which Tennyson has derived so much inspiration); "The Golden Legend;" and three curious treatises on

"Hunting, Hawking, and Fishing," partly written by Johanna Berners, a prioress of St. Alban's. In De Worde's "Collection of Christmas Carols" we find the words of that fine old song, still sung annually at Queen's College, Oxford,—

"The boar's head in hand bring I,
With garlands gay and rosemary."

De Worde also published some writings of Erasmus. The old printer was buried in the parish church of St. Bride's, before the high altar of St. Katharine; and he left land to the parish so that masses should be said for his soul. To his servants, not forgetting his bookbinder, Nowel, in Shoe Lane, he bequeathed books. De Worde lived near the Conduit, a little west of Shoe Lane. This conduit, which was begun in the year 1439 by Sir William Estfielde, a former Lord Mayor, and finished in 1471, was, according to Stow's account, a stone tower; on the top were images of St. Christopher and angels, who, on sweet-sounding bells, hourly chimed a hymn with hammers, thus anticipating the wonders of St. Dunstan's. These London conduits were great resorts for the apprentices, whom their masters sent with big leather and metal jugs to bring home the daily supply of water. Here these noisy, quarrelsome young rascals stayed to gossip, idle, and fight. At the coronation of Anne Boleyn this conduit was newly painted, all the arms and angels refreshed, and "the music melodiously sounding." Upon the conduit was raised a tower with four turrets, and in every turret stood one of the cardinal virtues, promising never to leave the queen, while, to the delight and wonder of thirsty citizens, the taps ran with claret and red wine. Fleet Street, according to Mr. Noble, was supplied in the Middle Ages with water from the conduit at Marylebone and the holy wells of St. Clement's and St. Bridget's. The tradition is that the latter well was drained dry for the supply of the coronation banquet of George IV. As early as 1358 the inhabitants of Fleet Street complained of aqueduct pipes bursting and flooding their cellars, upon which they were allowed the privilege of erecting a pent-house over an aqueduct opposite the tavern of John Walworth, and near the house of the Bishop of Salisbury. In 1478 a Fleet Street wax-chandler, having been detected tapping the conduit pipes for his own use, was sentenced to ride through the City with a vessel shaped like a conduit on his felonious head, and the City crier walking before him to proclaim his offence.

The "Castle Tavern," mentioned as early as 1432, stood at the south-west corner of Shoe Lane. Here the Clockmakers' Company held their meetings before the Great Fire, and in 1708 the "Castle" possessed the largest sign-board in London. Early in the last century, says Mr. Noble, its proprietor was Alderman Sir John Task, a wine merchant, who died in 1735 (George II.), worth, it was understood, a quarter of a million of money.

The *Morning Advertiser* (No. 127, north) was established in 1794, by the Society of Licensed Victuallers, on the mutual benefit society principle. Every member is bound to take in the paper and is entitled to a share in its profits. Members unsuccessful in business become pensioners on the funds of the institution. The paper, which took the place of the *Daily Advertiser*, and was the suggestion of Mr. Grant, a master printer, was an immediate success. Down to 1850 the *Morning Advertiser* circulated chiefly in public-houses and coffee-houses at the rate of nearly 5,000 copies a day. But in 1850, the circulation beginning to decline, the committee resolved to enlarge the paper to the size of the *Times*, and Mr. James Grant was appointed editor. The profits now increased, and the paper found its way to the clubs. The late Lord Brougham and Sir David Brewster contributed to the *Advertiser ;* and the letters signed "An Englishman" excited much interest. This paper has generally been Liberal. Mr. Grant remained the editor for twenty years : he died in 1879.

No. 91 (south side) was till lately the office of that old-established paper, *Bell's Weekly Messenger*. Mr. Bell, the spirited publisher who founded this paper, is delightfully sketched by Leigh Hunt in his autobiography.

"About the period of my writing the above essays," he says, in his easy manner, "circumstances introduced me to the acquaintance of Mr. Bell, the proprietor of the *Weekly Messenger*. In his house, in the Strand, I used to hear of politics and dramatic criticisms, and of the persons who wrote them. Mr. Bell had been well known as a bookseller and a speculator in elegant typography. It is to him the public are indebted for the small editions of the poets that preceded Cooke's. Bell was, upon the whole, a remarkable person. He was a plain man, with a red face and a nose exaggerated by intemperance ; and yet there was something not unpleasing in his countenance, especially when he spoke. He had sparkling black eyes, a good-natured smile, gentlemanly manners, and one of the most agreeable voices I ever heard. He had no acquirements—perhaps not even grammar ; but his taste in putting forth a publication and getting the best artists to adorn it was new in those times, and may be admired in any. Unfortunately for Mr. Bell, the Prince of

Wales, to whom he was bookseller, once did him the honour to partake of an entertainment or refreshment (I forget which—most probably the latter) at his house. He afterwards became a bankrupt. After his bankruptcy he set up a newspaper, which became profitable to everybody but himself."*

No. 93, Fleet Street (south side) is endeared to us by its connection with Charles Lamb. At that number, in 1823, that great humorist, the king of all London clerks that ever were or will be, published his "Elia," a collection of essays immortal as the language, full of quaint and tender thoughts and gleaming with cross-lights of humour as shot silk does with interchanging colours. In 1821, when the first editor was shot in a duel, the *London Magazine* fell into the hands of Messrs. Taylor & Hessey, of No. 93 ; but they published the excellent periodical and gave their "magazine dinners" at their publishing house in Waterloo Place.

Mr. John Scott, a man of great promise, the editor of the *London* for its first publishers—Messrs. Baldwin, Cradock, & Joy—met with a very tragic death in 1821. The duel in which he fell arose from a quarrel between the men on the *London* and some clever but bitter and unscrupulous writers in *Blackwood*, started in 1817. Lockhart, who had cruelly maligned Leigh Hunt and his set (the "Cockney School," as the Scotch Tories chose to call them), was sharply attacked in the *London*. Fiery and vindictive, Lockhart at once rushed up to town, and angrily demanded from Mr. Scott, the editor, an explanation, an apology, or a meeting. Mr. Scott declined giving an apology unless Mr. Lockhart would first deny that he was editor of *Blackwood*. Lockhart refused to give this denial, and retorted by expressing a mean opinion of Mr. Scott's courage. Lockhart and Scott both printed contradictory versions of the quarrel, which continued till at last Mr. Christie, a friend of Lockhart, challenged Scott ; and they met at Chalk Farm by moonlight on February 16th, at nine o'clock at night, attended by their seconds and surgeons, in the old business-like, bloodthirsty way. The first time Mr. Christie did not fire at Mr. Scott, a fact of which Mr. Patmore, the author, Scott's second, with most blamable indiscretion, did not inform his principal. At the second fire Christie's ball struck Scott just above the right hip, and he

* An intelligent compositor (Mr. J. P. S. Bicknell), who has been a noter of curious passages in his time, informs me that Bell was the first printer who confined the small letter "s" to its present shape, and rejected altogether the older form "ſ."—W. T.

fell. He lingered till the 27th. It was said at the time that Hazlitt, perhaps unintentionally, had driven Scott to fight by indirect taunts. "I don't pretend," Hazlitt is reported to have said, "to hold the principles of honour which you hold. I would neither give nor accept a challenge. You hold the opinions of the world; with you it is different. As for me, it would be nothing. I do not think as you and the world think," and so on. Poor Scott, not yet forty, had married the pretty daughter of Colnaghi, the print-seller in Pall Mall, and left two children.

For the five years it lasted, perhaps no magazine —not even the mighty *Maga* itself—ever drew talent towards it with such magnetic attraction. In Mr. Barry Cornwall's delightful memoir of his old friend Lamb, composed when the writer was in his seventy-third year, he has summarised the writers in the *London*, and shown how deep and varied was the intellect brought to bear on its production. First of all he mentions poor Scott, a shrewd, critical, rather hasty man, who wrote essays on Sir Walter Scott, Wordsworth, Godwin, Byron, Keats, Shelley, Leigh Hunt, and Hazlitt, his wonderful contemporaries, in a fruitful age. Hazlitt, glowing and capricious, produced the twelve essays of his "Table Talk," many dramatic articles, and papers on Beckford's Fonthill, the Angerstein pictures, and the Elgin marbles—pages wealthy with thought. Lamb contributed in three years all the matchless essays of "Elia." Mr. Thomas Carlyle, then only a promising young Scotch philosopher, wrote several articles on the "Life and Writings of Schiller." Mr. de Quincey, that subtle thinker and bitter Tory, contributed his wonderful "Confessions of an Opium-Eater." That learned and amiable man, the Rev. H. F. Cary, the translator of Dante, wrote several interesting notices of early French poets. Allan Cunningham, the vigorous Scottish bard, sent the romantic "Tales of Lyddal Cross" and a series of papers styled "Traditional Literature." Mr. John Poole—who died in 1872—(the author of *Paul Pry* and that humorous novel, "Little Pedlington," which is supposed to have furnished Mr. Charles Dickens with some suggestions for "Pickwick") wrote burlesque imitations of contemporaneous dramatic writers—Morton, Dibdin, Reynolds, Moncrieff, &c. Mr. J. H. Reynolds wrote, under the name of Henry Herbert, notices of contemporaneous events, such as a scene at the Cockpit, the trial of Thurtell, &c. That delightful punster and humorist, with pen or pencil, Tom Hood, the elder, sent to the *London* his first poems of any ambition or length—"Lycus

the Centaur," and "The Two Peacocks of Bedfont." Keats, "that sleepless soul that perished in its pride," and Montgomery, both contributed poems. Sir John Bowring, the accomplished linguist, wrote on Spanish poetry. Mr. Henry Southern, the projector of that excellent work, the *Retrospective Review*, contributed "The Conversations of Lord Byron." Mr. Walter Savage Landor, that very original and eccentric thinker, published in this magazine one at least of his admirable "Imaginary Conversations." Mr. Julius (afterwards Archdeacon) Hare reviewed in it the robust works of Landor. Mr. Elton contributed graceful translations from Catullus, Propertius, &c. Even among the lesser contributors there were very eminent writers, not forgetting Barry Cornwall, Hartley Coleridge, John Clare, the Northamptonshire peasant poet; and Bernard Barton, the Quaker poet. Nor must we omit that strange contrast to these pure-hearted and wise men, "Janus Weathercock" (Wainwright), the polished villain who murdered his young niece and most probably several other friends and relations, for the money insured upon their lives. This gay and evil being, by no means a dull writer upon art and the drama, was much liked by Lamb and the Russell Street set. The news of his cold-blooded crimes (transpiring in 1837) seem to have struck a deep horror among all the scoundrel's fashionable associates. Although when arrested in France it was discovered that Wainwright habitually carried strychnine about with him, he was only tried for forgery, and for that offence transported for life.

A fine old citizen of the last century, Joseph Brasbridge, who published his memoirs, kept a silversmith's shop at No. 98, several doors from Alderman Waithman's. At one time Brasbridge confesses he divided his time between the tavern club, the card party, the hunt, and the fight, and left his shop to be looked after by others, whilst he decided on the respective merits of Humphries and Mendoza, Cribb and Big Ben. Among Brasbridge's early customers were the Duke of Marlborough, the Duke of Argyle, and other men of rank, and he glories in having once paid an elaborate compliment to Lady Hamilton. The most curious story in Brasbridge's "Fruits of Experience" is the following, various versions of which have been paraphrased by modern writers. A surgeon in Gough Square had purchased for dissection the body of a man who had been hanged at Tyburn. The servant girl, wishing to look at the corpse, stole upstairs in the doctor's absence, and, to her horror, found the body sitting up on the board, wondering where it was. The girl almost threw herself down the stairs in her fright. The surgeon, on learning of the resuscitation of his subject, humanely concealed the man in the house till he could fit him out for America. The fellow proved as clever and industrious as he was grateful, and having amassed a fortune, he eventually left it all to his benefactor. The sequel is still more

the Strand, then came forward, and deposed that his wife and her mother, he remembered, used to visit the surgeon in Gough Square. On inquiry Mrs. Willcocks was proved the next of kin, and the base shoemaker returned to his last. The lucky Mr. Willcocks was the good-natured bookseller who lent Johnson and Garrick, when they first came up

ALDERMAN WAITHMAN, FROM AN AUTHENTIC PORTRAIT (*see page* 68).

curious. The surgeon dying some years after, his heirs were advertised for. A shoemaker at Islington eventually established a claim and inherited the money. Mean in prosperity, the *ci-devant* shoemaker then refused to pay the lawyer's bill, and, moreover, called him a rogue. The enraged lawyer replied, " I have put you into possession of this property by my exertions, now I will spend £100 out of my own pocket to take it away again, for you are not deserving of it." The lawyer accordingly advertised again for the surgeon's nearest of kin; Mr. Willcocks, a bookseller in

to London to seek their fortunes, £5 on their joint note.

Nos. 103 (afterwards the *Sunday Times* office) and 104 were the shop of that bustling politician, Alderman Waithman; and to his memory was erected the obelisk on the site of his first shop, formerly the north-west end of Fleet Market. Waithman, according to Mr. Timbs, had a genius for the stage, and especially shone as Macbeth. He was uncle to John Reeve, the comic actor. Cobbett, who hated Waithman, has left a portrait of the alderman, written in his usual racy English. " Among these persons," he says, talking of the Princess Caroline agitation, in 1813, "there was a common council-man named Robert Waithman, a man who for many years had taken a conspicuous part in the politics of the City; a man not destitute of the powers of utterance, and a man of sound prin-

Common Council, opposed it, and was defeated. On the appointed day the Princess was presented with the address, to the delight of the more zealous Radicals. The procession of more than one hundred carriages came back past Carlton House on their return from Kensington,

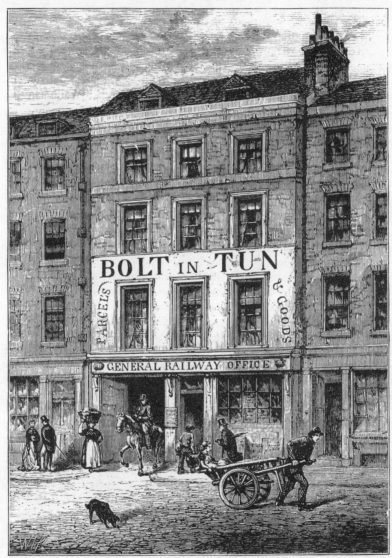

THE "BOLT-IN-TUN," 1859 (*see page* 53).
From a Water-Colour Drawing in Mr. Crace's Collection.

ciples also; but a man so enveloped, so completely swallowed up by self-conceit, who, though perfectly illiterate, though unable to give to three consecutive sentences a grammatical construction, seemed to look upon himself as the first orator, the first writer, and the first statesman of the whole world." According to Cobbett, Waithman, vexed that Alderman Wood had been the first to propose an address of condolence to the Princess at the

the people groaning and hissing, to torment the Regent.

Brasbridge, the Tory silversmith of Fleet Street, writes very contemptuously in his autobiography of Waithman. Sneering at his boast of reading, he says:—"I own my curiosity was a little excited to know when and where he began his studies. It could not be in his shop in Fleet Market, for there he was too busily employed in attending on the fishwomen and other ladies connected with the business of the market. Nor could it be at the corner of Fleet Street, where he was always no less assiduously engaged in ticketing his super-super calicoes at two and two pence, and cutting them off for two and twenty pence." According to Brasbridge, Waithman made his first speech in 1792, in Founder's Hall, Lothbury, "called by some at that time the cauldron of sedition." Waithman was Lord Mayor in 1823-24, and was returned to Parliament five times for the City. He died in 1833. His shop was pulled down about the year 1870, in order to make room for Ludgate Circus.

A short biography of this civic orator will not be uninteresting :—Robert Waithman was born of humble parentage, at Wrexham, in North Wales. Becoming an orphan when only four months old, he was placed at the school of a Mr. Moore by his uncle, on whose death, about 1778, he obtained a situation at Reading, whence he proceeded to London, and entered into the service of a respectable linen-draper, with whom he continued till he became of age. He then entered into business at the south end of Fleet Market, whence, some years afterwards, he removed to the corner of New Bridge Street. He appears to have commenced his political career about 1792, at the oratorical displays made in admiration and imitation of the proceedings of the French Revolutionists, at Founder's Hall, in Lothbury. In 1794 he brought forward a series of resolutions, at a common hall, animadverting upon the war with revolutionised France, and enforcing the necessity of a reform in Parliament. In 1796 he was first elected a member of the Common Council for the Ward of Farringdon Without, and became a very frequent speaker in that public body. It was supposed that Mr. Fox intended to have rewarded his political exertions by the place of Receiver-General of the Land Tax. In 1818, after having been defeated on several previous occasions, he was elected as one of the representatives in Parliament of the City of London, defeating the old member, Sir William Curtis.

Very shortly after, on the 4th of August, he was elected Alderman of his ward, on the death of Sir Charles Price, Bart. On the 25th of January, 1819, he made his maiden speech in Parliament, on the presentation of a petition praying for a revision of the criminal code, the existing state of which he severely censured. At the ensuing election of 1820 the friends of Sir William Curtis turned the tables upon him, Waithman being defeated. In this year, however, he attained the honour of the shrievalty; and in October, 1823, he

was chosen Lord Mayor. In 1826 he stood another contest for the City, with better success. In 1830, 1831, and 1832 he obtained his re-election with difficulty; but in 1831 he suffered a severe disappointment in losing the chamberlainship, in the competition for which Sir James Shaw obtained a large majority of votes.

We subjoin the remarks made on his death by the editor of the *Times* newspaper :—" The magistracy of London has been deprived of one of its most respectable members, and the City of one of its most upright representatives. Everybody knows that Mr. Alderman Waithman has filled a large space in City politics ; and most people who were acquainted with him will be ready to admit that, had his early education been better directed, or his early circumstances more favourable to his ambition, he might have become an important man in a wider and higher sphere. His natural parts, his political integrity, his consistency of conduct, and the energy and perseverance with which he performed his duties, placed him far above the common run of persons whose reputation is gained by their oratorical displays at meetings of the Common Council. In looking back at City proceedings for the last thirty-five or forty years, we find him always rising above his rivals as the steady and consistent advocate of the rights of his countrymen and the liberties and privileges of his fellow-citizens."

There is a curious story told of the Fleet Street crossing, opposite Waithman's corner. It was swept for years by an old black man named Charles M'Ghee, whose father had died in Jamaica at the age of 108. According to Mr. Noble, when he laid down his broom he sold his professional right for a very large sum. Retiring into private life much respected, he was always to be seen on Sundays at Rowland Hill's chapel. When in his seventy-third year his portrait was taken and hung in the parlour of the "Twelve Bells," Bride Lane. To Miss Waithman, who used to send him out soup and bread, he is, untruly, said to have left £7,000.

Mr. Diprose, in his "History of St. Clement," tells us more of this black sweeper. "Brutus Billy," or "Tim-buc-too," as he was generally called, lived in a passage leading from Stanhope Street into Drury Lane. He was a short, thick-set man, with his white-grey hair carefully brushed up into a toupee, the fashion of his youth. He was found in his shop, as he called his crossing, in all weathers, and was invariably civil. At night, after he had shut up shop (swept mud over his crossing), he carried round a basket of nuts and fruit to places of public entertainment, so that in time he laid by a considerable amount of money. Brutus Billy was brimful of story and anecdote. He died in Chapel Court in 1854, in his eighty-seventh year. This worthy man was perhaps the model for Billy Waters, the negro beggar in *Tom and Jerry*, who is so indignant at the beggars' supper on seeing " a turkey without sassenges."

In Garrick's time John Hardham, the well-known tobacconist, opened a shop at No. 106. There, at the sign of the "Red Lion," Hardham's Highlander kept steady guard at a doorway through which half the celebrities of the day made their exits and entrances. His celebrated " No. 37 " snuff was said, like the French millefleur, to be composed of a great number of ingredients, and Garrick in his kind way helped it into fashion by mentioning it favourably on the stage. Hardham, a native of Chichester, began life as a servant, wrote a comedy, acted, and at last became Garrick's "numberer," having a general's quick *coup d'œil* at gauging an audience, and so checking the money-takers. Garrick once became his security for a hundred pounds; but eventually Hardham grew rich, and died in 1772, bequeathing £22,289 to Chichester, 10 guineas to Garrick, and merely setting apart £10 for his funeral, only vain fools, as he said, spending more on such pageants. We can fancy the great actors of that day seated on Hardham's tobacco-chests discussing the drollery of Foote or the vivacity of Clive.

"It has long been a source of inquiry," says a writer in the *City Press*, "whence the origin of the cognomen, ' No. 37,' to the celebrated snuff compounded still under the name of John Hardham, in Fleet Street. There is a tradition that Lord Townshend, on being applied to by Hardham, whom he patronised, to name the snuff, suggested the cabalistic number of 37, it being the exact number of a majority obtained in some proceedings in the Irish Parliament whilst he was Lord Lieutenant of Ireland, and which was considered a triumph for his Government. The dates, however, do not serve this theory, as Lord Townshend was not viceroy till the years 1767–72, when the snuff must have been well established in public fame, and Hardham in the last years of his life. It has already been stated elsewhere that, on the famed snuff coming out in the first instance, David Garrick, hearing of it, called in Fleet Street, as he was wont frequently to do, and offered to bring it under the public notice in the most effectual manner, by introducing an incident in a new comedy then about to be produced by him, where he would, in his part in the play, offer another character a pinch of snuff, who would extol its excellence, whereupon Garrick arranged to continue the conversation by naming

the snuff as the renowned ' 37 of John Hardham.' But the enigma, even now, is not solved; so we will, for what it may be worth, venture our own explanation. It is well known that in most of the celebrated snuffs before the public a great variety of qualities and descriptions of tobacco, and of various ages, are introduced. Hardham, like the rest, never told his secret how the snuff was made, but left it as a heritage to his successors. It is very probable, therefore, that the mystic figures, 37, we have quoted represented the number of qualities, growths, and description of the 'fragrant weed' introduced by him into his snuff, and may be regarded as a sort of appellative rebus, or conceit, founded thereon."*

But Hardham occupied himself in other ways than in the making of snuff and of money—for the Chichester youth had now grown wealthy—and in extending his circle of acquaintances amongst dramatists and players he was abundantly distinguished for Christian charity; for, in the language of a contemporary writer, we find that "his deeds in that respect were extensive," and his bounty "was conveyed to many of the objects of it in the most delicate manner." From the same authority we find that Hardham once failed in business (we presume, as a lapidary) more creditably than he could have made a fortune by it. This spirit of integrity, which remained a remarkable feature in his character throughout life, induced him to be often resorted to by his wealthy patrons as trustee for the payment of their bounties to deserving objects; in many cases the patrons died before the recipients of their relief. With Hardham, however, this made no difference; the annuities once granted, although stopped by the decease of the donors, were paid ever after by Hardham so long as he lived; and his delicacy of feeling induced him even to persuade the recipients into the belief that they were still derived from the same source.

No. 102 (south) was opened as a shop, in 1719, by one Lockyer, who called it "Mount Pleasant." It then became a " saloop-house," where the poor purchased a beverage made out of sassafras chips. The proprietor, who began life, as Mr. Noble says, with half-a-crown, died in March, 1739, worth £1,000. Thomas Read was a later tenant. Charles Lamb mentions "saloop" in one of his essays, and says, " Palates otherwise not uninstructed in dietetical elegancies sup it up with avidity." Chimney-sweeps, beloved by Lamb, approved it, and eventually stalls were set up in the streets, as at present, to reach even humbler customers.

* The real fact is, the famous snuff was merely called from the number of the drawer that held it.

CHAPTER VI.

FLEET STREET (NORTHERN TRIBUTARIES—SHIRE LANE AND BELL YARD).

The Kit-Kat Club—The Toast for the Year—Little Lady Mary—Drunken John Sly—Garth's Patients—Club removed to Barn Elms—Steele at the "Trumpet"—Rogues' Lane—Murder—Beggars' Haunts—Thieves' Dens—Coiners—Theodore Hook in Hemp's Sponging-house—Pope in Bell Yard—Minor Celebrities—Apollo Court.

OPPOSITE Child's Bank, and almost within sound of the jingle of its gold, once stood Shire Lane, afterwards known as Lower Serle's Place. It latterly became a dingy, disreputable defile, where lawyers' clerks and the hangers-on of the law-courts were often allured and sometimes robbed; yet it had been in its day a place of great repute. In this lane the Kit-Kat, the great club of Queen Anne's reign, held its sittings, at the "Cat and Fiddle," the shop of a pastrycook named Christopher Kat. The house, according to local antiquaries, afterwards became the "Trumpet," a tavern mentioned by Steele in the *Tatler,* and latterly known as the "Duke of York." The Kit-Kats were originally Whig patriots, who, at the end of King William's reign, met in this out-of-the-way place to devise measures to secure the Protestant succession and keep out the pestilent Stuarts. Latterly they assembled for simple enjoyment; and there have been grave disputes as to whether the club took its name from the punning sign, the "Cat and Kit," or from the favourite pies which Christopher Kat had christened; and as this question will probably last the antiquaries another two centuries, we leave it alone. According to some verses by Arbuthnot, the chosen friend of Pope and Swift, the question was mooted even in his time, as if the very founders of the club had forgotten. Some think that the club really began with a weekly dinner given by Jacob Tonson, the great bookseller of Gray's Inn Lane, to his chief authors and patrons. This Tonson, one of the patriarchs of English booksellers, who published Dryden's "Virgil," purchased a share of Milton's works, and first made Shakespeare's works cheap enough to be accessible to the many, was secretary to the club from the commencement. An average of thirty-nine poets, wits, noblemen, and gentlemen formed the staple of the association. The noblemen were perhaps rather too numerous for that republican equality which often prevails in the best intellectual society; yet above all the dukes shine out Steele and Addison, the two great luminaries of the club. Among the Kit-Kat dukes was the great Marlborough; among the earls the poetic Dorset, the patron of Dryden and Prior; among the lords the wise Halifax; among the baronets bluff Sir Robert Walpole. Among the poets and wits there were

Congreve, the most courtly of dramatists; Garth, the poetical physician—"well-natured Garth," as Pope somewhat awkwardly calls him; and Vanbrugh, the writer of admirable comedies. Dryden could hardly have seriously belonged to a Whig club; Pope was inadmissible as a Catholic, and Prior as a renegade. Latterly objectionable men pushed in, worst of all, Lord Mohun, a disreputable debauchee and duellist, afterwards run through by the Duke of Hamilton in Hyde Park, the duke himself perishing in the encounter. When Mohun, in a drunken pet, broke a gilded emblem off a club chair, respectable old Tonson predicted the downfall of the society, and said with a sigh, "The man who would do that would cut a man's throat." Sir Godfrey Kneller, the great Court painter of the reigns of William and Anne, was a member; and he painted for his friend Tonson the portraits of forty-two gentlemen of the Kit-Kat, including Dryden, who died a year after it was started. The forty-two portraits, painted three-quarter size (hence called Kit-Kat), to suit the walls of Tonson's villa at Barn Elms, still exist, and are treasured by Mr. W. R. Baker, a connection of the Tonson family, at Hertingfordbury, in Hertfordshire. Among the lesser men of this distinguished club we must include Pope's friends, the "knowing Walsh" and "Granville the polite."

As at the "Devil," "the tribe of Ben" must have often discussed the downfall of Lord Bacon, the poisoning of Overbury, the war in the Palatinate, and the murder of Buckingham; so in Shire Lane, opposite, the talk must have run on Marlborough's victories, Jacobite plots, and the South-Sea Bubble; Addison must have discussed Swift, and Steele condemned the littleness of Pope. It was the custom of this aristocratic club every year to elect some reigning beauty as a toast. To the queen of the year the gallant members wrote epigrammatic verses, which were etched with a diamond on the club glasses. The most celebrated of these toasts were the four daughters of the Duke of Marlborough—Lady Godolphin, Lady Sunderland (generally known as "the Little Whig"), Lady Bridgewater, and Lady Monthermer. Swift's friend, Mrs. Long, was another; and so was a niece of Sir Isaac Newton. The verses

seem flat and dead now, like flowers found between the leaves of an old book; but in their
time no doubt they had their special bloom and
fragrance. The most tolerable are those written
by Lord Halifax on "the Little Whig":—

> " All nature's charms in Sunderland appear,
> Bright as her eyes and as her reason clear;
> Yet still their force, to man not safely known,
> Seems undiscovered to herself alone."

Yet how poor after all is this laboured compliment in comparison to a sentence of Steele's on
some lady of rank whose virtues he honoured,—
"that even to have known her was in itself a
liberal education."

But few stories connected with the Kit-Kat
meetings are to be dug out of books, though no
doubt many snatches of the best conversation
are embalmed in the *Spectator* and the *Tatler*.
Yet Lady Mary Wortley Montagu, whom Pope
first admired and then reviled, tells one pleasant
incident of her childhood that connects her with
the great club.

One evening when toasts were being chosen,
her father, Evelyn Pierpoint, Duke of Kingston,
took it into his head to nominate Lady Mary, then
a child only eight years of age. She was prettier,
he vowed, than any beauty on the list. "You
shall see her," cried the duke, and instantly sent a
chaise for her. Presently she came ushered in,
dressed in her best, and was elected by acclamation. The Whig gentlemen drank the little lady's
health up-standing, and, feasting her with sweet-
meats and passing her round with kisses, at once
inscribed her name with a diamond on a drinking-
glass. "Pleasure," she says, "was too poor a
word to express my sensations. They amounted
to ecstasy. Never again throughout my whole life
did I pass so happy an evening."

It used to be said that it took so much wine to
raise Addison to his best mood, that Steele generally got drunk before that golden hour arrived.
Steele, that warm-hearted careless fellow in whom
Thackeray so delighted, certainly shone at the Kit-
Kat; and an anecdote still extant shows him to
us with all his amiable weaknesses. On the night
of that great Whig festival—the celebration of King
William's anniversary—Steele and Addison brought
with them Dr. Hoadley, the Bishop of Bangor, and
solemnly drank "the immortal memory." Presently John Sly, an eccentric hatter and enthusiastic politician, crawled into the room on his
knees, in the old Cavalier fashion, and drank the
Orange toast in a tankard of foaming October. No
one laughed at the tipsy hatter; but Steele, kindly

even when in liquor, kept whispering to the
rather shocked prelate, "Do laugh; it is humanity
to laugh." The bishop soon put on his hat and
withdrew, and Steele by and by subsided under the
table. Picked up and crammed into a sedan-chair,
he insisted, late as it was, in going to the Bishop of
Bangor's to apologise. Eventually he was coaxed
home and went up-stairs, but then, in a gush of
politeness, he insisted on seeing the chairmen out;
after which he retired with self-complacency to
bed. The next morning, in spite of headache the
most racking, Steele sent the tolerant bishop the
following exquisite couplet, which covered a multitude of such sins:—

> "Virtue with so much ease on Bangor sits,
> All faults he pardons, though he none commits."

One night when amiable Garth lingered over the
Kit-Kat wine, though patients were pining for him,
Steele reproved the epicurean doctor. "Nay,
nay, Dick," said Garth, pulling out a list of fifteen,
"it's no great matter after all, for nine of them
have such bad constitutions that not all the physicians in the world could save them; and the
other six have such good constitutions that all the
physicians in the world could not kill them."

Three o'clock in the morning seems to have
been no uncommon hour for the Kit-Kat to break
up, and a Tory lampooner says that at this club
the youth of Anne's reign learned

> " To sleep away the days and drink away the nights."

The club latterly held its meetings at Tonson's
villa at Barn Elms, previously the residence of
Cowley, or at the "Upper Flask" tavern, on
Hampstead Heath. The club died out before
the year 1727; for Sir J. Vanbrugh, writing to
Tonson, says,—" Both Lord Carlisle and Cobham
expressed a great desire of having one meeting
next winter, not as a club, but as old friends
that have been of a club—and the best club that
ever met." In 1709 we find the Kit-Kat sub-
scribing 400 guineas for the encouragement of
good comedies. Altogether such a body of men
must have had great influence on the literature of
the age, for, in spite of the bitterness of party, there
was some generous *esprit de corps* then, and the
Whig wits and poets were a power, and were
backed by rank and wealth.

Whether the "Trumpet" (formerly half-way up
on the left-hand side ascending from Temple Bar)
was the citadel of the Kit-Kats or not, Steele introduces it as the scene of two of the best of his
Tatler papers. It was there, in October, 1709, that
he received his deputation of Staffordshire county

THE "TRUMPET," AFTERWARDS THE "DUKE OF YORK," SHIRE LANE, 1778 (*see page* 71).

ELIAS ASHMOLE'S HOUSE, FROM PRINTS IN MR. CRACE'S COLLECTION (*see page* 75).

gentlemen, delightful old fogies, standing much on form and precedence. There he prepares tea for Sir Harry Quickset, Bart.; Sir Giles Wheelbarrow; Thomas Rentfree, Esq., J.P.; Andrew Windmill, Esq., the steward, with boots and whip; and Mr. Nicholas Doubt, of the Inner Temple, Sir Harry's mischievous young nephew. After much dispute about precedence, the sturdy old fellows are taken

humour Steele sketches Sir Geoffrey Notch, the president, who had spent all his money on horses, dogs, and gamecocks, and who looked on all thriving persons as pitiful upstarts. Then comes Major Matchlock, who thought nothing of any battle since Marston Moor, and who usually began his story of Naseby at three-quarters past six. Dick Reptile was a silent man, with a nephew

BISHOP BUTLER (*see page* 77).

by Steele to "Dick's" Coffee-house for a morning draught; and safely, after some danger, effect the passage of Fleet Street, Steele rallying them at the Temple Gate. In Sir Harry we fancy we see a faint sketch of the more dignified Sir Roger de Coverley, whom Addison afterwards so exquisitely elaborated.

At the "Trumpet" Steele also introduces us to a delightful club of old citizens that met every evening precisely at six. The humours of the fifteen "Trumpeters" are painted with the breadth and vigour of Hogarth's best manner. With a delightful

whom he often reproved. The wit of the club, an old Temple bencher, never left the room till he had quoted ten distiches from " Hudibras " and told long stories of a certain extinct man about town named Jack Ogle. Old Reptile was extremely attentive to all that was said, though he had heard the same stories every night for twenty years, and upon all occasions winked oracularly to his nephew particularly to mind what passed. About ten the innocent twaddle closed by a man coming in with a lantern to light home old Bickerstaff. They were simple and happy times that Steele describes with such kindly humour; and the London of his days must have been full of such quiet, homely haunts.

Mr. R. Hills, of Colne Park, Essex, kindly informs us that as late as the year 1765 there was a club that still kept up the name of Kit-Kat. The members in 1765 included, among others, Lord Sandwich (Jemmy Twitcher, as he was generally called), Mr. Beard, Lord Weymouth, Lord Bolingbroke, the Duke of Queensberry, Lord Carysfort, Mr. Cadogan, the Marquis of Caracciollo, Mr. Seymour, and Sir George Armytage. One of the most active managers of the club was Richard Phelps (who, we believe, afterwards was secretary to Pitt). Among the letters and receipts preserved by Mr. Hills is one from Thomas Pingo, jeweller, of the "Golden Head," on the "Paved Stones," Gray's Inn Lane, for gold medals, probably to be worn by the members.

Even in the reign of James I. Shire Lane was christened Rogues' Lane, and, in spite of all the dukes and lords of the Kit-Kat, it never grew very respectable. In 1724 that incomparable young rascal, Jack Sheppard, used to frequent the "Bible" public-house—a printers' house of call—at No. 13. In one of the rooms there was a trap by which Jack could drop into a subterraneous passage leading to Bell Yard. The Tyburn gibbet cured Jack of this trick. In 1738 the lane went·from bad to worse, for there Thomas Carr (a low attorney, of Elm Court) and Elizabeth Adams robbed and murdered a gentleman named Quarrington at the "Angel and Crown" Tavern, and the miscreants were hung at Tyburn. Hogarth painted a portrait of the woman. One night, many years ago, a man was robbed, thrown downstairs, and killed, in one of the dens in Shire Lane. There was snow on the ground, and about two o'clock, when the watchmen grew drowsy and were a long while between their rounds, the frightened murderers carried the stiffened body up the lane and placed it bolt upright, near a dim oil lamp, at a neighbour's door. There the watchmen found it; but there was no clue to guide them, for nearly every house in the lane was infamous. Years after, two ruffianly fellows who were confined in the King's Bench were heard accusing each other of the murder in Shire Lane, and justice pounced upon her prey.

One thieves' house, the "Retreat," says Mr. Diprose, in his "St. Clement Danes," led by a back way into Crown Court; other dens had a passage into the Strand. Nos. 9, 10, and 11 were known as Cadgers' Hall, and were much frequented by beggars; and bushels of bread, thrown aside by the professional mendicants, were found there by the police.

The "Sun" Tavern, afterwards the "Temple Bar Stores," had been a great resort for the Tom and Jerry frolics of the Regency; and the "Anti-Gallican" Tavern was a haunt of low sporting men, being kept by Harry Lee, father of the first and original "tiger," invented and made fashionable by the notorious Lord Barrymore. During the Chartist times violent meetings were held at a club in Shire Lane. A good story is told of one of these. A detective in disguise attended an illegal meeting, leaving his comrades ready below. All at once a frantic hatter rose, denounced the detective as a spy, and proposed off-hand to pitch him out of window. Permitted by the more peaceable to depart, the policeman scuttled downstairs as fast as he could, and, not being recognised in his disguise, was instantly knocked down by his friends' prompt truncheons.

In Ship Yard, close to Shire Lane, once stood a block of disreputable, tumble-down houses, used by coiners, and known as the "Smashing Lumber." Every room had a secret trap, and from the workshop above a shaft reached the cellars to hurry away by means of a basket and pulley all the apparatus at the first alarm. The first man made his fortune, but the new police soon ransacked the den and broke up the business.

In August, 1823, Theodore Hook, the witty and the heartless, was brought to a sponging-house kept by a sheriff's officer named Hemp, at the upper end of Shire Lane, being under arrest for a Crown debt of £12,000, due to the Crown for defalcations during his careless treasurership at the Mauritius. He was editor of *John Bull* at the time, and continued while in this horrid den to write his "Sayings and Doings," and to pour forth for royal pay his usual scurrilous lampoons at all who supported poor, persecuted Queen Caroline. Dr. Maginn, who had just come over from Cork to practise Toryism, was his constant visitor, and Hemp's barred door no doubt often shook at their reckless laughter. Hook at length left Shire Lane for the Rules of the Bench, Temple Place, in April, 1824. Previously to his arrest he had been living in retirement at lodgings in Somers' Town, with a poor girl whom he had led astray. Here he renewed the mad scenes of his thoughtless youth with Terry, Matthews, and wonderful old Tom Hill; and here he resumed (but not at these revels) his former acquaintanceship with that mischievous obstructive, Wilson Croker. After he left Shire Lane and the Rules of the Bench he went to Putney.

In spite of all bad proclivities, Shire Lane had its fits of respectability. In 1603 there was living there Sir Arthur Atie, Knt., in early life secretary to the great Earl of Leicester, and afterwards attendant on his step-son, the luckless Earl of Essex. Elias Ashmole, the great antiquary and student in alchemy and astrology, also honoured this lane, but he gathered in the Temple those great collections of books and coins, some of which perished by fire, and some of which he afterwards gave to the University of Oxford, where they were placed in a building called, in memory of the illustrious collector, the Ashmolean Museum.

To Mr. Noble's research we are indebted for the knowledge that in 1767 Mr. Hoole, the translator of Tasso, was living in Shire Lane, and from thence wrote to Dr. Percy, who was collecting his "Ancient Ballads," to ask him Dr. Wharton's address. Hoole was at that time writing a dramatic piece called *Cyrus*, for Covent Garden Theatre. He seems to have been an amiable man but a feeble poet, was an esteemed friend of Dr. Johnson, and had a situation in the East India House.

Another illustrious tenant of Shire Lane was James Perry, the proprietor of the *Morning Chronicle*, who died, as it was reported, worth £130,000. That lively memoir-writer, Taylor, of the *Sun*, who wrote "Monsieur Tonson," describes Perry as living in the narrow part of Shire Lane, opposite a passage which led to the stairs from Boswell Court. He lodged with Mr. Lunan, a bookbinder, who had married his sister, who subsequently became the wife of that great Greek scholar, thirsty Dr. Porson. Perry had begun life as the editor of the *Gazeteer*, but being dismissed by a Tory proprietor, and on the *Morning Chronicle* being abandoned by Woodfall, some of Perry's friends bought the derelict for £210, and he and Gray, a friend of Barett, became the joint proprietors of the concern. Their printer, Mr. Lambert, lived in Shire Lane; and here the partners, too, lived for three or four years, when they removed to the corner-house of Lancaster Court, Strand.

Bell Yard can boast of but few associations; yet Pope often visited the dingy passage, because there for some years resided his old friend Fortescue, then a barrister, but afterwards a judge and Master of the Rolls. To Fortescue Pope dedicated his "Imitation of the First Satire of Horace," published in 1733. It contains what the late Mr. Rogers, the banker and poet, used to consider the best line Pope ever wrote, and it is certainly almost perfect,—

"Bare the mean heart that lurks behind a star."

In that delightful collection of Pope's "Table Talk," called "Spence's Anecdotes," we find that a chance remark of Lord Bolingbroke, on taking up a "Horace" in Pope's sick-room, led to those fine "Imitations of Horace" which we now possess. The "First Satire" consists of an imaginary conversation between Pope and Fortescue, who advises him to write no more dangerous invectives against vice or folly. It was Fortescue who assisted Pope in writing the humorous law-report of "Stradling *versus* Stiles," in "Scriblerus." The intricate case is this, and is worthy of Anstey himself: Sir John Swale, of Swale's Hall, in Swale Dale, by the river Swale, knight, made his last will and testament, in which, among other bequests, was this: "Out of the kind love and respect that I bear my much-honoured and good friend, Mr. Matthew Stradling, gent., I do bequeath unto the said Matthew Stradling, gent., all my black and white horses." Now the testator had six black horses, six white, and six pied horses. The debate, therefore, was whether the said Matthew Stradling should have the said pied horses, by virtue of the said bequest. The case, after much debate, is suddenly terminated by a motion in arrest of judgment that the pied horses were mares, and thereupon an inspection was prayed. This, it must be confessed, is admirable fooling. If the Scriblerus Club had carried out their plan of bantering the follies of the followers of every branch of knowledge, Fortescue would no doubt have selected the law as his special butt. "This friend of Pope," says Mr. Carruthers, "was consulted by the poet about all his affairs, as well as those of Martha Blount, and, as may be gathered, he gave him advice without a fee. The intercourse between the poet and his 'learned counsel' was cordial and sincere; and of the letters that passed between them sixty-eight have been published, ranging from 1714 to the last year of Pope's life. They are short, unaffected letters— more truly *letters* than any others in the series." Fortescue was promoted to the bench of the Exchequer in 1735, from thence to the Common Pleas in 1738, and in 1741 was made Master of the Rolls. Pope's letters are often addressed to "his counsel learned in the law, at his house at the upper end of Bell Yard, near unto Lincoln's Inn." In March, 1736, he writes of "that filthy old place, Bell Yard, which I want them and you to quit."

Apollo Court, next Bell Yard, has little about it worthy of notice beyond the fact that it derived its name from the great club-room at the "Devil" Tavern, that once stood on the opposite side of Fleet Street, and the jovialities of which we have already chronicled.

CHAPTER VII.

FLEET STREET (NORTHERN TRIBUTARIES—CHANCERY LANE).

The Asylum for Jewish Converts—The Rolls Chapel—Ancient Monuments—A Speaker Expelled for Bribery—" Remember Cæsar "—Trampling on a Master of the Rolls—Sir William Grant's Oddities—Sir John Leach—Funeral of Lord Gifford—Mrs. [Clark and the Duke of York— Wolsey in his Pomp—Strafford—" Honest Isaak "—The Lord Keeper—Lady Fanshawe—Jack Randal—Serjeants' Inn—An Evening with Hazlitt at the " Southampton "—Charles Lamb—Sheridan—The Sponging Houses—The Law Institute—A Tragical Story.

CHANCERY, or Chancellor's, Lane, as it was first called, must have been a mere quagmire, or cart-track, in the reign of Edward I., for Strype tells us that at that period it had become so impassable to knight, monk, and citizen, that John Breton, Custos of London, had it barred up, to "hinder any harm;" and the Bishop of Chichester, whose house was there (now Chichester Rents), kept up the bar for ten years ; at the end of that time, on an inquisition of the annoyances of London, the bishop was proscribed at an inquest for setting up two staples and a bar, "whereby men with carts and other carriages could not pass." The bishop pleaded John Breton's order, and the sheriff was then commanded to remove the annoyance, and the hooded men with their carts once more cracked their whips and whistled to their horses up and down the long disused lane.

Half-way up on the east side of Chancery Lane a dull archway, through which can be caught glimpses of the door of an old chapel, leads to the Rolls Court. On the site of that chapel, in the year 1233, history tells us that Henry III. erected a Carthusian house for the maintenance of converted Jews, who there lived under a Christian governor. At a time when Norman barons were not unaccustomed to pull out a Jew's teeth, or to fry him on gridirons till he paid handsomely for his release, conversion, which secured safety from such rough practices, may not have been unfrequent. However, the converts decreasing when Edward I., after hanging 280 Jews for clipping coin, banished the rest from the realm, half the property of the Jews who were hung stern Edward gave to the preachers who tried to convert the obstinate and stiff-necked generation, and half to the " Domus Conversorum," in Chancellor's Lane. In 1278 we find the converts calling themselves, in a letter sent to the king by John the Convert, " Pauperes Cœlicolæ Christi." In the reign of Richard II. a certain converted Jew received twopence a day for life ; and in the reign of Henry IV. we find the daughter of a rabbi paid by the keepers of the house of converts a penny a day for life, by special patent.

Edward III., in 1377, broke up the Jewish almshouse in Chancellor's Lane, and annexed the house and chapel to the newly-created office of Custos Rotulorum, or Keeper of the Rolls. Some of the stones which the old gaberdines have rubbed against are no doubt incorporated in the present chapel, which, however, has been so often altered, that, like the Highlandman's gun, it is "new stock and new barrel." The first Master of the Rolls, in 1377, was William Burstal; but till Thomas Cromwell, in 1534, the Masters of the Rolls were generally priests, and often king's chaplains.

The Rolls Chapel was built, says Pennant, by Inigo Jones, in 1617, at a cost of £2,000. Dr. Donne, the poet, preached the consecration sermon. One of the monuments belonging to the earlier chapel is that of Dr. John Yonge, Master of the Rolls in the reign of Henry VIII. Vertue and Walpole attribute the tomb to Torregiano, Michael Angelo's contemporary and the sculptor of the tomb of Henry VII. at Westminster. The master is represented by the artist (who starved himself to death at Seville) in effigy on an altar-tomb, in a red gown and deep square cap ; his hands are crossed, his face wears an expression of calm resignation and profound devotion. In a recess at the back is a head of Christ, and an angel's head appears on either side in high relief. Another monument of interest in this quiet, legal chapel is that of Sir Edward Bruce, created by James I. Baron of Kinloss. He was one of the crafty ambassadors sent by wily James to openly congratulate Elizabeth on the failure of the revolt of Essex, but secretly to commence a correspondence with Cecil. The place of Master of the Rolls was Bruce's reward for this useful service. The ex-master lies with his head resting on his hand, in the "toothache" attitude ridiculed by the old dramatists. His hair is short, his beard long, and he wears a long furred robe. Before him kneels a man in armour, possibly his son, Lord Kinloss, who, three years after his father's death, perished in a most savage duel with Sir Edward Sackville.

Another fine monument is that of Sir Richard Allington, of Horseheath, in Cambridgeshire, the

brother-in law of Sir William Cordall, a former
Master of the Rolls, who died in 1561. Clad in
armour, Sir Richard kneels,—

> "As for past sins he would atone,
> By saying endless prayers in stone."

His wife faces him, and beneath on a tablet kneel
their three daughters. Sir Richard's charitable
widow lived after his death in Holborn, in a house
long known as Allington Place. Many of the past
masters sleep within these walls, and amongst them
Sir John Trevor, who died in 1717 (George I.),
and Sir John Strange; but the latter has not had
inscribed over his bones, as Pennant remarks, the
old punning epitaph,—

> "Here lies an honest lawyer—that is *Strange*!"

The above-mentioned Sir John Trevor, while
Speaker of the House of Commons, being denounced
for bribery, was compelled himself to preside over
the subsequent debate—an unparalleled disgrace.
The indictment ran :—
"That Sir John Trevor, Speaker of the House,
receiving a gratuity of 1,000 guineas from the City
of London, after the passing of the Orphans' Bill,
is guilty of high crime and misdemeanour." Trevor
was himself, as Speaker, compelled to put this resolution from the chair. The "Ayes" were not met
by a single "No," and the culprit was required to
officially announce that, in the unanimous opinion
of the House over which he presided, he stood
convicted of a high crime. " His expulsion from
the House," says Mr. Jeaffreson, in his " Book
about Lawyers," "followed in due course. One
is inclined to think that in these days no English
gentleman could outlive such humiliation for four-
and-twenty hours. Sir John Trevor not only
survived the humiliation, but remained a personage
of importance in London society. Convicted of
bribery, he was not called upon to refund the
bribe ; and expelled from the House of Commons,
he was not driven from his judicial office. He
continued to be the Master of the Rolls till his
death, which took place on May 20, 1717, in his
official mansion in Chancery Lane. His retention
of office is easily accounted for. Having acted
as a vile negotiator between the two great political
parties, they were equally afraid of him. Neither
the Whigs nor the Tories dared to demand his
expulsion from office, fearing that in revenge he
would make revelations alike disgraceful to all
parties concerned."
The arms of Sir Robert Cecil and Sir Harbottle
Grimstone gleam in the chapel windows. Swift's
detestation, Bishop Burnet, the historian and friend

of William of Orange, was preacher here for nine
years, and here delivered his sermon on the text,
"Save me from the lion's mouth : thou hast heard
me from the horns of the unicorn." Burnet was
appointed by Sir Harbottle, who was Master of
the Rolls ; and in his " Own Times " he has inserted
a warm eulogy of Sir Harbottle as a worthy and
pious man. Atterbury, the Jacobite Bishop of
Rochester, was also preacher here ; nor can we
forget that amiable man and great theologian,
Bishop Butler, the author of the " Analogy of
Religion." Butler, the son of a Dissenting tradesman at Wantage, was for a long time lost in a
small country living, a loss to the Church which
Archbishop Blackburne lamented to Queen Caroline.
"Why, I thought he had been dead !" exclaimed
the queen. "No, madam," replied the archbishop; " he is only buried." In 1718 Butler was
appointed preacher at the Rolls by Sir Joseph
Jekyll. This excellent man afterwards became
Bishop of Bristol, and died Bishop of Durham.
A few anecdotes about past dignitaries at the
Rolls. Of Sir Julius Cæsar, Master of the Rolls in
the reign of Charles I., Lord Clarendon, in his
" History of the Rebellion," tells a story too good
to be passed by. This Sir Julius, having by right
of office the power of appointing the six clerks,
designed one of the profitable posts for his son,
Robert Cæsar. One of the clerks dying before
Sir Julius could appoint his son, the imperious
treasurer, Sir Richard Weston, promised his place
to a dependant, who gave him for it £6,000 down.
The vexation of old Sir Julius at this arbitrary
step so moved his friends, that King Charles
was induced to promise Robert Cæsar the next
post in the clerks' office that should fall vacant,
and the Lord Treasurer was bound by this promise. One day the Earl of Tullibardine, passion-
ately pressing the treasurer about his business, was
told by Sir Richard that he had quite forgotten
the matter, but begged for a memorandum, that
he might remind the king that very afternoon.
The earl then wrote on a small bit of paper the
words, " Remember Cæsar !" and Sir Richard,
without reading it, placed it carefully in a little
pocket, where he said he kept all the memorials
first to be transacted. Many days passed, and
the ambitious treasurer forgot all about Cæsar.
At length one night, changing his clothes, his
servant brought him the notes and papers from
his pocket, which he looked over according to his
custom. Among these he found the little billet
with merely the words "Remember Cæsar !" and
on the sight of this the arrogant yet timid courtier
was utterly confounded. Turning pale, he sent

OLD HOUSES IN FETTER LANE, WEST SIDE, NEAR THE RECORD OFFICE, FROM A DRAWING BY SHEPHERD, 1853 (*see page* 101).

for his bosom friends, showed them the paper, and held a solemn deliberation over it. It was decided that it must have been dropped into his hand by some secret friend, as he was on his way to the priory lodgings. Every one agreed that some conspiracy was planned against his life by his many and mighty enemies, and that Cæsar's fate might soon be his unless great precautions were taken. His friends therefore persuaded him to be at once indisposed, and not venture forth in that neighbourhood, nor to admit to an audience any but persons of undoubted affection. At night the gates were shut and barred early, and the porter solemnly enjoined not to open them to any one, or to venture on even a moment's sleep. Some servants were sent to watch with him, and the friends sat up all night to await the event. "Such houses," says Clarendon, who did not like the treasurer, "are always in the morning haunted by early suitors;" but it was very late before any one could now get admittance into the house, the porter having tasted some

IZAAK WALTON'S HOUSE (see page 82).

of the arrears of sleep which he owed to himself for his night watching, which he accounted for to his acquaintance by whispering to them "that his lord should have been killed that night, which had kept all the house from going to bed." Shortly afterwards, however, the Earl of Tullibardine asking the treasurer whether he had remembered Cæsar, the treasurer quickly recollecting the ground of his perturbation, could not forbear imparting it to his friends, and so the whole jest came to be discovered.

In 1614, £6 12s. 6d. was claimed by Sir Julius Cæsar for paving the part of Chancery Lane over against the Rolls Gate.

Sir Joseph Jekyll, the Master of the Rolls in the reign of George I., was an ancestor of that witty Jekyll, the friend and adviser of George IV. Sir Joseph was very active in introducing a Bill for increasing the duty on gin, in consequence of which he became so odious to the mob that they one day hustled and trampled on him in a riot in Lincoln's Inn Fields. Hogarth, who painted his "Gin Lane" to express his alarm and disgust at the growing intemperance of the London poor, has in one of his extraordinary pictures represented a low fellow writing J. J. under a gibbet.

Sir William Grant, who succeeded Lord Alvanley, was the last Master but one that resided in the Rolls. He had practised at the Canadian bar, and on returning to England attracted the attention of Lord Thurlow, then Chancellor. He was an admirable speaker in the House, and even Fox is said to have girded himself tighter for an encounter with such an adversary. "He used," says Mr. Cyrus Jay, in his amusing book, "The Law," "to sit from five o'clock till one, and seldom spoke during that time. He dined before going into court, his allowance being a bottle of Madeira at dinner and a bottle of port after. He dined alone, and the unfortunate servant was expected to anticipate his master's wishes by intuition. Sir William never spoke if he could help it. On one occasion, when the favourite dish of a leg of pork was on the table, the servant saw by Sir William's face that something was wrong, but he could not tell what. Suddenly a thought flashed upon him—the Madeira was not on the table. He at once placed the decanter before Sir William, who immediately flung it into the grate, exclaiming, "Mustard, you fool!"

Sir John Leach, another Master of the Rolls, was the son of a tradesman at Bedford, afterwards a merchant's clerk and an embryo architect. Mr. Canning appointed him Master of the Rolls, an office previously, it has been said, offered to Mr. Brougham. Leach was fond, says Mr. Jay, of saying sharp, bitter things in a bland and courtly voice. "No submission could ameliorate his temper, no opposition lend asperity to his voice.' In court two large fan shades were always placed in a way to shade him from the light, and to render Sir John entirely invisible. "After the counsel who was addressing the court had finished, and resumed his seat, there would be an awful pause for a minute or two, when at length out of the darkness which surrounded the chair of justice would come a voice, distinct, awful, solemn, but with the solemnity of suppressed anger—'the bill is dismissed with costs.'" No explanations, no long series of arguments were advanced by him to support the conclusion. The decision was given with the air of a man who knew he was right, and that only folly or villainy could doubt the propriety of his judgments. Sir John was the Prince Regent's great adviser during Queen Caroline's trial, and assisted in getting up the evidence. "How often," says Mr. Jay, "have I seen him, when walking through the Green Park between four and five o'clock in the afternoon, knock at the private door of Carlton Palace. I have seen him go in four or five days following."

Gifford was another eminent Master of the Rolls, though he did not hold the office long. He first attracted attention when a lawyer's clerk by his clever observations on a case in which he was consulted by his employers, in the presence of an important client. The high opinion which Lord Ellenborough formed of his talents induced Lord Liverpool to appoint him Solicitor-General. While in the House he had frequently to encounter Sir Samuel Romilly. Mr. Cyrus Jay has an interesting anecdote about the funeral of Lord Gifford, who is buried in the Rolls Chapel. "I was," he says, "in the little gallery when the procession came into the chapel, and Lord Eldon and Lord Chief Justice Abbott were placed in a pew by themselves. I could observe everything that took place in the pew, it being a small chapel, and noted that Lord Eldon was very shaky, and during the most solemn part of the service saw him touch the Chief Justice. I have no doubt he asked for his snuff-

box, for the snuff-box was produced, and he took a large pinch of snuff. The Chief Justice was a very great snuff-taker, but he only took it up one nostril. I kept my eye on the pinch of snuff, and saw that Lord Eldon, the moment he had taken it from the box, threw it away. I was sorry at the time, and was astonished at the deception practised by so great a man, with the grave yawning before him."

When Sir Thomas Plumer was Master of the Rolls, and gave a succession of dinners to the Bar, Romilly, alluding to Lord Eldon's stinginess, said, "Verily he is working off the arrears of the Lord Chancellor."

At the back of the Rolls Chapel, in Bowling-Pin Alley, Bream's Buildings (No. 28, Chancery Lane), there once lived, according to party calumny, a journeyman labourer, named Thompson, whose clever and pretty daughter, the wife of one Clark, a bricklayer, became the mischievous mistress of the good-natured but weak Duke of York. After making great scandal about the sale of commissions obtained by her influence, the shrewd woman wrote some memoirs, 10,000 copies of which were, in the next year, burnt at a printer's in Salisbury Square, upon condition of her debts being paid, and an annuity of £400 granted her.

Wilberforce's unscrupulous party statement, that Mrs. Clark was a low, vulgar, and extravagant woman, was entirely untrue. Mrs. Clark, however imprudent and devoid of virtue, was no more the daughter of a journeyman bricklayer than she was the daughter of a king. She was really, as Mr. Cyrus Redding, who knew most of the political secrets of his day, has proved, the unfortunate granddaughter of that unfortunate man, Theodore, King of Corsica, and daughter of even a more unhappy man, Colonel Frederick, a brave, well-read gentleman, who, under the pressure of a temporary monetary difficulty, occasioned by the dishonourable conduct of a friend, blew out his brains in the churchyard of St. Margaret's, Westminster. In 1798 a poem, written, we believe, by Mrs., then Miss Clark, called "Ianthe," was published by subscription at Hookham's, in New Bond Street, for the benefit of Colonel Frederick's daughter and children, and dedicated to the Prince of Wales. The girl married an Excise officer, much older than herself, and became the mistress of the Duke of York, to whom probably she had applied for assistance, or subscriptions to her poem. The fact is, the duke's vices were turned, as vices frequently are, into scourges for his own back. He was a jovial, good-natured, affable, selfish man, an incessant and reckless gambler, quite devoid of all conscience about debts, and, indeed, of moral principle in general. When he got tired of Mrs. Clark, he meanly and heartlessly left her, with a promised annuity which he never paid, and with debts mutually incurred at their house in Gloucester Place, which he shamefully allowed to fall upon her. In despair and revengeful rage the discarded mistress sought the eager enemies whom the duke's careless neglect had sown round him, and the scandal broke forth. The Prince of Wales, who was as fond of his brother as he could be of any one, was greatly vexed at the exposure, and sent Lord Moira to buy up the correspondence from the Radical bookseller, Sir Richard Phillips, who had advanced money upon it, and was glorying in the escapade.

Sir Richard Phillips himself used to narrate to his friends the strange and mysterious story of the real secret cause of the Duke of York scandal. The exposure originated in the resentment of one M'Callum against Sir Thomas Picton, who, as Governor of Trinidad, had, among other arbitrary acts, imprisoned M'Callum in an underground dungeon. On getting to England he sought justice; but, finding himself baffled, he first published his travels in Trinidad, to expose Picton; then ferreted out charges against the War Office, and at last, through Colonel Wardle, brought forward the notorious great-coat contract. This being negatived by a Ministerial majority, he then traced Mrs. Clark, and arranged the whole of the exposure for Wardle and others. To effect this in the teeth of power, though destitute of resources, he wrought night and day for months. He lodged in a garret in Hungerford Market, and often did not taste food for twenty-four hours. He lived to see the Duke of York dismissed from office, had time to publish a short narrative, then died of exhaustion and want.

An eye-witness of Mrs. Clark's behaviour at the bar of the House of Commons pronounced her replies as full of sharpness against the more insolent of her adversaries, but her bearing is described as being "full of grace." Mr. Redding, who had read twenty or thirty of this lady's letters, tells us that they showed a good education in the writer.

A writer who was present during her examination before the House of Commons, has pleasantly described the singular scene. "I was," he says, "in the House of Commons when Mary Anne Clark first made her appearance at the bar, dressed in her light-blue pelisse, light muff and tippet. She was a pretty woman, rather of a slender make. It was debated whether she should have a chair; this occasioned a hubbub, and she was asked who the

person with her deeply veiled was. She replied that she was her friend. The lady was instantly ordered to withdraw, then a chair was ordered for Mrs. Clark, and she seemed to pluck up courage, for when she was asked about the particulars of an annuity promised to be settled on her by the Duke of York, she said, pointing with her hand, 'You may ask Mr. William Adam there, as he knows all about it.' She was asked if she was quite certain that General Clavering ever was at any of her parties; she replied, 'So certain, that I always told him he need not use any ceremony, but come in his boots.' It will be remembered that General C. was sent to Newgate for prevarication on that account, *not having recollected in time* this circumstance.

"Perceval fought the battle manfully. The Duke of York could not be justified for some of his acts—for instance, giving a footboy of Mrs. Clark's a commission in the army, and allowing an improper influence to be exerted over him in his thoughtless moments; but that the trial originated in pique and party spirit, there can be no doubt; and, as he justly merited, Colonel Wardle, the prosecutor in the case, sunk into utter oblivion, whilst the Duke of York, the soldier's friend and the beloved of the army, was, after a short period (having been superseded by Sir David Dundas), replaced as commander-in-chief, and died deeply regretted and fully meriting the colossal statue erected to him, with his hand pointing to the Horse Guards."

Cardinal Wolsey lived, at some period of his extraordinary career, in a house in Chancery Lane, at the Holborn end, and on the east side, near the Six Clerks' Office. We do not know what rank the proud favourite held at this time, whether he was almoner to the king, privy councillor, Canon of Windsor, Bishop of Lincoln, Archbishop of York, or Cardinal of the Cecilia. We like to think that down that dingy legal lane he rode on his way to Westminster Hall, with all that magnificence described by his faithful gentleman usher, Cavendish. He would come out of his chamber, we read, about eight o'clock in his cardinal's robes of scarlet taffeta and crimson satin, with a black velvet tippet edged with sable round his neck, holding in his hand an orange filled with a sponge containing aromatic vinegar, in case the crowd of suitors should incommode him. Before him were borne the broad seal of England, and the scarlet cardinal's hat. A sergeant-at-arms preceded him bearing a great mace of silver, and two gentlemen carrying silver plates. At the hall-door he mounted his mule, trapped with crimson and having a saddle covered with crimson velvet, while the gentlemen ushers, bare-headed, cried,—" On, masters, before, and make room for my lord cardinal." When Wolsey was mounted he was preceded by his two cross-bearers and his two pillow-bearers, all upon horses trapped in scarlet ; and four footmen with pole-axes guarded the cardinal till he came to Westminster. And every Sunday, when he repaired to the king's court at Greenwich, he landed at the Three Cranes, in the Vintry, and took water again at Billingsgate. "He had," says Cavendish, "a long season, ruling all things in the realm appertaining to the king, by his wisdom, and all other matters of foreign regions with whom the king had any occasion to meddle, and then he fell like Lucifer, never to rise again. Here," says Cavendish, " is the end and fall of pride ; for I assure you he was in his time the proudest man alive, having more regard to the honour of his person than to his spiritual functions, wherein he should have expressed more meekness and humility."

One of the greatest names connected with Chancery Lane is that of the unfortunate Wentworth, Earl of Strafford, who, after leading his master, Charles I., on the path to the scaffold, was the first to lay his head upon the block. Wentworth, the son of a Yorkshire gentleman, was born in 1593 in Chancery Lane, at the house of Mr. Atkinson, his maternal grandfather, a bencher of Lincoln's Inn. At first an enemy of Buckingham, the king's favourite, and opposed to the Court, he was won over by a peerage and the counsels of his friend Lord Treasurer Weston. He soon became a headlong and unscrupulous advocate of arbitrary power, and, as Lord Deputy of Ireland, did his best to raise an army for the king and to earn his Court name of " Thorough." Impeached for high treason, and accused by Sir Henry Vane of a design to subdue England by force, he was forsaken by the weak king and condemned to the block. " Put not your trust in princes," he said, when he heard of the king's consent to the execution of so faithful a servant, " nor in any child of man, for in them is no salvation." He died on Tower Hill, with calm and undaunted courage, expressing his devotion to the Church of England, his loyalty to the king, and his earnest desire for the peace and welfare of the kingdom.

Of this steadfast and dangerous man Clarendon has left one of those Titianesque portraits in which he excelled. " He was a man," says the historian, " of great parts and extraordinary endowment of nature, and of great observation and a piercing judgment both into things and persons ; but his too good skill in persons made him judge the

worse of things, and so that upon the matter he wholly relied upon himself ; and discerning many defects in most men, he too much neglected what they said or did. Of all his passions his pride was most predominant, which a moderate exercise of ill fortune might have corrected and reformed ; and which was by the hand of Heaven strangely punished by bringing his destruction on him by two things that he most despised—the people and Sir Harry Vane. In a word, the epitaph which Plutarch records that Sylla wrote for himself may not be unfitly applied to him—' that no man did ever pass him either in doing good to his friends or in doing harm to his enemies.' "

Izaak Walton, that amiable old angler, lived for some years (1627 to 1644) of his happy and contented life in a house (No. 120) at the west corner of Chancery Lane and Fleet Street. This was many years before he published his " Complete Angler," which did not, indeed, appear till the year before the Restoration. Yet we imagine that at this time the honest citizen often sallied forth to the Lea banks with his friends, the Roes, on those fine cool May mornings upon which he expatiates so pleasantly. A quiet man and a lover of peace was old Izaak ; and we may be sure no jingle of money ever hurried him back from the green fields where the lark, singing as she ascended higher and higher into the air, and nearer to the heavens, excelled, as he says, in her simple piety " all those little nimble musicians of the air (her fellows) who warble forth their various ditties with which Nature has furnished them, to the shame of art." Refreshed and exhilarated by the pure country air, we can fancy Walton returning homeward to his Chancery Lane shop, humming to himself that fine old song of Marlowe's which the milkmaid sung to him as he sat under the honeysuckle-hedge out of the shower,—

"Come live with me and be my love,
And we will all the pleasures prove
That valleys, groves, or hills, or field,
Or woods, or steepy mountain, yield."

How Byron had the heart to call a man who loved such simple pleasures, and was so guileless and pure-hearted as Walton, "a cruel old coxcomb," and to wish that in his gullet he had a hook, and " a strong trout to pull it," we never could understand ; but Byron was no angler, and we suppose he thought Walton's advice about sewing up frogs' mouths lovingly somewhat hard-hearted.

North, in his life of that faithful courtier of Charles II., Lord Keeper Guildford, mentions that his lordship "settled himself in the great brick house in Serjeants' Inn, near Chancery Lane, which was formerly the Lord Chief Justice Hyde's, and that he held it till he had the Great Seal, and some time after. When his lordship lived in this house, before his lady began to want her health, he was in the height of all the felicity his nature was capable of. He had a seat in St. Dunstan's Church appropriated to him, and constantly kept the church in the mornings, and so his house was to his mind; and having, with leave, a door into Serjeants' Inn garden, he passed daily with ease to his chambers, dedicated to business and study. His friends he enjoyed at home, and politic ones often found him out at his chambers." He rebuilt Serjeants' Inn Hall, which had become poor and ruinous, and improved all the dwellings in Chancery Lane from Jackanapes Alley down to Fleet Street. He also drained the street for the first time, and had a rate levied on the unwilling inhabitants, after which his at first reluctant neighbours thanked him warmly. This same Lord Keeper, a time-server and friend of arbitrary power, according to Burnet, seems to have been a learned and studious man, for he encouraged the sale of barometers and wrote a philosophical essay on music. It was this timid courtier that unscrupulous Jeffreys vexed by spreading a report that he had been seen riding on a rhinoceros, then one of the great sights of London. Jeffreys was at the time hoping to supersede the Lord Keeper in office, and was anxious to cover him with ridicule.

Besides the Cæsars, Cecils, Throckmortons, Lincolns, Sir John Franklin, and Edward Reeve, who, as it would appear, all resided in Chancery Lane when it was a fashionable legal quarter, we must not forget that on the site of No. 115 lived Sir Richard Fanshawe, the ambassador sent by Charles II. to arrange his marriage with the Portuguese princess. This accomplished man, who translated Guarini's "Pastor Fido," and the "Lusiad" of Camoens, died at Madrid in 1666. His brave yet gentle wife, who wrote some interesting memoirs, gives a graphic account of herself and her husband taking leave of his royal master, Charles I., at Hampton Court. At parting, the king saluted her, and she prayed God to preserve his majesty with long life and happy years. The king stroked her on the cheek, and said, "Child, if God pleaseth, it shall be so; but both you and I must submit to God's will, for you know whose hands I am in." Then turning to Sir Richard, Charles said, "Be sure, Dick, to tell my son all that I have said, and deliver these letters to my wife. Pray God bless her; and I hope I shall do well." Then, embracing Sir Richard, the king added, "Thou hast ever been an honest man, and

I hope God will bless thee, and make thee a happy servant to my son, whom I have charged in my letter to continue his love and trust to you; and I do promise you, if I am ever restored to my dignity, I will bountifully reward you both for your services and sufferings." "Thus," says the noble Royalist lady, enthusiastically, "did we part from that glorious sun that within a few months after was extinguished, to the grief of all Christians who are not forsaken of their God."

No. 45 (east side) is the "Hole in the Wall" Tavern, kept early in the century by Jack Randal, *alias* "Nonpareil," a fighting man, whom Tom Moore visited, says Mr. Noble, to get materials for his "Tom Cribb's Memorial to Congress," "Randal's Diary," and other satirical poems. Hazlitt, when living in Southampton Buildings, describes going to this haunt of the fancy the night before the great fight between Neate, the Bristol butcher, and Hickman, the gas-man, to find out where the encounter was to take place, although Randal had once rather too forcibly expelled him for some trifling complaint about a chop. Hazlitt went down to the fight with Thurtell, the betting man, who afterwards murdered Mr. Weare, a gambler and bill-discounter of Lyon's Inn. In Byron's early days taverns like Randal's were frequented by all the men about town, who considered that to wear bird's-eye handkerchiefs and heavy-caped box coats was the height of manliness and fashion.

Chichester Rents, a sorry place now, preserves a memory of the site of the town-house of the Bishops of Chichester. It was originally built in a garden belonging to one John Herberton, granted the bishops by Henry III., who excepted it out of the charter of the Jew converts' house, now the Rolls Chapel.

Serjeants' Inn, originally designed for serjeants alone, was subsequently open to all students, though it more especially affected the Freres Serjens, or Fratres Servientes, who derived their name originally from being the lower grade or servitors of the Knights Templars. Serjeants still address each other as "brother," and indeed, as far as Cain and Abel go, the brotherhood of lawyers cannot be disputed. The old formula at Westminster, when a new serjeant approached the judges, was, "I think I see a brother."

One of Chaucer's Canterbury pilgrims was a "serjeant of law." This inn dates back as early as the reign of Henry IV., when it was held under a lease from the Bishop of Ely. In 1442 a William Antrobus, citizen and taylor of London, held it at the rent of ten marks a year. In the hall windows are emblazoned the arms of Lord Keeper

Guildford (1684). The inn was rebuilt, all but the old dining-hall, by Sir Robert Smirke, in 1837–38. In 1878 the inn was broken up, and the buildings sold to Mr. Serjeant Cox.

The humours of Southampton Buildings, Chancery Lane, have been admirably described by essayist, fine-art and theatrical critic, thoughtful metaphysician, and miserable man, William Hazlitt. He lodged at the house of Mr. Walker, a tailor, who was blessed with two fair daughters, with one of whom, Sarah, Hazlitt, then a married man, fell madly in love. He declared she was like the

OLD SERJEANTS' INN (see page 83).

Hazlitt, and are thus condensed by a contemporaneous writer.

"In 1820 a ray of light strikes the Buildings, for one of the least popular, but by no means the least remarkable, of the Charles Lamb set came to lodge at No. 9, half-way down on the right-hand side as you come from Holborn. There for four years lived, taught, wrote, and suffered that admirable Madonna—she seems really to have been a cold, calculating flirt, rather afraid of her wild lover. To his 'Liber Amoris,' a most stultifying series of dialogues between himself and the lodging-house keeper's daughter, the author appended a drawing of an antique gem (Lucretia), which he declared to be the very image of the obdurate tailor's daughter. This untoward but remarkably gifted man, whom

Lamb admired, if he did not love, and whom Leigh Hunt regarded as a spirit highly endowed, usually spent his evenings at the 'Southampton,' an hotel or coffee-house on the left hand, near the Patent Office. The 'Southampton' is now a most unpretending public-house, with its dull, quiet, bald-looking coffee-room altered; but still one likes to wander past the

admired by William, the sleek, neat waiter (who had a music-master to teach him the flageolet two hours every morning before the maids were up), for his temper in managing an argument. Mr. Kirkpatrick was one of those bland, simpering, self-complacent men, who, unshakable from the high tower of their own self-satisfaction, look down upon your arguments from their magnificent

HAZLITT (*see page* 87).

place and think that Hazlitt, his hand still warm with the grip of Lamb, has often entered it. In an essay on 'Coffee-House Politicians,' in the second volume of his 'Table Talk,' Hazlitt has sketched the coterie at the 'Southampton' in a manner not unworthy of Steele. The picture wants Sir Richard's mellow, Jan Steen colour, but it possesses much of Wilkie's dainty touch and keen appreciation of character. Let us call up, he says, the old customers at the 'Southampton' from the dead, and take a glass with them. First of all comes Mr. George Kirkpatrick, so much

elevation. 'I will explain,' was his condescending phrase. If you corrected the intolerable magnifico, he corrected your correction; if you hinted at an obvious blunder, he was always aware what your mistaken objection would be. He and his clique would spend a whole evening on a wager as to whether the first edition of Dr. Johnson's 'Dictionary' was quarto or folio. The confident assertions, the cautious ventures, the length of time demanded to ascertain the fact, the precise terms of the forfeit, the provisoes for getting out of paying it at last, led to a long and inextricable discussion. Kirkpatrick's vanity, however, one night led him into a terrible pitfall. He recklessly ventured money on the fact that *The Mourning Bride* was written by Shakespeare; headlong he fell, and ruefully he partook of the bowl of punch for which he had to pay. As a rule his nightly outlay seldom exceeded sevenpence. Four hours' good conversation for sevenpence made the 'Southampton' the cheapest of London clubs.

"Kirkpatrick's brother Roger was the Mercutio to his Shallow. Roger was a rare fellow, 'of the driest humour and the nicest tact, of infinite sleights and evasions, of a picked phraseology, and the very soul of mimicry.' He had the mind of a harlequin; his wit was acrobatic, and threw somersaults. He took in a character at a glance, and threw a pun at you as dexterously as a fly-fisher casts his fly over a trout's nose. 'How finely,' says Hazlitt, in his best and heartiest mood; 'how finely, how truly, how gaily he took off the company at the "Southampton!" Poor and faint are my sketches compared to his! It was like looking into a camera-obscura—you saw faces shining and speaking. The smoke curled, the lights dazzled, the oak wainscoting took a higher polish. There was old S., tall and gaunt, with his couplet from Pope and case at Nisi Prius; Mudford, eyeing the ventilator and lying perdu for a moral; and H. and A. taking another friendly finishing glass. These and many more windfalls of character he gave us in thought, word, and action. I remember his once describing three different persons together to myself and Martin Burney [a bibulous nephew of Madame d'Arblay and a great friend of Charles Lamb], namely, the manager of a country theatre, a tragic and a comic performer, till we were ready to tumble on the floor with laughing at the oddity of their humours, and at Roger's extraordinary powers of ventriloquism, bodily and mental; and Burney said (such was the vividness of the scene) that when he awoke the next morning he wondered what three amusing characters he had been in company with the evening before.' He was fond also of imitating old Mudford, of the *Courier*, a man of letters, who had left the *Morning Chronicle* in 1814, just as Hazlitt joined it, and was renowned for having written a reply to 'Cœlebs.' He would enter a room, fold up his great-coat, take out a little pocket volume, lay it down to think, rubbing all the time the fleshy calf of his leg with dull gravity and intense and stolid self-complacency, and start out of his reveries when addressed with the same inimitable vapid exclamation of 'Eh!' Dr. Whittle, a large, plain-faced Moravian preacher, who had turned physician, was another of his chosen impersonations. Roger represented the honest, vain, empty man purchasing an ounce of tea by stratagem to astonish a favoured guest; he portrayed him on the summit of a narrow, winding, and very steep staircase, contemplating in airy security the imaginary approach of duns. This worthy doctor on one occasion, when watching Sarratt, the great chess-player, turned suddenly to Hazlitt, and said, 'I think I could dance. I'm sure I could; aye, I could dance like Vestris.' Such were the odd people Roger caricatured on the memorable night he pulled off his coat to eat beef-steaks on equal terms with Martin Burney.

"Then there was C., who, from his slender neck, shrillness of voice, and his ever-ready quibble and laugh. at himself, was for some time taken for a lawyer, with which folk the Buildings were then, as now, much infested. But on careful inquiry he turned out to be a patent-medicine seller, who at leisure moments had studied Blackstone and the statutes at large from mere sympathy with the neighbourhood. E. came next, a rich tradesman, Tory in grain, and an everlasting babbler on the strong side of politics; querulous, dictatorial, and with a peevish whine in his voice like a beaten schoolboy. He was a stout advocate for the Bourbons and the National Debt, and was duly disliked by Hazlitt, we may feel assured. The Bourbons he affirmed to be the choice of the French people, the Debt necessary to the salvation of these kingdoms. To a little inoffensive man, 'of a saturnine aspect but simple conceptions,' Hazlitt once heard him say grandly, 'I will tell you, sir. I will make my proposition so clear that you will be convinced of the truth of my observation in a moment. Consider, sir, the number of trades that would be thrown out of employ if the Debt were done away with. What would become of the porcelain manufacture without it?' He would then show the company a flower, the production of his own garden, calling it a unique and curious exotic, and hold forth on his carnations, his country-house, and his old English hospitality, though he never invited a friend to come down to a Sunday's dinner. Mean and ostentatious, insolent and servile, he did not know whether to treat those he conversed with as if they were his porters or his customers. The 'prentice boy was not yet ground out of him, and his imagination hovered between his grand new country mansion and the workhouse. Opposed to him and every one else was K., a Radical reformer and tedious logician, who wanted to make short work of the taxes and National Debt, reconstruct the Government from first principles, and shatter the Holy Alliance at a blow. He was for crushing out the future prospects of society as with a machine, and for starting where the French Revolution had begun five-and-twenty years before. He was a born disturber, and never agreed to more than half a proposition at a time. Being very stingy, he generally brought a bunch of radishes with him for economy, and would give a penny to a band of musicians at the door, observing that he liked their performance better than all the opera-squalling. His objections to the National Debt arose from motives of personal economy; and he objected to Mr. Canning's pension because it took a farthing a year out of his own pocket.

"Another great sachem at the 'Southampton' was Mr. George Mouncey, of the firm of Mouncey & Gray, solicitors, Staple's Inn. 'He was,' says Hazlitt, 'the oldest frequenter of the place and the latest sitter-up; well-informed, unobtrusive, and that sturdy old English character, a lover of truth and justice. Mouncey never approved of anything unfair or illiberal, and, though good-natured and gentleman-like, never let an absurd or unjust proposition pass him without expressing dissent.' He was much liked by Hazlitt, for they had mutual friends, and Mouncey had been intimate with most of the wits and men about town for twenty years before. 'He had in his time known Tobin, Wordsworth, Porson, Wilson, Paley, and Erskine. He would speak of Paley's pleasantry and unassuming manners, and describe Porson's deep potations and long quotations at the "Cider Cellars."' Warming with his theme, Hazlitt goes on in his essay to etch one memorable evening at the 'Southampton.' A few only were left, 'like stars at break of day,' the discourse and the ale were growing sweeter; but Mouncey, Hazlitt, and a man named Wells, alone remained. The conversation turned on the frail beauties of Charles II.'s Court, and from thence passed to Count Grammont, their gallant, gay, and not over-scrupulous historian. Each one cited his favourite passage in turn; from Jacob Hall, the rope-dancer, they progressed by pleasant stages of talk to pale Miss Churchill and her fortunate fall from her horse. Wells then spoke of 'Apuleius and his Golden Ass,' 'Cupid and Psyche,' and the romance of 'Heliodorus, Theogenes, and Chariclea,' which, as he affirmed, opened with a pastoral landscape equal to one of Claude's. 'The night waned,' says the delightful essayist, 'but our glasses brightened, enriched with the pearls of Grecian story. Our cup-bearer slept in a corner of the room, like another Endymion, in the pale rays of a half-extinguished lamp, and, starting up at a fresh summons for a further supply, he swore it was too late, and was inexorable to entreaty. Mouncey sat with his hat on and a hectic flush in his face while any hope remained, but as soon as we rose to go, he dashed out of the room as quick as lightning, determined not to be the last. I said some time after to the waiter that " Mr. Mouncey was no flincher." " Oh, sir !" says he, " you should have known him formerly. Now he is quite another man : he seldom stays later than one or two ; then he used to help sing catches, and all sorts."'

"It was at the 'Southampton' that George Cruikshank, Hazlitt, and Hone used to often meet, to discuss subjects for Hone's squibs on the Queen's trial (1820). Cruikshank would sometimes dip his finger in ale and sketch a suggestion on the table.

"While living in a state of half-assumed love-frenzy at No. 9, Southampton buildings, Hazlitt produced some of his best work. His noble lectures on the age of Elizabeth had just been delivered, and he was writing for the *Edinburgh Review*, the *New Monthly*, and the *London Magazine*, in conjunction with Charles Lamb, Reynolds, Barry Cornwall, De Quincey, and Wainwright ('Janus Weathercock') the poisoner. In 1821 he published his volume of 'Dramatic Criticisms,' and his subtle 'Table Talk;' in 1823, his foolish 'Liber Amoris;' and in 1824, his fine 'Sketches of the Principal English Picture Galleries.'

"Hazlitt, who was born in 1778 and died in 1830, was the son of a Unitarian minister of Irish descent. Hazlitt was at first intended for an artist, but, coming to London, soon drifted into literature. He became a parliamentary reporter to the *Morning Chronicle* in 1813, and in that wearing occupation injured his naturally weak digestion. In 1814 he succeeded Mudford as theatrical critic on Perry's paper. In 1815 he joined the *Champion*, and in 1818 wrote for the *Yellow Dwarf*. Hazlitt's habits at No. 9 were enough to have killed a rhinoceros. He sat up half the night, and rose about one or two. He then remained drinking the strongest black tea, nibbling a roll, and reading (no appetite, of course) till about five p.m. At supper at the 'Southampton,' his jaded stomach then rousing, he ate a heavy meal of steak or game, frequently drinking during his long and suicidal vigils three or four quarts of water. Wine and spirits he latterly never touched. Morbidly self-conscious, touchy, morose, he believed that his aspect and manner were strange and disagreeable to his friends, and that every one was perpetually insulting him. He had a magnificent forehead, regular features, pale as marble, and a profusion of curly black hair, but his eyes were shy and suspicious. His manner when not at his ease Mr. P. G. Patmore describes as worthy of Apemantus himself. He would enter a room as if he had been brought in in custody. He shuffled sidelong to the nearest chair, sat down on the extreme corner of it, dropped his hat on the floor, buried his chin in his stock, vented his usual pet phrase on such occasions, 'It's a fine day,' and resigned himself moodily to social misery. If the talk did not suit him, he bore it a certain time, silent, self-absorbed, as a man condemned to death, then suddenly, with a brusque 'Well, good morning,' shuffled to the door and blundered his way out, audibly cursing himself for his folly in voluntarily making himself the laughing-stock of an idiot's critical servants. It must have been hard to bear with such a man, whatever might be his talent; and yet his dying words were, 'I've led a happy life.'"

That delightful humorist, Lamb, lived in Southampton Buildings, in 1800, coming from Pentonville, and moving to Mitre Court Buildings, Fleet Street. Here, then, must have taken place some of those enjoyable evenings which have been so pleasantly sketched by Hazlitt, one of the most favoured of Lamb's guests :—

"At Lamb's we used to have lively skirmishes, at the Thursday evening parties. I doubt whether the small-coal man's musical parties could exceed them. Oh, for the pen of John Buncle to consecrate a *petit souvenir* to their memory! There was Lamb himself, the most delightful, the most provoking, the most witty, and the most sensible of men. He always made the best pun and the best remark in the course of the evening. His serious conversation, like his serious writing, is the best. No one ever stammered out such fine, piquant, deep, eloquent things, in half-a-dozen sentences, as he does. His jests scald like tears, and he probes a question with a play upon words. What a keen-laughing, hair-brained vein of home-felt truth! What choice venom! How often did we cut into the haunch of letters! how we skimmed the cream of criticism! How we picked out the marrow of authors! Need I go over the names? They were but the old, everlasting set—Milton and Shakespeare, Pope and Dryden, Steele and Addison, Swift and Gay, Fielding, Smollet, Sterne, Richardson, Hogarth's prints, Claude's landscapes, the Cartoons at Hampton Court, and all those things that, having once been, must ever be. The Scotch novels had not then been heard of, so we said nothing about them. In general we were hard upon the moderns. The author of the *Rambler* was only tolerated in Boswell's life of him; and it was as much as anyone could do to edge in a word for Junius. Lamb could not bear ' Gil Blas;' this was a fault. I remember the greatest triumph I

ever had was in persuading him, after some years' difficulty, that Fielding was better than Smollett. On one occasion he was for making out a list of persons famous in history that one would wish to see again, at the head of whom were Pontius Pilate, Sir Thomas Browne, and Dr. Faustus; but we black-balled most of his list. But with what a gusto he would describe his favourite authors, Donne or Sir Philip Sidney, and call their most crabbed passages *delicious*. He tried them on his palate, as epicures taste olives, and his observations had a smack in them like a roughness on the tongue. With what discrimination he hinted a defect in what he admired most, as in saying the display of the sumptuous banquet in ' Paradise Regained' was not in true keeping, as the simplest fare was all that was necessary to tempt the extremity of hunger, and stating that Adam and Eve, in ' Paradise Lost,' were too much like married people. He has furnished many a text for Coleridge to preach upon. There was no fuss or cant about him; nor were his sweets or sours ever diluted with one particle of affectation."

Towards the unhappy close of Sheridan's life, when weighed down by illness and debt, having just lost the election at Stafford, and the clouds and darkness gathering closer round him, he was thrown for several days (about 1814) into a sponging-house in Tooke's Court, Cursitor Street, Chancery Lane. Tom Moore describes meeting him shortly before with Lord Byron, at the table of Rogers; and some days after Sheridan burst into tears on hearing that Byron had said that he (Sheridan) had written the best comedy, the best operetta, the best farce, the best address, and delivered the best oration ever produced in England. Sheridan's books and pictures had been sold; and from his sordid prison he wrote a piteous letter to his kind but severely business-like friend, Whitbread, the brewer. "I have done everything," he says, "to obtain my release, but in vain; and, Whitbread, putting all false professions of friendship and feeling out of the question, you have no right to keep me here, for it is in truth your act; if you had not forcibly withheld from me the £12,000, in consequence of a letter from a miserable swindler, whose claim you in particular know to be a lie, I should at least have been out of the reach of this miserable insult; for that, and that only, lost me my seat in Parliament."

Even in the depths of this den, however, Sheridan still remained sanguine; and when Whitbread came to release him, he found him confidently calculating on the representation of Westminster, then about to become vacant by the unjust disgrace of Lord Cochrane. On his return home to his wife, fortified perhaps by wine, Sheridan burst into a long and passionate fit of weeping, at the profanation, as he termed it, which his person had suffered.

In Lord Eldon's youth, when he was simply plain John Scott, of the Northern Circuit, he lived with the pretty little wife with whom he had run away, in very frugal and humble lodgings in Cursitor Street, just opposite No. 2, the chained and barred door of Sloman's sponging-house, on the northern side. Here, in after life he used to boast, although his struggles had really been very few, that he used to run out into Clare Market for sixpennyworth of sprats.

Mr. Disraeli, in "Henrietta Temple," an early novel written in the Theodore Hook manner, has sketched Sloman's with a remarkable *verve* and intimate knowledge of the place :—

"In pursuance of this suggestion, Captain Armine was ushered into the best drawing-room with barred windows and treated in the most aristocratic manner. It was evidently the chamber reserved only for unfortunate gentlemen of the utmost distinction; it was simply furnished with a mirror, a loo-table, and a very hard sofa. The walls were hung with old-fashioned caricatures by Bunbury; the fire-irons were of polished brass; over the mantelpiece was the portrait of the master of the house, which was evidently a speaking likeness, and in which Captain Armine fancied he traced no slight resemblance to his friend Mr. Levison; and there were also some sources of literary amusement in the room, in the shape of a Hebrew Bible and the Racing Calendar.

"After walking up and down the room for an hour, meditating over the past—for it seemed hopeless to trouble himself any further with the future —Ferdinand began to feel very faint, for it may be recollected that he had not even breakfasted. So, pulling the bell-rope with such force that it fell to the ground, a funny little waiter immediately appeared, awed by the sovereign ring, and having indeed received private intelligence from the bailiff that the gentleman in the drawing-room was a regular nob.

"And here, perhaps, I should remind the reader that of all the great distinctions in life none, perhaps, is more important than that which divides mankind into the two great sections of *nobs* and *snobs*. It might seem at the first glance that if there were a place in the world which should level all distinctions, it would be a debtors' prison; but this would be quite an error. Almost at the very moment that Captain Armine arrived at his sorrowful hotel, a poor devil of a tradesman, who had been arrested for fifty pounds and torn from his

wife and family, had been forced to retire to the same asylum. He was introduced into what is styled the coffee-room, being a long, low, unfurnished, sanded chamber, with a table and benches; and being very anxious to communicate with some friend, in order, if possible, to effect his release, and prevent himself from being a bankrupt, he had continued meekly to ring at intervals for the last half-hour, in order that he might write and forward his letter. The waiter heard the coffee-room bell ring, but never dreamed of noticing it; though the moment the signal of the private room sounded, and sounded with so much emphasis, he rushed upstairs three steps at a time, and instantly appeared before our hero; and all this difference was occasioned by the simple circumstance that Captain Armine was a *nob*, and the poor tradesman a *snob*.

"'I am hungry,' said Ferdinand. 'Can I get anything to eat at this place?'

"'What would you like, sir? Anything you choose, sir—mutton chop, rump steak, weal cutlet? Do you a fowl in a quarter of an hour—roast or boiled, sir?'

"'I have not breakfasted yet; bring me some breakfast.'

"'Yes, sir,' said the waiter. 'Tea, sir? coffee, eggs, toast, buttered toast, sir? Like any meat, sir? ham, sir? tongue, sir? Like a devil, sir?'

"'Anything—everything; only be quick.'

"'Yes, sir,' responded the waiter. 'Beg pardon, sir. No offence, I hope; but custom to pay here, sir. Shall be happy to accommodate you, sir. Know what a gentleman is.'

"'Thank you, I will not trouble you,' said Ferdinand. 'Get me that note changed.'

"'Yes, sir,' replied the little waiter, bowing very low, as he disappeared.

"'Gentleman in best drawing-room wants breakfast. Gentleman in best drawing-room wants change for a ten-pound note. Breakfast immediately for gentleman in best drawing-room. Tea, coffee, toast, ham, tongue, and a devil. A regular nob!'"

Sloman's has been sketched both by Mr. Disraeli and by Thackeray. In "Vanity Fair" we find it described as the temporary abode of the impecunious Colonel Crawley, and Moss describes his uncomfortable past and present guests in a manner worthy of Fielding himself. There is the "Honourable Capting Famish, of the Fiftieth Dragoons, whose 'mar' had just taken him out after a fortnight, jest to punish him, who punished the champagne, and had a party every night of regular tip-top swells down from the clubs at the West End; and Capting Ragg and the Honourable

Deuceace, who lived, when at home, in the Temple. There's a doctor of divinity upstairs, and five gents in the coffee-room who know a good glass of wine when they see it. There is a tably d'hote at half-past five in the front parlour, and cards and music afterwards." Moss's house of durance the

for visitors, and a dark-eyed maid in curling-papers brings in the tea."

The Law Institute, that Grecian temple which has wedged itself into the south-west end of Chancery Lane, was built in the stormy year of 1830. On the Lord Mayor's day that year there

CLIFFORD'S INN (*see page* 92).

great novelist describes as splendid with dirty huge old gilt cornices, dingy yellow satin hangings, while the barred-up windows contrasted with "vast and oddly-gilt picture-frames surrounding pieces sporting and sacred, all of which works were by the greatest masters, and fetched the greatest prices, too, in the bill transactions, in the course of which they were sold and bought over and over again. A quick-eyed Jew boy locks and unlocks the door

was a riot; the Reform Bill was still pending, and it was feared might not pass, for the Lords were foaming at the mouth. The Iron Duke was detested as an opposer of all change, good or bad; the new police were distasteful to the people; above all, there was no Lord Mayor's show, and no men in brass armour to look at. The rioters assembled outside No. 62, Fleet Street, were there harangued by some dirty-faced demagogue, and

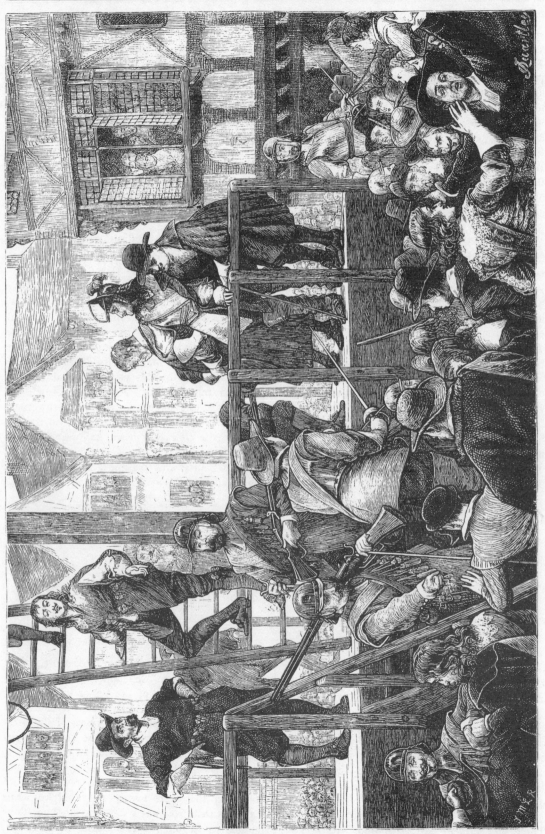

EXECUTION OF TOMKINS AND CHALLONER (*see page* 95).

then marched westward. At Temple Bar the zealous new Police slammed the old muddy gates, to stop the threatening mob; but the City Marshal, red in the face at this breach of City privilege, re-opened them, and the mob roared approval from a thousand distorted mouths. The more pugnacious reformers now broke the scaffolding at the Law Institute into dangerous cudgels, and some 300 of the unwashed patriots dashed through the Bar towards Somerset House, full of vague notions of riot, and perhaps (delicious thought!) of plunder. But at St. Mary's, Commissioner Mayne and his men in the blue tail-coats received the roughs in battle array, and at the first charge the coward mob broke and fled.

In 1815, No. 68, Chancery Lane, not far from the north-east corner, was the scene of an event which terminated in the legal murder of a young and innocent girl. It was here, at Olibar Turner's, a law stationer's, that Eliza Fenning lived, whom we have already mentioned when we entered Hone's shop, in Fleet Street. This poor girl, on the eve of a happy marriage, was hanged at Newgate, on the 26th of July, 1815, for attempting to poison her master and mistress. The trial took place at the Old Bailey on April 11th of the same year, and Mr. Gurney conducted the prosecution before that rough, violent, unfeeling man, Sir John Sylvester (*alias* Black Jack), Recorder of London, who, it is said, used to call the calendar "a bill of fare." The arsenic for rats, kept in a drawer by Mr. Turner, had been mixed with the dough

of some yeast dumplings, of which all the family, including the poor servant, freely partook. There was no evidence of malice, no suspicion of any ill-will, except that Mrs. Turner had once scolded the girl for being free with one of the clerks. It was, moreover, remembered that the girl had particularly pressed her mistress to let her make some yeast dumplings on the day in question. The defence was shamefully conducted. No one pressed the fact of the girl having left the dough in the kitchen for some time untended; nor was weight laid on the fact of Eliza Fenning's own danger and sufferings. All the poor, half-paralysed, Irish girl could say was, "I am truly innocent of the whole charge—indeed I am. I liked my place. I was very comfortable." And there was pathos in those simple, stammering words, more than in half the self-conscious diffuseness of tragic poetry. In her white bridal dress (the cap she had joyfully worked for herself) she went to her cruel death, still repeating the words, "I am innocent." The funeral, at St. George the Martyr, was attended by 10,000 people. Curran used to declaim eloquently on her unhappy fate, and Mr. Charles Phillips wrote a glowing rhapsody on this victim of legal dulness. But such mistakes not even Justice herself can correct. A city mourned over her early grave; but the life was taken, and there was no redress. Gadsden, the clerk, whom she had warned not to eat any dumpling, as it was heavy (this was thought, suspicious), afterwards became a wealthy solicitor in Bedford Row.

CHAPTER VIII.

FLEET STREET (NORTHERN TRIBUTARIES—*continued*).

Clifford's Inn—Dyer's Chambers—The Settlement after the Great Fire—Peter Wilkins and his Flying Wives—Fetter Lane—Waller's Plot and its Victims—Praise-God Barebone and his Doings—Charles Lamb at School—Hobbes the Philosopher—A Strange Marriage—Mrs. Brownrigge—Paul Whitehead—The Moravians—The Record Office and its Treasures—Rival Poets.

CLIFFORD'S INN, originally a town house of the Lords Clifford, ancestors of the Earls of Cumberland, given to them by Edward II., was first let to the students of law in the eighteenth year of King Edward III., at a time when might was too often right, and hard knocks decided legal questions oftener than deed or statute. Harrison the regicide was in youth clerk to an attorney in Clifford's Inn, but when the Civil War broke out he rode off and joined the Puritan troopers.

Clifford's Inn is the oldest Inn in Chancery. There was formerly, we learn from Mr. Jay, an

office there, out of which were issued writs, called "Bills of Middlesex," the appointment of which office was in the gift of the senior judge of the Queen's Bench. "But what made this Inn once noted was that all the six attorneys of the Marshalsea Court (better known as the Palace Court) had their chambers there, as also had the satellites, who paid so much per year for using their names and looking at the nature of their practice. I should say that more misery emanated from this small spot than from any one of the most populous counties in England. The causes in this court were obliged to be tried in the city of Westminster, near the Palace, and it was a melancholy sight (except to lawyers) to observe in the court the crowd of every description of persons suing one another. The most remarkable man in the court was the extremely fat prothonotary, Mr. Hewlett, who sat under the judge or the judge's deputy, with a wig on his head like a thrush's nest, and with only one book before him, which was one of the volumes of 'Burns' Justice.' I knew a respectable gentleman (Mr. G. Dyer) who resided here in chambers (where he died) over a firm of Marshalsea attorneys. This gentleman, who wrote a history of Cambridge University and a biography of Robinson of Cambridge, had been a Bluecoat boy, went as a Grecian to Cambridge, and, after the University, visited almost every celebrated library in Europe. It often struck me what a mighty difference there was between what was going on in the one set of chambers and the other underneath. At Mr. Dyer's I have seen Sir Walter Scott, Southey, Coleridge, Lamb, Talfourd, and many other celebrated literati, 'all benefiting by hearing, which was but of little advantage to the owner.' In the lawyers' chambers below were people wrangling, swearing, and shouting, and some, too, even fighting, the only relief to which was the eternal stamping of cognovits, bound in a book as large as a family Bible." The Lord Chief Justice of the Common Pleas and Lord Chelmsford both at one time practised in the County Court, purchased their situations for large sums, and afterwards sold them. "It was not a bad nursery for a young barrister, as he had an opportunity of addressing a jury. There were only four counsel who had a right to practise in this court, and if you took a first-rate advocate in there specially, you were obliged to give briefs to two of the privileged four. On the tombstone of one of the compensated Marshalsea attorneys is cut the bitterly ironical epitaph, 'Blessed are the peacemakers: for they shall be called the children of God.'"

The George Dyer mentioned by Mr. Jay was not the author of "The Fleece," but that eccentric and amiable old scholar sketched by Charles Lamb in "The Essays of Elia." Dyer was a poet and an antiquary, and edited for Valpy nearly all the 140 volumes of the Delphin Classics. Alternately writer, Baptist minister, and reporter, he eventually settled down in the monastic solitude of Clifford's Inn to compose verses, annotate Greek plays, and write for the magazines. How the worthy, simple-hearted bookworm once walked straight from Lamb's parlour in Colebrooke Row into the New River, and was then fished out and

restored with brandy-and-water, Lamb was never tired of telling. In the latter part of his life poor old Dyer became totally blind. He died in 1841.

Coke, that great luminary of English jurisprudence, resided at Clifford's Inn for a year, and then entered himself at the Inner Temple. Coke, it will be remembered, conducted the prosecutions of both Essex and Raleigh; in both cases he was grossly unfeeling to fallen great men.

The hall of Clifford's Inn is memorable as being the place where Sir Matthew Hale and seventeen other wise and patient judges sat, after the Great Fire of 1666, to adjudicate upon the claims of the landlords and tenants of burned houses, and prevent future lawsuits. The difficulty of discovering the old boundaries, under the mountains of ashes, must have been great; and forty thick folio volumes of decisions, now preserved in the British Museum, tell of many a legal headache in Clifford's Inn.

A very singular custom, and probably of great antiquity, prevails after the dinners at Clifford's Inn. The society is divided into two sections—the Principal and Aules, and the Juniors or "Kentish Men." When the meal is over, the chairman of the Kentish Men, standing up at the Junior table, bows gravely to the Principal, takes from the hand of a servitor standing by four small rolls of bread, silently dashes them three times on the table, and then pushes them down to the further end of the board, from whence they are removed. Perfect silence is preserved during this mystic ceremony, which some antiquary who sees deeper into millstones than his brethren thinks typical of offerings to Ceres, who first taught mankind the use of laws and originated those peculiar ornaments of civilisation, their expounders, the lawyers.

In the hall is preserved an old oak folding case, containing the forty-seven rules of the institution, now almost defaced, and probably of the reign of Henry VIII. The hall casement contains armorial glass with the bearings of Baptist Hicks, Viscount Campden, &c.

Robert Pultock, the almost unknown author of that graceful story, "Peter Wilkins," from whose flying women Southey drew his poetical notion of the Glendoveer, or flying spirit, in his wild poem of "The Curse of Kehama," lived in this Inn, paced on its terrace, and mused in its garden. "'Peter Wilkins' is to my mind," says Coleridge (in his "Table Talk"), "a work of uncommon beauty, and yet Stothard's illustrations have *added* beauties to it. If it were not for a certain tendency to affectation, scarcely any praise could be too high for Stothard's designs. They give me great pleasure. I believe that 'Robinson Crusoe' and ' Peter Wilkins' could only have been written by islanders. No continentalist could have conceived either tale. Davis's story is an imitation of ' Peter Wilkins ;' but there are many beautiful things in it, especially his finding his wife crouching by the fireside, she having, in his absence, plucked out all her feathers, to be like him ! It would require a very peculiar genius to add another tale, *ejusdem generis*, to ' Peter Wilkins' and ' Robinson Crusoe.' I once projected such a thing, but the difficulty of a pre-occupied ground stopped me. Perhaps La Motte Fouqué might effect something ; but I should fear that neither he nor any other German could entirely understand what may be called the ' *desert island* ' feeling. I would try the marvellous line of ' Peter Wilkins,' if I attempted it, rather than the *real* fiction of ' Robinson Crusoe.'"

The name of the author of " Peter Wilkins" was discovered only a few years ago. In the year 1835 Mr. Nicol, the printer, sold by auction a number of books and manuscripts in his possession, which had formerly belonged to the well-known publisher, Dodsley ; and in arranging them for sale, the original agreement for the sale of the manuscript of " Peter Wilkins," by the author, " Robert Pultock, of Clifford's Inn," to Dodsley, was discovered. From this document it appears that Mr. Pultock received twenty pounds, twelve copies of the work, and " the cuts of the first impression "—*i.e.*, a set of proof impressions of the fanciful engravings that professed to illustrate the first edition of the work—as the price of the entire copyright. This curious document had been sold afterwards to John Wilkes, Esq., M.P.

Inns of Chancery, like Clifford's Inn, were originally law schools, to prepare students for the larger Inns of Court.

Fetter Lane did not derive its name from the manufacture of Newgate fetters. Stow, who died early in the reign of James I., calls it " Fewtor Lane," from the Norman-French word " fewtor " (idle person, loafer), perhaps analogous to the even less complimentary modern French word " foutre," blackguard. Mr. Jesse, however, derives the word " fetter" from the Norman " defaytor " (defaulter), as if the lane had once been a sanctuary for skulking debtors. In either case the derivation is somewhat ignoble, but the inhabitants have long since lived it down. Stow says it was once a mere byway leading to gardens (*quantum mutatus !*) If men of the Bobadil and Pistol character ever did look over the garden-gates and puff their Trinidado in the faces of respectable passers-by, the lane at least regained its character later, when

poets and philosophers condescended to live in it, and persons of considerable consequence rustled their silks and trailed their velvet along its narrow roadway.

During the Middle Ages Fetter Lane slumbered, but it woke up on the breaking out of the Civil War, and in 1643 became unpleasantly celebrated as the spot where Waller's plot disastrously terminated.

In the second year of the war between King and Parliament, the Royal successes at Bath, Bristol, and Cornwall, as well as the partial victory at Edgehill, had roused the moderate party and chilled many lukewarm adherents of the Puritans. The distrust of Pym and his friends soon broke out into a reactionary plot, or, more probably, two plots, in one or both of which Waller, the poet, was dangerously mixed up. The chief conspirators were Tomkins and Challoner, the former Waller's brother-in-law, a gentleman living in Holborn, near the end of Fetter Lane, and a secretary to the Commissioners of the Queen's Revenues ; the latter an eminent citizen, well known on 'Change. Many noblemen and Cavalier officers and gentlemen had also a whispering knowledge of the ticklish affair. The projects of these men, or of some of the more desperate, at least, were—(1) to secure the king's children ; (2) to seize Mr. Pym, Colonel Hampden, and other members of Parliament specially hostile to the king ; (3) to arrest the Puritan Lord Mayor, and all the sour-faced committee of the City Militia ; (4) to capture the outworks, forts, magazines, and gates of the Tower and City, and to admit 3,000 Cavaliers sent from Oxford by a pre-arranged plan ; (5) to resist all payments imposed by Parliament for support of the armies of the Earl of Essex. Unfortunately, just as the white ribbons were preparing to tie round the arms of the conspirators, to mark them on the night of action, a treacherous servant of Mr. Tomkins, of Holborn, overheard Waller's plans from behind a convenient arras, and disclosed them to the angry Parliament. In a cellar at Tomkins's the soldiers who rummaged it found a commission sent from the king by Lady Aubigny, whose husband had been recently killed at Edgehill.

Tomkins and Challoner were hung at the Holborn end of Fetter Lane. On the ladder, Tomkins said :—" Gentlemen, I humbly acknowledge, in the sight of Almighty God (to whom, and to angels, and to this great assembly of people, I am now a spectacle), that my sins have deserved of Him this untimely and shameful death ; and, touching the business for which I suffer, I acknowledge that affection to a brother-in-law, and affection and gratitude to the king, whose bread I have eaten now about twenty-two years (I have been servant to him when he was prince, and ever since : it will be twenty-three years in August next)—I confess these two motives drew me into this foolish business. I have often since declared to good friends that I was glad it was discovered, because it might have occasioned very ill consequences ; and truly I have repented having any hand in it."

Challoner was equally fatal against Waller, and said, when at the same giddy altitude as Tomkins, "Gentlemen, this is the happiest day that ever I had. I shall now, gentlemen, declare a little more of the occasion of this, as I am desired by Mr. Peters [the famous Puritan divine, Hugh Peters] to give him and the world satisfaction in it. It came from Mr. Waller, under this notion, that if we could make a moderate party here in London, and stand betwixt and in the gap to unite the king and the Parliament, it would be a very acceptable work, for now the three kingdoms lay a-bleeding ; and unless that were done, there was no hopes to unite them," &c.

Waller had a very narrow escape, but he extricated himself with the most subtle skill, perhaps secretly aided by his kinsman, Cromwell. He talked of his "carnal eye," of his repentance, of the danger of letting the army try a member of the House. As Lord Clarendon says : "With incredible dissimulation he acted such a remorse of conscience, that his trial was put off, out of Christian compassion, till he could recover his understanding." In the meantime he bribed the Puritan preachers, and listened with humble deference to their prayers for his repentance. He bent abjectly before the house ; and eventually, with a year's imprisonment and a fine of £10,000, obtained leave to retire to France. Having spent all his money in Paris, Waller at last gained permission from Cromwell to return to England. "There cannot," says Clarendon, "be a greater evidence of the inestimable value of his (Waller's) parts, than that he lived after this in the good esteem and affection of many, the pity of most, and the reproach and scorn of few or none." The body of the unlucky Tomkins was buried in the churchyard of St. Andrew's, Holborn.

According to Peter Cunningham, that shining light of the Puritan party in the early days of Cromwell, "Praise-God Barebone," was a leather-seller in Fetter Lane, having a house, either at the same time or later, called the "Lock and Key," near Crane Court, at which place his son, a great speculator and builder, afterwards resided. Barebone (probably Barbon, of a French Huguenot family) was one of those gloomy religionists who looked on surplices, plum-porridge, theatres, dances, Christmas pudding, and homicide as equally detestable, and did his best to shut out all sunshine from that long, rainy, stormy day that is called life. He was at the head of that fanatical, tenderconscienced Parliament of 1653 which Cromwell convened from among the elect in London, after untoward Sir Harry Vane had been expelled from Westminster at the muzzles of Pride's muskets. Of Barebone, also, and his crochety, impracticable fellows, Cromwell had soon enough; and, in despair of all aid but from his own brain and hand, he then took the title of Lord Protector, and became the most inflexible and ablest monarch we have ever had, or indeed ever hope to have. Barebone is first heard of in local history as preaching in 1641, together with Mr. Greene, a felt-maker, at a conventicle in Fetter Lane, a place always renowned for its heterodoxy. The thoughtless Cavaliers, who did not like long sermons, and thought all religion but their own hypocrisy, delighted in gaunt Barebone's appropriate name, and made fun of him in those ribald ballads in which they consigned rednosed Noll, the brewer, to the reddest and hottest portion of the unknown world. At the Restoration, when all Fleet Street was ablaze with bonfires to roast the Rumps, the street boys, always on the strongest side, broke poor Barebone's windows, though he had been constable and commoncouncilman, and was a wealthy leather-seller to boot. But he was not looked upon as of the regicide or extreme dangerous party, and a year afterwards attended a vestry-meeting unmolested. After the Great Fire he came to the Clifford's Inn Appeal Court about his Fleet Street house, which had been burnt over the heads of his tenants, and eventually he rebuilt it.

In Irving's "History of Dissenters" there is a curious account, taken from an old pamphlet entitled "New Preachers," "of Barebone, Greene the felt-maker, Spencer the horse-rubber, Quartermaine the brewer's clerk, and some few others, who are mighty sticklers in this new kind of talking trade, which many ignorant coxcombs call preaching ; whereunto is added the last tumult in Fleet Street, raised by the disorderly preachment, pratings, and prattlings of Mr. Barebone the leather-seller, and Mr. Greene the felt-maker, on Sunday last, the 19th December."

The tumult alluded to is thus described : "A brief touch in memory of the fiery zeal of Mr. Barebone, a reverend unlearned leather-seller, who with Mr. Greene the felt-maker were both taken preaching or prating in a conventicle amongst a hundred persons, on Sunday, the 19th of December last, 1641."

One of the pleasantest memories of Fetter Lane is that which connects it with the school-days of that delightful essay-writer, Charles Lamb. He himself, in one of Hone's chatty books, has described the school, and Bird, its master, in his own charming way.

Both Lamb and his sister, says Mr. Fitzgerald, in his Memoir of Lamb, went to a school where Starkey had been usher about a year before they

were not frequent; but when they took place, the correction was performed in a private room adjoining, whence we could only hear the plaints, but saw nothing. This heightened the decorum and solemnity." He then describes the ferule—"that almost obsolete weapon now." "To make him look more formidable—if a pedagogue had need of these heightenings—Bird wore one of those flowered Indian gowns formerly in use with schoolmasters, the strange figures upon which we used to interpret into hieroglyphics of pain and suffering." This

ROASTING THE RUMPS IN FLEET STREET (FROM AN OLD PRINT) (*see page* 95).

came to it—a room that looked into "a discoloured, dingy garden, in the passage leading from Fetter Lane into Bartlett's Buildings. This was close to Holborn. Queen Street, where Lamb lived when a boy, was in Holborn." Bird is described as an "eminent writer" who taught mathematics, which was no more than "cyphering." "Heaven knows what languages were taught there. I am sure that neither my sister nor myself brought any out of it but a little of our native English. It was, in fact, a humble day-school." Bird and Cook, he says, were the masters. Bird had "that peculiar mild tone—especially when he was inflicting punishment—which is so much more terrible to children than the angriest looks and gestures." Whippings

is in Lamb's most delightful vein. So, too, with other incidents of the school, especially "our little leaden ink-stands, not separately subsisting, but sunk into the desks; and the agonising benches on which we were all cramped together, and yet encouraged to attain a free hand, unattainable in this position." Lamb recollected even his first copy—"Art improves nature," and could look back with "pardonable pride to his carrying off the first premium for spelling. Long after, certainly thirty years, the school was still going on, only there was a Latin inscription over the entrance in the lane, unknown in our humbler days." In the evening was a short attendance of girls, to which Miss Lamb went, and she recollected the theatricals, and even *Cato* being performed by the young gentlemen. "She describes the cast of the characters with relish. 'Martha,' by the handsome Edgar Hickman, who afterwards went to Africa."

The Starkey mentioned by Lamb was a poor, crippled dwarf, generally known at Newcastle in his old age as "Captain Starkey," the butt of the street-boys and the pensioner of benevolent citizens. In 1818, when he had been an inmate of the Freemen's Hospital, Newcastle, for twenty-six

was lodging in Fetter Lane when he published his "Leviathan." He was not there, however, in 1660, at the Restoration, since we are told that on that *glorious* occasion he was standing at the door of Salisbury House, the mansion of his kind and generous patron, the Earl of Devonshire; and that the king, formerly Hobbes's pupil in mathematics, nodded to his old tutor. A short sketch of Hobbes himself may not be uninteresting. This sceptical philosopher, hardened into dogmatic selfishness

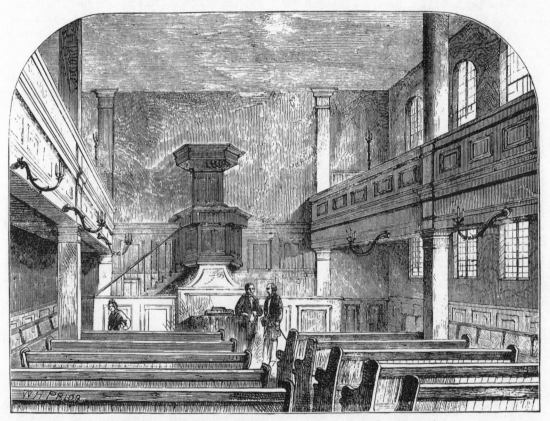

INTERIOR OF THE MORAVIAN CHAPEL IN FETTER LANE (*see page* 100).

years, the poor old ex-usher of the Fetter Lane school wrote "The Memoirs of his Life," a small pamphlet of only fourteen pages, upon which Hone good-naturedly penned an article which educed Lamb's pleasant postscript. Starkey, it appears, had been usher, not in Lamb's own time, but in that of Mary Lamb's, who came after her brother had left. She describes Starkey running away on one occasion, being brought back by his father, and sitting the remainder of the day with his head buried in his hands, even the most mischievous boys respecting his utter desolation.

That clever but mischievous advocate of divine right and absolute power, Hobbes of Malmesbury,

by exile, was the son of a Wiltshire clergyman, and he first saw the light in the year of the Armada, his mother being prematurely confined during the first panic of the Spanish invasion. Hobbes, with that same want of self-respect and love of independence which actuated Gay and Thomson, remained his whole life a tolerated pensioner of his former pupil, the Earl of Devonshire; bearing, no doubt, in his time many rebuffs; for pride will be proud, and rich men require wisdom, when in their pay, to remember its place. Hobbes in his time was a friend of, and, it is said, a translator for, Lord Bacon; and Ben Jonson, that ripe scholar, revised his sound translation of "Thucydides." He sat at the feet of Galileo and by the side of Gassendi and Descartes. While in Fetter Lane he associated with Harvey, Selden, and Cowley. He talked and wrangled with the wise men of half Europe. He had sat at Richelieu's table and been loaded with honours by Cosmo de Medici. The laurels Hobbes won in the schools he lost on Parnassus. His translation of Homer is tasteless and contemptible. In mathematics, too, he was dismounted by Wallis and others. Personally he had weaknesses. He was afraid of apparitions, he dreaded assassination, and had a fear that Burnet and the bishops would burn him as a heretic. His philosophy, though useful, as Mr. Mill says, in expanding free thought and exciting inquiry, was based on selfishness. Nothing can be falser and more detestable than the maxims of this sage of the Restoration and of reaction. He holds the natural condition of man to be a state of war—a war of all men against all men; might making right, and the conqueror trampling down all the rest. The civil laws, he declares, are the only standards of good or evil. The sovereign, he asserts, possesses absolute power, and is not bound by any compact with the people, who pay him as their head servant. Nothing he does can be wrong. The sovereign has the right of interpreting Scripture; and he thinks that Christians are bound to obey the laws of an infidel king, even in matters of religion. He sneers at the belief in a future state, and hints at materialism. These monstrous doctrines, which even Charles II. would not fully sanction, were naturally battered and bombarded by Harrington, Dr. Henry More, and others. Hobbes was also vehemently attacked by that disagreeable Dr. Fell, the subject of the well-known epigram,—

> "I do not like thee, Dr. Fell;
> The reason why I cannot tell;
> But this I know, and know full well,
> I do not like thee, Dr. Fell,"

who rudely called Hobbes "*irritabile illud et vanissimum Malmsburiense animal.*" The philosopher of Fetter Lane, who was short-sighted enough to deride the early efforts of the Royal Society, though they were founded on the strict inductive Baconian theory, seems to have been a vain man, loving paradox rather than truth, and desirous of founding, at all risks, a new school of philosophy. The Civil War had warped him; solitary thinking had turned him into a cynical dogmatiser. He was timid as Erasmus; and once confessed that if he was cast into a deep pit, and the devil should put down his hot cloven foot, he would take hold of it to draw himself out. This was not the metal that such men as Luther and Latimer were made of; but it served for the Aristotle of Rochester and Buckingham. A wit of the day proposed as Hobbes's epitaph the simple words, "The philosopher's stone."

Hobbes's professed rule of health was to dedicate the morning to his exercise and the afternoon to his studies. At his first rising, therefore, he walked out and climbed any hill within his reach; or, if the weather was not dry, he fatigued himself within doors by some exercise or other, in order to perspire, recommending that practice upon this opinion, that an old man had more moisture than heat, and therefore by such motion heat was to be acquired and moisture expelled. After this he took a comfortable breakfast, then went round the lodgings to wait upon the earl, the countess, the children, and any considerable strangers, paying some short addresses to all of them. He kept these rounds till about twelve o'clock, when he had a little dinner provided for him, which he ate always by himself, without ceremony. Soon after dinner he retired to his study, and had his candle, with ten or twelve pipes of tobacco, laid by him; then, shutting his door, he fell to smoking, thinking, and writing for several hours.

At a small coal-shed (not unlike the sheds still to be seen at the south-west end) in Fetter Lane, Dr. Johnson's friend, the poor apothecary, Levett, met a woman of bad character, who duped him into marriage. The whole story, Dr. Johnson used to say, was as marvellous as any page of "The Arabian Nights." Lord Macaulay, in his highly-coloured and somewhat exaggerated way, calls Levett "an old quack doctor, who bled and dosed coal-heavers and hackney-coachmen, and received for fees crusts of bread, bits of bacon, glasses of gin, and a little copper." Levett, however, was neither a quack nor a doctor, but an honest man and an apothecary, and the list of his patients is entirely hypothetical. This simple-hearted, benevolent man was persuaded by the proprietress of the coal-shed that she had been defrauded of her birthright by her kinsman, a man of fortune. Levett, then nearly sixty, married her; and four months after, a writ was issued against him for debts contracted by his wife, and he had to lie close to avoid the gaol. Not long afterwards his amiable wife ran away from him, and, being taken up for picking pockets, was tried at the Old Bailey, where she defended herself, and was acquitted. Dr. Johnson then, touched by Levett's misfortunes and goodness, took him to his own home at Bolt Court.

It was in a house on the east side of this lane, looking into Fleur-de-Lys Court, that (in 1767)

Elizabeth Brownrigge, midwife to the St. Dunstan's workhouse and wife of a house-painter, cruelly ill-used her two female apprentices. Mary Jones, one of these unfortunate children, after being often beaten, ran back to the Foundling, from whence she had been taken. On the remaining one, Mary Mitchell, the wrath of the avaricious hag now fell with redoubled severity. The poor creature was perpetually being stripped and beaten, was frequently chained up at night nearly naked, was scratched, and her tongue cut with scissors. It was the constant practice of Mrs. Brownrigge to fasten the girl's hands to a rope slung from a beam in the kitchen, after which this old wretch beat her four or five times in the same day with a broom or a whip. The moanings and groans of the dying child, whose wounds were mortifying from neglect, aroused the pity of a baker opposite, who sent the overseers of the parish to see the child, who was found hid in a buffet cupboard. She was taken to St. Bartholomew's Hospital, and soon died. Brownrigge was at once arrested; but Mrs. Brownrigge and her son, disguising themselves in Rag Fair, fled to Wandsworth, and there took lodgings in a chandler's shop, where they were found. The woman was tried at the Old Bailey sessions, and found guilty of murder. Mr. Silas Told, an excellent Methodist preacher, who attended her in the condemned cell, has left a curious, simple-hearted account of her behaviour and of what he considered her repentance. She *talked* a great deal of religion, and stood much on the goodness of her past life. The mob raged terribly as she passed through the streets on her way to Tyburn. The women especially screamed, "Tear off her hat; let us see her face! The devil will fetch her!" and threw stones and mud, pitiless in their hatred. After execution her corpse was thrust into a hackney-coach and driven to Surgeons' Hall for dissection; the skeleton is still preserved in a London collection. The cruel hag's husband and son were sentenced to six months' imprisonment. A curious old drawing is still extant, representing Mrs. Brownrigge in the condemned cell. She wears a large, broad-brimmed gipsy hat, tied under her chin, and a cape; and her long, hard face wears a horrible smirk of resigned hypocrisy. Canning, in one of his bitter banters on Southey's republican odes, writes,—

> " For this act
> Did Brownrigge swing. Harsh laws! But time shall come
> When France shall reign, and laws be all repealed."

In Castle Street, an offshoot of Fetter Lane, in 1709–10 (Queen Anne), at the house of his father, a master tailor, was born a very small poet, Paul Whitehead. This poor satirist and worthless man became a Jacobite barrister and protégé of Bubb Doddington and the Prince of Wales and his Leicester Fields Court. For libelling Whig noblemen, in his poem called "Manners," Dodsley, Whitehead's publisher, was summoned by the Ministers, who wished to intimidate Pope, before the House of Lords. He appears to have been an atheist, and was a member of the infamous Hell-Fire Club, that held its obscene and blasphemous orgies at Medmenham Abbey, in Buckinghamshire, the seat of Sir Francis Dashwood, where every member assumed the name of an Apostle. Later in life Whitehead was bought off by the Ministry, and then settled down at a villa on Twickenham Common, where Hogarth used to visit him. If Whitehead is ever remembered, it will be only for that splash of vitriol which Churchill threw in his face, when he wrote of the turncoat,—

> " May I—can worse disgrace on manhood fall?—
> Be born a Whitehead and baptised a Paul."

It was this Whitehead, with Carey, the surgeon of the Prince of Wales, who got up a mock procession, in ridicule of the Freemasons' annual cavalcade from Brooke Street to Haberdashers' Hall. The ribald procession consisted of shoe-blacks and chimney-sweeps, in carts drawn by asses, followed by a mourning-coach with six horses, each of a different colour. The City authorities very properly refused to let them pass through Temple Bar, but they waited there and saluted the Masons. Hogarth published a print of "The Scald Miserables," which is coarse, and even dull. The Prince of Wales, with more good sense than usual, dismissed Carey for this offensive buffoonery. Whitehead bequeathed his heart to Lord De Spenser, who buried it in his mausoleum with absurd ceremonial.

At Pemberton Row, formerly Three-Leg Alley, Fetter Lane, lived that very indifferent poet but admirable miniature-painter of Charles II.'s time, Flatman. He was a briefless barrister of the Inner Temple, and resided with his father till the period of his death. Anthony Wood tells us that having written a scurrilous ballad against marriage, beginning,—

> " Like a dog with a bottle tied close to his tail,
> Like a Tory in a bog, or a thief in a jail,"

his comrades serenaded him with the song on his wedding-night. Rochester wrote some vigorous lines on Flatman, which are not unworthy even of Dryden himself,—

> " Not that slow drudge, in swift Pindaric strains,
> Flatman, who Cowley imitates with pains,
> And drives a jaded Muse, whipt with loose reins."

We find Dr. Johnson quoting these lines with approval, in a conversation in which he suggested that Pope had partly borrowed his "Dying Christian" from Flatman.

"The chapel of the United Brethren, or Moravians, 32, Fetter Lane," says Smith, in his "Streets of London," "was the meeting-house of the celebrated Thomas Bradbury. During the riots which occurred on the trial of Dr. Sacheveral, this chapel was assaulted by the mob and dismantled, the preacher himself escaping with some difficulty. The other meeting-houses that suffered on this occasion were those of Daniel Burgess, in New Court, Carey Street; Mr. Earl's, in Hanover Street, Long Acre; Mr. Taylor's, Leather Lane; Mr. Wright's, Great Carter Lane; and Mr. Hamilton's, in St. John's Square, Clerkenwell. With the benches and pulpits of several of these, the mob, after conducting Dr. Sacheveral in triumph to his lodgings in the Temple, made a bonfire in the midst of Lincoln's Inn Fields, around which they danced with shouts of 'High Church and Sacheveral,' swearing, if they found Daniel Burgess, that they would roast him in his own pulpit in the midst of the pile."

This Moravian chapel was one of the original eight conventicles where Divine worship was permitted. Baxter preached here in 1672, and Wesley and Whitefield also struck great blows at the devil in this pulpit, where Zinzendorf's followers afterwards prayed and sang their fervent hymns.

Count Zinzendorf, the poet, theologian, pastor, missionary, and statesman, who first gave the Moravian body a vital organisation, and who preached in Fetter Lane to the most tolerant class of all Protestants, was born in Dresden in 1700. His ancestors, originally from Austria, had been Crusaders and Counts of Zinzendorf. One of the Zinzendorfs had been among the earliest converts to Lutheranism, and became a voluntary exile for the faith. The count's father was one of the Pietists, a sect protected by the first king of Prussia, the father of Frederick the Great. The founder of the Pietists laid special stress on the doctrine of conversion by a sudden transformation of the heart and will. It was a young Moravian missionary to Georgia who first induced Wesley to embrace the vital doctrine of justification by faith. For a long time there was a close kinsmanship maintained between Whitefield, the Wesleys, and the Moravians; but eventually Wesley pronounced Zinzendorf to be verging on anti-Moravianism, and Zinzendorf objected to Wesley's doctrine of sinless perfection. In 1722 Zinzendorf gave an asylum to two families of persecuted Moravian brothers, and built houses for them on a spot he called Hernhut

("watched of the Lord"), a marshy tract in Saxony, near the main road to Zittau. These simple and pious men were Taborites, a section of the old Hussites, who had renounced obedience to the Pope and embraced the Vaudois doctrines. This was the first formation of the Moravian sect.

"On January 24th, 1672–73," says Baxter, "I began a Tuesday lecture at Mr. Turner's church, in New Street, near Fetter Lane, with great convenience and God's encouraging blessing; but I never took a penny for it from any one." The chapel in which Baxter officiated in Fetter Lane is that between Nevil's Court and New Street, once occupied by the Moravians. It appears to have existed, though perhaps in a different form, before the Great Fire of London. Turner, who was the first minister, was a very active man during the plague. He was ejected from Sunbury, in Middlesex, and continued to preach in Fetter Lane till towards the end of the reign of Charles II., when he removed to Leather Lane. Baxter carried on the Tuesday morning lecture till the 24th of August, 1682. The church which then met in it was under the care of Mr. Lobb, whose predecessor had been Thankful Owen, president of St. John's College, Oxford. Ejected by the commissioners in 1660, he became a preacher in Fetter Lane. "He was," says Calamy, "a man of genteel learning and an excellent temper, admir'd for an uncommon fluency and easiness and sweetness in all his composures. After he was ejected he retired to London, where he preached privately and was much respected. He dy'd at his house in Hatton Garden, April 1, 1681. He was preparing for the press, and had almost finished, a book entituled 'Imago Imaginis,' the design of which was to show that Rome Papal was an image of Rome Pagan."

At No. 96, Fetter Lane is an Independent Chapel, whose first minister was Dr. Thomas Goodwin, 1660–1681—troublous times for Dissenters. Goodwin had been a pastor in Holland and a favourite of Cromwell. The Protector made him one of his commissioners for selecting preachers, and he was also President of Magdalen College, Oxford. When Cromwell became sick unto death, Goodwin boldly prophesied his recovery, and when the great man died, in spite of him, he is said to have exclaimed, "Thou hast deceived us, and we are deceived;" which is no doubt a Cavalier calumny. On the Restoration, the Oxford men showed Goodwin the door, and he retired to the seclusion of Fetter Lane. He seems to have been a good scholar and an eminent Calvinist divine, and he left on Puritan shelves five ponderous folio volumes of his works. The present chapel, says Mr. Noble, dates from

1732, and one of its pastors was the Rev. John Spurgeon, the father of the eloquent Baptist preacher, the Rev. C. H. Spurgeon.

The disgraceful disorder of our national records had long been a subject of regret among English antiquaries. There was no certainty of finding any required document among such a mass of ill-stored, dusty, unclassified bundles and rolls— many of them never opened since the day King John sullenly signed Magna Charta. We are a great conservative people, and abuses take a long time ripening before they seem to us fit for removal, so it happened that this evil went on several centuries before it roused the attention of Parliament, and then it was talked over and over, till in 1850 something was at last done. It was resolved to build a special storehouse for national records, where the various collections might be united under one roof, and there be arranged and classified by learned men. The first stone of a magnificent Gothic building was therefore laid by Lord Romilly on 24th May, 1851, on the west side of Fetter Lane, and slowly and surely the walls grew till, in the summer of 1866, all the new Search Offices were formally opened, to the great convenience of all students of records. The architect, Sir James Pennethorne, has produced a stately building, useful for its purpose, but not very remarkable for picturesque light and shade, and tame, as all imitations of bygone ages, adapted for bygone uses, must ever be. The number of records stored within this building can only be reckoned by "*hundreds of millions.*" These are Sir Thomas Duffus Hardy's own words. There, in cramped bundles and rolls, dusty as papyri, lie charters and official notices that once made mailed knights tremble and proud priests shake in their sandals. Now—the magic gone, the words powerless—they lie in their several binns in strange companionship. Many years will elapse before these State records and Government documents can be classified; but the small staff is as industrious as Sir Thomas Hardy could have wished, and in time the Augean stable of crabbed writings will be cleansed and ranged in order. The useful and accurate calendars of Everett Green, John Bruce, &c., are books of reference invaluable to historical students; and the old chronicles published by order of Lord Romilly, so long Master of the Rolls and Keeper of the Records, are most useful mines for the Froudes and Freemans of the future. In time it is hoped that all the episcopal records of England will be gathered together in this great treasure-house, and that many of our English noblemen will imitate the patriotic generosity of Lord Shaftesbury, in contributing their family papers to the same Gaza in Fetter Lane. Under the concentrated gaze of learned eyes, family papers, valueless and almost unintelligible to their original possessors, often reveal very curious and important facts. Mere lumber in the manor-house, fit only for the butterman, sometimes turns to leaves of gold when submitted to such microscopic analysis. It was such a gift that led to the discovery of the Locke papers among the records of the nobleman above mentioned. The pleasant rooms of the Record Office are open to all applicants; nor is any reference or troublesome preliminary form required from those wishing to consult Court rolls or State papers over twenty years old. Among other priceless treasures the Record Office contains the original, uninjured, Domesday Book, compiled by order of William the Conqueror. It is written throughout in a beautiful clerkly hand, in close fine character, and is in a perfect state of preservation. It is in two volumes, the covers of which are cut with due economy from the same skin of parchment. Bound in massive board covers, and kept with religious care under glass cases, the precious volumes seem indeed likely to last to the very break of doom. It is curious to remark that London occupies only some three or four pages. There is also preserved the original Papal Bull sent to Henry VIII., with a golden seal attached to it, the work of Benvenuto Cellini. The same collection contains the celebrated Treaty of the Field of the Cloth of Gold, the initial portrait of Francis I. being beautifully illuminated and the vellum volume adorned by an exquisite gold seal, in the finest relievo, also by Benvenuto Cellini. The figures in this seal are so perfect in their finish, that even the knee-cap of one of the nymphs is shaped with the strictest anatomical accuracy. The visitor should also see the interesting Inventory Books relating to the foundation of Henry VII.'s chapel.

The national records were formerly bundled up anyhow in the Rolls Chapel, the White Tower, the Chapter House, Westminster Abbey, Carlton Ride in St. James's Park, the State Paper Office, and the Prerogative Will Office. No one knew where anything was. They were unnoticed—mere dusty lumber, in fact—useless to men or printers' devils. Hot-headed Hugh Peters, during the Commonwealth, had, in his hatred of royalty, proposed to make one great heap of them and burn them up in Smithfield. In that way he hoped to clear the ground of many mischievous traditions. This desperate act of Communism that tough-headed old lawyer, Prynne, opposed tooth and nail.

In 1656 he wrote a pamphlet, which he called "A Short Demurrer against Cromwell's Project of Recalling the Jews from their Banishment," and in this work he very nobly epitomizes the value of these treasures ; indeed, there could not be found a more lucid syllabus of the contents of the present Record Office than Prynne has there set forth.

breakfast with the Duke of Buckingham." "The deuce he is," said Otway, and, actuated either by envy, pride, or disappointment, in a kind of involuntary manner, he took up a piece of chalk which lay on a table which stood upon the landing-place, near Dryden's chamber, and wrote over the door,—

"Here lives Dryden, a poet and a wit."

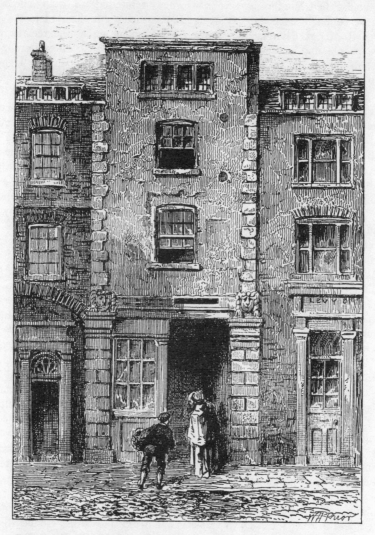

HOUSE SAID TO HAVE BEEN OCCUPIED BY DRYDEN IN FETTER LANE.

Dryden and Otway were contemporaries, and lived, it is said, for some time opposite to each other in Fetter Lane. One morning the latter happened to call upon his brother bard about breakfast-time, but was told by the servant that his master was gone to breakfast with the Earl of Pembroke. "Very well," said Otway, "tell your master that I will call to-morrow morning." Accordingly he called about the same hour. "Well, is your master at home now?" "No, sir; he is just gone to

The next morning, at breakfast, Dryden recognised the handwriting, and told the servant to go to Otway and desire his company to breakfast with him. In the meantime, to Otway's line of

"Here lives Dryden, *a poet and a wit*,"
he added,—

"This was written by Otway, *opposite*."

When Otway arrived he saw that his line was linked with a rhyme, and being a man of rather

RIVAL POETS.

A MEETING OF THE ROYAL SOCIETY IN CRANE COURT (see p. 106).

petulant disposition, he took it in dudgeon, and, turning upon his heel, told Dryden " that he was welcome to keep his wit and his breakfast to himself."

A curious old book, a *vade mecum* for malt worms, *temp*. George I., thus immortalises the patriotism of a tavern-keeper in Fetter Lane :—

" Though there are some who, with invidious look,
  Have styl'd this bird more like a Russian duck
Than what he stands depicted for on sign,
  He proves he well has croaked for prey within,
From massy tankards, formed of silver plate,
  That walk throughout this noted house in state,
Ever since *Englesfield*, in *Anna's* reign,
  To compliment each fortunate campaign,
Made one be hammered out for ev'ry town was ta'en."

CHAPTER IX.

FLEET STREET TRIBUTARIES—CRANE COURT, JOHNSON'S COURT, BOLT COURT.

Removal of the Royal Society from Gresham College—Opposition to Newton—Objections to Removal—The First Catalogue—Swift's Jeer at the Society—Franklin's Lightning Conductor and King George III.—Sir Hans Sloane insulted—The Scottish Society—Wilkes's Printer—The Delphin Classics—Johnson's Court—Johnson's Opinion on Pope and Dryden—His Removal to Bolt Court—The *John Bull*—Hook and Terry—Prosecutions for Libel—Hook's Impudence.

IN the old times, when newspapers could not legally be published without a stamp, " various ingenious devices," says a writer in the *Bookseller* (1867), " were employed to deceive and mislead the officers employed by the Government. Many of the unstamped papers were printed in Crane Court, Fleet Street; and there, on their several days of publication, the officers of the Somerset House solicitor would watch, ready to seize them immediately they came from the press. But the printers were quite equal to the emergency. They would make up sham parcels of waste-paper, and send them out with an ostentatious show of secrecy. The officers —simple fellows enough, though they were called 'Government spies,' 'Somerset House myrmidons,' and other opprobrious names, in the unstamped papers—duly took possession of the parcels, after a decent show of resistance by their bearers, while the real newspapers intended for sale to the public were sent flying by thousands down a shoot in Fleur-de-Lys Court, and thence distributed in the course of the next hour or two all over the town."

The Royal Society came to Crane Court from Gresham College in 1710, and removed in 1782 to Somerset House. This society, according to Dr. Wallis, one of the earliest members, originated in London in 1645, when Dr. Wilkins and certain philosophical friends met weekly to discuss scientific questions. They afterwards met at Oxford, and in Gresham College, till that place was turned into a Puritan barrack. After the Restoration, in 1662, the king, wishing to turn men's minds to philosophy —or, indeed, anywhere away from politics—incor-

porated the members into what Boyle has called " the Invisible College," and gave it the name of the Royal Society. In 1710, the Mercers' Company growing tired of their visitors, the society moved to a house rebuilt by Wren in 1670, and purchased by the members for £1,450. It had been the residence, before the Great Fire, of Dr. Nicholas Barebone (son of Praise-God Barebone), a great building speculator, who had much property in the Strand, and who was the first promoter of the Phœnix Fire Office. It seems to have been thought at the time that Newton was somewhat despotic in his announcement of the removal, and the members in council grumbled at the new house, and complained of it as small, inconvenient, and dilapidated. Nevertheless, Sir Isaac, unaccustomed to opposition, overruled all these objections, and the society flourished in this Fleet Street " close " seventy-two years. Before the society came to Crane Court, Pepys and Wren had been presidents; while at Crane Court the presidents were—Newton (1703–1727), Sir Thomas Hoare, Matthew Ffolkes, Esq. (whose portrait Hogarth painted), the Earl of Macclesfield, the Earl of Morton, James Burrow, Esq., James West, Esq., Sir John Pringle, and Sir Joseph Banks. The earliest records of this useful society are filled with accounts of experiments on the Baconian inductive principle, many of which now appear to us puerile, but which were valuable in the childhood of science. Among the labours of the society while in Fleet Street, we may enumerate its efforts to promote inoculation, 1714–1722; electrical experiments on fourteen miles of wires near Shooter's Hill, 1745;

ventilation, *apropos* of gaol fever, 1750; discussions on Cavendish's improved thermometers, 1757; a medal to Dollond for experiments on the laws of light, 1758; observations on the transit of Venus, in 1761; superintendence of the Observatory at Greenwich, 1765; observations of the transit of Venus in the Pacific, 1769 (Lieutenant Cook commenced the expedition); the promotion of an Arctic expedition, 1773; the *Racehorse* meteorological observations, 1773; experiments on lightning conductors by Franklin, Cavendish, &c., 1772. The removal of the society was, as we have said, at first strongly objected to, and in a pamphlet published at the time, the new purchase is thus described : "The approach to it, I confess, is very fair and handsome, through a long court; but, then, they have no other property in this than in the street before it, and in a heavy rain a man may hardly escape being thoroughly wet before he can pass through it. The front of the house towards the garden is nearly half as long again as that towards Crane Court. Upon the ground floor there is a little hall, and a direct passage from the stairs into the garden, and on each side of it a little room. The stairs are easy, which carry you up to the next floor. Here there is a room fronting the court, directly over the hall; and towards the garden is the meeting-room, and at the end another, also fronting the garden. There are three rooms upon the next floor. These are all that are as yet provided for the reception of the society, except you will have the garrets, a platform of lead over them, and the usual cellars, &c., below, of which they have more and better at Gresham College."

When the society got settled, by Newton's order the porter was clothed in a suitable gown and provided with a staff surmounted by the arms of the society in silver, and on the meeting nights a lamp was hung out over the entrance to the court from Fleet Street. The repository was built at the rear of the house, and thither the society's museum was removed. The first catalogue, compiled by Dr. Green, contains the following, among many other marvellous notices :—

"The quills of a porcupine, which on certain occasions the creature can shoot at the pursuing enemy and erect at pleasure.

"The flying squirrel, which for a good nut-tree will pass a river on the bark of a tree, erecting his tail for a sail.

"The leg-bone of an elephant, brought out of Syria for the thigh-bone of a giant. In winter, when it begins to rain, elephants are mad, and so continue from April to September, chained to some tree, and then become tame again.

"Tortoises, when turned on their backs, will sometimes fetch deep sighs and shed abundance of tears.

"A humming-bird and nest, said to weigh but twelve grains; his feathers are set in gold, and sell at a great rate.

"A bone, said to be taken out of a mermaid's head.

"The largest whale—liker an island than an animal.

"The white shark, which sometimes swallows men whole.

"A siphalter, said with its sucker to fasten on a ship and stop it under sail.

"A stag-beetle, whose horns, worn in a ring, are good against the cramp.

"A mountain cabbage—one reported 300 feet high."

The author of "Hudibras," who died in 1680, attacked the Royal Society for experiments that seemed to him futile and frivolous, in a severe and bitter poem, entitled, "The Elephant in the Moon," the elephant proving to be a mouse inside a philosopher's telescope. The poem expresses the current opinion of the society, on which King Charles II. is once said to have played a joke.

In 1726–27 Swift, too, had his bitter jeer at the society. In Laputa, he thus describes the experimental philosophers :—

"The first man I saw," he says, "was of a meagre aspect, with sooty hands and face, his hair and beard long, ragged, and singed in several places. His clothes, shirt, and skin, were all of the same colour. He had been eight years upon a project for extracting sunbeams out of cucumbers, which were to be put in phials hermetically sealed, and let out to warm the air in raw, inclement summers. He told me he did not doubt that, in eight years more, he should be able to supply the governor's gardens with sunshine at a reasonable rate; but he complained that his stock was low, and entreated me 'to give him something as an encouragement to ingenuity, especially since this had been a very dear season for cucumbers.' I made him a small present, for my lord had furnished me with money on purpose, because he knew their practice of begging from all who go to see them. I saw another at work to calcine ice into gunpowder, who likewise showed me a treatise he had written concerning the 'Malleability of Fire,' which he intended to publish.

"There was a most ingenious architect, who had contrived a new method of building houses, by beginning at the roof and working downward to the foundation ; which he justified to me by the like practice of those two prudent insects, the bee and the spider. I went into another room, where the walls and ceilings were all hung round with cobwebs, except a narrow passage for the architect to go in and out. At my entrance, he called aloud to me 'not to disturb his webs.' He lamented 'the fatal mistake the world had been so long in, of using silk-worms, while we had such plenty of domestic insects who infinitely excelled the former, because they understood how to weave as well as spin.' And he proposed, farther, 'that, by employing spiders, the charge of dyeing silks would be wholly saved;' whereof I was fully convinced when he showed me a vast number of flies, most beautifully coloured, wherewith he fed his spiders, assuring us, 'that the webs would take a tincture from them ;' and, as he had them of all hues, he hoped to fit everybody's fancy, as soon as he could find proper food for the flies, of certain gums, oils, and other glutinous matter, to give a strength and consistence to the threads."

Mr. Grosley, who, in 1770, at Lausanne, published a book on London, has drawn a curious picture of the society at that date. "The Royal Society," he says, "combines within itself the purposes of the Parisian Academy of Sciences and that of Inscriptions ; it cultivates, in fact, not only the higher branches of science, but literature also. Every one, whatever his position, and whether English or foreign, who has made observations which appear to the society worthy of its attention, is allowed to submit them to it either by word of mouth or in writing. I once saw a joiner, in his working clothes, announce to the society a means he had discovered of explaining the causes of tides. He spoke a long time, evidently not knowing what he was talking about; but he was listened to with the greatest attention, thanked for his confidence in the value of the society's opinion, requested to put his ideas into writing, and conducted to the door by one of the principal members.

"The place in which the society holds its meetings is neither large nor handsome. It is a long, low, narrow room, only furnished with a table (covered with green cloth), some morocco chairs, and some wooden benches, which rise above each other along the room. The table, placed in front of the fire-place at the bottom of the room, is occupied by the president (who sits with his back to the fire) and the secretaries. On this table is placed a large silver-gilt mace, similar to the one in use in the House of Commons,

and which, as is the case with the latter, is laid at the foot of the table when the society is in committee. The president is preceded on his entrance and departure by the beadle of the society, bearing this mace. He has beside him, on his table, a little wooden mallet for the purpose of imposing silence when occasion arises, but this is very seldom the case. With the exception of the secretaries and the president, every one takes his place hap-hazard, at the same time taking great pains to avoid causing any confusion or noise. The society may be said to consist, as a body corporate, of a committee of about twenty persons, chosen from those of its associates who have the fuller opportunities of devoting themselves to their favourite studies. The president and the secretaries are *ex-officio* members of the committee, which is renewed every year—an arrangement which is so much the more necessary that, in 1765, the society numbered 400 British members, of whom more than forty were peers of the realm, five of the latter being most assiduous members of the committee.

"The foreign honorary members, who number about 150, comprise within their number all the most famous learned men of Europe, and amongst them we find the names of D'Alembert, Bernouilli, Bonnet, Buffon, Euler, Jussieu, Linné, Voltaire, &c.; together with those, in simple alphabetical order, of the Dukes of Braganza, &c., and the chief Ministers of many European sovereigns."

During the dispute about lightning conductors (after St. Bride's Church was struck in 1764), in the year 1772, George III. (says Mr. Weld, in his "History of the Royal Society") is stated to have taken the side of Wilson—not on scientific grounds, but from political motives ; he even had blunt conductors fixed on his palace, and actually endeavoured to make the Royal Society rescind their resolution in favour of pointed conductors. The king, it is declared, had an interview with Sir John Pringle, during which his Majesty earnestly entreated him to use his influence in supporting Mr. Wilson. The reply of the president was highly honourable to himself and the society whom he represented. It was to the effect that duty as well as inclination would always induce him to execute his Majesty's wishes to the utmost of his power; "But, sire," said he, "I cannot reverse the laws and operations of Nature." It is stated that when Sir John regretted his inability to alter the laws of Nature, the king replied, "Perhaps, Sir John, you had better resign." It was shortly after this occurrence that a friend of Dr. Franklin's wrote this epigram :—

" While you, great George, for knowledge hunt,
And sharp conductors change for blunt,
The nation's out of joint ;
Franklin a wiser course pursues,
And all your thunder useless views,
By keeping to the point."

A strange scene in the Royal Society in 1710 (Queen Anne) deserves record. It ended in the expulsion from the council of that irascible Dr. Woodward who once fought a duel with Dr. Mead inside the gate of Gresham College. "The sense," says Mr. Ward, in his "Memoirs," "entertained by the society of Sir Hans Sloane's services and virtues was evinced by the manner in which they resented an insult offered him by Dr. Woodward, who, as the reader is aware, was expelled the council. Sir Hans was reading a paper of his own composition, when Woodward made some grossly insulting remarks. Dr. Sloane complained, and moreover stated that Dr. Woodward had often affronted him by making grimaces at him; upon which Dr. Arbuthnot rose and begged to be 'informed what distortion of a man's face constituted a grimace.' Sir Isaac Newton was in the chair when the question of expulsion was agitated, and when it was pleaded in Woodward's favour that 'he was a good natural philosopher,' Sir Isaac remarked that in order to belong to that society a man ought to be a good moral philosopher as well." The house was burnt down in 1877.

The Scottish Society held its meetings in Crane Court. "Elizabeth," says Mr. Timbs, "kept down the number of Scotsmen in London to the astonishingly small one of fifty-eight; but with James I. came such a host of traders and craftsmen, many of whom failing to obtain employment, gave rise, as early as 1613, to the institution of the 'Scottish Box,' a sort of friendly society's treasury, when there were no banks to take charge of money. In 1638 the company, then only twenty, met in Lamb's Conduit Street. In this year upwards of 300 poor Scotsmen, swept off by the great plague of 1665-66, were buried at the expense of the 'box,' while numbers more were nourished during their sickness, without subjecting the parishes in which they resided to the smallest expense.

"In the year 1665 the 'box' was exalted into the character of a corporation by a royal charter, the expenses attendant on which were disbursed by gentlemen who, when they met at the ' Cross Keys,' in Covent Garden, found their receipts to be £116 8s. 5d. The character of the times is seen in one of their regulations, which imposed a fine of 2s. 6d. for every oath used in the course of their quarterly business.

"Presents now flocked in. One of the corporation gave a silver cup ; another, an ivory mallet or hammer for the chairman ; and among the contributors we find Gilbert Burnet, afterwards bishop, giving £1 half-yearly. In no very Scotsman-like spirit the governors distributed each quarter-day all that had been collected during the preceding interval. But in 1775 a permanent fund was established. The hospital now distributes about £2,200 a year, chiefly in £10 pensions to old people ; and the princely bequest of £76,495 by Mr. W. Kinloch, who had realised a fortune in India, allows of £1,800 being given in pensions of £4 to disabled soldiers and sailors.

"All this is highly honourable to those connected, by birth or otherwise, with Scotland. The monthly meetings of the society are preceded by divine service in the chapel, which is in the rear of the house in Crane Court. Twice a year is held a festival, at which large sums are collected. On St. Andrew's Day, 1863, Viscount Palmerston presided, with the brilliant result of the addition of £1,200 to the hospital fund."

Appended to the account of the society already quoted we find the following remarkable "note by an Englishman" :—

"It is not one of the least curious particulars in the history of the Scottish Hospital that it substantiates by documentary evidence the fact that Scotsmen who have gone to England occasionally find their way back to their own country. It appears from the books of the corporation that in the year ending 30th November, 1850, the sum of £30 16s. 6d. was spent in passages from London to Leith ; and there is actually a corresponding society in Edinburgh to receive the *revenants* and pass them on to their respective districts."

In Crane Court, says Mr. Timbs, lived Dryden Leach, the printer, who, in 1763, was arrested on a general warrant upon suspicion of having printed Wilkes's *North Briton*, No. 45. Leach was taken out of his bed in the night, his papers were seized, and even his journeymen and servants were apprehended, the only foundation for the arrest being a hearsay report that Wilkes had been seen going into Leach's house. Wilkes had been sent to the Tower for his share in producing No. 45. He obtained a verdict of £4,000, and Leach £300, damages from three of the king's messengers, who had executed the illegal warrant. Kearsley, the bookseller, of Fleet Street (whom we recollect by his tax-tables), had been taken up for publishing No. 45, when also at Kearsley's were seized the letters of Wilkes, which seemed to fix upon him the writing of the blasphemous "Essay on Woman," of which he was convicted in the Court of King's Bench, and for which he was expelled the House of Commons. The author of this "indecent patchwork" was not Wilkes (says Walpole), but Thomas Potter, the wild son of the learned Archbishop of Canterbury,

George Dyer, of Clifford's Inn, laboriously edited, and which opened the eyes of the subscribers very wide indeed as to the singular richness of ancient literature. At the press of an eminent printer in this court, that useful and perennial serial the *Gentleman's Magazine* (started in 1731) was partly

THE ROYAL SOCIETY'S HOUSE IN CRANE COURT (*see page* 104).

who had tried to fix the authorship on the learned and arrogant Warburton—a piece of matchless impudence worthy of Wilkes himself.

Red Lion Court (No. 169), though an unlikely spot, has been, of all the side binns of Fleet Street, one of the most specially favoured by Minerva. Here Valpy published that interminable series of Latin and Greek authors, which he called the "Delphin Classics," which Lamb's eccentric friend,

printed from 1779 to 1781, and entirely printed from 1792 to 1820.

Johnson's Court, Fleet Street (a narrow court on the north side of Fleet Street, the fourth from Fetter Lane, eastward), was not named from Dr. Johnson, although inhabited by him.

Dr. Johnson was living in Johnson's Court in 1765, after he left No. 1, Inner Temple Lane, and before he removed to Bolt Court. In Johnson's

Court he made the acquaintance of Murphy, and he worked at his edition of "Shakespeare." He saw much of Reynolds and Burke. On the accession of George III. a pension of £300 a year had been bestowed on him, and thenceforward he became comparatively an affluent man. In 1763 Boswell had become acquainted with Dr. Johnson,

"He" (Johnson), says Hawkins, "removed from the Temple into a house in Johnson's Court, Fleet Street, and invited thither his friend Mrs. Williams. An upper room, which had the advantage of a good light and free air, he fitted up for a study and furnished with books, chosen with so little regard to editions or their external appearances

Theodore E. Hook (See page 110.)

and from that period his wonderful conversations are recorded. The indefatigable biographer describes, in 1763, being taken by Mr. Levett to see Dr. Johnson's library, which was contained in his garret over his Temple chambers, where the son of the well-known Lintot used to have his warehouse. The floor was strewn with manuscript leaves; and there was an apparatus for chemical experiments, of which Johnson was all his life very fond. Johnson often hid himself in this garret for study, but never told his servant, as the Doctor would never allow him to say "not at home" when he was within.

as showed they were intended for use, and that he disdained the ostentation of learning."

"I returned to London," says Boswell, "in February, 1766, and found Dr. Johnson in a good house in Johnson's Court, Fleet Street, in which he had accommodated Mrs. Williams with an apartment on the ground-floor, while Mr. Levett occupied his post in the garret. His faithful Francis was still attending upon him. He received me with much kindness. The fragments of our first conversation, which I have preserved, are these :— I told him that Voltaire, in a conversation with me, had distinguished Pope and Dryden, thus : ' Pope drives a handsome chariot, with a couple of neat, trim nags; Dryden, a coach and six stately horses.' Johnson: 'Why, sir, the truth is, they both drive coaches and six, but Dryden's horses are either galloping or stumbling ; Pope's go at a steady, even trot.' He said of Goldsmith's 'Traveller,' which had been published in my absence, 'There's not been so fine a poem since Pope's time.' Dr. Johnson at the same time favoured me by marking the lines which he furnished to Goldsmith's 'Deserted Village,' which are only the last four :—

> 'That trade's proud empire hastes to swift decay,
> As ocean sweeps the labour'd mole away ;
> While self-dependent power can time defy,
> As rocks resist the billows and the sky.'

At night I supped with him at the 'Mitre' tavern, that we might renew our social intimacy at the original place of meeting. But there was now considerable difference in his way of living. Having had an illness, in which he was advised to leave off wine, he had, from that period, continued to abstain from it, and drank only water or lemonade."

"Mr. Beauclerk and I," says Boswell, in another place, "called on him in the morning. As we walked up Johnson's Court, I said, 'I have a veneration for this court,' and was glad to find that Beauclerk had the same reverential enthusiasm." The Doctor's removal Boswell thus duly chronicles :—" Having arrived," he says, "in London late on Friday, the 15th of March, 1776, I hastened next morning to wait on Dr. Johnson, at his house, but found he was removed from Johnson's Court, No. 7, to Bolt Court, No. 8, still keeping to his favourite Fleet Street. My reflection at the time, upon this change, as marked in my journal, is as follows: 'I felt a foolish regret that he had left a court which bore his name ; but it was not foolish to be affected with some tenderness of regard for a place in which I had seen him a great deal, from whence I had often issued a better and a happier man than when I went in ; and which had often appeared to my imagination, while I trod its pavement in the solemn darkness of the night, to be sacred to wisdom and piety.'"

Johnson was living in Johnson's Court when he was introduced to George III., an interview in which he conducted himself, considering he was an ingrained Jacobite, with great dignity, self-respect, and good sense.

That clever, but most shameless and scurrilous, paper, *John Bull*, was started in Johnson's Court, at the close of 1820. Its specific and real object was to slander unfortunate Queen Caroline and to torment, stigmatise, and blacken "the Brandenburg House party," as her honest sympathisers were called. Theodore Hook was chosen editor, because he knew society, was quick, witty, satirical, and thoroughly unscrupulous. For his " splendid abuse"—as his biographer, the unreverend Mr. Barham, calls it—he received the full pay of a greedy hireling. Tom Moore and the Whigs now met with a terrible adversary. Hook did not hew or stab, like Churchill and the old rough lampooners of earlier days, but he filled crackers with wild fire, or laughingly stuck the enemies of George IV. over with pins. Hook had only a year before returned from the Treasuryship of the Mauritius, charged with a defalcation of £12,000—the result of the grossest and most culpable neglect. Hungry for money, as he had ever been, he was eager to show his zeal for the master who had hired his pen. Hook and Daniel Terry, the comedian, joined to start the new satirical paper ; but Miller, a publisher in the Burlington Arcade, was naturally afraid of libel, and refused to have anything to do with the new venture. With Miller, as Hook said in his clever, punning way, all argument in favour of it proved Newgate-ory. Hook at first wanted to start a magazine upon the model of *Blackwood*, but the final decision was for a weekly newspaper, to be called *John Bull*, a title already discussed for a previous scheme by Hook and Elliston. The first number appeared on Saturday, December 16, 1820, in the publishing office, No. 11, Johnson's Court. The modest projectors only printed seven hundred and fifty copies of the first number, but the sale proved considerable. By the sixth week the sale had reached ten thousand weekly. The first five numbers were reprinted, and the first two actually stereotyped.

Hook's favourite axiom—worthy of such a satirist—was "that there was always a concealed wound in every family, and the point was to strike exactly at the source of pain." Hook's clerical elder brother, Dr. James Hook, the author of "Pen Owen" and other novels, and afterwards Dean of Worcester, assisted him ; but Terry was too busy in what Sir Walter Scott, his great friend and sleeping partner, used to call " *Terry*fying the novelists by not very brilliant adaptations of their works." Dr. Maginn, summoned from Cork to edit a newspaper for Hook (who had bought up two dying newspapers for the small expenditure of three hundred guineas), wrote only one article for the *Bull*. Mr. Haynes Bayley contributed some of his graceful verses, and Ingoldsby (Barham) some of his rather ribald fun. The anonymous editor of *John Bull* became for a time as much talked about as "Junius" in earlier times. By many witty James Smith was suspected, but his fun had not malignity enough for the Tory purposes of those bitter days. Latterly Hook let Alderman Wood alone, and set all his staff on Hume, the great economist, and the Hon. Henry Grey Bennett.

Several prosecutions followed, says Mr. Barham, that for libel on the Queen among the rest; but the grand attempt on the part of the Whigs to crush the paper was not made till the 6th of May, 1821. A short and insignificant paragraph, containing some observations upon the Hon. Henry Grey Bennett, a brother of Lord Tankerville, was selected for attack, as involving a breach of privilege; in consequence of which the printer, Mr. H. F. Cooper, the editor, and Mr. Shackell were ordered to attend at the bar of the House of Commons. A long debate ensued, during which Ministers made as fair a stand as the nature of the case would admit in behalf of their guerrilla allies, but which terminated at length in the committal of Cooper to Newgate, where he was detained from the 11th of May till the 11th of July, when Parliament was prorogued.

Meanwhile the most strenuous exertions were made to detect the real delinquents—for, of course, honourable gentlemen were not to be imposed upon by the unfortunate "men of straw" who had fallen into their clutches, and who, by the way, suffered for an offence of which their judges and accusers openly proclaimed them to be not only innocent, but incapable. The terror of imprisonment and the various arts of cross-examination proving insufficient to elicit the truth, recourse was had to a simpler and more conciliatory mode of treatment—bribery. The storm had failed to force off the editorial cloak—the golden beams were brought to bear upon it. We have it for certain that an offer was made to a member of the establishment to stay all impending proceedings, and, further, to pay down a sum of £500 on the names of the actual writers being given up. It was rejected with disdain, while such were the precautions taken that it was impossible to fix Hook, though suspicion began to be awakened, with any share in the concern. In order, also, to cross the scent already hit off, and announced by sundry deep-mouthed pursuers, the following "Reply"—framed upon the principle, we presume, that in literature, as in love, everything is fair—was thrown out in an early number :—

"MR. THEODORE HOOK.

"The conceit of some people is amazing, and it has not been unfrequently remarked that conceit is in abundance where talent is most scarce. Our readers will see that we have received a letter from Mr. Hook, disowning and disavowing all connection with this paper. Partly out of good nature, and partly from an anxiety to show the gentleman how little desirous we are to be associated with him, we have made a declaration which will doubtless be quite satisfactory to his morbid sensibility and affected squeamishness. We are free to confess that two things surprise us in this business : the first, that anything which we have thought worth giving to the public should have been mistaken for Mr. Hook's; and, secondly, that *such a person* as Mr. Hook should think himself disgraced by a connection with *John Bull.*"

For sheer impudence this, perhaps, may be admitted to "defy competition"; but in point of tact and delicacy of finish it falls infinitely short of a subsequent notice, a perfect gem of its class, added by way of clenching the denial :—

"We have received Mr. Theodore Hook's second letter. We are ready to confess that we may have appeared to treat him too unceremoniously, but we will put it to his own feelings whether the terms of his denial were not, in some degree, calculated to produce a little asperity on our part. We shall never be ashamed, however, to do justice, and we readily declare that we meant no kind of imputation on Mr. Hook's personal character."

The ruse answered for awhile, and the paper went on with unabated audacity.

The death of the Queen, in the summer of 1821, produced a decided alteration in the tone and temper of the paper. In point of fact, its occupation was now gone. The main, if not the sole, object of its establishment had been brought about by other and unforeseen events. The combination it had laboured so energetically to thwart was now dissolved by a higher and resistless agency. Still, it is not to be supposed that a machine which brought in a profit of something above £4,000 per annum, half of which fell to the share of Hook, was to be lightly thrown up, simply because its original purpose was attained. The dissolution of the "League" did not exist then as a precedent. The Queen was no longer to be feared; but there were Whigs and Radicals enough to be held in check, and, above all, there was a handsome income to be realised.

"Latterly Hook's desultory nature made him

wander from the *Bull*, which might have furnished the thoughtless and heartless man of pleasure with an income for life. The paper naturally lost sap and vigour, at once declined in sale, and sank into a mere respectable club-house and party organ." "Mr. Hook," says Barham, "received to the day of his death a fixed salary, but the proprietorship had long since passed into other hands."

CHAPTER X.

FLEET STREET TRIBUTARIES.

Dr. Johnson in Bolt Court—His motley Household—His Life there—Still existing—The gallant "Lumber Troop"—Reform Bill Riots—Sir Claudius Hunter—Cobbett in Bolt Court—The Bird Boy—The Private Soldier—In the House—Dr. Johnson in Gough Square—Busy at the Dictionary—Goldsmith in Wine Office Court—Selling "The Vicar of Wakefield"—Goldsmith's Troubles—Wine Office Court—The Old "Cheshire Cheese."

OF all the nooks of London associated with the memory of that good giant of literature, Dr. Johnson, not one is more sacred to those who love that great and wise man than Bolt Court. To this monastic court Johnson came in 1776, and remained till that December day in 1784, when a procession of all the learned and worthy men who honoured him followed his body to its grave in the Abbey, near the feet of Shakespeare and by the side of Garrick. The great scholar, whose ways and sayings, whose rough hide and tender heart, are so familiar to us—thanks to that faithful parasite who secured an immortality by getting up behind his triumphal chariot—came to Bolt Court from Johnson's Court, whither he had flitted from Inner Temple Lane, where he was living when the young Scotch barrister who was afterwards his biographer first knew him. His strange household of fretful and disappointed almspeople seems as well known as our own. At the head of these pensioners was the daughter of a Welsh doctor, (a blind old lady named Williams), who had written some trivial poems; Mrs. Desmoulins, an old Staffordshire lady, her daughter, and a Miss Carmichael. The relationships of these fretful and quarrelsome old maids Dr. Johnson has himself sketched, in a letter to Mr. and Mrs. Thrale:—"Williams hates everybody; Levett hates Desmoulins, and does not love Williams; Desmoulins hates them both; Poll (Miss Carmichael) loves none of them." This Levett was a poor eccentric apothecary, whom Johnson supported, and who seems to have been a charitable man.

The annoyance of such a menagerie of singular oddities must have driven Johnson more than ever to his clubs, where he could wrestle with the best intellects of the day, and generally retire victorious. He had done nearly all his best work by this time, and was sinking into the sere and yellow leaf, not, like Macbeth, with the loss of honour, but with love, obedience, troops of friends, and golden opinions from all sorts of people. His Titanic labour, the Dictionary, he had achieved chiefly in Gough Square; his "Rasselas"—that grave and wise Oriental story—he had written in a few days, in Staple's Inn, to defray the expenses of his mother's funeral. In Bolt Court he, however, produced his "Lives of the Poets," a noble compendium of criticism, defaced only by the bitter Tory depreciation of Milton, and injured by the insertion of many worthless and the omission of several good poets.

It is pleasant to think of some of the events that happened while Johnson lived in Bolt Court. Here he exerted himself with all the ardour of his nature to soothe the last moments of that wretched man, Dr. Dodd, who was hanged for forgery. From Bolt Court he made those frequent excursions to the Thrales, at Streatham, where the rich brewer and his brilliant wife gloried in the great London lion they had captured. To Bolt Court came Johnson's friends Reynolds and Gibbon, and Garrick, and Percy, and Langton; but poor Goldsmith had died before Johnson left Johnson's Court. To Bolt Court he stalked home the night of his memorable quarrel with Dr. Percy, no doubt regretting the violence and boisterous rudeness with which he had attacked an amiable and gifted man. From Bolt Court he walked to service at St. Clement's Church on the day he rejoiced in comparing the animation of Fleet Street with the desolation of the Hebrides. It was from Bolt Court Boswell drove Johnson to dine with General Paoli, a drive memorable for the fact that on that occasion Johnson uttered his first and only recorded pun.

Johnson was at Bolt Court when the Gordon Riots broke out, and he describes them to Mrs. Thrale.

Boswell gives a pleasant sketch of a party at Bolt Court, when Mrs. Hall (a sister of Wesley) was there, and Mr. Allen, a printer; Johnson produced his silver salvers, and it was "a great day." It was on this occasion that the conversation fell on apparitions, and Johnson, always superstitious to the last degree, told the story of hearing his mother's voice call him one day at Oxford (probably at a time when his brain was overworked). On this great occasion also, Johnson, talked at by Mrs. Hall and Mrs. Williams at the same moment, gaily quoted the line from the *Beggar's Opera*,—

"But two at a time there's no mortal can bear,"

and Boswell playfully compared the great man to Captain Macheath. Imagine Mrs. Williams, old and peevish; Mrs. Hall, lean, lank, and preachy; Johnson, rolling in his chair like Polyphemus at a debate; Boswell, stooping forward on the perpetual listen; Mr. Levett, sour and silent; Frank, the black servant, proud of the silver salvers—and you have the group as in a picture.

In Bolt Court we find Johnson now returning from pleasant dinners with Wilkes and Garrick, Malone and Dr. Burney; now sitting alone over his Greek Testament, or praying with his black servant, Frank. We like to picture him on that Good Friday morning (1783), when he and Boswell, returning from service at St. Clement's, rested on the stone seat at the garden-door in Bolt Court, talking about gardens and country hospitality.

Then, finally, we come to almost the last scene of all, when the sick man addressed to his kind physician, Brocklesby, that pathetic passage of Shakespeare's,—

"Canst thou not minister to a mind diseased;
Pluck from the memory a rooted sorrow;
Raze out the written troubles of the brain;
And with some sweet oblivious antidote
Cleanse the stuffed bosom of that perilous stuff
Which weighs upon the heart?"

Round Johnson's dying bed gathered many wise and good men. To Burke he said, "I must be in a wretched state indeed, when your company would not be a delight to me." To another friend he remarked solemnly, but in his old grand manner, "Sir, you cannot conceive with what acceleration I advance towards death." Nor did his old vehemence and humour by any means forsake him, for he described a man who sat up to watch him "as an idiot, sir; awkward as a turnspit when first put into the wheel, and sleepy as a dormouse." His remaining hours were spent in fervent prayer. The last words he uttered were those of benediction upon the daughter of a friend who came to ask his blessing.

Some years before Dr. Johnson's death, when the poet Rogers was a young clerk of literary proclivities at his father's bank, he one day stole surreptitiously to Bolt Court, daringly to show some of his fledgeling poems to the great Polyphemus of literature. He and young Maltby, the father of the late Bishop of Durham, crept blushingly through the quiet court, and on arriving at the sacred door on the west side, ascended the steps and knocked at the door; but the awful echo of that knocker struck terror to the young *débutants*' hearts, and before Frank Barber, the Doctor's old negro footman, could appear, the two lads, like street-boys who had perpetrated a mischievous runaway knock, took to their heels and darted back into noisy Fleet Street. Mr. Jesse, who has collected so many excellent anecdotes, some even original, in his three large volumes on "London's Celebrated Characters and Places," says that the elder Mr. Disraeli, singularly enough, used in society to relate an almost similar adventure as a youth. Eager for literary glory, but urged towards the counter by his sober-minded relations, he enclosed some of his best verses to the celebrated Dr. Johnson, and modestly solicited from the terrible critic an opinion of their value. Having waited some time in vain for a reply, the ambitious Jewish youth at last, December 13, 1784, resolved to face the lion in his den, and rapping tremblingly (as his predecessor, Rogers), heard with dismay the knocker echo on the metal. We may imagine the feelings of the young votary at the shrine of learning, when the servant (probably Frank Barber), who slowly opened the door, informed him that Dr. Johnson had breathed his last only a few short hours before.

Mr. Timbs reminds us of another story of Dr. Johnson, which will not be out of place here. It is an excellent illustration of the keen sagacity and forethought of that great man's mind. One evening Dr. Johnson, looking from his dim Bolt Court window, saw the slovenly lamp-lighter of those days ascending a ladder (just as Hogarth has drawn him in the "Rake's Progress"), and fill the little receptacle in the globular lamp with detestable whale-oil. Just as he got down the ladder the dull light wavered out. Skipping up the ladder again, the son of Prometheus lifted the cover, thrust the torch he carried into the heated vapour rising from the wick, and instantly the ready flame sprang restored to life. "Ah," said the old seer, "one of these days the streets of London will be lighted by smoke."

Johnson's house (No. 8), according to Mr. Noble, was not destroyed by fire in 1819, as Mr. Timbs and other writers assert. The house destroyed was Bensley the printer's (next door to No. 8), the successor of Johnson's friend, Allen, who in 1772 published Manning's Saxon, Gothic, and Latin

been founded—*sic itur ad astra*. The back room, first floor, in which the great man died, had been pulled down by Mr. Bensley, to make way for a staircase. Bensley was one of the first introducers of the German invention of steam-printing.

At "Dr. Johnson's" tavern, established some half

OLD HOUSE STILL STANDING IN BOLT COURT (*see page* 112).

Dictionary, and died in 1780. In Bensley's destructive fire all the plates and stock of Dallaway's "History of Sussex" were consumed. Johnson's house, says Mr. Noble, was in 1858 purchased by the Stationers' Company, and fitted up as a school (the fee, two pounds a quarter). In 1861 Mr. Foss, Master of the Company, initiated a fund, and since then eight university scholarships have

a century ago, the well-known society of the "Lumber Troop" once drained their porter and held their solemn smokings. This gallant force of supposititious fighting men "came out" with great force during the Reform Riots of 1830. These useless disturbances originated in a fussy, foolish warning letter, written by Sir John Key, Lord Mayor elect (he was generally known in the City as Don

DR. JOHNSON'S HOUSE IN THE TEMPLE.

Key after this), to the Duke of Wellington, then as terribly unpopular with the English Reformers as he had been with the French after the battle of Waterloo, urging him (the duke) if he came with King William and Queen Adelaide to dine with the new Lord Mayor, (his worshipful self), to come "strongly and sufficiently guarded." This imprudent step greatly offended the people, who were also just then much vexed with the severities of Peel's obnoxious new police. The result was that the new king and queen (for the not over-beloved George IV. had only died in June of that year) thought it better to decline coming to the City festivities altogether. Great, then, was even the Tory indignation, and the fattest alderman trotted about, eager to discuss the grievance, the waste of half-cooked turtle, and the general folly and enormity of the Lord Mayor elect's conduct. Sir Claudius Hunter, who had shared in the Lord Mayor's fears, generously marched to his aid. In a published statement that he made, he enumerated the force available for the defence of the (in his mind) endangered City in the following way:—

Ward Constables	400
Fellowship, Ticket, and Tackle Porters ...	250
Firemen...	150
Corn Porters	100
Extra men hired	130
City Police or own men	54
Tradesmen with emblems in the procession...	300
Some gentlemen called the Lumber Troopers	150
The Artillery Company	150
The East India Volunteers	600
Total of all comers 2,284	

In the same statement Sir Claudius says:— "The Lumber Troop are a respectable smoking club, well known to every candidate for a seat in Parliament for London, and most famed for the quantity of tobacco they consume and the porter they drink, which, I believe, from my own observation, made nineteen years ago, when I was a candidate for that office, is the only liquor allowed. They were to have had no pay, and I am sure they would have done their best."

Along the line of procession, to oppose this civic force, the right worshipful but foolish man reckoned there would be some 150,000 persons. With all these aldermanic fears, and all these irritating precautions, a riot naturally took place. On Monday, November 8th, that glib, unsatisfactory man, Orator Hunt, the great demagogue of the day, addressed a Reform meeting at the Rotunda, in Blackfriars Road. At half-past eleven, when the Radical gentleman, famous for his white hat

the lode-star of faction, retired, a man suddenly waved a tricolour flag (it was the year, remember, of the Revolution in Paris), with the word "Reform" painted upon it, and a preconcerted cry was raised by the more violent of, "Now for the West End!" About one thousand men then rushed over Blackfriars bridge, shouting, "Reform!" "Down with the police!" "No Peel!" "No Wellington!" Hurrying along the Strand, the mob first proceeded to Earl Bathurst's, in Downing Street. A foolish gentleman of the house, hearing the cries, came out on the balcony, armed with a brace of pistols, and declared he would fire on the first man who attempted to enter the place. Another gentleman at this moment came out, and very sensibly took the pistols from his friend, on which the mob retired. The rioters were then making for the House of Commons, but were stopped by a strong line of police, just arrived in time from Scotland Yard. One hundred and forty more men soon joined the constables, and a general fight ensued, in which many heads were quickly broken, and the Reform flag was captured. Three of the rioters were arrested, and taken to the watch-house in the Almonry in Westminster. A troop of Royal Horse Guards (blue) remained during the night ready in the court of the Horse Guards, and bands of policemen paraded the streets.

On Tuesday the riots continued. About half-past five p.m., 300 or 400 persons, chiefly boys, came along the Strand, shouting, "No Peel!" "Down with the raw lobsters!" (the new police); "This way, my lads; we'll give it them!" At the back of the menageries at Charing Cross the police rushed upon them, and after a skirmish put them to flight. At seven o'clock the vast crowd by Temple Bar compelled every coachman and passenger in a coach, as a passport, to pull off his hat and shout "Huzza!" Stones were thrown, and attempts were made to close the gates of the Bar. The City marshals, however, compelled them to be reopened, and opposed the passage of the mob to the Strand, but the pass was soon forced. The rioters in Pickett Place pelted the police with stones and pieces of wood, broken from the scaffolding of the Law Institute, then building in Chancery Lane. Another mob of about 500 persons ran up Piccadilly to Apsley House and hissed and hooted the stubborn, unprogressive old Duke, Mr. Peel, and the police; the constables, however, soon dispersed them. The same evening dangerous mobs collected in Bethnal Green, Spitalfields, and Whitechapel, one party of them displaying tricoloured flags. They broke a lamp and a window or two, but did little else. Alas for poor Sir Claudius and his profound computations! His 2,284 loyal fighting men dwindled down to 600, including even those strange hybrids, the firemen-watermen ; and as for the gallant Lumber Troop, they were nowhere visible to the naked eye.

To Bolt Court that scourge of King George III., William Cobbett, came from Fleet Street to sell his Indian corn, for which no one cared, and to print and publish his twopenny *Political Register*, for which the London Radicals of that day hungered. Nearly opposite the office of "this good hater," says Mr. Timbs, Wright (late Kearsley) kept shop, and published a searching criticism on Cobbett's excellent English Grammar as soon as it appeared. We only wonder that Cobbett did not reply to him as Johnson did to a friend after he knocked Osborne (the grubbing bookseller of Gray's Inn Gate) down with a blow—"Sir, he was impertinent, and I beat him."

A short biographical sketch of Cobbett will not be inappropriate here. This sturdy Englishman, born in the year 1762, was the son of an honest and industrious yeoman, who kept an inn called the "Jolly Farmer," at Farnham, in Surrey. "My first occupation," says Cobbett, "was driving the small birds from the turnip seed and the rooks from the peas. When I first trudged a-field with my wooden bottle and my satchel over my shoulder, I was hardly able to climb the gates and stiles." In 1783 the restless lad (a plant grown too high for the pot) ran away to London, and turned lawyer's clerk. At the end of nine months he enlisted, and sailed for Nova Scotia. Before long he became sergeant-major, over the heads of thirty other non-commissioned officers. Frugal and diligent, the young soldier soon educated himself. Discharged at his own request in 1791, he married a respectable girl, to whom he had before entrusted £150 hard-earned savings. Obtaining a trial against four officers of his late regiment for embezzlement of stores, for some strange reason Cobbett fled to France on the eve of the trial, but finding the king of that country dethroned, he started at once for America. At Philadelphia he boldly began as a high Tory bookseller, and denounced Democracy in his virulent "Porcupine Papers." Finally, overwhelmed with actions for libel, Cobbett in 1800 returned to England. Failing with a daily paper and a bookseller's shop, Cobbett then started his *Weekly Register*, which for thirty years continued to express the changes of his honest but impulsive and vindictive mind. Gradually—it is said, owing to some slight shown him by Pitt (more probably from real conviction)—

Cobbett grew Radical and progressive, and in 1809 was fined £500 for libels on the Irish Government. In 1817 he was fined £1,000 and imprisoned two years for violent remarks about some Ely militiamen who had been flogged under a guard of fixed bayonets. This punishment he never forgave. He followed up his *Register* by his *Twopenny Trash*, of which he eventually sold 100,000 a number. The Six Acts being passed—as he boasted, to gag him—he fled, in 1817, again to America. The persecuted man returned to England in 1819, bringing with him, much to the amusement of the Tory lampooners, the bones of that foul man, Tom Paine, the infidel, whom (in 1796) this changeful politician had branded as "base, malignant, treacherous, unnatural, and blasphemous." During the Queen Caroline trial Cobbett worked heart and soul for that questionable martyr. He went out to Shooter's Hill to welcome her to London, and boasted of having waved a laurel bough above her head.

In 1825 he wrote a scurrilous "History of the Reformation" (by many still attributed to a priest), in which he declared Luther, Calvin, and Beza to be the greatest ruffians that ever disgraced the world. In his old age, too late to be either brilliant or useful, Cobbett got into Parliament, being returned in 1832, thanks to the Reform Bill, member for Oldham. He died at his house near Farnham, in 1835. Cobbett was an egotist, it must be allowed, and a violent-tempered, vindictive man ; but his honesty, his love of truth and liberty, few who are not blinded by party opinion can doubt. His writings are remarkable for vigorous and racy Saxon, as full of vituperation as Rabelais's, and as terse and simple as Swift's.

Mr. Grant, in his pleasant book, "Random Recollections of the House of Commons," written *circa* 1834, gives us an elaborate full-length portrait of old Cobbett. He was, he says, not less than six feet high, and broad and athletic in proportion. His hair was silver-white, his complexion ruddy as a farmer's. Till his small eyes sparkled with laughter, he looked a mere dull-pated clodpole. His dress was a light, loose, grey tail-coat, a white waistcoat, and sandy kerseymere breeches, and he usually walked about the House with both his hands plunged into his breeches pockets. He had an eccentric, half-malicious way of sometimes suddenly shifting his seat, and on one important night, big with the fate of Peel's Administration, deliberately anchored down in the very centre of the disgusted Tories and at the very back of Sir Robert's bench, to the infinite annoyance of the somewhat supercilious party.

We next penetrate into Gough Square, in search of the great lexicographer.

As far as can be ascertained from Boswell, Dr. Johnson resided in Gough Square from 1748 to 1758, an eventful period of his life, and one of struggle, pain, and difficulty. In this gloomy side square near Fleet Street, he achieved many results and abandoned many hopes. Here he nursed his hypochondria—the nightmare of his life —and sought the only true relief in hard work. Here he toiled over books, drudging for Cave and Dodsley. Here he commenced both the *Rambler* and the *Idler*, and formed his acquaintance with Bennet Langton. Here his wife died, leaving him more than ever a prey to his natural melancholy; and here he toiled on his great work, the Dictionary, in which he and six amanuenses effected what it took all the French Academicians to perform for their language.

A short epitome of what this great man accomplished while in Gough Square will clearly recall to our readers his way of life while in that locality. In 1749, Johnson formed a quiet club in Ivy Lane, wrote that fine paraphrase of Juvenal, "The Vanity of Human Wishes," and brought out, with dubious success, under Garrick's auspices, his tragedy of *Irene*. In 1750, he commenced the *Rambler*. In 1752, the year his wife died, he laboured on at the Dictionary. In 1753, he became acquainted with Bennet Langton. In 1754 he wrote the life of his early patron, Cave, who died that year. In 1755, the great Dictionary, begun in 1747, was at last published, and Johnson wrote that scathing letter to the Earl of Chesterfield, who, too late, thrust upon him the patronage the poor scholar had once sought in vain. In 1756, the still struggling man was arrested for a paltry debt of £5 18s., from which Richardson the worthy relieved him. In 1758, when he began the *Idler*, Johnson is described as "being in as easy and pleasant a state of existence as constitutional unhappiness ever permitted him to enjoy."

While the Dictionary was going forward, "Johnson," says Boswell, "lived part of the time in Holborn, part in Gough Square (Fleet Street); and he had an upper room fitted up like a counting-house for the purpose, in which he gave to the copyists their several tasks. The words, partly taken from other dictionaries and partly supplied by himself, having been first written down with space left between them, he delivered in writing their etymologies, definitions, and various significations. The authorities were copied from the books themselves, in which he had marked the passages with a black-lead pencil, the traces of which could be easily effaced. I have seen several of them in which that trouble had not been taken, so that they were just as when used by the copyists. It is remarkable that he was so attentive to the choice of the passages in which words were authorised, that one may read page after page of his Dictionary with improvement and pleasure; and it should not pass unobserved, that he has quoted no author whose writings had a tendency to hurt sound religion and morality."

To this account Bishop Percy adds a note of great value for its lucid exactitude. "Boswell's account of the manner in which Johnson compiled his Dictionary," he says, "is confused and erroneous. He began his task (as he himself expressly described to me) by devoting his first care to a diligent perusal of all such English writers as were most correct in their language, and under every sentence which he meant to quote he drew a line, and noted in the margin the first letter of the word under which it was to occur. He then delivered these books to his clerks, who transcribed each sentence on a separate slip of paper and arranged the same under the word referred to. By these means he collected the several words, and their different significations, and when the whole arrangement was alphabetically formed, he gave the definitions of their meanings, and collected their etymologies from Skinner, and other writers on the subject." To these accounts, Hawkins adds his usual carping, pompous testimony. "Dr. Johnson," he says, "who, before this time, together with his wife, had lived in obscurity, lodging at different houses in the courts and alleys in and about the Strand and Fleet Street, had, for the purpose of carrying on this arduous work, and being near the printers employed in it, taken a handsome house in Gough Square, and fitted up a room in it with books and other accommodations for amanuenses, whom, to the number of five or six, he kept constantly under his eye. An interleaved copy of 'Bailey's Dictionary,' in folio, he made the repository of the several articles, and these he collected by incessantly reading the best authors in our language, in the practice whereof his method was to score with a black-lead pencil the words by him selected. The books he used for this purpose were what he had in his own collection, a copious but a miserably ragged one, and all such as he could borrow; which latter, if ever they came back to those that lent them, were so defaced as to be scarce worth owning, and yet some of his friends were glad to receive and entertain them as curiosities."

" Mr. Burney," says Boswell, "during a visit to the capital, had an interview with Johnson in Gough Square, where he dined and drank tea with him, and was introduced to the acquaintance of Mrs. Williams. After dinner Mr. Johnson proposed to Mr. Burney to go up with him into his garret, which being accepted, he found there about five or six Greek folios, a poor writing-desk, and a chair and a half. Johnson, giving to his guest the entire seat, balanced himself on one with only three legs and one arm. Here he gave Mr. Burney Mrs. Williams's history, and showed him some notes on Shakespeare already printed, to prove that he was in earnest. Upon Mr. Burney's opening the first volume at the *Merchant of Venice* he observed to him that he seemed to be more severe on Warburton than on Theobald. 'Oh, poor Tib!' said Johnson, 'he was nearly knocked down to my hands; Warburton stands between me and him.' 'But, sir,' said Mr. Burney, 'You'll have Warburton on your bones, won't you?' 'No, sir; he'll not come out; he'll only growl in his den.' 'But do you think, sir, Warburton is a superior critic to Theobald?' 'Oh, sir, he'll make two-and-fifty Theobalds cut into slices! The worst of Warburton is that he has a rage for saying something when there's nothing to be said.' Mr. Burney then asked him whether he had seen the letter Warburton had written in answer to a pamphlet addressed 'to the most impudent man alive.' He answered in the negative. Mr. Burney told him it was supposed to be written by Mallet. A controversy now raged between the friends of Pope and Bolingbroke, and Warburton and Mallet were the leaders of the several parties. Mr. Burney asked him then if he had seen Warburton's book against Bolingbroke's philosophy! 'No, sir; I have never read Bolingbroke's impiety, and therefore am not interested about its refutation.'"

Goldsmith appears to have resided at No. 6, Wine Office Court from 1760 to 1762, during which period he earned a precarious livelihood by writing for the booksellers.

They still point out Johnson and Goldsmith's favourite seats in the north-east corner of the window of that cozy though utterly unpretentious tavern, the " Cheshire Cheese," in this court.

It was while living in Wine Office Court that Goldsmith is supposed to have partly written that delightful novel, " The Vicar of Wakefield," which he had begun at Canonbury Tower. We like to think that, seated at the " Cheese," he perhaps espied and listened to the worthy but credulous vicar and his gosling son attending to the profound theories of the learned and philosophic but shifty

Mr. Jenkinson. We think now by the window, with a cross light upon his coarse Irish features, and his round prominent brow, we see the watchful poet sit eyeing his prey, secretly enjoying the grandiloquence of the swindler and the admiration of the honest country parson.

"One day," says Mrs. Piozzi, "Johnson was called abruptly from our house at Southwark, after dinner, and, returning in about three hours, said he had been with an enraged author, whose landlady pressed him within doors while the bailiffs beset him without; that he was drinking himself drunk with Madeira to drown care, and fretting over a novel which, when finished, was to be his whole fortune; but he could not get it done for distraction, nor dared he stir out of doors to offer it for sale. Mr. Johnson, therefore," she continues, "sent away the bottle and went to the bookseller, recommending the performance, and devising some immediate relief; which, when he brought back to the writer, the latter called the woman of the house directly to partake of punch and pass their time in merriment. It was not," she concludes, "till ten years after, I dare say, that something in Dr. Goldsmith's behaviour struck me with an idea that he was the very man; and then Johnson confessed that he was so."

"A more scrupulous and patient writer," says the admirable biographer of the poet, Mr. John Forster, "corrects some inaccuracies of the lively little lady, and professes to give the anecdote authentically from Johnson's own exact narration. 'I received one morning,' Boswell represents Johnson to have said, 'a message from poor Goldsmith, that he was in great distress, and, as it was not in his power to come to me, begging that I would come to him as soon as possible. I sent him a guinea, and promised to come to him directly. I accordingly went as soon as I was dressed, and found that his landlady had arrested him for his rent, at which he was in a violent passion. I perceived that he had already changed my guinea, and had got a bottle of Madeira and a glass before him. I put the cork into the bottle, desired he would be calm, and began to talk to him of the means by which he might be extricated. He then told me that he had a novel ready for the press, which he produced to me. I looked into it and saw its merits, told the landlady I should soon return, and, having gone to a bookseller, sold it for £60. I brought Goldsmith the money, and he discharged his rent, not without rating his landlady in a high tone for having used him so ill.'"

The arrest is plainly connected with Newbery's reluctance to make further advances, and of all

Mrs. Fleming's accounts found among Goldsmith's papers, the only one unsettled is that for the summer months preceding the arrest. The manuscript of the novel seems by both statements, in would surely have carried it to the elder Newbery. He did not do this. He went with it to Francis Newbery, the nephew; does not seem to have given a very brilliant account of the "merit" he

GOUGH SQUARE (*see page* 118).

which the discrepancies are not so great but that Johnson himself may be held accountable for them, to have been produced reluctantly, as a last resource; and it is possible, as Mrs. Piozzi intimates, that it was still regarded as unfinished. But if strong adverse reasons had not existed, Johnson had perceived in it—four years after its author's death he told Reynolds that he did not think it would have had much success—and rather with regard to Goldsmith's immediate want than to any confident sense of the value of the copy, asked and obtained the £60. "And, sir," he said afterwards, "a sufficient price, too, when it was sold, for then the fame of Goldsmith had not been elevated, as it afterwards was, by his 'Traveller,' and the bookseller had faint hopes of profit by his bargain. After 'The Traveller,' to be sure, it was accidentally worth more money."

fears which centred in it doubtless mingled on that miserable day with the fumes of the Madeira. In the excitement of putting it to press, which followed immediately after, the nameless novel recedes altogether from the view, but will reappear in due time. Johnson approved the verses more

WINE OFFICE COURT AND THE "CHESHIRE CHEESE" (*see page* 122).

On the poem, meanwhile, the elder Newbery *had* consented to speculate, and this circumstance may have made it hopeless to appeal to him with a second work of fancy. For, on that very day of the arrest, "The Traveller" lay completed in the poet's desk. The dream of eight years, the solace and sustainment of his exile and poverty, verged at last to fulfilment or extinction, and the hopes and

than the novel; read the proof-sheets for his friend; substituted here and there, in more emphatic testimony of general approval, a line of his own; prepared a brief but hearty notice for the *Critical Review*, which was to appear simultaneously with the poem, and, as the day of publication drew near, bade Goldsmith be of good heart.

Oliver Goldsmith came first to London in 1756,

a raw Irish student, aged twenty-eight. He was just fresh from Italy and Switzerland. He had heard Voltaire talk, had won a degree at Louvain or Padua, had been "bear leader" to the stingy nephew of a rich pawnbroker, and had played the flute at the door of Flemish peasants for a draught of beer and a crust of bread. No city of golden pavement did London prove to those worn and dusty feet. Almost a beggar had Oliver been, then an apothecary's journeyman and quack doctor; next a reader of proofs for Richardson, the novelist and printer; after that a tormented and jaded usher at a Peckham school; last, and worst of all, a hack writer of articles for Griffith's *Monthly Review*, then being opposed by Smollett in a rival publication. In Green Arbour Court Goldsmith spent the roughest part of the toilsome years before he became known to the world. There he formed an acquaintance with Johnson and his set, and wrote essays for Smollett's *British Magazine*.

Wine Office Court is supposed to have derived its name from an office where licences to sell wine were formerly issued. "In this court," says Mr. Noble, "once flourished a fig-tree, planted a century ago by the Vicar of St. Bride's, who resided, with an absence of pride suitable, if not common, to Christianity, at No. 12. It was a slip from another exile of a tree, formerly flourishing, in a sooty kind of grandeur, at the sign of the 'Fig Tree,' in Fleet Street. This tree was struck by lightning in 1820, but slips from the growing stump were planted in 1822, in various parts of England."

The old-fashioned and changeless character of the "Cheese," in whose low-roofed and sanded rooms Goldsmith and Johnson have so often hung up their cocked hats and sat down facing each other to a snug dinner, not unattended with punch, has been capitally sketched by a modern essayist, who possesses a thorough knowledge of the physiology of London. In an admirable paper entitled "Brain Street," Mr. George Augustus Sala thus describes Wine Office Court and the "Cheshire Cheese":—

"The vast establishments," says Mr. Sala, "of Messrs. Pewter & Antimony, typefounders (Alderman Antimony was Lord Mayor in the year '46); of Messrs. Quoin, Case, & Chappell, printers to the Board of Blue Cloth; of Messrs. Cutedge & Treecalf, bookbinders; with the smaller industries of Scawper & Tinttool, wood-engravers; and Treacle, Gluepot, & Lampblack, printing-roller makers, are packed together in the upper part of the court as closely as herrings in a cask. The 'Cheese' is at the Brain Street end.

It is a little lop-sided, wedged-up house, that always reminds you, structurally, of a high-shouldered man with his hands in his pockets. It is full of holes and corners and cupboards and sharp turnings; and in ascending the stairs to the tiny smoking-room you must tread cautiously, if you would not wish to be tripped up by plates and dishes, momentarily deposited there by furious waiters. The waiters at the 'Cheese' are always furious. Old customers abound in the comfortable old tavern, in whose sanded-floored eating-rooms a new face is a rarity; and the guests and the waiters are the oldest of familiars. Yet the waiter seldom fails to bite your nose off as a preliminary measure when you proceed to pay him. How should it be otherwise when on that waiter's soul there lies heavy a perpetual sense of injury caused by the savoury odour of steaks, and 'muts' to follow; of cheese-bubbling in tiny tins—the 'specialty' of the house; of floury potatoes and fragrant green peas; of cool salads, and cooler tankards of bitter beer; of extra-creaming stout and 'goes' of Cork and 'rack,' by which is meant gin; and, in the winter-time, of Irish stew and rump-steak pudding, glorious and grateful to every sense? To be compelled to run to and fro with these succulent viands from noon to late at night, without being able to spare time to consume them in comfort—where do waiters dine, and when, and how?—to be continually taking other people's money only for the purpose of handing it to other people—are not these grievances sufficient to cross-grain the temper of the mildest-mannered waiter? Somebody is always in a passion at the 'Cheese:' either a customer, because there is not fat enough on his 'point'-steak, or because there is too much bone in his mutton-chop; or else the waiter is wroth with the cook; or the landlord with the waiter, or the barmaid with all. Yes, there is a barmaid at the 'Cheese,' mewed up in a box not much bigger than a birdcage, surrounded by groves of lemons, 'ones' of cheese, punch-bowls, and cruets of mushroom-catsup. I should not care to dispute with her, lest she should quoit me over the head with a punch-ladle, having a William-the-Third guinea soldered in the bowl.

"Let it be noted in candour that Law finds its way to the 'Cheese' as well as Literature; but the Law is, as a rule, of the non-combatant and, consequently, harmless order. Literary men who have been called to the bar, but do not practise; briefless young barristers, who do not object to mingling with newspaper men; with a sprinkling of retired solicitors (amazing dogs these for old port-wine; the landlord has some of the same bin which served as Hippocrene to Judge Blackstone when he wrote his 'Commentaries')—these make up the legal element of the 'Cheese.' Sharp attorneys in practice are not popular there. There is a legend that a process-server once came in at a back door to serve a writ; but being detected by a waiter, was skilfully edged by that wary retainer into Wine Bottle Court, right past the person on whom he was desirous to inflict the 'Victoria, by the grace, &c.' Once in the court, he was set upon by a mob of inky-faced boys just released from the works of Messrs. Ball, Roller, & Scraper, machine printers, and by the skin of his teeth only escaped being converted into 'pie.'"

Mr. William Sawyer has also written a very admirable sketch of the "Cheese" and its old-fashioned, conservative ways, which we cannot resist quoting :—

"We are a close, conservative, inflexible body —we, the regular frequenters of the 'Cheddar,'" says Mr. Sawyer. "No new-fangled notions, new usages, new customs, or new customers for us. We have our history, our traditions, and our observances, all sacred and inviolable. Look around! There is nothing new, gaudy, flippant, or effeminately luxurious here. A small room with heavily-timbered windows. A low planked ceiling. A huge, projecting fire-place, with a great copper boiler always on the simmer, the sight of which might have roused even old John Willett, of the 'Maypole,' to admiration. High, stiff-backed, inflexible 'settles,' hard and grainy in texture, box off the guests, half-a-dozen each to a table.

Sawdust covers the floor, giving forth that peculiar faint odour which the French avoid by the use of the vine sawdust with its pleasant aroma. The only ornament in which we indulge is a solitary picture over the mantelpiece, a full-length of a now departed waiter, whom in the long past we caused to be painted, by subscription of the whole room, to commemorate his virtues and our esteem. He is depicted in the scene of his triumphs—in the act of giving change to a customer. We sit bolt upright round our tables, waiting, but not impatient. A time-honoured solemnity is about to be observed, and we, the old stagers, is it for us to precipitate it? There are men in this room who have dined here every day for a quarter of a century —aye, the whisper goes that one man did it even on his wedding-day! In all that time the more staid and well-regulated among us have observed a steady regularity of feeding. Five days in the week we have our 'Rotherham steak'—that mystery of mysteries—or our 'chop and chop to follow,' with the indispensable wedge of Cheddar—unless it is preferred stewed or toasted—and on Saturday decorous variety is afforded in a plate of the world-renowned 'Cheddar' pudding. It is of this latter luxury that we are now assembled to partake, and that with all fitting ceremony and observance. As we sit, like pensioners in hall, the silence is broken only by a strange sound, as of a hardly human voice, muttering cabalistic words, 'Ullo mul lum de loodle wumble jum!' it cries, and we know that chops and potatoes are being ordered for some benighted outsider, ignorant of the fact that it is pudding-day."

CHAPTER XI.

FLEET STREET TRIBUTARIES—SHOE LANE.

The First Lucifers—Perkins' Steam Gun—A Link between Shakespeare and Shoe Lane—Florio and his Labours—"Cogers' Hall"—Famous "Cogers"—A Saturday Night's Debate—Gunpowder Alley—Richard Lovelace, the Cavalier Poet—"To Althea, from Prison"—Lilly the Astrologer, and his Knaveries—A Search for Treasure with Davy Ramsay—Hogarth in Harp Alley—The "Society of Sign Painters"—Hudson, the Song Writer—"Jack Robinson"—The Bishop's Residence—Bangor House—A Strange Story of Unstamped Newspapers—Oldbourne Hall—Chatterton's Death—Curious Legend of his Burial—A well-timed Joke.

AT the east corner of Peterborough Court (says Mr. Timbs) was one of the earliest shops for the instantaneous light apparatus, "Hertner's Eupyrion" (phosphorus and oxymuriate matches, to be dipped in sulphuric acid and asbestos), the costly predecessor of the lucifer match. Nearly opposite were the works of Jacob Perkins, the engineer of the steam gun exhibited at the Adelaide Gallery, Strand, and which the Duke of Wellington truly foretold would never be advantageously employed in battle.

One golden thread of association links Shakespeare to Shoe Lane. Slight and frail is the thread, yet it has a double strand. In this narrow side-aisle of Fleet Street, in 1624, lived John Florio, the compiler of our first Italian Dictionary. Now it is more than probable that our great poet knew this industrious Italian, as we shall presently show. Florio was a Waldensian teacher, no doubt driven to England by religious persecution. He taught French and Italian with success at Oxford, and finally was appointed tutor to that generous-minded, hopeful, and unfortunate Prince Henry, son of James I. Florio's "Worlde of Wordes" (a most copious and exact dictionary in Italian and English) was printed in 1598, and published by Arnold Hatfield for Edward Church, and "sold at his shop over against the north door of Paul's Church." It is dedicated to "The Right Honourable Patrons of Virtue, Patterns of Honour, Roger Earle of Rutland, Henrie Earle of Southampton, and Lucie Countess of Bedford." In the dedication, worthy of the fantastic author of "Euphues" himself, the author says:—" My hope springs out of three stems—your Honours' naturall benignitie; your able emploiment of such servitours; and the towardly like-lie-hood of this springall to do you honest service. The first, to vouchsafe all; the second, to accept this; the third, to applie it selfe to the first and second. Of the first, your birth, your place, and your custome; of the second, your studies, your conceits, and your exercise; of the thirde, my endeavours, my proceedings, and my project giues assurance. Your birth, highly noble, more than gentle; your place, above others, as in degree, so in height of bountie, and other vertues; your custome, never wearie of well doing; your studies much in all, most in Italian excellence; your conceits, by understanding others to worke above them in your owne; your exercise, to read what the world's best writers have written, and to speake as they write. My endeavour, to apprehend the best, if not all; my proceedings, to impart my best, first to your Honours, then to all that emploie me; my proiect in this volume to comprehend the best and all, in truth, I acknowledge an entyre debt, not only of my best knowledge, but of all, yea, of more than I know or can, to your bounteous lordship, most noble, most vertuous, and most Honorable Earle of Southampton, in whose paie and patronage I haue liued some yeeres; to whom I owe and vowe the yeeres I haue to live. . . . . Good parts imparted are not empaired; your springs are first to serue yourself, yet may yeelde your neighbours sweete water; your taper is to light you first, and yet it may light your neighbour's candle. . . . . Accepting, therefore, of the childe, I hope your Honors' wish as well to the Father, who to your Honors' all deuoted wisheth meede of your merits, renowne of your vertues, and health

of your persons, humblie with gracious leave kissing your thrice-honored hands, protesteth to continue euer your Honors' most humble and bounden in true seruice, JOHN FLORIO."

And now to connect Florio with Shakespeare. The industrious Savoyard, besides his Dictionary—of great use at a time when the tour to Italy was a necessary completion of a rich gallant's education—translated the Essays of that delightful old Gascon egotist, Montaigne. Now in a copy of Florio's "Montaigne" there was found some years ago one of the very few genuine Shakespeare signatures. Moreover, as Florio speaks of the Earl of Southampton as his steady patron, we may fairly presume that the great poet, who must have been constantly at Southampton's house, often met there the old Italian master. May not the bard in those conversations have perhaps gathered some hints for the details of *Cymbeline, Romeo and Juliet, Othello,* or *The Two Gentlemen of Verona,* and had his attention turned by the old scholar to fresh chapters of Italian story?

No chronicle of Shoe Lane would be complete without some mention of the "Cogers' Discussion Hall," formerly at No. 10. This useful debating society—a great resort for local politicians—was founded by Mr. Daniel Mason as long ago as 1755, and among its most eminent members it glories in the names of John Wilkes, Judge Keogh, Daniel O'Connell, and the eloquent Curran. The word "Coger" does not imply "codger," or a drinker of cogs, but comes from *cogito,* to cogitate. The Grand, Vice-Grand, and secretary were elected on the night of every 14th of June by show of hands. The room was open to strangers, but the members had the right to speak first. The society was Republican in the best sense, for side by side with master tradesmen, shopmen, and mechanics, reporters and young barristers gravely sipped their grog, and abstractedly emitted wreathing columns of tobacco-smoke from their pipes. Mr. J. Parkinson has sketched the little parliament very pleasantly in the columns of a contemporary.

"A long low room," says the writer, "like the saloon of a large steamer. Wainscoat dimmed and ornaments tarnished by tobacco-smoke and the lingering dews of steaming compounds. A room with large niches at each end, like shrines for full-grown saints, one niche containing 'My Grand' in a framework of shabby gold, the other 'My Grand's Deputy' in a bordering more substantial. More than one hundred listeners are waiting patiently for My Grand's utterances this Saturday night, and are whiling away the time philosophically with bibulous and nicotian refreshment. The narrow tables of

the long room are filled with students and per-
formers, and quite a little crowd is congregated
at the door and in a room adjacent until places
can be found for them in the presence-chamber.
'Established 1755' is inscribed on the ornamental
signboard above us, and 'Instituted 1756' on
another signboard near. Dingy portraits of departed Grands and Deputies decorate the walls.
Punctually at nine My Grand opens the proceedings amid profound silence. The deputy buries
himself in his newspaper, and maintains as profound a calm as the Speaker 'in another place.'
The most perfect order is preserved. The Speaker
or deputy, who seems to know all about it, rolls
silently in his chair : he is a fat dark man, with a
small and rather sleepy eye, such as I have seen
come to the surface and wink lazily at the fashionable people clustered round a certain tank in the
Zoological Gardens. He re-folds his newspaper
from time to time until deep in the advertisements.
The waiters silently remove empty tumblers and
tankards, and replace them full. But My Grand
commands profound attention from the room,
and a neighbour, who afterwards proved a perfect Boanerges in debate, whispered to us concerning his vast attainments and high literary
position.

"This chieftain of the Thoughtful Men is, we
learn, the leading contributor to a newspaper of
large circulation, and, under his signature of
'Locksley Hall,' rouses the sons of toil to a sense
of the dignity and rights of labour, and exposes the
profligacy and corruption of the rich to the extent
of a column and a quarter every week. A shrewd,
hard-headed man of business, with a perfect knowledge of what he had to do, and with a humorous
twinkle of the eye, My Grand went steadily through
his work, and gave the Thoughtful Men his epitome
of the week's intelligence. It seemed clear
that the Cogers had either not read the newspapers, or liked to be told what they already knew.
They listened with every token of interest to facts
which had been published for days, and it seemed
difficult to understand how a debate could be carried on when the text admitted so little dispute.
But we sadly underrated the capacity of the orators
near us. The sound of My Grand's last sentence
had not died out when a fresh-coloured, rather
aristocratic-looking elderly man, whose white hair
was carefully combed and smoothed, and whose
appearance and manner suggested a very different
arena to the one he waged battle in now, claimed
the attention of the Thoughtful ones. Addressing
'Mee Grand' in the rich and unctuous tones which
a Scotchman and Englishman might try for in vain,

this orator proceeded, with every profession of
respect, to contradict most of the chief's statements,
to ridicule his logic, and to compliment him with
much irony on his overwhelming goodness to the
society 'to which I have the honour to belong.
Full of that hard *northern* logic' (much emphasis
on 'northern,' which was warmly accepted as a hit
by the room)—'that hard northern logic which
demonstrates everything to its own satisfaction ;
abounding in that talent which makes you, sir, a
leader in politics, a guide in theology, and generally
an instructor of the people ; yet even you, sir, are
perhaps, if I may say so, somewhat deficient in the
lighter graces of pathos and humour. Your
speech, sir, has commanded the attention of the
room. Its close accuracy of style, its exactitude
of expression, its consistent argument, and its
generally transcendant ability will exercise, I doubt
not, an influence which will extend far beyond this
chamber, filled as this chamber is by gentlemen of
intellect and education, men of the time, who both
think and feel, and who make their feelings and
their thoughts felt by others. Still, sir,' and the
orator smiles the smile of ineffable superiority,
'grateful as the members of the society you have
so kindly alluded to ought to be for your countenance and patronage, it needed not' (turning to
the Thoughtful Men generally, with a sarcastic
smile)—'it needed not even Mee Grand's enco-
miums to endear this society to its people, and to
strengthen their belief in its efficacy in time of
trouble, its power to help, to relieve, and to
assuage. No, Mee Grand, an authoritee whose
dictum even you will accept without dispute—mee
Lord Macaulee—that great historian whose un-
dying pages record those struggles and trials of
constitutionalism in which the Cogers have borne
no mean part—me Lord Macaulee mentions, with
a respect and reverence not exceeded by Mee
Grand's utterances of to-night' (more smiles of
mock humility to the room) 'that great association
which claims me as an unworthy son. We could,
therefore, have dispensed with the recognition
given us by Mee Grand ; we could afford to wait
our time until the nations of the earth are fused by
one common wish for each other's benefit, when
the principles of Cogerism are spread over the
civilised world, when justice reigns supreme, and
loving-kindness takes the place of jealousy and
hate.' We looked round the room while these
fervid words were being triumphantly rolled forth,
and were struck with the calm impassiveness of the
listeners. There seemed to be no partisanship
either for the speaker or the Grand. Once, when
the former was more than usually emphatic in his

denunciations, a tall pale man, with a Shakespeare forehead, rose suddenly, with a determined air, as if about to fiercely interrupt; but it turned out he only wanted to catch the waiter's eye, and this done, he pointed silently to his empty glass, and remarked, in a hoarse whisper, 'Without sugar, as before.'"

Gunpowder Alley, a side-twig of Shoe Lane, leads us to the death-bed of an unhappy poet, poor Richard Lovelace, the Cavalier, who, dying here only to waste his fortune in Royalist plots. He served in the French army, raised a regiment for Louis XIII., and was left for dead at Dunkirk. On his return to England, he found Lucy Sacheverell—his "Lucretia," the lady of his love—married, his death having been reported. All went ill. He was again imprisoned, grew penniless, had to borrow, and fell into a consumption from despair for love and loyalty. "Having consumed all his estate," says Anthony Wood, "he grew very

COGERS' HALL, FROM AN OLD PRINT (see page 124).

two years before the Stuart Restoration, in a very mean lodging, was buried at the west end of St. Bride's Church. The son of a knight, and brought up at Oxford, Anthony Wood describes the gallant and hopeful lad at sixteen, when presented at the Court of Charles I., as "the most amiable and beautiful youth that eye ever beheld. A person, also, of innate modesty, virtue, and courtly deportment, which made him then, but specially after, when he retired to the great city, much admired and adored by the female sex." Presenting a daring petition from Kent in favour of the king, the Cavalier poet was thrown into prison by the Long Parliament, and was released melancholy, which at length brought him into a consumption; became very poor in body and purse, was the object of charity, went in ragged clothes (whereas when he was in his glory he wore cloth of gold and silver), and mostly lodged in obscure and dirty places, more befitting the worst of beggars than poorest of servants." There is a doubt, however, as to whether Lovelace died in such abject poverty, poor, dependent, and unhappy as he might have been. Lovelace's verse is often strained, affected, and wanting in judgment; but at times he mounts a bright-winged Pegasus, and with plume and feather flying, tosses his hand up, gay and chivalrous as Rupert's bravest. His verses to Lucy

OLDBOURNE HALL, SHOE LANE, 1823. (See page 134.)

Sacheverell, on leaving her for the French camp, are worthy of Montrose himself. The last two lines—

> " I could not love thee, dear, so much,
> Lov'd I not honour more "—

contain the thirty-nine articles of a soldier's faith. And what Wildrake could have sung in the Gate House or the Compter more gaily of liberty than Lovelace, when he wrote,—

> " Stone walls do not a prison make,
>   Nor iron bars a cage ;
>   Minds innocent and quiet take
>   That for a hermitage.
>   If I have freedom in my love,
>   And in my soul am free,
>   Angels alone, that soar above,
>   Enjoy such liberty " ?

Whenever we read the stanza that begins,—

> " When love, with unconfinèd wings,
>   Hovers within my gates,
>   And my divine Althea brings,
>   To whisper at my grates,"

the scene rises before us ; we see a fair pale face, with its aureole of golden hair gleaming between the rusty bars of the prison door, and the worn visage of the wounded Cavalier turning towards it as the flower turns to the sun. And surely Master Wildrake himself, with his glass of sack half-way to his mouth, never put it down to sing a finer Royalist stave than Lovelace's " To Althea, from Prison,"—

> " When, linnet-like, confined, I
>   With shriller note shall sing
>   The mercy, sweetness, majesty,
>   And glories of my king ;
>   When I shall voice aloud how good
>   He is, how great should be,
>   Th' enlarged winds that curl the flood
>   Know no such liberty."

In the Cromwell times there resided in Gunpowder Alley, probably to the scorn of poor dying Lovelace, that remarkable cheat and early medium, Lilly the astrologer, the "Sidrophel" of "Hudibras." This rascal, who supplied the King and Parliament alternately with equally veracious predictions, was in youth apprenticed to a mantua-maker in the Strand, and on his master's death married his widow. Lilly studied astrology under one Evans, an ex-clergyman, who told fortunes in Gunpowder Alley. Besotted by the perusal of Cornelius Agrippa and other such trash, Lilly found fools plenty, and the stars, though potent in their spheres, unable to contradict his lies. This artful cheat was consulted as to the most propitious day and hour for Charles's escape from Carisbrook, and was even

sent for by the Puritan generals to encourage their men before Colchester. Lilly was a spy of the Parliament, yet at the Restoration professed to disclose the fact that Cornet Joyce had betrayed Charles. Whenever his predictions or his divining-rod failed, he always attributed his failures, as the modern spiritualists, the successors of the old wizards, still conveniently do, to want of faith in the spectators. By means of his own shrewdness, rather than by stellar influence, Lilly obtained many useful friends, among whom we may specially particularise the King of Sweden, Lenthal the Puritan Speaker, Bulstrode, Whitelocke (Cromwell's Minister), and the learned but credulous Elias Ashmole. Lilly's Almanac, the predecessor of Moore's and Zadkiel's, was carried on by him for six-and-thirty years. He claimed to be a special *protégé* of an angel called Salmonæus, and to have a more than bowing acquaintance with Salmael and Malchidael, the guardian angels of England. Among his works are his autobiography, and his " Observations on the Life and Death of Charles, late King of England." The remainder of his effusions are pretentious, mystical, muddle-headed rubbish, half nonsense, half knavery ; as " The White King's Prophecy," " Supernatural Light," " The Starry Messenger," and " Annus Tenebrosus, or the Black Year." The rogue's starry mantle descended on his adopted son, a tailor, whom he named Merlin Junior. The credulity of the atheistical times of Charles II. is equalled only by that of our own day.

Lilly himself, in his amusing, half-knavish autobiography, has described his first introduction to the Welsh astrologer of Gunpowder Alley :—

" It happened," he says, " on one Sunday, 1632, as myself and a justice of peace's clerk were, before service, discoursing of many things, he chanced to say that such a person was a great scholar—nay, so learned that he could make an almanac, which to me then was strange ; one speech begot another, till, at last, he said he could bring me acquainted with one Evans, in Gunpowder Alley, who had formerly lived in Staffordshire, that was an excellent wise man, and studied the black art. The same week after we went to see Mr. Evans. When we came to his house, he, having been drunk the night before, was upon his bed, if it be lawful to call that a bed whereon he then lay. He roused up himself, and after some compliments he was content to instruct me in astrology. I attended his best opportunities for seven or eight weeks, in which time I could set a figure perfectly. Books he had not any, except Haly, ' De Judiciis Astrorum,' and Orriganus's ' Ephemerides ;' so that as often as I entered his house I thought I was in the wilderness. Now, something of the man. He was by birth a Welshman, a master of arts, and in sacred orders. He had formerly had a cure of souls in Staffordshire, but now was come to try his fortunes at London, being in a manner enforced to fly, for some offences very scandalous committed by him in those parts where he had lately lived; for he gave judgment upon things lost, the only shame of astrology. He was the most saturnine person my eye ever beheld, either before I practised or since; of a middle stature, broad forehead, beetle-browed, thick shoulders, flat-nosed, full lips, down-looked, black, curling, stiff hair, splay-footed. To give him his right, he had the most piercing judgment naturally upon a figure of theft, and many other questions, that I ever met withal; yet for money he would willingly give contrary judgments; was much addicted to debauchery, and then very abusive and quarrelsome; seldom without a black eye or one mischief or other. This is the same Evans who made so many antimonial cups, upon the sale whereof he chiefly subsisted. He understood Latin very well, the Greek tongue not all; he had some arts above and beyond astrology, for he was well versed in the nature of spirits, and had many times used the circular way of invocating, as in the time of our familiarity he told me."

One of Lilly's most impudent attempts to avail himself of demoniacal assistance was when he dug for treasure (like Scott's Dousterswivel) with David Ramsay, one dark and stormy night, in the cloisters at Westminster.

"Davy Ramsay," says the arch-rogue, "his majesty's clockmaker, had been informed that there was a great quantity of treasure buried in the cloisters of Westminster Abbey; he acquaints Dean Williams therewith, who was also then Bishop of Lincoln; the dean gave him liberty to search after it, with this proviso, that if any was discovered his church should have a share of it. Davy Ramsay finds out one John Scott,* who pretended the use of the Mosaical rods, to assist him therein. I was desired to join with him, unto which I consented. One winter's night Davy Ramsay,† with several gentlemen, myself, and Scott, entered the cloisters; upon the west side of the cloisters the rods turned one over another, an argument that the treasure was there. The labourers digged at least six feet deep, and then we met with a coffin, but in regard it was not heavy, we did not open, which we after-

* "This Scott lived in Pudding Lane, and had some time been a page (or such-like) to the Lord Norris."

† "Davy Ramsay brought a half-quartern sack to put the treasure in."

wards much repented. From the cloisters we went into the abbey church, where upon a sudden (there being no wind when we began) so fierce, so high, so blustering and loud a wind did rise, that we verily believed the west-end of the church would have fallen upon us; our rods would not move at all; the candles and torches, all but one, were extinguished, or burned very dimly. John Scott, my partner, was amazed, looked pale, knew not what to think or do, until I gave directions and command to dismiss the demons, which when done all was quiet again, and each man returned unto his lodging late, about twelve o'clock at night. I could never since be induced to join with any in such-like actions.

"The true miscarriage of the business was by reason of so many people being present at the operation, for there was about thirty—some laughing, others deriding us; so that if we had not dismissed the demons, I believe most part of the abbey church had been blown down. Secrecy and intelligent operators, with a strong confidence and knowledge of what they are doing, are best for this work."

In the last century, when every shop had its sign and London streets were so many out-of-door picture-galleries, a Dutchman named Vandertrout opened a manufactory of these pictorial advertisements in Harp Alley, Shoe Lane, a dirty passage now laid open to the sun and air on the east of the new St. Bride's Street, running from Ludgate Circus to Holborn. In ridicule of the spurious black, treacly old masters then profusely offered for sale by the picture-dealers of the day, Hogarth and Bonnell Thornton opened an exhibition of shop-signs. In Nicholls and Stevens' "Life of Hogarth" there is a full and racy account of this sarcastic exhibition:—"At the entrance of the large passage-room was written, 'N.B. That the merit of the *modern masters* may be fairly examined into, it has been thought proper to place some admired works of the most eminent *old masters* in this room, and along the passage through the yard.' Among these are 'A Barge' in still life, by Vandertrout. He cannot be properly called an English artist; but not being sufficiently encouraged in his own country, he left Holland with William the Third, and was the first artist who settled in Harp Alley. An original half-length of Camden, the great historian and antiquary, in his herald's coat; by Vandertrout. As this artist was originally colour-grinder to Hans Holbein, it is conjectured there are some of that great master's touches in this piece. 'Nobody, *alias* Somebody,' a character. (The figure of an officer, all head, arms, legs, and thighs. This piece has a very odd effect, being so drolly executed that you do not miss the body.) 'Somebody, *alias* Nobody,' a caricature, its companion; both these by Hagarty. (A rosy figure, with a little head and a huge body, whose belly sways over almost quite down to his shoe-buckles. By the staff in his hand, it appears to be intended to represent a constable. It might else have been intended for an eminent justice of peace.) 'A Perspective View of Billingsgate, or Lectures on Elocution;' and 'The True Robin Hood Society, a Conversation or Lectures on Elocution,' its companion; these two by Barnsley. (These two strike at a famous lecturer on elocution and the reverend projector of a rhetorical academy, are admirably conceived and executed, and—the latter more especially—almost worthy the hand of Hogarth. They are full of a variety of droll figures, and seem, indeed, to be the work of a great master struggling to suppress his superiority of genius, and endeavouring to paint *down* to the common style and manner of sign-painting.)

"At the entrance to the *grand room :*—'The Society of Sign Painters take this opportunity of refuting a most malicious suggestion that their exhibition is designed as a ridicule on the exhibitions of the Society for the Encouragement of Arts, &c., and of the artists. They intend theirs only as an appendix or (in the style of painters) a companion to the other. There is nothing in their collection which will be understood by any candid person as a reflection on anybody, or any body of men. They are not in the least prompted by any mean jealousy to depreciate the merit of their brother artists. Animated by the same public spirit, their sole view is to convince foreigners, as well as their own blinded countrymen, that however inferior this nation may be unjustly deemed in other branches of the polite arts, the palm for sign-painting must be ceded to *us*, the Dutch themselves not excepted.' Projected in 1762 by Mr. Bonnel Thornton, of festive memory; but I am informed that he contributed no otherwise towards this display than by a few touches of chalk. Among the heads of distinguished personages, finding those of the King of Prussia and the Empress of Hungary, he changed the cast of their eyes, so as to make them leer significantly at each other. Note.—These (which in the catalogue are called an original portrait of the present Emperor of Prussia and ditto of the Empress Queen of Hungary, its antagonist) were two old signs of the "Saracen's Head" and Queen Anne. Under the first was written 'The Zarr,' and under the other 'The Empress Quean.' They were lolling their tongues

out at each other; and over their heads ran a wooden label, inscribed, 'The present state of Europe.'

"In 1762 was published, in quarto, undated, 'A Catalogue of the Original Paintings, Busts, and Carved Figures, &c. &c., now Exhibiting by the Society of Sign-painters, at the Large Room, the upper end of Bow Street, Covent Garden, nearly opposite the Playhouse.'"

At 98, Shoe Lane lived, now some sixty years ago, a tobacconist named Hudson, a great humorist, a fellow of infinite fancy, and the writer of half the comic songs that once amused festive London. Hudson afterwards, we believe, kept the "Kean's Head" tavern, in Russell Court, Drury Lane, and about 1830 had a shop of some kind or other in Museum Street, Bloomsbury. Hudson was one of those professional song-writers and vocalists who used to be engaged to sing at such supper-rooms and theatrical houses as Offley's, in Henrietta Street (north-west end), Covent Garden; the "Coal Hole," in the Strand; and the "Cider Cellars," Maiden Lane. Sitting among the company, Hudson used to get up at the call of the chairman and "chant" one of his lively and really witty songs. The platform belongs to "Evans's" and a later period. Hudson was at his best long after Captain Morris's day, and at the time when Moore's melodies were popular. Many of the melodies Hudson parodied very happily, and with considerable tact and taste. Many of Hudson's songs, such as "Jack Robinson" (infinitely funnier than most of Dibdin's), became coined into catch-words and street sayings of the day. "Before you could say Jack Robinson" is a phrase, still current, derived from this highly droll song. The verse in which Jack Robinson's "engaged" apologises for her infidelity is as good as anything that James Smith ever wrote. To the returned sailor,—

" Says the lady, says she, 'I've changed my state.'
    'Why, you don't mean,' says Jack, 'that you've got a mate ?
You know you promised me.' Says she, 'I couldn't wait,
For no tidings could I gain of you, Jack Robinson.
And somebody one day came to me and said
That somebody else had somewhere read,
In some newspaper, that you was somewhere dead.'—
' I've not been dead at all,' says Jack Robinson."

Another song, "The Spider and the Fly," is still often sung; and "Going to Coronation" is by no means forgotten in Yorkshire. "There was a Man in the West Countrie" figures in most current collections of songs. Hudson particularly excelled in stage-Irishman songs, which were then popular; and some of these, particularly one that ends with the refrain, "My brogue and my blarney and bothering ways," have real humour in them. Many of these Irish songs were written for and sung ·by the late Mr. Fitzwilliam, the comedian, as others of Hudson's songs were by Mr. Rayner. Collectors of comic ditties will not readily forget "Walker, the Twopenny Postman," or "The Dogs'-meat Man" —rough caricatures of low life, unstained by the vulgarity of many of the modern music-hall ditties. In the motto to one of his collections of poems, Hudson borrows from Churchill an excuse for the rough, humorous effusions that he scattered broadcast over the town,—

"When the mad fit comes on, I seize the pen,
　Rough as they run, the rapid thoughts set down ;
Rough as they run, discharge them on the town.
Hence rude, unfinished brats, before their time,
Are born into this idle world of rhyme ;
And the poor slattern muse is brought to bed,
With all her imperfections on her head."

We subjoin a very good specimen of Hudson's songs, from his once very popular "Coronation of William and Adelaide" (1830), which, we think, will be allowed to fully justify our praise of the author :—

"And when we got to town, quite tired,
　The bells all rung, the guns they fired,
　The people looking all bemired,
　　　　In one conglomeration.
Soldiers red, policemen blue,
Horse-guards, foot-guards, and blackguards too,
Beef-eaters, dukes, and Lord knows who,
　　　　To see the Coronation.

"While Dolly bridled up, so proud,
　At us the people laughed aloud ;
　Dobbin stood in thickest crowd,
　　　　Wi' quiet resignation.
To move again he warn't inclined ;
'Here's a chap !' says one behind,
'He's brought an old horse, lame and blind,
　　　　To see the Coronation'

"Dolly cried, 'Oh ! dear, oh ! dear,
　I wish I never had come here,
　To suffer every jibe and jeer,
　　　　In such a situation.'
While so busy, she and I
To get a little ease did try,
By goles ! the king and queen went by,
　　　　And all the Coronation.

"I struggled hard, and Dolly cried ;
　And tho' to help myself I tried,
　We both were carried with the tide,
　　　　Against our inclination.
'The reign's begun !' folks cried ; ''tis true ;'
'Sure,' said Dolly, 'I think so too ;
'The rain's begun, for I'm wet thro',
　　　　All through the Coronation.'

"We bade good-bye to Lunnun town ;
　The king and queen they gain'd a crown ;
　Dolly spoilt her bran-new gown,
　　　　To her mortification.
I'll drink our king and queen wi' glee,
In home-brewed ale, and so will she ;
But Doll and I ne'er want to see
　　　　Another Coronation."

Our English bishops, who had not the same taste as the Cistercians in selecting pleasant places for their habitations, seem during the Middle Ages to have much affected the neighbourhood of Fleet Street. Ely Place still marks the residence of one rich prelate. In Chichester Rents we have already met with the humble successors of the netmaker of Galilee. In a siding on the north-west side of Shoe Lane the Bishops of Bangor lived, with their spluttering and choleric Welsh retinue, as early as 1378. Recent improvements have laid open the miserable "close" called Bangor Court, that once glowed with the reflections of scarlet hoods and jewelled copes ; and a schoolhouse of bastard Tudor architecture, with sham turrets and flimsy mullioned windows, now occupies the site of the Christian prelate's old palace. Bishop Dolben, who died in 1633 (Charles I.), was the last Welsh bishop who deigned to reside in a neighbourhood from which wealth and fashion was fast ebbing. Brayley says that a part of the old episcopal garden, where the ecclesiastical subjects of centuries had been discussed by shaven men and frocked scholars, still existed in 1759 (George II.) ; and, indeed, as Mr. Jesse records, even as late as 1828 (George IV.) a portion of the old mansion, once redolent with the stupefying incense of the unreformed Church, still lingered. Old Bangor House, according to Mr. J. T. Smith, is mentioned in the Patent Rolls as early as Edward III. The lawyers' barbarous dog-Latin of an old deed describe "unum messuag, unum placeam terræ, ac unam gardniam, cum aliis edificiis," in Shoe Lane, London. In 1647 (Charles I.) Sir John Birkstead purchased of the Parliamentary trustees the bishop's lands, that had probably been confiscated, to build streets upon the site. But Sir John went on paving the old place, and never built at all. Cromwell's Act of 1657, to check the increase of London, entailed a special exemption in his favour. At the Restoration the land returned to its Welsh bishop ; but it had degenerated : the palace was divided into several residences, and mean buildings sprang up like fungi around it. A drawing by Malcolm, early in the century, shows us its two Tudor windows. Latterly it became divided into wretched rooms, and two or three hundred poor people, chiefly Irish, herded in them. The house was entirely pulled down in the autumn of 1828.

Mr. Grant, that veteran of the press, tells a capital story, in his "History of the Newspaper Press," about one of the early vendors of unstamped newspapers in Shoe Lane :—

a time to elude their vigilance ; and in order to prevent the seizure of his paper, he resorted to an expedient which was equally ingenious and laughable. Close by his little shop in Shoe Lane there was an undertaker, whose business, as might be inferred from the neighbourhood, as well as from

BANGOR HOUSE, 1818 (see page 131).

"*Cleave's Police Gazette*," says Mr. Grant, "consisted chiefly of reports of police cases. It certainly was a newspaper to all intents and purposes, and was ultimately so declared to be in a court of law by a jury. But in the meantime, while the action was pending, the police had instructions to arrest Mr. John Cleave, the proprietor, and seize all the copies of the paper as they came out of his office in Shoe Lane. He contrived for

his personal appearance and the homeliness of his shop, was exclusively among the lower and poorer classes of the community. With him Mr. Cleave made an arrangement to construct several coffins of the plainest and cheapest kind, for purposes which were fully explained. The 'undertaker,' whose ultra-republican principles were in perfect unison with those of Mr. Cleave, not only heartily undertook the work, but did so on terms so moderate that he would not ask for nor accept any profit. He, indeed, could imagine no higher nor holier duty than that of assisting in the dissemination of a paper which boldly and energetically preached the extinction of the aristocracy and the perfect equality in social position, and in property too, of all classes of the community. Accordingly the coffins, with a rudeness in make and material which were in perfect keeping with the purpose to which they were to be applied, were got ready; and Mr. Cleave, in the dead of night,

readiness to render a similar service to Mr. Cleave and the cause of red Republicanism when the next *Gazette* appeared.

"In this way Mr. Cleave contrived for some time to elude the vigilance of the police and to sell about 50,000 copies weekly of each impression of his paper. But the expedient, ingenious and eminently successful as it was for a time, failed at last. The people in Shoe Lane and the neighbourhood began to be surprised and alarmed at the number of funerals, as they believed them to be, which the

OLD ST. DUNSTAN'S CHURCH, 1814 (*see page* 135).

got them filled with thousands of his *Gazettes*. It had been arranged beforehand that particular houses in various parts of the town should be in readiness to receive them with blinds down, as if some relative had been dead, and was about to be borne away to the house appointed for all living. The deal coffin was opened, and the contents were taken out, tied up in a parcel so as to conceal from the prying curiosity of any chance person that they were *Cleave's Police Gazettes*, and then sent off to the railway stations most convenient for their transmission to the provinces. The coffins after this were returned in the middle of next night to the 'undertaker's' in Shoe Lane, there to be in

departure of so many coffins from the 'undertaker's' necessarily implied. The very natural conclusion to which they came was, that this supposed sudden and extensive number of deaths could only be accounted for on the assumption that some fatal epidemic had visited the neighbourhood, and there made itself a local habitation. The parochial authorities, responding to the prevailing alarm, questioned the 'undertaker' friend and fellow-labourer of Mr. Cleave as to the causes of his sudden and extensive accession of business in the coffin-making way; and the result of the close questions put to him was the discovery of the whole affair. It need hardly be added that an immediate and complete collapse took place in Mr. Cleave's business, so far as his *Police Gazette* was concerned. Not another number of the publication ever made its appearance, while the coffin-trade of the 'undertaker' all at once returned to its normal proportions."

On the east side of Shoe Lane formerly stood an antiquated building, called Oldbourne Hall, of which we give an engraving on page 127. The edifice is mentioned by Stow in his "Survey of London" (1598) as being even at that time "letten out into tenements."

One especially sad association attaches to Shoe Lane, and that is the burial in the workhouse graveyard (the site of the late Farringdon Market) of that unhappy child of genius, Chatterton the poet. In August, 1770, the poor lad, who had come from Bristol full of hope and ambition to make his fortune in London by his pen, broken-hearted and maddened by disappointment, destroyed himself in his mean garret-lodging in Brooke Street, Holborn, by swallowing arsenic. Mr. John Dix, his very unscrupulous biographer, has noted down a curious legend about the possible removal of the poet's corpse from London to Bristol, which, doubtful as it is, is at least interesting as a possibility :—

"I found," says Mr. Dix, "that Mrs. Stockwell, of Peter Street, wife of Mr. Stockwell, a basket-maker, was the person who had communicated to Sir R. Wilmot her grounds for believing Chatterton to have been so interred ; and on my requesting her to repeat to me what she knew of that affair, she commenced by informing me that at ten years of age she was a scholar of Mrs. Chatterton, his mother, where she was taught plain work, and remained with her until she was near twenty years of age ; that she slept with her, and found her kind and motherly, insomuch that there were many things which in moments of affliction Mrs. C. communicated to her, that she would not have wished to have been generally known ; and among others, she often repeated how happy she was that her unfortunate son lay buried in Redcliff, through the kind attention of a friend or relation in London, who, after the body had been cased in a parish shell, had it properly secured and sent to her by the waggon ; that when it arrived it was opened, and the corpse found to be black and half putrid (having been burst with the motion of the carriage, or from some other cause), so that it became necessary to inter it speedily; and that it was early interred by Phillips, the sexton, who was of her family. That the effect of the loss of her son was a nervous disorder, which never quitted her, and she was often seen weeping at the bitter remembrance of her misfortune. She described the poet as having been sharp-tempered, but that it was soon over ; and she often said he had cost her many uneasy hours, from the apprehension she entertained of his going mad, as he was accustomed to remain fixed for above an hour at a time quite motionless, and then he would snatch up a pen and write incessantly ; but he was always, she added, affectionate. . . . .

"In addition to this, Mrs. Stockwell told the writer that the grave was on the right-hand side of the lime-tree, middle paved walk, in Redcliff Churchyard, about twenty feet from the father's grave, which is, she says, in the paved walk, and where now Mrs. Chatterton and Mrs. Newton, her daughter, also lie. Also, that Mrs. Chatterton gave a person leave to bury his child over her son's coffin, and was much vexed to find that he afterwards put the stone over it, which, when Chatterton was buried, had been taken up for the purpose of digging the grave, and set against the church-wall ; that afterwards, when Mr. Hutchinson's or Mr. Taylor's wife died, they buried her also in the same grave, and put this stone over with a new inscription. (Query, did he erase the first, or turn the stone ?—as this might lead to a discovery of the spot.) . . . .

"Being referred to Mrs. Jane Phillips, of Rolls Alley, Rolls Lane, Great Gardens, Temple Parish (who is sister to that Richard Phillips who was sexton at Redcliff Church in the year 1772), she informed me that his widow and a daughter were living in Cathay ; the widow is sexton, a Mr. Perrin, of Colston's Parade, acting for her. She remembers Chatterton having been at his father's school, and that he always called Richard Phillips, her brother, 'uncle,' and was much liked by him. He liked him for his spirit, and there can be no doubt he would have risked the privately burying him on that account. When she heard he was gone to London she was sorry to hear it, for all loved him, and thought he could get no good there.

"Soon after his death her brother, R. Phillips, told her that poor Chatterton had killed himself ; on which she said she would go to Madam Chatterton's, to know the rights of it ; but that he forbade her, and said, if she did so he should be sorry he had told her. She, however, did go, and asking if it was true that he was dead, Mrs. Chatterton began to weep bitterly, saying, 'My son indeed is dead !' and when she asked her where he was buried, she replied, 'Ask me nothing ; he is dead and buried.'"

Poppin's Court (No. 109) marks the site of the ancient hostel (hotel) of the Abbots of Cirencester —though what they did there, when they ought to have been on their knees in their own far-away Gloucestershire abbey, history does not choose to record. The sign of their inn was the "Poppin-gaye" (popinjay, parrot), and in 1602 (last year of Elizabeth) the alley was called Poppingay Alley. That excellent man Van Mildert (then a poor curate, living in Ely Place, afterwards Bishop of Durham—a prelate remarkable for this above all his many other Christian virtues, that he was not proud) was once driven into this alley with a young barrister friend by a noisy illumination-night crowd. The street boys began firing a volley of squibs at the young curate, who found all hope of escape barred, and dreaded the pickpockets, who take rapid advantage of such temporary embarrassments; but his good-natured exclamation, "Ah! here you are, popping away in Poppin's Court!" so pleased the crowd that they at once laughingly opened a passage for him. "Sic me servavit Apollo," he used afterwards to add when telling the story.

CHAPTER XII.

FLEET STREET TRIBUTARIES—SOUTH.

Worthy Mr. Fisher—Lamb's Wednesday Evenings—Persons one would wish to have seen—Ram Alley—Serjeants' Inn—The *Daily News*— "Memory" Woodfall—A Mug-House Riot—Richardson's Printing Office—Fielding and Richardson—Johnson's Estimate of Richardson—. Hogarth and Richardson's Guest—An Egotist Rebuked—The King's "Housewife"—Caleb Colton: his Life, Works, and Sentiments.

FALCON COURT, Fleet Street, took its name from an inn which bore the sign of the "Falcon." This passage formerly belonged to a gentleman named Fisher, who, out of gratitude to the Cordwainers' Company, bequeathed it to them by will. His gratitude is commonly said to have arisen from the number of good dinners that the Company had given him. However this may be, the Cordwainers are the present owners of the estate, and are under the obligation of having a sermon preached annually at the neighbouring church of St. Dunstan, on the 10th of July, when certain sums are given to the poor. Formerly it was the custom to drink sack in the church to the pious memory of Mr. Fisher, but this appears to have been discontinued for a considerable period. This Fisher was a jolly fellow, if all the tales are true which are related of him, as, besides the sack-drinking, he stipulated that the Cordwainers should give a grand feast on the same day yearly to all their tenants. What a quaint picture might be made of the churchwardens in the old church drinking to the memory of Mr. Fisher! Wynkyn de Worde, the father of printing in England, lived in Fleet Street, at his messuage or inn known by the sign of the Falcon. Whether it was the inn that stood on the site of Falcon Court is not known with certainty, but most probably it was.

Charles Lamb came to 16, Mitre Court Buildings in 1800, after leaving Southampton Buildings, and remained in that quiet harbour out of Fleet Street till 1809, when he removed to Inner Temple Lane.

It was whilst Lamb was residing in Mitre Court Buildings that those Wednesday evenings of his were in their glory. In two of Mr. Hazlitt's papers are graphic pictures of these delightful Wednesdays and the Wednesday men, and admirable notes of several choice conversations. There is a curious sketch in one of a little tilt between Coleridge and Holcroft, which must not be omitted. "Coleridge was riding the high German horse, and demonstrating the 'Categories of the Transcendental Philosophy' to the author of *The Road to Ruin*, who insisted on his knowledge of German and German metaphysics, having read the 'Critique of Pure Reason' in the original. 'My dear Mr. Holcroft,' said Coleridge, in a tone of infinitely provoking conciliation, 'you really put me in mind of a sweet pretty German girl of about fifteen, in the Hartz Forest, in Germany, and who one day, as I was reading "The Limits of the Knowable and the Unknowable," the profoundest of all his works, with great attention, came behind my chair, and leaning over, said, "What! you read Kant? Why, I, that am a German born, don't understand him!"' This was too much to bear, and Holcroft, starting up, called out, in no measured tone, 'Mr. Coleridge, you are the most eloquent man I ever met with, and the most troublesome with your eloquence.' Phillips held the cribbage-peg, that was to mark the game, suspended in his hand, and the whist-table was silent for a moment. I saw Holcroft downstairs, and on coming to the landing-place in Mitre Court he stopped me to observe that he thought Mr. Coleridge a very clever man, with a great command of language, but that he feared he did not always affix very proper ideas to the words he used. After he was gone we had our laugh out, and went on with the argument on 'The Nature of Reason, the Imagination, and the Will.' . . . . It would make a supplement to the 'Biographia Literaria,' in a volume and a half, octavo."

It was at one of these Wednesdays that Lamb started his famous question as to persons " one would wish to have seen." It was a suggestive topic, and proved a fruitful one. Mr. Hazlitt, who was there, has left an account behind him of the kind of talk which arose out of this hint, so lightly thrown out by the author of " Elia," and it is worth giving in his own words :—

" On the question being started, Ayrton said, 'I suppose the two first persons you would choose to see would be the two greatest names in English literature, Sir Isaac Newton and Locke?' In this Ayrton, as usual, reckoned without his host. Every one burst out a-laughing at the expression of Lamb's face, in which impatience was restrained by courtesy. 'Y—yes, the greatest names,' he stammered out hastily ; 'but they were not persons —not persons.' 'Not persons?' said Ayrton, looking wise and foolish at the same time, afraid his triumph might be premature. 'That is,' rejoined Lamb, 'not characters, you know. By Mr. Locke and Sir Isaac Newton you mean the "Essay on the Human Understanding" and "Principia," which we have to this day. Beyond their contents, there is nothing personally interesting in the men. But what we want to see any one *bodily* for is when there is something peculiar, striking in the individuals, more than we can learn from their writings and yet are curious to know. I dare say Locke and Newton were very like Kneller's portraits of them ; but who could paint Shakespeare ?' 'Ay,' retorted Ayrton, 'there it is. Then I suppose you would prefer seeing him and Milton instead?' 'No,' said Lamb, 'neither; I have seen so much of Shakespeare on the stage.' . . . . 'I shall guess no more,' said Ayrton. 'Who is it, then, you would like to see " in his habit as he lived," if you had your choice of the whole range of English literature ?' Lamb then named Sir Thomas Brown and Fulke Greville, the friend of Sir Philip Sidney, as the two worthies whom he should feel the greatest pleasure to encounter on the floor of his apartment in their night-gowns

and slippers, and to exchange friendly greeting with them. At this Ayrton laughed outright, and conceived Lamb was jesting with him ; but as no one followed his example he thought there might be something in it, and waited for an explanation in a state of whimsical suspense. . . . .

" When Lamb had given his explanation, some one inquired of him if he could not see from the window the Temple walk in which Chaucer used to take his exercise, and on his name being put to the vote I was pleased to find there was a general sensation in his favour in all but Ayrton, who said something about the ruggedness of the metre, and even objected to the quaintness of the orthography. . . . .

" Captain Burney muttered something about Columbus, and Martin Burney hinted at the Wandering Jew ; but the last was set aside as spurious, and the first made over to the New World.

" ' I should like,' said Mr. Reynolds, ' to have seen Pope talking with Patty Blount, and I *have* seen Goldsmith.' Every one turned round to look at Mr. Reynolds, as if by so doing they too could get a sight of Goldsmith. . . . .

" Erasmus Phillips, who was deep in a game of piquet at the other end of the room, whispered to Martin Burney to ask if Junius would not be a fit person to invoke from the dead. ' Yes,' said Lamb, ' provided he would agree to lay aside his mask.'

" We were now at a stand for a short time, when Fielding was mentioned as a candidate. Only one, however, seconded the proposition. ' Richardson?' ' By all means ; but only to look at him through the glass-door of his back-shop, hard at work upon one of his novels (the most extraordinary contrast that ever was presented between an author and his works), but not to let him come behind his counter, lest he should want you to turn customer ; nor to go upstairs with him, lest he should offer to read the first manuscript of " Sir Charles Grandison," which was originally written in twenty-eight volumes octavo ; or get out the letters of his female correspondents to prove that " Joseph Andrews " was low.'

" There was but one statesman in the whole of English history that any one expressed the least desire to see—Oliver Cromwell, with his fine, frank, rough, pimply face and wily policy—and one enthusiast, John Bunyan, the immortal author of ' The Pilgrim's Progress.' . . . .

" Of all persons near our own time, Garrick's name was received with the greatest enthusiasm. He presently superseded both Hogarth and

Handel, who had been talked of, but then it was on condition that he should sit in tragedy and comedy, in the play and the farce,—Lear and Wildair, and Abel Drugger. . . . .

"Lamb inquired if there was any one that was hanged that I would choose to mention, and I answered, 'Eugene Aram.'"

The present Hare Place was the once disreputable Ram Alley, the scene of a comedy of that name, written by Lodowick Barry and dramatised in the reign of James I.; the plot Killigrew afterwards used in his vulgar *Parson's Wedding*. Barry, an Irishman, of whom nothing much is known, makes one of his roystering characters say,—

> "And rough Ram Alley stinks with cooks' shops vile ;
> Yet, stay, there's many a worthy lawyer's chamber
> 'Buts on Ram Alley."

As a precinct of Whitefriars, Ram Alley enjoyed the mischievous privilege of sanctuary for murderers, thieves, and debtors—indeed, any class of rascals except traitors—till the fifteenth century. After this it sheltered only debtors. Barry speaks of its cooks, salesmen, and laundresses ; and Shadwell classes it (Charles II.) with Pye Corner, as the resort of "rascally stuff." Lord Clarendon, in his autobiography, describes the Great Fire as burning on the Thames side as far as the "new buildings of the Inner Temple next to Whitefriars," striking next on some of the buildings which joined to Ram Alley, and sweeping all those into Fleet Street. In the reign of George I. Ram Alley was full of public-houses, and was a place of no reputation, having passages into the Temple and Serjeants' Inn. "A kind of privileged place for debtors," adds Hatton, "before the late Act of Parliament (9 & 10 William III. c. 17, s. 15) for taking them away." This useful Act swept out all the London sanctuaries, those vicious relics of monastic rights, including Mitre Court, Salisbury Court (Fleet Street), the Savoy, Fulwood Rents (Holborn), Baldwin's Gardens (Gray's Inn Lane), the Minories, Deadman's Place, Montague Close (Southwark), the Clink, and the Mint in the same locality. The Savoy and the Mint, however, remained disreputable a generation or two later.

Serjeants' Inn, Fleet Street, now deserted by the faithless serjeants, is supposed to have been given to the Dean and Chapter of York in 1409 (Henry IV.). It then consisted of shops, &c. In 1627 (Charles I.) the inn began its legal career by being leased for forty years to nine judges and fifteen serjeants. In this hall, in 1629, the judges in full bench struck a sturdy blow at feudal privi-

leges by agreeing that peers might be attached upon process for contempt out of Chancery. In 1723 (George I.) the inn was highly aristocratic, its inmates being the Lord Chief Justice, the Lord Chief Baron, justices, and serjeants. In 1730, however, the fickle serjeants removed to Chancery Lane, and Adam, the architect of the Adelphi, designed the present nineteen houses and the present street frontage. On the site of the hall arose the Amicable Assurance Society, which in 1865 transferred its business to the Economic, and the house is now the Norwich Union Office. The inn is a parish in itself, making its own assessment, and contributing to the City rates. Its pavement, which had been part of the stonework of Old St. Paul's, was not replaced till 1860. The conservative old inn retained its old dim lamps long after the introduction of gas.

The arms of Serjeants' Inn, worked into the iron gate opening on Fleet Street, are a dove and a serpent, the serpent twisted into a kind of true lover's knot. The lawyers of Serjeants' Inn, no doubt, unite the wisdom of the serpent with the guilelessness of the dove. Singularly enough Dr. Dodd, the popular preacher, who was hanged, bore arms nearly similar.

Half way down Bouverie Street, in the centre of old Whitefriars, is the office of the *Daily News*. The first number of this popular and influential paper appeared on January 21, 1846. The publishers, and part proprietors, were Messrs. Bradbury and Evans ; the principal editor was Charles Dickens ; the manager was Dickens's father ; the second, or assistant editor, Douglas Jerrold ; and among the other "leader" writers and contributors were Albany Fonblanque and John Forster, both of the *Examiner*. "Father Prout" (Mahoney) acted as Roman correspondent. The musical critic was the late Mr. George Hogarth, Dickens's father-in-law ; and the new journal had an "Irish Famine Commissioner" in the person of Mr. R. H. Horne, the poet. Miss Martineau wrote leading articles in the new paper for several years, and Mr. M'Cullagh Torrens was also a recognised contributor. The staff of Parliamentary reporters was said to be the best in London, several having been taken, at advanced salaries, off the *Times*.

"The speculative proprietorship," says Mr. Grant, in his "History of the Newspaper Press," was divided into one hundred shares, some of which were held by Sir William Jackson, M.P., Sir Joshua Watkins, and the late Sir Joseph Paxton. Mr. Charles Dickens, as editor, received a salary of £2,000 a year."

The early numbers of the paper contained

instalments of Dickens's "Pictures from Italy;" yet the new venture did not succeed. Charles Dickens and Douglas Jerrold took the night-work on alternate days; but Dickens, who never made politics a special study, very soon retired from the editorship altogether, and Jerrold was chief editor for a little while, till he left to set up his paper, was in effect three halfpence. One of the features of the new plan was that the sheet should vary in size, according to the requirements of the day—with an eye, nevertheless, at all times to selection and condensation. It was a bold attempt, carried out with great intelligence and spirit; but it was soon found necessary to put

THE DORSET GARDENS THEATRE, WHITEFRIARS (*see page* 140).

Weekly Newspaper. Mr. Forster also held the editorship for a short period, and the paper then fell into the hands of the late Mr. Dilke, of the *Athenæum*, who excited some curiosity by extensively advertising these words: "See the *Daily News* of June 1st." The *Daily News* of June 1, 1846 (which began No. 1 again), was a paper of four pages, issued at 2½d., which, deducting the stamp, at that time affixed to every copy of every news-paper, on another halfpenny, and in a year or two the *Daily News* was obliged to return to the usual price of "dailies" at that time—fivepence. The chief editors of the paper, besides those already mentioned, have been Mr. Eyre Evans Crowe, Mr. Frederick Knight Hunt, Mr. Weir, and Mr. Thomas Walker, who retired in January, 1870, on receiving the editorship of the *London Gazette*. The journal came down to a penny in June, 1868.

SERJEANTS' INN, FLEET STREET. (*See page* 137.)

The *Daily News*, at the beginning, inspired the *Times* with some dread of rivalry; and it is noteworthy that, for several years afterwards, the great journal was very unfriendly in its criticisms on Dickens's books.

There is no doubt that, over-sanguine of success, the *Daily News* proprietors began by sinking too much money in the foundations. In 1846, the *Times'* reporters received on an average only five guineas a week, while the *Daily News* gave seven; but the pay was soon of necessity reduced. Mr. Grant computes the losses of the *Daily News* for the first ten years at not much less than £200,000. The talent and enterprise of this paper during the German invasion of France in 1871-2, and the excellence of their correspondents in either camp, is said to have trebled its circulation, which Mr. Grant computes at a daily issue of 90,000. As an organ of the highest and most enlightened form of Liberalism and progress, the *Daily News* now stands pre-eminent.

Many actors, poets, and authors dwelt in Salisbury Court in Charles II.'s time, and the great Betterton, Underhill, and Sandford affected this neighbourhood, to be near the theatres. Lady Davenant here presided over the Dorset Gardens Company; Shadwell, "round as a butt and liquored every chink," nightly reeled home to the same precinct, unsteadily following the guidance of a will-o'-the-wisp link-boy; and in the square lived and died Sir John King, the Duke of York's solicitor-general.

If Salisbury Square boasts of Richardson, the respectable citizen and admirable novelist, it must also plead guilty to having been the residence of that not very reputable personage, Mr. John Eyre, who, although worth, as it was said, some £20,000, was transported on November 1, 1771 (George III.) for systematic pilfering of paper from the alderman's chamber, in the justice room, Guildhall. This man, led away by the thirst for money, had an uncle who made two wills, one leaving Eyre all his money, except a legacy of £500 to a clergyman; another leaving the bulk to the clergyman, and £500 only to his nephew. Eyre, not knowing of the second will, destroyed the first, in order to cancel the vexatious bequest. When the real will was produced his disappointment and selfish remorse must have produced an expression of repressed rage worthy of Hogarth's pencil.

In Salisbury Square Mr. Clark's disagreeable confessions about the Duke of York were publicly burned, on the very spot (says Mr. Noble) where the zealous radical demagogue, Waithman, subsequently addressed the people from a temporary platform, not being able to obtain the use of St. Bride's Vestry. Nor must we forget to chronicle No. 53 as the house of Tatum, a silversmith, to whom, in 1812, that eminent man, Michael Faraday, acted as humble friend and assistant. How often does young genius act the herdsman, as Apollo did when he tended the kine of Admetus!

The Woodfalls, too, in their time, lent celebrity to Salisbury Square. The first Woodfall who became eminent was Henry Woodfall, at the "Elzevir's Head" at Temple Bar. He commenced business under the auspices of Pope. His son Henry, who rose to be a Common Councilman and Master of the Stationers' Company, bought of Theophilus Cibber, in 1736-37, one-third of a tenth share of the London *Daily Post*, an organ which gradually grew into the *Public Advertiser*, that daring paper in which the celebrated letters of "Junius" first appeared. Those letters, scathing and full of Greek fire, brought down Lords and Commons, King's Bench and Old Bailey, on Woodfall, and he was fined and imprisoned. Whether Burke, Barré, Chatham, Horne Tooke, or Sir Philip Francis wrote them, will now probably never be known. The stern writer in the iron mask went down into the grave shrouded in his own mystery, and that grave no inquisitive eyes will ever find. "I am the sole depository of my secret," he wrote, "and it shall perish with me." The "Junius" Woodfall died in 1805. William Woodfall, the younger brother, was born in 1745, and educated at St. Paul's School. He was editor and printer of the *Morning Chronicle*, and in 1790 had his office in Dorset Street, Salisbury Square. "Memory" Woodfall, as William was generally called, acquired fame by his extraordinary power of reporting from memory the speeches he heard in the House of Commons. His practice during a debate (says his friend Mr. Taylor, of the *Sun*) was to close his eyes and lean with both hands upon his stick. He was so well acquainted with the tone and manner of the several speakers that he seldom changed his attitude but to catch the name of a new member. His memory was as accurate as it was capacious, and, what was almost miraculous, he could retain full recollection of any particular debate for a full fortnight, and after many long nights of speaking. Woodfall used to say he could put a speech away on a corner shelf of his mind for future reference. This is an instance of power of memory scarcely equalled by Fuller, who, it is said, could repeat the names of all the shops down the Strand (at a time every shop had a sign) in regular and correct sequence; and it even surpasses "Memory" Thompson, who used to boast he could remember every shop from Ludgate Hill to the end of Piccadilly. Yet, with all his sensitively retentive memory, Woodfall did not care for slight interruptions during his writing. Dr. Johnson used to write abridged reports of debates for the *Gentleman's Magazine* from memory ; but, then, reports at that time were short and trivial. Woodfall was also a most excellent dramatic critic— slow to censure, yet never sparing in just rebuke. At the theatre his extreme attention gave his countenance a look of gloom and severity. Mr. J. Taylor, of the *Sun*, describes Kemble as watching Woodfall in one of those serious moods, and saying to a friend, " How applicable to that man is the passage in *Hamlet*,—'thoughts black, hands apt.'"

Finding himself hampered on the *Morning Chronicle*, Woodfall started a new daily paper, with the title of the *Diary*, but eventually he was overpowered by his competitors and their large staff of reporters. His eldest son, who displayed great abilities, went mad. Mr. Woodfall's hospitable parties at his house at Kentish Town are sketched for us by Mr. J. Taylor. On one particular occasion he mentions meeting Mr. Tickell, Richardson (a partner in " The Rolliad "), John Kemble, Perry (of the *Chronicle*), Dr. Glover (a humorist of the day), and John Coust.' Kemble and Perry fell out over their wine, and Perry was rude to the stately tragedian. Kemble, eyeing him with the scorn of Coriolanus, exclaimed, in the words of Zanga,—

" A lion preys not upon carcases."

Perry very naturally effervesced at this, and war would have been instantly proclaimed between the belligerents had not Coust and Richardson promptly interposed. The warlike powers were carefully sent home in separate vehicles.

Mr. Woodfall had a high sense of the importance of a Parliamentary reporter's duties, and once, during a heavy week, when his eldest son came to town to assist him, he said, " And Charles Fox to have a debate on a Saturday ! What ! does he think that reporters are made of iron ? " Woodfall used to tell a characteristic story of Dr. Dodd. When that miserable man was in Newgate waiting sentence of death, he sent earnestly for the editor of the *Morning Chronicle*. Woodfall, a kind and unselfish man, instantly hurried off, expecting that Dodd wished his serious advice. In the midst of Woodfall's condolement he was stopped by the Doctor, who said he had wished to see him' on quite a different subject. Knowing Woodfall's judgment in dramatic matters, he was anxious to have his opinion on a comedy which he had

written, and to request his interest with a manager to bring it on the stage. Woodfall was the more surprised and shocked, as on entering Newgate he had been informed by Ackerman, the keeper of Newgate, that the order for Dr. Dodd's execution had just arrived.

Before parting with the Woodfall family, we may mention that it is quite certain that Henry Sampson Woodfall did not know who the author of " Junius " was. Long after the letters appeared he used to say, " I hope and trust ' Junius' is not dead, as I think he would have left me a legacy ; for though I derived much honour from his preference, I suffered much by the freedom of his pen."

The grandson of William, Henry Dick Woodfall, died at Nice, April 13, 1869, aged sixty-nine, carrying to the grave (says Mr. Noble) the last chance of discovering one of the best kept secrets ever known.

The Whig " mug-house " of Salisbury Court deserves notice. The death of Queen Anne (1714) roused the hopes of the Jacobites. The rebellion of 1715 proved how bitterly they felt the peaceful accession of the Elector of Hanover. The northern revolt convinced them of their strength, but its failure taught them no lesson. They attributed its want of success to the rashness of the leaders and the absence of unanimity in their followers; to the outbreak not being simultaneous ; to every cause, indeed, but the right one. It was about this time that the Whig gentlemen of London, to unite their party and to organise places of gathering, established " mug-houses " in various parts of the City. At these places, " free-and-easy " clubs were held, where Whig citizens could take their mug of ale, drink loyal toasts, sing loyal songs, and arrange party processions. These assemblies, not always very just or forbearing, soon led to violent retaliations on the part of the Tories, attacks were made on several of the mug-houses, and dangerous riots naturally ensued. From the papers of the time we learn that the Tories wore white roses, or rue, thyme, and rosemary in their hats, flourished oak branches and green ribbons, and shouted " High Church ;" " Ormond for ever ;" " No King George ;" " Down with the Presbyterians ;" " Down with the mug-houses." The Whigs, on the other side, roared " King George for ever," displayed orange cockades, with the motto,—

" With heart and hand
By George we'll stand,"

and did their best on royal birthdays and other thanksgivings, by illuminations and blazing bonfires outside the mug-house doors, to irritate their adversaries and drive them to acts of illegal violence. The chief Whig mug-houses were in Long Acre, Cheapside, St. John's Lane (Clerkenwell), Tower Street, and Salisbury Court.

Mackey, a traveller, who wrote "A Journey through England" about this time, describes the mug-houses very lucidly :—

"The most amusing and diverting of all," he says, "is the 'Mug-House Club,' in Long Acre, where every Wednesday and Saturday a mixture of gentlemen, lawyers, and tradesmen meet in a great room, and are seldom under a hundred. They have a grave old gentleman in his own grey hairs, now within a few months of ninety years old, who is their president, and sits in an armed-chair some steps higher than the rest of the company, to keep the whole room in order. A harp always plays all the time at the lower end of the room, and every now and then one or other of the company rises and entertains the rest with a song; and, by-the-by, some are good masters. Here is nothing drank but ale; and every gentleman hath his separate mug, which he chalks on the table where he sits as it is brought in, and every one retires when he pleases, as in a coffee-house. The room is always so diverted with songs, and drinking from one table to another to one another's healths, that there is no room for politics, or anything that can sour conversation. One must be up by seven to get room, and after ten the company are, for the most part, gone. This is a winter's amusement that is agreeable enough to a stranger for once or twice, and he is well diverted with the different humours when the mugs overflow."

An attack on a Whig mug-house, the "Roebuck," in Cheapside, June, 1716, was followed by a still more stormy assault on the Salisbury Court mug-house in July of the same year. The riot began on a Friday, but the Whigs kept a resolute face, and the mob dwindled away. On the Monday they renewed the attack, declaring that the Whigs were drinking "Down with the Church," and reviling the memory of Queen Anne; and they swore they would level the house and make a bonfire of the timber in the middle of Fleet Street. But the wily Whigs, barricading the door, slipped out a messenger at a back door, and sent to a mug-house in Tavistock Street, Covent Garden, for reinforcements. Presently a band of Whig bludgeon-men arrived, and the Whigs of Salisbury Court then snatched up pokers, tongs, pitchforks, and legs of stools, and sallied out on the Tory mob, who soon fled before them. For two days the Tory mob seethed, fretted, and swore revenge. But the report of a squadron of horse being drawn up at Whitehall ready to ride down on the City kept them gloomily quiet. On the third day a Jacobite, named Vaughan, formerly a Bridewell boy, led them on to revenge; and on Tuesday they stormed the place in earnest. "The best of the Tory mob," says a Whig paper of the day, "were High Church scaramouches, chimney-sweeps, hackney coachmen, foot-boys, tinkers, shoe-blacks, street idlers, ballad singers, and strumpets." The contemporaneous account will most vividly describe the scene.

The *Weekly Journal* (a Whig paper) of July 28, 1716, says: "The Papists and Jacobites, in pursuance of their rebellious designs, assembled a mob on Friday night last, and threatened to attack Mr. Read's mug-house in Salisbury Court, in Fleet Street; but, seeing the loyal gentlemen that were there were resolved to defend themselves, the cowardly Papists and Jacobites desisted for that time. But on Monday night the villains meeting together again in a most rebellious manner, they began first to attack Mr. Goslin's house, at the sign of the 'Blew Boar's Head,' near Water Lane, in Fleet Street, breaking the windows thereof, for no other reason but because he is well-affected to his Majesty King George and the present Government. Afterwards they went to the above-said mug-house in Salisbury Court; but the cowardly Jacks not being able to accomplish their hellish designs that night, they assembled next day in great numbers from all parts of the town, breaking the windows with brick-bats, broke open the cellar, got into the lower rooms, which they robb'd, and pull'd down the sign, which was carried in triumph before the mob by one Thomas Bean, servant to Mr. Carnegie and Mr. Cassey, two rebels under sentence of death, and for which he is committed to Newgate, as well as several others, particularly one Hook, a joyner, in Blackfriars, who is charged with acting a part in gutting the mug-house. Some of the rioters were desperately wounded, and one Vaughan, a seditious weaver, formerly an apprentice in Bridewell, and since employed there, who was a notorious ringleader of mobs, was kill'd at the aforesaid mug-house. Many notorious Papists were seen to abet and assist in this villanous rabble, as were others, who call themselves Churchmen, and are like to meet with a suitable reward in due time for their assaulting gentlemen who meet at these mug-houses only to drink prosperity to the Church of England as by law established, the King's health, the Prince of Wales's, and the rest of the Royal Family, and those of his faithful and loyal Ministers. But it is farther to be observed that women of mean, scandalous lives, do frequently point, hiss, and cry out 'Whigs' upon his Majesty's good and loyal subjects, by which, raising a mob, they are often insulted by them. But 'tis hoped the magistrates will take such methods which may prevent the like insults for the future.

"Thursday last the coroner's inquest sat on the body of the person killed in Salisbury Court, who were for bringing in their verdict, wilful murder against Mr. Read, the man of the mug-house; but some of the jury stick out, and will not agree with that verdict; so that the matter is deferr'd till Monday next."

"On Tuesday last," says the same paper (August 4, 1716), "a petition, signed by some of the inhabitants of Salisbury Court, was deliver'd to the Court of Aldermen, setting forth some late riots occasioned by the meeting of some persons at the mug-house there. The petition was referr'd to, and a hearing appointed the same day before the Lord Mayor. The witnesses on the side of the petition were a butcher woman, a barber's 'prentice, and two or three other inferior people. These swore, in substance—that the day the man was killed there, they saw a great many people gathered together about the mug-house, throwing stones and dirt, &c.; that about twelve o'clock they saw Mr. Read come out with a gun, and shoot a man who was before the mob at some distance, and had no stick in his hand. Those who were call'd in Mr. Read's behalf depos'd that a very great mob attacked the house, crying, 'High Church and Ormond; No Hanover; No King George;' that then the constable read the Proclamation, charging them to disperse, but they still continued to cry, 'Down with the mug-house;' that two soldiers then issued out of the house, and drove the mob into Fleet Street; but by throwing sticks and stones, they drove these two back to the house, and the person shot returned at the head of the mob with a stick in his hand flourishing, and crying, 'No Hanover; No King George;' and 'Down with the mug-house.' That then Mr. Read desired them to disperse, or he would shoot amongst them, and the deceased making at him, he shot him and retired indoors; that then the mob forced into the house, rifled all below stairs, took the money out of the till, let the beer about the cellar, and what goods they could not carry away, they brought into the streets and broke to pieces; that they would have forced their way up stairs and murdered all in the house, but that a person who lodged in the house made a barricade at the stair-head, where he defended himself above half an hour against all the mob, wounded some of them, and compelled them to give over the

assault. There were several very credible witnesses to these circumstances, and many more were ready to have confirmed it, but the Lord Mayor thought sufficient had been said, and the following gentlemen, who are men of undoubted reputation and worth, offering to be bail for Mr. Read, namely, Mr. Johnson, a justice of the peace, and Colonels Coote and Westall, they were accepted, and accordingly entered into a recognisance."

Five of the rioters were eventually hung at Tyburn Turnpike, in the presence of a vast crowd. According to Mr. J. T. Smith, in his "Streets of London," a Whig mug-house existed as early as 1694. It has been said the slang word "mug" owes its derivation to Lord Shaftesbury's "ugly mug," which the beer cups were moulded to resemble.

In the *Flying Post* of June 30, 1716, we find a doggerel old mug-house ballad, which is so characteristic of the violence of the times that it is worth preserving:—

"Since the Tories could not fight,
    And their master took his flight,
They labour to keep up their faction;
    With a bough and a stick,
    And a stone and a brick,
They equip their roaring crew for action.

"Thus in battle array
    At the close of the day,
After wisely debating their deep plot,
    Upon windows and stall,
    They courageously fall,
And boast a great victory they have got.

"But, alas! silly boys,
    For all the mighty noise,
Of their 'High Church and Ormond for ever,'
    A brave Whig with one hand,
    At George's command,
Can make their mightiest hero to quiver."

Richardson's printing office was at the north-west corner of Salisbury Square, communicating with the court, No. 76, Fleet Street. Here the thoughtful old citizen wrote "Pamela," and here, in 1756, Oliver Goldsmith acted as his "reader." Richardson seems to have been an amiable and benevolent man, kind to his compositors and servants, and beloved by children. All the anecdotes relating to his private life are pleasant. He used to encourage early rising among his workmen by hiding half-crowns among the disordered type, so that the earliest comer might find his virtue rewarded; and he would frequently bring up fruit from the country to give to those of his servants who had been zealous and good-tempered.

Samuel Richardson, the author of "Pamela" and "Clarissa," was the son of a Derbyshire joiner. He was born in 1689, and died in 1761. Apprenticed to a London printer, he rose by steady industry and prudence to be the manager of a large business, printer of the Journals of the House of Commons, Master of the Stationers' Company, and joint-printer to the king. In 1741, at the age of fifty-two, publishers urging the thriving citizen to write them a book of moral letters, Richardson produced "Pamela," a novel which ran through five editions the first year, and became the rage of the town. Ladies carried the precious volumes to

from the foolish romances of his day. In "Pamela" he rewarded struggling virtue; in "Clarissa" he painted the cruel selfishness of vice; in "Sir Charles" he tried to represent the perfect Christian gentleman. Coleridge said that to read Fielding after Richardson was like emerging from a sick room, heated by stoves, into an open lawn on a breezy May morning. Richardson, indeed, wrote more for women than for men. Fielding was coarser, but more manly; he had humour, but no moral

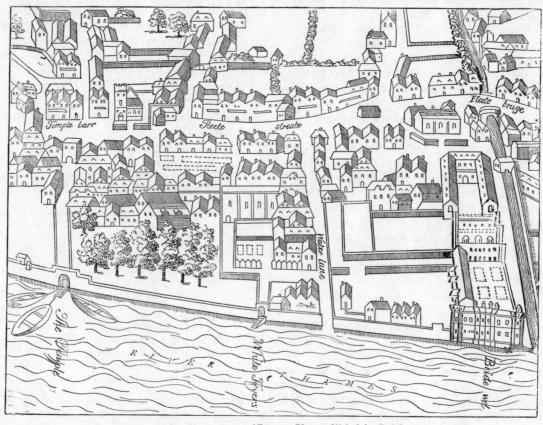

FLEET STREET, THE TEMPLE, ETC. (*From a Plan published by Ralph Aggas*, 1563.)

Ranelagh, and held them up in smiling triumph to each other. Pope praised the novel as more useful than twenty volumes of sermons, and Dr. Sherlock gravely recommended it from the pulpit. In 1749 Richardson wrote "Clarissa Harlowe," his most perfect work, and in 1753 his somewhat tedious "Sir Charles Grandison" (7 vols.). In "Pamela" he drew a servant, whom her master attempts to seduce and eventually marries, but in "Clarissa" the heroine, after harrowing misfortunes, dies unrewarded. Richardson had always a moral end in view. He hated vice and honoured virtue, but he is too often prolix and wearisome. He wished to write novels that should wean the young

purpose at all. The natural result was that Fielding and his set looked on Richardson as a grave, dull, respectable old prig; Richardson on Fielding as a low rake, who wrote like a man who had been an ostler born in a stable, or a runner in a sponging-house. "The virtues of Fielding's heroes," the vain old printer used to say to his feminine clique, "are the vices of a truly good man."

Dr. Johnson, who had been befriended by Richardson, was never tired of depreciating Fielding and crying up the author of "Pamela." "Sir," he used to thunder out, "there is as much difference between the two as between a man who knows how a watch is made and a man who can merely tell the hour on the dial-plate." He called Fielding a "barren rascal." "Sir, there is more knowledge of the heart in one letter of Richardson's than in all 'Tom Jones.'" Some one present here mildly suggested that Richardson was very tedious. "Why, sir," replied Johnson, "if you were to read Richardson for the story, your impatience would be so great that you would hang yourself. But you must read him for the sentiment, and consider the story as only giving occasion to the

partisan of George II., he observed to Richardson that certainly there must have been some very unfavourable circumstances lately discovered in this particular case which had induced the king to approve of an execution for rebellion so long after the time it was committed, as this had the appearance of putting a man to death in cold blood, and was very unlike his majesty's usual clemency. While he was talking he perceived a person standing at a window in the room shaking his head

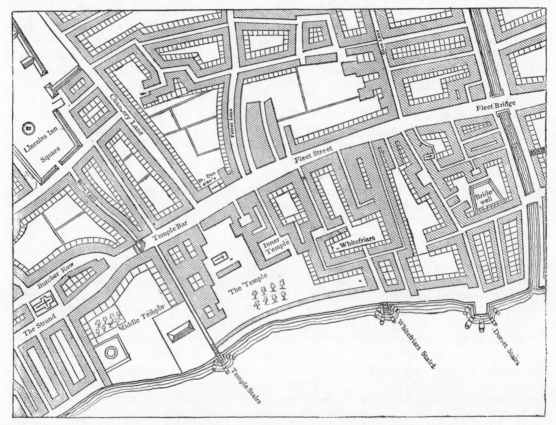

FLEET STREET, THE TEMPLE, ETC., FROM A MAP OF LONDON, PUBLISHED 1720.

sentiment." After all, it must be considered that, old-fashioned as Richardson's novels have now become, the old printer dissected the human heart with profound knowledge and exquisite care, and that in the back shop in Salisbury Court, amid the jar of printing-presses, the quiet old citizen drew his ideal beings with far subtler lines and touches than any previous novelist had done.

On one occasion at least Hogarth and Johnson met at Richardson's house.

"Mr. Hogarth," says Nichols, "came one day to see Richardson, soon after the execution of Dr. Cameron, for having taken arms for the house of Stuart in 1745–46 ; and, being a warm

and rolling himself about in a ridiculous manner. He concluded he was an idiot, whom his relations had put under the care of Mr. Richardson as a very good man. To his great surprise, however, this figure stalked forward to where he and Mr. Richardson were sitting, and all at once took up the argument, and burst out into an invective against George II., as one who, upon all occasions, was unrelenting and barbarous ; mentioning many instances, particularly that, where an officer of high rank had been acquitted by a court martial, George II. had, with his own hand, struck his name off the list. In short, he displayed such a power of eloquence that

Hogarth looked at him in astonishment, and actually imagined that this idiot had been at the moment inspired. Neither Johnson nor Hogarth were made known to each other at this interview."

Boswell tells a good story of a rebuke that Richardson's amiable but inordinate egotism on one occasion received, much to Johnson's secret delight, which is certainly worth quoting before we dismiss the old printer altogether. "One day," says Boswell, "at his country house at Northend, where a large company was assembled at dinner, a gentleman who was just returned from Paris, wishing to please Richardson, mentioned to him a flattering circumstance, that he had seen his 'Clarissa' lying on the king's brother's table. Richardson observing that part of the company were engaged in talking to each other, affected then not to attend to it; but by and bye, when there was a general silence, and he thought that the flattery might be fully heard, he addressed himself to the gentleman: 'I think, sir, you were saying somewhat about'—pausing in a high flutter of expectation. The gentleman provoked at his inordinate vanity resolved not to indulge it, and with an exquisitely sly air of indifference answered, 'A mere trifle, sir; not worth repeating.' The mortification of Richardson was visible, and he did not speak ten words more the whole day. Dr. Johnson was present, and appeared to enjoy it much."

At one corner of Salisbury Square (says Mr. Timbs) are the premises of Peacock, Bampton, & Mansfield, the famous pocket-book makers, whose "Polite Repository" for 1778 is "the patriarch of all pocket-books." Its picturesque engravings have never been surpassed, and their morocco and russia bindings scarcely equalled. In our time Queen Adelaide and her several maids of honour used the "Repository." George IV. was provided by the firm with a ten-guinea housewife (an antique-looking pocket-book, with gold-mounted scissors, tweezers, &c.); and Mr. Mansfield relates that on one occasion the king took his housewife from his pocket and handed it round the table to his guests, and next day the firm received orders for twenty-five, "just like the king's."

In St. Bride's Passage, westward (says Mr. Timbs), was a large dining-house, where, some forty years ago, Colton, the author, used to dine, and publicly boast that he wrote the whole of his "Lacon; or, Many Things in Few Words," upon a small rickety deal table, with one pen. Another frequenter of this place was one Webb, who seems to have been so well up in the topics of the day

that he was a sort of walking newspaper: he was much with the King and Queen of the Sandwich Islands when they visited England in 1825.

This Caleb Colton, mentioned by Mr. Timbs, was that most degraded being, a disreputable clergyman, with all the vices but little of the genius of Churchill, and had been, in his flourishing time, vicar of Kew and Petersham. He was educated at Eton, and eventually became Fellow of King's College, Cambridge. He wrote "A Plain and Authentic Narrative of the Stamford Ghost," "Remarks on the Tendencies of 'Don Juan,'" a poem on Napoleon, and a satire entitled "Hypocrisy." His best known work, however, was "Lacon; or, Many Things in Few Words," published in 1820. These aphorisms want the terse brevity of Rochefoucauld, and are in many instances vapid and trivial. A passion for gaming at last swallowed up Colton's other vices, and becoming involved, he cut the Gordian knot of debt in 1828 by absconding; his living was then seized and given to another. He fled to America, and from there returned to that syren city, Paris, where he is said in two years to have won no less than £25,000. The miserable man died by his own hand at Fontainebleau, in 1832. In his "Lacon" is the subjoined passage, that seems almost prophetic of the miserable author's miserable fate:—

"The gamester, if he die a martyr to his profession, is doubly ruined. He adds his soul to every loss, and by the act of suicide renounces earth to forfeit heaven." . . . . "Anguish of mind has driven thousands to suicide, anguish of body none. This proves that the health of the mind is of far more consequence to our happiness than the health of the body, although both are deserving of much more attention than either of them receive."

And here is a fine sentiment, worthy of Dr. Dodd himself:—

"There is but one pursuit in life which it is in the power of all to follow and of all to attain. It is subject to no disappointments, since he that perseveres makes every difficulty an advancement and every contest a victory—and this the pursuit of virtue. Sincerely to aspire after virtue is to gain her, and zealously to labour after her wages is to receive them. Those that seek her early will find her before it is late; her reward also is with her, and she will come quickly. For the breast of a good man is a little heaven commencing on earth, where the Deity sits enthroned with unrivalled influence, every subjugated passion, 'like the wind and storm, fulfilling his word.'"

CHAPTER XIII.

THE TEMPLE.—GENERAL INTRODUCTION.

Origin of the Order of Templars—First Home of the Order—Removal to the Banks of the Thames—Rules of the Order—The Templars at the Crusades, and their Deeds of Valour—Decay and Corruption of the Order—Charges brought against the Knights—Abolition of the Order.

THE Order of Knights Templars, established by Baldwin, King of Jerusalem, in 1118, to protect Christian pilgrims on their road to Jerusalem, first found a home in England in 1128 (Henry I.), when Hugh de Payens, the first Master of the Order, visited our shores to obtain succours and subsidies against the Infidel.

The proud, and at first zealous, brotherhood originally settled on the south side of Holborn, without the Bars. Indeed, about a century and a half ago, part of a round chapel, built of Caen stone, was found under the foundation of some old houses at the Holborn end of Southampton Buildings. In time, however, the Order amassed riches, and, growing ambitious, purchased a large space of ground extending from Fleet Street to the river, and from Whitefriars to Essex House in the Strand. The new Temple was a vast monastery, fitted for the residence of the prior, his chaplain, serving brethren and knights; and it boasted a council-chamber, a refectory, a barrack, a church, a range of cloisters, and a river terrace for religious meditation, military exercise, and the training of chargers. In 1185 Heraclius, the Patriarch of Jerusalem, who had come to England with the Masters of the Temple and the Hospital to procure help from Henry II. against the victorious Saladin, consecrated the beautiful river-side .church, which the proud Order had dedicated to the Virgin Lady Mary. The late Master of the Temple had only recently died in a dungeon at Damascus; and the new Master of the Hospital, after the great defeat of the Christians at Jacob's Ford, on the Jordan, had swam the river covered with wounds, and escaped to the Castle of Beaufort.

The singular rules of the " Order of the Poor Fellow-Soldiers of Jesus Christ and of the Temple of Solomon," were revised by the first Abbot of Clairvaux, St. Bernard himself. Extremely austere and earnest, they were divided into seventy-two heads, and enjoined severe and constant devotional exercises, self-mortification, fasting, prayer, and regular attendance at matins, vespers, and all the services of the Church. Dining in one common refectory, the Templars were to make known wants that could not be expressed by signs, in a gentle, soft, and private way. Two and two were in general to live together, so that one might watch the other. After departing from the supper hall to bed it was not permitted them to speak again in public, except upon urgent necessity, and then only in an undertone. All scurrility, jests, and idle words were to be avoided; and after any foolish saying, the repetition of the Lord's Prayer was enjoined. All professed knights were to wear white garments, both in summer and winter, as emblems of chastity. The esquires and retainers were required to wear black, or, in provinces where that coloured cloth could not be procured, brown. No gold or silver was to be used in bridles, breast-plates, or spears; and if ever that furniture was given them in charity, it was to be discoloured to prevent an appearance of superiority or arrogance. No brother was to receive or despatch letters without the leave of the master or procurator, who might read them if he chose. No gift was to be accepted by a Templar till permission was first obtained from the Master. No knight should talk to any brother of his previous frolics and irregularities in the world. No brother, in pursuit of worldly delight, was to hawk, to shoot in the woods with long or cross-bow, to halloo to dogs, or to spur a horse after game. There might be married brothers, but they were to leave part of their goods to the chapter, and not to wear the white habit. Widows were not to dwell in the Preceptories. When travelling, Templars were to lodge only with men of the best repute, and to keep a light burning all night "lest the dark enemy, from whom God preserve us, should find some opportunity." Unrepentant brothers were to be cast out. Last of all, every Templar was to shun "feminine kisses," whether from widow, virgin, mother, sister, aunt, or any other woman.

During six of the seven Crusades (1096–1272), during which the Christians of Europe endeavoured, with tremendous yet fitful energy, to wrest the birthplace of Christianity from the equally fanatic Moslems, the Knights Templars fought bravely among the foremost. Whether by the side of Godfrey of Bouillon, Louis VII., Philip V., Richard Cœur de Lion, Louis IX., or Prince Edward, the stern, sunburnt men in the white mantles were ever foremost in the shock of spears. Under many a clump of palm trees, in many a scorched desert track, by many a hill fortress, smitten with sabre or pierced with arrow, the holy brotherhood dug the graves of their slain companions.

A few of the deeds, which must have been so often talked of upon the Temple terrace and in the Temple cloister, must be narrated, to show that, however mistaken was the ideal of the Crusaders, these monkish warriors fought their best to turn it into a reality. In 1146 the whole brotherhood joined the second Crusade, and protected the rear of the Christian army in its toilsome march through Asia Minor. In 1151, the Order saved Jerusalem, and drove back the Infidels with terrible slaughter. Two years later the Master of the Temple was slain, with many of the white mantles, in fiercely essaying to storm the walls of Ascalon. Three years after this 300 Templars were slain in a Moslem ambuscade, near Tiberias, and 87 were taken prisoners. We next find the Templars repelling the redoubtable Saladin from Gaza ; and in a great battle near Ascalon, in 1177, the Master of the Temple and ten knights broke through the Mameluke Guards, and all but captured Saladin in his tent. The Templars certainly had their share of Infidel blows; for, in 1178, the whole Order was nearly slain in a battle with Saladin ; and in another fierce conflict, only the Grand Master and two knights escaped; while again at Tiberias, in 1187, they received a cruel repulse, and were all but totally destroyed.

In 1187, when Saladin took Jerusalem, he next besieged the great Templar stronghold of Tyre ; and soon after a body of the knights, sent from London, attacked Saladin's camp in vain, and the Grand Master and nearly half of the Order perished. In the subsequent siege of Acre the Crusaders lost nearly 100,000 men in nine pitched battles. In 1191, however, Acre was taken, and the Kings of France and England, and the Masters of the Temple and the Hospital, gave the throne of the Latin kingdom to Guy de Lusignan. When Richard Cœur de Lion had cruelly put to death 2,000 Moslem prisoners, we find the Templars interposing to prevent Richard and the English fighting against the Austrian allies ; and soon after the Templars bought Cyprus of Richard for 300,000 livres of gold. In the advance to Jerusalem the Templars led the van of Richard's army. When the attack on Jerusalem was suspended, the Templars followed Richard to Ascalon, and soon afterwards gave Cyprus to Guy de Lusignan, on condition of his surrendering the Latin crown. When Richard abandoned the Crusade, after his treaty with Saladin, it was the Templars who gave him a galley and the disguise of a Templar's white robe to secure his safe passage to an Adriatic port. Upon Richard's departure they erected many fortresses in Palestine, especially one on Mount Carmel, which they named Pilgrim's Castle.

The fourth Crusade was looked on unfavourably by the brotherhood, who now wished to remain at peace with the Infidel; but they nevertheless soon warmed to the fighting, and we find a band of the white mantles defeated and slain at Jaffa. With a second division of Crusaders the Templars quarrelled, and were then deserted by them. Soon after the Templars and Hospitallers, now grown corrupt and rich, quarrelled about lands and fortresses; but they were still favoured by the Pope, and helped to maintain the Latin throne. In 1209 they were strong enough to resist the interdict of Pope Innocent ; and in the Crusade of 1217 they invaded Egypt, and took Damietta by assault, but, at the same time, to the indignation of England, wrote home urgently for more money. An attack on Cairo proving disastrous, they concluded a truce with the Sultan in 1221. In the Crusade of the Emperor Frederick the Templars refused to join an excommunicated man. In 1240, the Templars wrested Jerusalem from the Sultan of Damascus, but, in 1243, were ousted by the Sultan of Egypt and the Sultan of Damascus, and were almost exterminated in a two days' battle ; and, in 1250, they were again defeated at Mansourah. When King Louis was taken prisoner, the Infidels demanded the surrender of all the Templar fortresses in Palestine, but eventually accepted Damietta alone and a ransom, which Louis exacted from the Templars. In 1257 the Moguls and Tartars took Jerusalem, and almost annihilated the Order, whose instant submission they required. In 1268 Pope Urban excommunicated the Marshal of the Order, but the Templars nevertheless held by their comrade, and Bendocdar, the Mameluke, took all the castles belonging to the Templars in Armenia, and also stormed Antioch, which had been a Christian city 170 years.

After Prince Edward's Crusade the Templars were close pressed. In 1291, Aschraf Khalil besieged the two Orders and 12,000 Christians in Acre for six terrible weeks. The town was stormed, and all the Christian prisoners, who flew to the Infidel camp, were ruthlessly beheaded. A few of the Templars flew to the Convent of the Temple, and there perished ; the Grand Master had already fallen ; a handful of the knights only escaping to Cyprus.

The persecution of the now corrupt and useless Order commenced sixteen years afterwards. In 1306, both in London and Paris, terrible murmurs arose at their infidelity and their vices. At the Church of St. Martin's, Ludgate, where the English Templars were accused, the following strange charges were brought against them :—

1. That at their first reception into the Order, they were admonished by those who had received them within the bosom of the fraternity to deny Christ, the crucifixion, the blessed Virgin, and all the saints. 5. That the receivers instructed those that were received that Christ was not the true God. 7. That they said Christ had not suffered for the redemption of mankind, nor been crucified but for His own sins. 9. That they made those they received into the Order spit upon the cross. 10. That they caused the cross itself to be trampled under foot. 11. That the brethren themselves did sometimes trample on the same cross. 14. That they worshipped a cat, which was placed in the midst of the congregation. 16. That they did not believe the sacrament of the altar, nor the other sacraments of the Church. 24. That they believed that the Grand Master of the Order could absolve them from their sins. 25. That the visitor could do so. 26. That the preceptors, of whom many were laymen, could do it. 36. That the receptions of the brethren were made clandestinely. 37. That none were present but the brothers of the said Order. 38. That for this reason there has for a long time been a vehement suspicion against them. 46. That the brothers themselves had idols in every province, viz., heads, some of which had three faces, and some one, and some a man's skull. 47. That they adored that idol, or those idols, especially in their great chapters and assemblies. 48. That they worshipped them. 49. As their God. 50. As their saviour. 51. That some of them did so. 52. That the greater part did. 53. They said those heads could save them. 54. That they could produce riches. 55. That they had given to the Order all its wealth. 56. That they caused the earth to bring forth seed. 57. That they made the trees to flourish. 58. That they bound or touched the heads of the said idols with cords, wherewith they bound themselves about their shirts, or next their skins. 59. That at their reception, the aforesaid little cords, or others of the same length, were delivered to each of the brothers. 61. That it was enjoined them to gird themselves with the said little cords, as before mentioned, and continually to wear them. 62. That the brethren of the Order were generally received in that manner. 63. That they did these things out of devotion. 64. That they did them everywhere. 65. That the greater part did. 66. That those who refused the things above mentioned at their reception, or to observe them afterwards, were killed or cast into prison.

The Order grew proud and arrogant, and had many enemies. The Order was rich, and spoil would reward its persecutors. The charges against the knights were eagerly believed; many of the Templars were burned at the stake in Paris, and many more in various parts of France. In England their punishment seems to have been less severe. The Order was formally abolished by Pope Clement V., in the year 1312.

CHAPTER XIV.

THE TEMPLE CHURCH AND PRECINCT.

The Temple Church—Its Restorations—Discoveries of Antiquities—The Penitential Cell—Discipline in the Temple—The Tombs of the Templars in the " Round "—William and Gilbert Marshall—Stone Coffins in the Churchyard—Masters of the Temple—The " Judicious " Hooker—Edmund Gibbon, the Historian—The Organ in the Temple Church—The Rival Builders—" Straw Bail "—History of the Precinct—Chaucer and the Friar—His Mention of the Temple—The Serjeants—Erection of New Buildings—The " Roses "—Sumptuary Edicts—The Flying Horse.

THE round church of the Temple is the finest of the four round churches still existing in England. The Templars did not, however, always build their churches with round towers, though such was generally their practice. The restoration of this beautiful relic was one of the first symptoms of the modern Gothic revival in London.

In the reign of Charles II. the body of the church was filled with formal pews, which concealed the bases of the columns, while the walls were encumbered, to the height of eight feet from the ground, with oak wainscoting, which was carried entirely round the church, so as to hide the elegant marble piscina, the interesting almeries over the high altar, and the *sacrarium* on the eastern side of the edifice. The elegant Gothic arches connecting the round with the square church were choked up with an oak screen and glass windows and doors, and with an organ gallery adorned with Corinthian columns, pilasters, and Grecian ornaments, which divided the building into two parts, altogether altered its original character and appearance, and sadly marring its architectural beauty. The eastern end of the church was at the same time disfigured by an enormous altar-piece in the *classic style*, decorated with Corinthian columns and Grecian cornices and entablatures, and with enrichments of cherubims and wreaths of fruit, flowers, and leaves, heavy and cumbrous, and quite at variance with the Gothic character of the building. A large pulpit and carved sounding-board were erected in the middle of the building, and the walls were encrusted and disfigured with a number of hideous mural monuments and pagan trophies of forgotten wealth and vanity.

The following account of the earliest repairs of the Temple Church is given in "The New View of London": "Having narrowly escaped the flames in 1666, it was in 1682 beautified, and the curious wainscot screen set up. The south-west part was, in the year 1695, new built with stone. In the year 1706 the church was wholly new whitewashed, gilt, and painted within, and the pillars of the round tower wainscoted with a new battlement and buttresses on the south side, and other parts of the outside were well repaired. Also the figures of the Knights Templars were cleaned and painted, and the iron-work enclosing them new painted and gilt with gold. The east end of the church was repaired and beautified in 1707." In 1737 the exterior of the north side and east end were again repaired.

The first step towards the real restoration of the Temple Church was made in 1825. It had been generally repaired in 1811, but in 1825 Sir Robert Smirke restored the whole south side externally and the lower part of the circular portion of the round church. The stone seat was renewed, the arcade was restored, the heads which had been defaced or removed were supplied. The wain-

A KNIGHT TEMPLAR.

scoting of the columns was taken away, the monuments affixed to some of the columns were removed, and the position of others altered. There still remained, however, monuments in the round church materially affecting the relative proportions of the two circles; the clustered columns still retained their incrustations of paint, plaster, and whitewash; the three archway entrances into the oblong church remained in their former state, detaching the two portions from each other, and entirely destroying the perspective which those arches afforded.

When the genuine restoration was commenced in 1845, the removal of the *beautifications and adornments* which had so long disfigured the Temple Church, was regarded as an act of vandalism. Seats were substituted for pews, and a smaller pulpit and reading-desk supplied more appropriate to the character of the building. The pavement was lowered to its original level; and thus the bases of the columns became once more visible. The altar screen and railing were taken down. The organ was removed, and thus all the arches from the round church to the body of the oblong church were thrown open. By this alteration the character of the church was shown in its original beauty.

In the summer of 1840, the two Societies of the Inner and Middle Temple had the paint and whitewash scraped off the marble columns and ceiling. The removal of the modern oak wainscoting led to the discovery of a very beautiful double marble piscina near the east end of the south side of the building, together with an adjoining elegantly-shaped recess, and also a picturesque Gothic niche on the north side of the church.

On taking up the modern floor, remains of the original tesselated pavement were discovered. When the whitewash and plaster were removed from the ceiling it was found in a dangerous condition. There were also found there remains of ancient

INTERIOR OF THE TEMPLE CHURCH, 1870 (*see page* 150).

decorative paintings and rich ornaments worked in gold and silver; but they were too fragmentary to give an idea of the general pattern. Under these circumstances it was resolved to redecorate the ceiling in a style corresponding with the ancient decorative paintings observable in many Gothic churches in Italy and France.

As the plaster and whitewash were removed it was found that the columns were of the most beautiful Purbeck marble. The six elegant clustered columns in the round tower had been concealed with a thick coating of Roman cement, which had altogether concealed the graceful form of the mouldings and carved foliage of their capitals. Barbarous slabs of Portland stone had been cased round their bases and entirely altered their character. All this modern patchwork was thrown away; but the venerable marble proved so mutilated that new columns were found necessary to support the fabric. These are exact imitations of the old ones. The six elegant clustered columns already alluded to, however, needed but slight repair. Almost all the other marble-work required renewal, and a special messenger was despatched to Purbeck to open the ancient quarries.

Above the western doorway was discovered a beautiful Norman window, composed of Caen stone. The porch before the western door of the Temple Church, which formerly communicated with an ancient cloister leading to the hall of the Knights Templars, had been filled up with rubbish to a height of nearly two feet above the level of the ancient pavement, so that all the bases of the magnificent Norman doorway were entirely hidden from view.

Previous to the recent restoration the round tower was surmounted by a wooden, flat, whitewashed ceiling, altogether different from the ancient roof. This ceiling and the timber roof above it have been entirely removed, and replaced by the present elegant and substantial roof, which is composed of oak, protected externally by sheet copper, and has been painted by Mr. Willement in accordance with an existing example of decorative painting in an ancient church in Sicily. Many buildings were also removed to give a clearer view of the fine old church.

"Among the many interesting objects," says Mr. Addison, "to be seen in the ancient church of the Knights Templars is a *penitential cell*, a dreary place of solitary confinement formed within the thick wall of the building, only four feet six inches long and two feet six inches wide, so narrow and small that a grown person cannot lie down within it. In this narrow prison the disobedient brethren of the ancient Templars were temporarily confined in chains and fetters, ' in order that their souls might be saved from the eternal prison of hell.' The hinges and catch of a door, firmly attached to the doorway of this dreary chamber, still remain, and at the bottom of the staircase is a stone recess or cupboard, where bread and water were placed for the prisoner. In this cell Brother Walter le Bacheler, Knight, and Grand Preceptor of Ireland, is said to have been starved to death for disobedience to his superior, the Master of the Temple. His body was removed at daybreak and buried by Brother John de Stoke and Brother Radulph de Barton in the middle of the court between the church and the hall."

The Temple discipline in the early times was very severe: disobedient brethren were scourged by the Master himself in the Temple Church, and frequently whipped publicly on Fridays in the church. Adam de Valaincourt, a deserter, was sentenced to eat meat with the dogs for a whole year, to fast four days in the week, and every Monday to present himself naked at the high altar to be publicly scourged by the officiating priest.

At the time of the restoration of the church stained glass windows were added, and the panels of the circular vaulting were emblazoned with the lamb and horse—the devices of the Inner and Middle Temple—and the Beauseant, or black and white banner of the Templars.

The mail-clad effigies on the pavement of the "Round" of the Temple Church are not monuments of Knights Templars, but of "Associates of the Temple," persons only partially admitted to the privileges of the powerful Order. During the last repairs there were found two Norman stone coffins and four ornamented leaden coffins in small vaults beneath these effigies, but not in their original positions. Stow, in 1598, speaks of eight images of armed knights in the round walk. The effigies have been restored by Mr. Richardson, the sculptor. The most interesting of these represents Geoffrey de Magnaville, Earl of Essex, a bold baron, who fought against King Stephen, sacked Cambridge, and plundered Ramsey Abbey. He was excommunicated, and while besieging Burwell Castle was struck by an arrow from a crossbow just as he had taken off his helmet to get air. The Templars, not daring to bury him, soldered him up in lead, and hung him on a crooked tree in their riverside orchard. The corpse being at last absolved, the Templars buried it before the west door of their church. He is to be known by a long, pointed shield charged with rays on a diamonded field. The next figure, of Purbeck marble in low relief, is supposed to be the most ancient of all. The shield is kite-shaped, the armour composed of rude rings—name unknown. Vestiges of gilding were discovered upon this monument. The two effigies on the north-east of the "Round" are also anonymous. They are the tallest of all the stone brethren : one of them is straight-legged ; the crossed legs of his comrade denote a Crusading vow. The feet of the first rests on two grotesque human heads, probably Infidels ; the second wears a mouth guard like a respirator. Between the two figures is the copestone lid of an ancient sarcophagus, probably that of a Master or Visitor-General of the Templars, as it has the head of the cross which decorates it adorned with a lion's head, and the foot rests on the head of a lamb, the joint emblems of the Order of the Templars. During the excavations in the "Round," a magnificent Purbeck marble sarcophagus, the lid decorated with a foliated cross, was dug up and re-interred.

On the south side of the "Round," between two columns, his feet resting upon a lion, reposes a great historical personage, William Marshall, the Protector of England during the minority of King Henry III., a warrior and a statesman whose name is sullied by no crimes. The features are handsome, and the whole body is wrapped in chain mail. A Crusader in early life, the earl became one of Richard Cœur de Lion's vice-gerents during his absence in Palestine. He fought in Normandy for King John, helped in the capture of Prince Arthur and his sister, urged the usurper to sign Magna Charta, and secured the throne for Prince Henry. Finally, he defeated the French invaders, routed the French at sea, and died, in the fulness of years, a warrior whose deeds had been notable, a statesman whose motives could seldom be impugned. Shakespeare, with ever a keen eye for great men, makes the earl the interceder for Prince Arthur. He was a great benefactor of the brethren of the Chivalry of the Temple.

By the side of the earl reposes his warlike son William Marshall the younger, cut in freestone. He was one of the chief leaders of the Barons against John, and in Henry's reign he overthrew Prince Llewellyn, and slew 8,000 wild Welsh. He fought with credit in Brittany and Ireland, and eventually married Eleanor, the king's sister. He gave an estate to the Templars. The effigy is clad in a shirt of ring mail, above which is a loose garment, girded at the waist. The shield on the left arm bears a lion rampant.

Near the western doorway reclines the mailed effigy of Gilbert Marshall, Earl of Pembroke, third son of the Protector. He is in the act of drawing a sword, and his left foot rests on a winged dragon. This earl, at the murder of a brother in Ireland, succeeded to the title, and married Margaret, a daughter of the King of Scotland. He was just starting for the Crusades, when he was killed by a fall from his horse, in a tournament held at Ware, (1241). Like the other Marshalls, he was a bene-factor of the Temple, and, like all the four sons of the Protector, died without issue, in the reign of Henry III., the family becoming extinct with him. Matthew Paris declared that the race had been cursed by the Bishop of Ferns, from whom the Protector had stolen lands. The bishop, says the chronicler, with great awe came with King Henry to the Temple Church, and, standing at the earl's tomb, promised the dead man absolution if the lands were returned. No restitution was made, so the curse fell on the doomed race. All these Pembrokes wear chain hoods and have animals recumbent at their feet.

The name of a beautiful recumbent mailed figure next Gilbert Marshall is unknown ; and near him, on the south side of the "Round," rests the ever-praying effigy of Robert, Lord de Ros. This lord was no Templar, for he has no beard, and wears flowing hair, contrary to the rules of the Order. His shield bears three water buckets. The figure is cut out of yellow Roach Abbey stone. The armour is linked. This knight was fined £800 by Richard Cœur de Lion for allowing a French prisoner of consequence to escape from his custody. He married a daughter of a King of Scotland, was Sheriff of Cumberland, helped to extort Magna Charta from King John, and gave much public property to the Templars.

During the repairs of the round tower several sarcophagi of Purbeck marble were discovered. On the coffins being removed while the tower was being propped, the bodies all crumbled to dust. The sarcophagi were all reinterred in the centre of the "Round."

During the repairs of 1850 the workmen dis-covered and stole an ancient seal of the Order; it had the name of Berengarius, and on one side was represented the Holy Sepulchre. "The churchyard abounds," Mr. Addison says, "with ancient stone coffins. According to Burton, an antiquary of Elizabeth's time, there then existed in the Temple Church a monument to a Visitor-General of the Order. Among other distinguished persons buried in the Temple Church, for so many ages a place of special sanctity, was William Plantagenet, fifth son of Henry III., who died when a youth. Henry III. himself, had at one time resolved to be buried " with the brethren of the Chivalry of the Temple, expecting and hoping that, through our Lord and Saviour, it will greatly contribute to the salvation of our soul." Queen Eleanor also provided for her interment in the Temple, but it was otherwise decreed.

In the triforium of the Temple Church have been packed away, like lumber, the greater part of the clumsy monuments that once disfigured the walls and columns below. In this strange museum lord chancellors, councillors of state, learned benchers, barons of the exchequer, masters of the rolls, treasurers, readers, prothonotaries, poets, and authors jostle each other in dusty confusion. At the entrance, under a canopy, is the recumbent figure of the great lawyer of Elizabeth's time, Edmund Plowden. This grave and wise man, being a staunch Romanist, was slighted by the Protestant Queen. It is said that he was so studious in his youth that at one period he never went out of the Temple precincts for three whole years. He was Treasurer of the Middle Temple when the Hall was built.

Selden (that great writer on international law, whose "Mare clausum" was a reply to the "Mare liberum" of Grotius) is buried to the left of the altar, the spot being marked by a monument of white marble. "His grave," says Aubrey, "was about ten feet deepe or better, walled up a good way with bricks, of which also the bottome was paved, but the sides at the bottome for about two foot high were of black polished marble, wherein his coffin (covered with black bayes) lyeth, and upon that wall of marble was presently lett downe a huge black marble stone of great thicknesse, with this inscription—'Hic jacet corpus Johannis Seldeni, qui obijt 30 die Novembris, 1654.' Over this was turned an arch of brick (for the house would not lose their ground), and upon that was throwne the earth," &c.

There is a monument in the triforium to Edmund Gibbon, a herald and an ancestor of the historian. The great writer alluding to this monument says, "My family arms are the same which were borne by the Gibbons of Kent, in an age when the College of Heralds religiously guarded the distinctions of blood and name—a lion rampant gardant between three schollop shells argent, on a field azure. I should not, however, have been tempted to blazon my coat of arms were it not connected with a whimsical anecdote. About the reign of James I., the three harmless schollop shells were changed by Edmund Gibbon, Esq., into three ogresses, or female cannibals, with a design of stigmatising three ladies, his kinswomen, who had

provoked him by an unjust lawsuit. But this singular mode of revenge, for which he obtained the sanction of Sir William Seager, King-at-Arms, soon expired with its author; and on his own monument in the Temple Church the monsters vanish, and the three schollop shells resume their proper and hereditary place."

At the latter end of Charles II.'s reign the organ in the Temple Church became the subject of a singular contest, which was decided by a most remarkable judge. The benchers had determined to have the best organ in London; the competitors for the building were Smith and Harris. Father Smith, a German, was renowned for his care in choosing wood without knot or flaw, and for throwing aside every metal or wooden pipe that was not perfect and sound. His stops were also allowed by all to be singularly equal and sweet in tone. The two competitors were each to erect an organ in the Temple Church, and the best one was to be retained. The competition was carried on with such violence that some of the partisans almost ruined themselves by the money they expended. The night preceding the trial the too zealous friends of Harris cut the bellows of Smith's organ, and rendered it for the time useless. Drs. Blow and Purcell were employed to show the powers of Smith's instrument, and the French organist of Queen Catharine performed on Harris's. The contest continued, with varying success, for nearly a twelvemonth. At length Harris challenged ' is redoubtable r.val to make certain additional reed stops, vox humana, cremona, double bassoon and other stops, within a given time. The controversy was at last terminated by Lord Chief Justice Jefferies—the cruel and debauched Jefferies, who was himself an accomplished musician—deciding in favour of Father Smith. Part of Harris's rejected organ was erected at St. Andrew's, Holborn, part at Christ Church Cathedral, Dublin. Father Smith, in consequence of his success at the Temple, was employed to build an organ for St. Paul's, but Sir Christopher Wren would never allow the case to be made large enough to receive all the stops. "The sound and general mechanism of modern instruments," says Mr. Burge, "are certainly superior to those of Father Smith's, but for sweetness of tone I have never met in any part of Europe with pipes that have equalled his."

In the reign of James I. there was a great dispute between the Custos of the Temple and the two Societies. This sinecure office, the gift of the Crown, was a rectory without tithes, and the Custos was dependent upon voluntary contributions. The benchers, irritated at Dr. Micklethwaite's arrogant pretensions, shut the doctor out from their dinners. In the reign of Charles I., the doctor complained to the king that he received no tithes, was refused precedence as Master of the Temple, was allowed no share in the deliberations, was not paid for his supernumerary sermons, and was denied ecclesiastical jurisdiction. The doctor thereupon locked up the church and took away the keys; but Noy, the Attorney-General, snubbed him, and called him "*elatus et superbus;*" and he got nothing, after all, but hard words for his petition.

The learned and judicious Hooker, author of "The Ecclesiastical Polity," was for six years Master of the Temple—"a place," says Izaak Walton, "which he accepted rather than desired." Travers, a disciple of Cartwright the Nonconformist, was the lecturer; so Hooker, it was said, preached Canterbury in the forenoon, and Travers Geneva in the afternoon. The benchers were divided, and Travers being at last silenced by the archbishop, Hooker resigned, and in his quiet parsonage of Bishopsbourne renewed the contest in print, in his "Ecclesiastical Polity."

When Bishop Sherlock was Master of the Temple, the sees of Canterbury and London were vacant about the same time (1748); this occasioned an epigram upon Sherlock,—

> "At the Temple one day Sherlock taking a boat,
> The waterman asked him, 'Which way will you float?'
> 'Which way?' says the Doctor; 'why, fool, with the stream!
> To St. Paul's or to Lambeth was all one to him."

The tide in favour of Sherlock was running to St. Paul's. He was made Bishop of London. Most of his successors in the Mastership have been men of eminence.

During the repairs of 1827 the ancient freestone chapel of St. Anne, which stood on the south side of the "Round," was removed. The upper storey communicated with the Temple Church by a staircase opening on the west end of the south aisle of the choir; the lower joined the "Round" by a doorway under one of the arches of the circular arcade. The chapel anciently opened upon the cloisters, and formed a private way from the convent to the church. Here the Papal legate and the highest bishops frequently held conferences; and on Sunday mornings the Master of the Temple held chapters, enjoined penances, made up quarrels, and pronounced absolution. The chapel of St. Anne was in the old time much resorted to by barren women, who there prayed for children.

In Charles II.'s time, according to "Hudibras," "straw bail" and low rascals of that sort lingered about the Round, waiting for hire. Butler says:—

> "Retain all sorts of witnesses
> That ply i' the Temple, under trees;
> Or walk the Round with Knights o' th' Posts,
> About the cross-legg'd knights, their hosts;
> Or wait for customers between
> The pillar rows in Lincoln's Inn."

In James I.'s time the Round, as we find in Ben Jonson, was a place for appointments; and in 1681 Otway describes bullies of Alsatia, with flapping hats pinned up on one side, sandy, weather-beaten periwigs, and clumsy iron swords clattering at their heels, as conspicuous personages among the Knights of the Posts and the other peripatetic philosophers of the Temple walks.

We must now turn to the history of the whole precinct. When the proud Order was abolished by the Pope, Edward II. granted the Temple to Aymer de Valence, Earl of Pembroke, who, however, soon surrendered it to the king's cousin, the Earl of Lancaster, who let it, at their special request, to the students and professors of the common laws; the colony then gradually became an organised and collegiate body, Edward I. having authorised laymen for the first time to read and plead causes.

Hugh le Despenser for a time held the Temple, and on his execution Edward III. appointed the Mayor of London its guardian. The mayor, by closing the water-gate, caused much vexation to the lawyers rowing by boat to Westminster, and the king had to interfere. In 1333 the king farmed out the Temple rents at £25 a year. In the meantime, the Knights Hospitallers, affecting to be offended at the desecration of holy ground—the Bishop of Ely's lodgings, a chapel dedicated to à Becket, and the door to the Temple Hall—claimed the forfeited spot. The king granted their request, the annual revenue of the Temple then being £73 6s. 11d., equal to about £1,000 of our present money. In 1340, in consideration of £100 towards an expedition to France, the warlike king made over the residue of the Temple to the Hospitallers, who instantly endowed the church with lands and one thousand fagots a year from Lillerton Wood to keep up the church fires.

In this reign Chaucer, who is supposed to have been a student of the Middle Temple, and who is said to have once beaten an insolent Franciscan friar in Fleet Street, gives a eulogistic sketch of a Temple manciple or purveyor of provisions, in the prologue to his wonderful "Canterbury Tales."

> " A gentil manciple was there of the Temple,
> Of whom achatours mighten take ensample,
> For to ben wise in bying of vitàille;
> For, whether that he paid or toke by taille.

Algate he waited so in his achate
That he was aye before in good estate.
Now is not that of God a full fayre grace
That swiche a lewèd mannès wit shall face
The wisdom of an hepe of lerned men?

" Of maisters had he more than thries ten,
That were of law expert and curious;
Of which there was a dosein in that hous
Worthy to ben stewardes of rent and land
Of any lord that is in Engleland :
To maken him live by his propre good,
In honour detteles ; but if he were wood,
Or live as scarsly as him list desire,
And able for to helpen all a shire,
In any cos that mighte fallen or happe :
And yet this manciple sett 'hir aller cappe."

serjeants-at-law exactly resembles that once used for receiving "Fratres Servientes" into the fraternity of the Temple.

In Wat Tyler's rebellion the wild men of Kent poured down on the dens of the Temple lawyers, pulled down their houses, carried off the books, deeds, and rolls of remembrance, and burnt them in Fleet Street, to spite the Knights Hospitallers. Walsingham, the chronicler, indeed, says that the rebels—who, by the by, claimed only their rights—had resolved to decapitate all the lawyers of London, to put an end to all the laws that had oppressed them, and to clear the ground for better times. In the reign of Henry VI. the overgrown

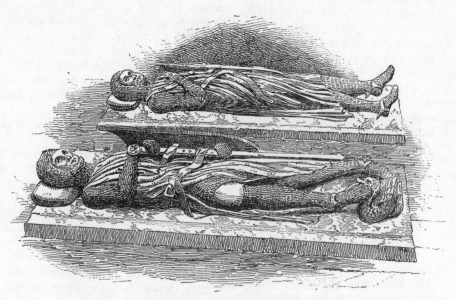

TOMBS OF KNIGHTS TEMPLARS (*see page* 152).

In the Middle Temple Chaucer is supposed to have formed the acquaintanceship of his graver contemporary, " the moral Gower."

Many of the old retainers of the Templars became servants of the new lawyers, who had ousted their masters. The attendants at table were still called paniers, as they had formerly been. The dining in pairs, the expulsion from hall for misconduct, and the locking out of chambers were old customs also kept up. The judges of Common Pleas retained the title of " knight," and the " Fratres Servientes" of the Templars arose again in the character of learned serjeants-at-law, the coif of the modern serjeant being the linen coif of the old " Freres Serjens" of the Temple. The coif was never, as some suppose, intended to hide the tonsure of priests practising law contrary to ecclesiastical prohibition. The old ceremony of creating

society of the Temple divided into two Halls, or rather the original two Halls of the knights and "Fratres Servientes" separated into two societies. Brooke, the Elizabethan antiquary, says : " To this day, in memory of the old custom, the benchers or ancients of the one society dine once every year in the Hall of the other society."

Sir John Fortescue, Chief Justice of the King's Bench in the reign of Henry VI., computed the annual expenses of each law student at more than £28, or about " £450 of our present money." The students were all gentlemen by birth, and at each Inn of Court there was an academy, where singing, music, and dancing were taught. On festival days, after the offices of the Church, the students employed themselves in the study of history and in reading the Scriptures. Any student expelled one society was refused admission to any of the other societies. A manuscript (*temp.* Henry VIII.) in the Cottonian Library dwells much on the readings, mootings, boltings, and other practices of the Temple students, and analyses the various classes of benchers, readers, cupboard-men, inner barristers, outer barristers, and students. The writer also mentions the fact that in term times the students met to talk law and confer on business in the church, which was, he says, as noisy as St. Paul's. When the plague broke out the students went home to the country.

The attention paid by the governors of the house both to the morals and dress of its members is evidenced by the imposition, in the thirteenth year of the reign of Henry VIII., of a fine of 6s. 8d. on any one who should exercise the plays of "shove-grote" or "slyp-grote," and by the mandate afterwards issued in the thirty-eighth year of the same reign, that students should reform themselves in their cut, or disguised apparel, and should not have long beards.

It is in the Temple Gardens that Shakespeare—

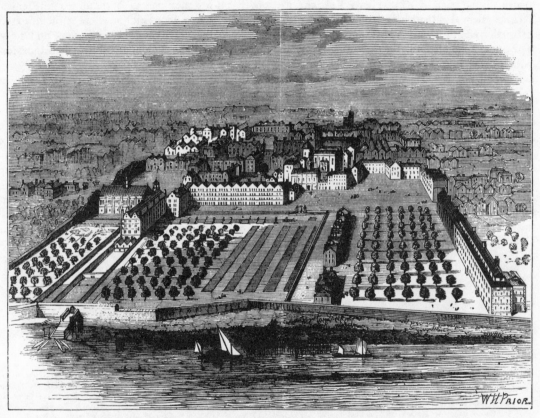

THE TEMPLE IN 1671.   (FROM AN OLD BIRD'S-EYE VIEW IN THE INNER TEMPLE.)

The Society of the Inner Temple was very active (says Mr. Foss) during the reign of Henry VIII. in the erection of new buildings. Several houses for chambers were constructed near the Library, and were called Pakington's Rents, from the name of the Treasurer who superintended them. Henry Bradshaw, Treasurer in the twenty-sixth year, gave his name to another set then built, which it kept until Chief Baron Tanfield resided there in the reign of James I., since which it has been called Tanfield Court. Other improvements were made about the same period, one of these being the construction of a new ceiling to the hall and the erection of a wall between the garden and the Thames.

relying, probably, on some old tradition which does not exist in print—has laid one of the scenes of his *King Henry VI.*—that, namely, in which the partisans of the rival houses of York and Lancaster first assume their distinctive badges of the white and red roses :—

> "*Suffolk.* Within the Temple Hall we were too loud :
> The garden here is more convenient.
>
>   *   *   *   *
>
> "*Plantagenet.* Let him that is a true-born gentleman,
> And stands upon the honour of his birth,
> If he suppose that I have pleaded truth,
> From off this brier pluck a white rose with me.
> "*Somerset.* Let him that is no coward, nor no flatterer,

But dare maintain the party of the truth,
Pluck a red rose from off this thorn with me.

　　　*　　　*　　　*　　　*

" *Plantagenet.* Hath not thy rose a canker, Somerset?
" *Somerset.* Hath not thy rose a thorn, Plantagenet?

　　　*　　　*　　　*　　　*

" *Warwick.*　　　　　　　　This brawl to-day,
Grown to this faction in the Temple Garden,
Shall send, between the red rose and the white,
A thousand souls to death and deadly night."

　　　　　　　King Henry VI., Part I., Act ii., sc. 4.

The books of the Middle Temple do not commence till the reign of King Henry VII., the first Treasurer named in them being John Brooke, in the sixteenth year of Henry VII. (1500-1). Readers were not appointed till the following year, the earliest being John Vavasour—probably son of the judge, and not, as Dugdale calls him, the judge himself, who had then been on the bench for twelve years. Members of the house might be excused from living in common on account of their wives being in town, or for other special reasons.

In the last year of Philip and Mary (1558) eight gentlemen of the Temple were expelled the society and committed to the Fleet for wilful disobedience to the Bench, but on their humble submission they were readmitted. A year before this a severe Act of Parliament was passed, prohibiting Templars wearing beards of more than three weeks' growth, upon pain of a forty-shilling fine, and double for every week after monition. The young lawyers were evidently getting too foppish. They were required to cease wearing Spanish cloaks, swords, bucklers, rapiers, gowns, hats, or daggers at their girdles. Only knights and benchers were to display doublets or hose of any light colour, except scarlet and crimson, or to affect velvet caps, scarf-wings to their gowns, white jerkins, buskins, velvet shoes, double shirt-cuffs, or feathers or ribbons in their caps. Moreover, no attorney was to be admitted into either house. These monastic rules were intended to preserve the gravity of the profession, and must have pleased the Poloniuses and galled the Mercutios of those troublous days.

In Elizabeth's days Master Gerard Leigh, a pedantic scholar of the College of Heralds, persuaded the misguided Inner Temple to abandon the old Templar arms—a plain red cross on a shield argent, with a lamb bearing the banner of the sinless profession, surmounted by a red cross. The heraldic euphuist substituted for this a flying Pegasus striking out the fountain of Hippocrene with its hoofs, with the appended motto of " Volat ad astra virtus," a recondite allusion to men like Chaucer and Gower, who, it is said, had turned from lawyers to poets.

CHAPTER XV.

THE TEMPLE (*continued*).

The Middle Temple Hall: its Roof, Busts, and Portraits—Manningham's Diary—Fox Hunts in Hall—The Grand Revels—Spenser—Sir J. Davis—A Present to a King—Masques and Royal Visitors at the Temple—Fires in the Temple—The Last Great Revel in the Hall—Temple Anecdotes—The Gordon Riots—John Scott and his Pretty Wife—Colman " Keeping Terms "—Blackstone's " Farewell "—Burke—Sheridan—A Pair of Epigrams—Hare Court—The Barber's Shop—Johnson and the Literary Club—Charles Lamb—Goldsmith : his Life, Troubles, and Extravagances—" Hack Work " for Booksellers—*The Deserted Village—She Stoops to Conquer*—Goldsmith's Death and Burial.

IN the glorious reign of Elizabeth the old Middle Temple Hall was converted into chambers, and a new Hall built. The present roof (says Mr. Peter Cunningham) is the best piece of Elizabethan architecture in London. The screen, in the Renaissance style, was long supposed to be an exact copy of the Strand front of Old Somerset House; but this is a vulgar error; nor could it have been made of timber from the Spanish Armada, for the simple reason that it was set up thirteen years before the Armada was organised. The busts of "doubting" Lord Eldon and his brother, Lord Stowell, the great Admiralty judge, are by Behnes. The portraits are chiefly second-rate copies. The exterior was cased with stone, in " wretched taste," in 1757. The diary of an Elizabethan barrister, named Manningham, preserved in the Harleian Miscellany, has revealed the interesting fact that in this hall in February, 1602—probably, says Mr. Collier, six months after its first appearance at the Globe—Shakespeare's *Twelfth Night* was acted.

" Feb. 2, 1601 (2).—At our feast," says Manningham, " we had a play called *Twelve Night, or What you Will*, much like the *Comedy of Errors* or *Menæchmi in Plautus*, but most like and neere to that in Italian called *Inganni*. A good practice in it is to make the steward believe his lady widdowe was in love with him, by counterfayting a letter, as from his lady, in generall terms telling him what shee liked best in him, and prescribing his gestures, inscribing his apparaile, &c., and then, when he came to practise, making him believe they tooke him to be mad."

The Temple Revels in the olden time were indeed gorgeous outbursts of mirth and hospitality. One of the most splendid of these took place in the fourth year of Elizabeth's reign, when the queen's favourite, Lord Robert Dudley (afterwards the great Earl of Leicester) was elected Palaphilos, constable or marshal of the inn, to preside over the Christmas festivities. He had lord chancellor and judges, eighty guards, officers of the household, and other distinguished persons to attend him ; and another of the queen's subsequent favourites, Christopher Hatton—a handsome youth, remarkable for his skill in dancing—was appointed master of the games. The daily banquets of the Constable were announced by the discharge of a double cannon, and drums and fifes summoned the mock court to the common hall, while sackbuts, cornets, and recorders heralded the arrival of every course. At the first remove a herald at the high table cried,— "The mighty Palaphilos, Prince of Sophie, High Constable, Marshal of the Knights Templars, Patron of the Honourable Order of Pegasus !— a largesse ! a largesse !" upon which the Prince of Sophie tossed the man a gold chain worth a thousand talents. The supper ended, the king-at-arms entered, and, doing homage, announced twenty-four special gentlemen, whom Pallas had ordered him to present to Palaphilos as knights-elect of the Order of Pegasus. The twenty-four gentlemen at once appeared, in long white vestures with scarves of Pallas's colours, and the king-at-arms, bowing to each, explained to them the laws of the new order.

For every feast the steward provided five fat hams, with spices and cakes, and the chief butler seven dozen gilt and silver spoons, twelve damask table-cloths, and twenty candlesticks. The Constable wore gilt armour and a plumed helmet, and bore a pole-axe in his hands. On St. Thomas's Eve a parliament was held, when the two youngest brothers, bearing torches, preceded the procession of benchers, the officers' names were called, and the whole society passed round the hearth singing a carol. On Christmas Eve the minstrels, sounding, preceded the dishes, and, dinner done, sang a song at the high table; after dinner the oldest master of the revels and other gentlemen sang songs.

On Christmas Day the feast grew still more feudal and splendid. At the great meal at noon the minstrels and a long train of servitors bore in the blanched boar's head, with a golden lemon in its jaws, the trumpeters being preceded by two gentlemen in gowns, bearing four torches of white wax. On St. Stephen's Day the younger Templars waited at table upon the Benchers. At the first course the Constable entered, to the sound of horns, preceded by sixteen swaggering trumpeters, while the halberdiers bore "the tower" on their shoulders and marched gravely three times round the fire.

On St. John's Day the Constable was up at seven, and personally called and reprimanded any tardy officers, who were sometimes committed to the Tower for disorder. If any officer absented himself at meals, any one sitting in his place was compelled to pay his fee and assume his office. Any offender, if he escaped into the oratory, could claim sanctuary, and was pardoned if he returned into the hall humbly and as a servitor, carrying a roll on the point of a knife. No one was allowed to sing after the cheese was served.

On Childermas Day, New Year's Day, and Twelfth Night the same costly feasts were continued, only that on Thursday there was roast beef and venison pasty for dinner, and mutton and roast hens were served for supper. The final banquet closing all was preceded by a dance, revel, play, or mask, the gentlemen of every Inn of Court and Chancery being invited, and the hall furnished with side scaffolds for the ladies, who were feasted in the library. The Lord Chancellor and the "ancients" feasted in the hall, the Templars serving. The feast over, the Constable, in his gilt armour, ambled into the hall on a caparisoned mule, and arranged the sequence of sports.

The Constable then, with three reverences, knelt before the King of the Revels, and, delivering up his naked sword, prayed to be taken into the royal service. Next entered Hatton, the Master of the Game, clad in green velvet, his rangers arrayed in green satin. Blowing "a blast of venery" three times on their horns, and holding green-coloured bows and arrows in their hands, the rangers paced three times round the central fire, then knelt to the King of the Revels, and desired admission into the royal service. Next ensued a strange and barbarous ceremony. A huntsman entered with a live fox and cat and nine or ten couple of hounds, and, to the blast of horns and wild shouting, the poor creatures were torn to shreds, for the amusement of the applauding Templars. At supper the Constable entered to the sound of drums, borne upon a scaffold by four men, and as he was carried three times round the hearth every one shouted, "A lord ! a lord !"

He then descended, called together his mock court, by such fantastic names as—

"Sir Francis Flatterer, of Fowlershurst, in the county of Buckingham;

Sir Randal Rakabite, of Rascal Hall, in the county of Rakebell;

Sir Morgan Mumchance, of Much Monkery, in the county of Mad Mopery;"

and the banquet then began, every man having a gilt pot full of wine, and each one paying sixpence for his repast. That night, when the lights were put out, the noisy, laughing train passed out of the portal, and the long revels were ended.

"Sir Edward Coke," says Lord Campbell, writing of this period, "first evinced his forensic powers when deputed by the students to make a representation to the benchers of the Inner Temple respecting the bad quality of their *commons* in the hall. After laboriously studying the facts and the law of the case, he clearly proved that the cook had broken his engagement, and was liable to be dismissed. This, according to the phraseology of the day, was called 'the cook's case, and he was said to have argued it with so much quickness of penetration and solidity of judgment, that he gave entire satisfaction to the students, and was much admired by the Bench."

In his exquisite "Prothalamion" Spenser alludes to the Temple as if he had sketched it from the river, after a visit to his great patron, the Earl of Essex,—

> "Those bricky towers,
> The which on Thames' broad, aged back doe ride,
> Where now the studious lawyers have their bowers,
> There whilom wont the Templar Knights to bide,
> Till they decayed through pride."

Sir John Davis, the author of "Nosce Teipsum," that fine mystic poem on the immortality of the soul, and of that strange philosophical rhapsody on dancing, was expelled the Temple in Elizabeth's reign, for thrashing his friend, another royster of the day, Mr. Richard Martin, in the Middle Temple Hall; but afterwards, on proper submission, he was readmitted. Davis afterwards reformed, and became the wise Attorney-General of Ireland. His biographer says, that the preface to his "Irish Reports" vies with Coke for solidity and Blackstone for elegance. Martin (whose monument is now hoarded up in the Triforium) also became a learned lawyer and a friend of Selden, and was the person to whom Ben Jonson dedicated his bitter play, *The Poetaster*. In the dedication the poet says, "For whose innocence as for the author's you were once a noble and kindly undertaker: signed, your true lover, BEN JONSON."

On the accession of James I. some of his hungry Scotch courtiers attempted to obtain from the king a grant of the fee-simple of the Temple; upon which the two indignant societies made "humble suit" to the king, and obtained a grant of the property to themselves. The grant was signed in 1609, the benchers paying £10 annually to the king for the Inner Temple, and £10 for the Middle. In gratitude for this concession, the two loyal societies presented his majesty with a stately gold cup, weighing 200½ ounces, which James "most graciously" accepted. On one side was engraved a temple, on the other a flaming altar, with the words *nil nisi vobis;* on the pyramidical cover stood a Roman soldier leaning on his shield. This cup the bibulous monarch ever afterwards esteemed as one of his rarest and richest jewels. In 1623 James issued one of his absurd and trumpery sumptuary edicts, recommending the ancient way of wearing caps, and requesting the Templars to lay aside their unseemly boots and spurs, the badges of "roarers, rakes, and bullies."

The Temple feasts continued to be as lavish and magnificent as in the days of Queen Mary, when no reader was allowed to contribute less than fifteen bucks to the hall dinner, and many during their readings gave fourscore or a hundred.

On the marriage (1613) of the Lady Elizabeth, daughter of King James I., with Prince Frederick, the unfortunate Elector-Palatine, the Temple and Gray's Inn men gave a masque, of which Sir Francis Bacon was the chief contriver. The masque came to Whitehall by water from Winchester Place, in Southwark; three peals of ordnance greeting them as they embarked with torches and lamps, as they passed the Temple Garden, and as they landed. This short trip cost £300. The king, after all, was so tired, and the hall was so crowded, that the masque was adjourned till the Saturday following, when all went well. The next night the king gave a supper to the forty masquers; Prince Charles and his courtiers, who had lost a wager to the king at running at the ring, paid for the banquet, £30 a man. The masquers, who dined with forty of the chief nobles, kissed his majesty's hand. Shortly after this twenty Templars fought at barriers, in honour of Prince Charles, the benchers contributing thirty shillings each to the expenses; the barristers of seven years' standing, fifteen shillings; and the other gentlemen in commons, ten shillings.

One of the grandest masques ever given by the Templars was one which cost £21,000, and was presented, in 1633, to Charles I. and his French queen. Bulstrode Whitelock, then in his youth, gives a vivid picture of this pageant, which was meant to refute Prynne's angry "Histro-Mastix." Noy and Selden were members of the committee, and many grave heads met together to discuss the dances, dresses, and music. The music was written by Milton's friend, Lawes, the libretto by Shirley. The procession set out from Ely House, in Holborn, on Candlemas Day, in the evening. The four chariots that bore the sixteen masquers were preceded by twenty footmen in silver-laced scarlet liveries, who carried torches and cleared the way. After these rode 100 gentlemen from the Inns of Court, mounted and richly clad, every gentleman having two lackeys with torches and a page to carry his cloak. Then followed the other masquers— beggars on horseback and boys dressed as birds. The colours of the first chariot were crimson and silver, the four horses being plumed and trapped in parti-coloured tissue. The Middle Temple rode next, in blue and silver; and the Inner Temple and Lincoln's Inn followed in equal bravery, 100 of the suits being reckoned to have cost £10,000. The masque was most perfectly performed in the Banqueting House at Whitehall, the Queen dancing with several of the masquers, and declaring them to be as good dancers as ever she saw.

The year after the Restoration Sir Heneage Finch, afterwards Earl of Nottingham, kept his "reader's feast" in the great hall of the Inner Temple. At that time of universal vice, luxury, and extravagance, the banquet lasted from the 4th to the 17th of August. It was, in fact, open house to all London. The first day came the nobles and privy councillors; the second, the Lord Mayor and aldermen; the third, the whole College of Physicians, attired in their caps and gowns; the fourth, the doctors and advocates of civil law; on the fifth day, the archbishops, bishops, and obsequious clergy; and on the fifteenth, as a last grand display, the King, the Duke of York, the Duke of Buckingham, and half the peers. An entrance was made from the river through the wall of the Temple Garden, the King being received on landing by the Reader and the Lord Chief Justice of the Common Pleas; the path from the garden to the wall was lined with the Reader's servants, clad in scarlet cloaks and white doublets; while above them stood the benchers, barristers, and students, music playing all the while, and twenty violins welcoming Charles into the hall with unanimous scrape and quaver. Dinner was served by fifty young students in their gowns, no meaner servants appearing. In the November following the Duke of York, the Duke of Buckingham, and the Earl of Dorset were admitted members of the Society of the Inner

Temple. Six years after, Prince Rupert, then a grizzly old cavalry soldier, and addicted to experiments in chemistry and engraving in his house in the Barbican, received the same honour.

The great fire of 1666, says Mr. Jeaffreson, in his "Law and Lawyers," was stayed in its westward course at the Temple; but it was not suppressed until the flames had consumed many sets of chambers, had devoured the title-deeds of a vast number of valuable estates, and had almost licked the windows of the Temple Church. Clarendon has recorded that on the occasion of this stupendous calamity, which occurred when a large proportion of the Templars were out of town, the lawyers in residence declined to break open the chambers and rescue the property of absent members of their society, through fear of prosecution for burglary. Another great fire, some years later (January, 1678–79), destroyed the old cloisters and part of the old hall of the Inner Temple, and the greater part of the residential buildings of the "Old Temple." Breaking out at midnight, and lasting till noon of next day, it devoured, in the Middle Temple, the whole of Pump Court (in which locality it originated), Elm-tree Court, Vine Court, and part of Brick Court; in the Inner Temple the cloisters, the greater part of Hare Court, and part of the hall. The night was bitterly cold, and the Templars, aroused from their beds to preserve life and property, could not get an adequate supply of water from the Thames, which the unusual severity of the season had frozen. In this difficulty they actually brought barrels of ale from the Temple butteries, and fed the engines with the malt liquor. Of course this supply of fluid was soon exhausted, so the fire spreading eastward, the lawyers fought it by blowing up the buildings that were in immediate danger. Gunpowder was more effectual than beer; but the explosions were sadly destructive to human life. Amongst the buildings thus demolished was the library of the Inner Temple. Naturally, but with no apparent good reason, the sufferers by the fire attributed it to treachery on the part of persons unknown, just as the citizens attributed the fire of 1666 to the Papists. It is more probable that the calamity was caused by some such accident as that which occasioned the fire which, during Lord Campbell's attorney-generalship, destroyed a large amount of property, and, according to one story, had its origin in the clumsiness of a barrister, who upset a vessel full of spirit. Of this same fire he himself observes:—"When I was Attorney-General, my chambers in Paper Buildings, Temple, were burnt to the ground in the night-time, and all my books and manuscripts, with some valuable official papers, were consumed. Above all, I had to lament a collection of letters written to me by my dear father, from the time of my going to college till his death in 1824. All lamented this calamity except the claimant of a peerage, some of whose documents (suspected to chambers, which latter had been for the benefit of the Middle Temple; but, in regard that it could not be done without the consent of the Inner Houses, the masters of the Middle Houses waited upon the then Mr. Attorney Finch to desire the concurrence of his society upon a proposition of

THE OLD HALL OF THE INNER TEMPLE (*see page* 164).

be forged) he hoped were destroyed; but fortunately they had been removed into safe custody a few days before, and the claim was dropped." The fire here alluded to broke out in the chambers of Mr. (afterwards Judge) Maule.

"I remember," says North in his "Life of Lord Keeper Guildford," "that after the fire of the Temple it was considered whether the old cloister walks should be rebuilt or rather improved into some benefit to be thrown in on his side. But Mr. Attorney would by no means give way to it, and reproved the Middle Templars very bitterly and eloquently upon the subject of students walking in evenings there, and putting 'cases,' which, he said, 'was done in his time, mean and low as the buildings were then. However, it comes,' he said, 'that such a benefit to students is now made little account of. And thereupon the cloisters, by the

1. Door from the Middle Temple.
2. Wig-Shop in the Middle Temple.
3. Door from the Inner Temple.
4. Screen of the Middle Temple Hall.
5. Fireplace in the Inner Temple.
6. Buttery of the Inner Temple.

order and disposition of Sir Christopher Wren, were built as they now stand."

The last revel in any of the Inns of Court was held in the Inner Temple, February, 1733 (George II.), in honour of Mr. Talbot, a bencher of that house, accepting the Great Seal. The ceremony is described by an eye-witness in "Wynne's Eunomus." "The Lord Chancellor arrived at two o'clock, preceded by Mr. Wollaston, Master of the Revels, and followed by Dr. Sherlock, Bishop of Bangor, Master of the Temple, and the judges and serjeants formerly of the Inner Temple. There was an elegant dinner provided for them and the chancellor's officers, but the barristers and students had only the usual meal of grand days, except that each man was furnished with a flask of claret besides the usual allowance of port and sack. Fourteen students waited on the Bench table : among them was Mr. Talbot, the Lord Chancellor's eldest son, and by their means any special dish was easily obtainable from the upper table. A large gallery was built over the screen for the ladies ; and music, placed in the little gallery at the upper end of the hall, played all dinner-time. As soon as dinner was over, the play of *Love for Love* and the farce of *The Devil to Pay* were acted, the actors coming from the Haymarket in chaises, all ready-dressed. It was said they refused all gratuity, being satisfied with the honour of performing before such an audience. After the play, the Lord Chancellor, the Master of the Temple, the judges and benchers retired into their parliament chamber, and in about half an hour afterwards came into the hall again, and a large ring was formed round the fire-place (but no fire nor embers were in it). Then the Master of the Revels, who went first, took the Lord Chancellor by the right hand, and he with his left took Mr. J [ustice] Page, who, joined to the other judges, serjeants, and benchers present, danced, or rather walked, round about the coal fire, according to the old ceremony, three times, during which they were aided in the figure of the dance by Mr. George Cooke, the prothonotary, then upwards of sixty ; and all the time of the dance the *ancient song*, accompanied with music, was sung by one Tony Aston (an actor), dressed in a bar gown, whose father had been formerly Master of the Plea Office in the King's Bench. When this was over, the ladies came down from the gallery, went into the parliament chamber, and stayed about a quarter of an hour, while the hall was putting in order. Then they went into the hall and danced a few minutes. Country dances began about ten, and at twelve a very fine collation was provided for the whole company, from which they

returned to dancing. The Prince of Wales honoured the performance with his company part of the time. He came into the music gallery wing about the middle of the play, and went away as soon as the farce of walking round the coal fire was over."

Mr. Peter Cunningham, *apropos* of these revels, mentions that when the floor of the Middle Temple Hall was taken up in 1764 there were found nearly one hundred pair of very small dice, yellowed by time, which had dropped through the chinks above. The same writer caps this fact by one of his usually apposite quotations. Wycherly, in his *Plain Dealer* (1676—Charles II.), makes Freeman, one of his characters, say :—"Methinks 'tis like one of the Halls in Christmas time, whither from all parts fools bring their money to try the dice (nor the worst judges), whether it shall be their own or no."

The Inner Temple Hall (the refectory of the ancient knights) was almost entirely rebuilt in 1816. The roof was overloaded with timber, the west wall was cracking, and the wooden cupola of the bell let in the rain. The pointed arches and rude sculpture at the entrance doors showed great antiquity, but the northern wall had been rebuilt in 1680. The incongruous Doric screen was surmounted by lions' heads, cones, and other anomalous devices, and in 1741 low, classic windows had been inserted in the south front. Of the old hall, where the Templars frequently held their chapters, and at different times entertained King John, King Henry III., and several of the legates, several portions still remain. A very ancient groined Gothic arch forms the roof of the present buttery, and in the apartment beyond there is a fine groined and vaulted ceiling. In the cellars below are old walls of vast thickness, part of an ancient window, a curious fire-place, and some pointed arches, partly choked with modern brick partitions and dusty staircases. These vaults formerly communicated by a cloister with the chapel of St. Anne, on the south side of the church. In the reign of James I. some brick chambers, three storeys high, were erected over the cloister, but were burnt down in 1678. In 1681 the cloister chambers were again rebuilt.

During the formation of the present new entrance to the Temple by the church at the bottom of Inner Temple Lane, when some old houses were removed, the masons came on a strong ancient wall of chalk and ragstone, supposed to have been the ancient northern boundary of the convent.

Let us cull a few Temple anecdotes from various ages :—

In November, 1819, Erskine, in the House of Lords, speaking upon Lord Lansdowne's motion for an inquiry into the state of the country, condemned the conduct of the yeomanry at the "Manchester massacre." "By an ordinary display of spirit and resolution," observed the brilliant egotist to his brother peers (who were so impressed by his complacent volubility and good-humoured self-esteem, that they were for the moment ready to take him at his own valuation), "insurrection may be repressed without violating the law or the constitution. In the riots of 1780, when the mob were preparing to attack the house of Lord Mansfield, I offered to defend it with a small military force; but this offer was unluckily rejected. Afterwards, being in the Temple when the rioters were preparing to force the gate and had fired several times, I went to the gate, opened it, and showed them a field-piece, which I was prepared to discharge in case the attack was persisted in. They were daunted, fell back, and dispersed."

Judge Burrough (says Mr. Jeaffreson, in his "Law and Lawyers") used to relate that when the Gordon Rioters besieged the Temple he and a strong body of barristers, headed by a sergeant of the Guards, were stationed in Inner Temple Lane, and that, having complete confidence in the strength of their massive gate, they spoke bravely of their desire to be fighting on the other side. At length the gate was forced. The lawyers fell into confusion and were about to beat a retreat, when the sergeant, a man of infinite humour, cried out in a magnificent voice, "Take care no gentleman fires from behind." The words struck awe into the assailants and caused the barristers to laugh. The mob, who had expected neither laughter nor armed resistance, took to flight, telling all whom they met that the bloody-minded lawyers were armed to the teeth and enjoying themselves. The Temple was saved. When these Gordon Rioters filled London with alarm, no member of the junior bar was more prosperous and popular than handsome Jack Scott, and as he walked from his house in Carey Street to the Temple, with his wife on his arm, he returned the greetings of the barristers, who, besides liking him for a good fellow, thought it prudent to be on good terms with a man sure to achieve eminence. Dilatory in his early as well as his later years, Scott left his house that morning half an hour late. Already it was known to the mob that the Templars were assembling in their college, and a cry of "The Temple! kill the lawyers!" had been raised in Whitefriars and Essex Street. Before they reached the Middle Temple gate Mr. and Mrs. Scott were assaulted more than once. The man who won Bessie Surtees from a host of rivals and carried her away against the will of her parents and the wishes

of his own father, was able to protect her from serious violence. But before the beautiful creature was safe within the Temple her dress was torn, and when at length she stood in the centre of a crowd of excited and admiring barristers, her head was bare and her ringlets fell loose upon her shoulders. "The scoundrels have got your hat, Bessie," whispered John Scott; "but never mind—they have left you your hair."

In Lord Eldon's "Anecdote Book" there is another gate story amongst the notes on the Gordon Riots. "We youngsters," says the aged lawyer, "at the Temple determined that we would not remain inactive during such times; so we introduced ourselves into a troop to assist the military. We armed ourselves as well as we could, and next morning we drew up in the court ready to follow out a troop of soldiers who were on guard. When, however, the soldiers had passed through the gate it was suddenly shut in our faces, and the officer in command shouted from the other side, 'Gentlemen, I am much obliged to you for your intended assistance; but I do not choose to allow my soldiers to be shot, so I have ordered you to be locked in.'" And away he galloped.

The elder Colman decided on making the younger one a barrister; and after visits to Scotland and Switzerland, the son returned to Soho Square, and found that his father had taken for him chambers in the Temple, and entered him as a student at Lincoln's Inn, where he afterwards kept a few terms by eating oysters. Upon this Mr. Peake notes :—"The students of Lincoln's Inn keep term by dining, or pretending to dine, in the hall during the term time. Those who feed there are accommodated with wooden trenchers instead of plates, and previously to the dinner oysters are served up by way of prologue to the play. Eating the oysters, or going into the hall without eating them, if you please, and then departing to dine elsewhere, is quite sufficient for term-keeping." The chambers in King's Bench Walk were furnished with a tent-bedstead, two tables, half-a-dozen chairs, and a carpet as much too scanty for the boards as Sheridan's "rivulet of rhyme" for its "meadow of margin." To these the elder Colman added £10 worth of law books which had been given to him in his own Lincoln's Inn days by Lord Bath; then enjoining the son to work hard, the father left town upon a party of pleasure.

Colman had sent his son to Switzerland to get him away from a certain Miss Catherine Morris, an actress of the Haymarket company. This answered for a time, but no sooner had the father left the son in the Temple than he set off with Miss Morris to Gretna Green, and was there married, in 1784; and four years after, the father's sanction having been duly obtained, they were publicly married at Chelsea Church.

In the same staircase with Colman, in the Temple, lived the witty Jekyll, who, seeing in Colman's chambers a round cage with a squirrel in it, looked for a minute or two at the little animal, which was performing the same operation as a man in the treadmill, and then quietly said, " Ah, poor devil! he is going the Home Circuit;" the locality where it was uttered—the Temple—favouring this technical joke.

On the morning when young Colman began his studies (Dec. 20, 1784) he was interrupted by the intelligence that the funeral procession of the great Dr. Johnson was on its way from his late residence, Bolt Court, through Fleet Street, to Westminster Abbey. Colman at once threw down his pen, and ran forth to see the procession, but was disappointed to find it much less splendid and imposing than the sepulchral pomp of Garrick five years before.

Dr. Dibdin thus describes the Garden walks in the last century:—" Towards evening it was the fashion for the leading counsel to promenade during the summer months in the Temple Gardens. Cocked hats and ruffles, with satin small-clothes and silk stockings, at this time constituted the usual evening dress. Lord Erskine, though a great deal shorter than his brethren, somehow always seemed to take the lead, both in place and in discourse, and shouts of laughter would frequently follow his dicta."

" Ugly" Dunning, afterwards the famous Lord Ashburton, entered the Middle Temple in 1752, and was called four years later, in 1756. Lord Chancellor Thurlow used to describe him wittily as " the knave of clubs."

Horne Tooke, Dunning, and Kenyon were accustomed to dine together, during the vacation, at a little eating-house in the neighbourhood of Chancery Lane for the sum of sevenpence-halfpenny each. " As to Dunning and myself," said Tooke, " we were generous, for we gave the girl who waited upon us a penny a piece; but Kenyon, who always knew the value of money, sometimes rewarded her with a halfpenny, and sometimes with a promise."

Blackstone, before dedicating his powers finally to the study of the law in which he afterwards became so famous, wrote in Temple chambers his " Farewell to the Muse:"—

" Lulled by the lapse of gliding floods,
Cheer'd by the warbling of the woods,

How blest my days, my thoughts how free,
In sweet society with thee!
Then all was joyous, all was young,
And years unheeded roll'd along;
But now the pleasing dream is o'er—
These scenes must charm me now no more.
Lost to the field, and torn from you,
Farewell!—a long, a last adieu!
*   *   *   *
Then welcome business, welcome strife,
Welcome the cares, the thorns of life,
The visage wan, the purblind sight,
The toil by day, the lamp by night,
The tedious forms, the solemn prate,
The pert dispute, the dull debate,
The drowsy bench, the babbling hall,—
For thee, fair Justice, welcome all!"

That great orator, Edmund Burke, was entered at the Middle Temple in 1747, when the heads of the Scotch rebels of 1745 were still fresh on the spikes of Temple Bar, and he afterwards came to keep his terms in 1750. In 1756 he occupied a two-pair chamber at the " Pope's Head," the shop of Jacob Robinson, the Twickenham poet's publisher, just within the Inner Temple gateway. Burke took a dislike, however, perhaps fortunately for posterity, to the calf-skin books, and was never called to the bar.

Richard Brinsley Sheridan, an Irishman even more brilliant, but unfortunately far less prudent, than Burke, entered his name in the Middle Temple books a few days before his elopement with Miss Linley.

" A wit," says Archdeacon Nares, in his pleasant book, " Heraldic Anomalies," " once chalked the following lines on the Temple gate :"—

" As by the Templars' hold you go,
The horse and lamb display'd
In emblematic figures show
The merits of their trade.

" The clients may infer from thence
How just is their profession;
The lamb sets forth their innocence,
The horse their expedition.

" Oh, happy Britons! happy isle!
Let foreign nations say,
Where you get justice without guile
And law without delay."

A rival wag replied to these lively lines by the following severer ones :—

" Deluded men, these holds forego,
Nor trust such cunning elves;
These artful emblems tend to show
Their clients—not themselves.

" 'Tis all a trick; these are all shams
By which they mean to cheat you:
But have a care—for you're the lambs,
And they the wolves that eat you.

" Nor let the thought of ' no delay '
    To these their courts misguide you ;
'Tis you're the showy *horse*, and *they*
    The *jockeys* that will ride you."

Hare Court is said to derive its name from Sir Nicholas Hare, who was Privy Councillor to Henry VIII. the despotic, and Master of the Rolls to Queen Mary the cruel. Heaven only knows what stern decisions and anti-heretical indictments have not been drawn up in that quaint enclosure. The immortal pump, which stands as a special feature of the court, has been mentioned by the poet Garth in his " Dispensary :"—

" And dare the college insolently aim,
    To equal our fraternity in fame ?
Then let crabs' eyes with pearl for virtue try,
    Or Highgate Hill with lofty Pindus vie ;
So glowworms may compare with Titan's beams,
And Hare Court pump with Aganippe's streams."

In Essex Court one solitary barber remains : his shop is the last wigwam of a departing tribe. Dick Danby's, in the cloisters, used to be famous. In his " Lives of the Chief Justices," Lord Campbell has some pleasant gossip about Dick Danby, the Temple barber. In our group of antiquities of the Temple on page 163 will be found an engraving of the existing barber's shop.

" One of the most intimate friends," he says, " I have ever had in the world was Dick Danby, who kept a hairdresser's shop under the cloisters in the Inner Temple. I first made his acquaintance from his assisting me, when a student at law, to engage a set of chambers. He afterwards cut my hair, made my bar wigs, and aided me at all times with his valuable advice. He was on the same good terms with most of my forensic contemporaries. Thus he became master of all the news of the profession, and he could tell who were getting on, and who were without a brief—who succeeded by their talents, and who hugged the attorneys—who were desirous of becoming puisne judges, and who meant to try their fortunes in Parliament—which of the chiefs was in a failing state of health, and who was next to be promoted to the collar of S.S. Poor fellow ! he died suddenly, and his death threw a universal gloom over Westminster Hall, unrelieved by the thought that the survivors who mourned him might pick up some of his business—a consolation which wonderfully softens the grief felt for a favourite Nisi Prius leader."

In spite of all the great lawyers who have been nurtured in the Temple, it has derived its chief fame from the residence within its precincts of three civilians — Dr. Johnson, Goldsmith, and Charles Lamb.

Dr. Johnson came to the Temple (No. 1, Inner Temple Lane) from Gray's Inn in 1760, and left it for Johnson's Court (Fleet Street) about 1765. When he first came to the Temple he was loitering over his edition of " Shakespeare." In 1762 a pension of £300 a year for the first time made him independent of the booksellers. In 1763 Boswell made his acquaintance and visited Ursa Major in his den.

" It must be confessed," says Boswell, " that his apartments, furniture, and morning dress were sufficiently uncouth. His brown suit of clothes looked very rusty ; he had on a little old shrivelled, unpowdered wig, which was too small for his head ; his shirt neck and the knees of his breeches were loose, his black worsted stockings ill drawn up, and he had a pair of unbuckled shoes by way of slippers."

At this time Johnson generally went abroad at four in the afternoon, and seldom came home till two in the morning. He owned it was a bad habit. He generally had a levee of morning visitors, chiefly men of letters—Hawkesworth, Goldsmith, Murphy, Langton, Stevens, Beauclerk, &c.—and sometimes learned ladies. " When Madame de Boufflers (the mistress of the Prince of Conti) was first in England," said Beauclerk, " she was desirous to see Johnson. I accordingly went with her to his chambers in the Temple, where she was entertained with his conversation for some time. When our visit was over, she and I left him, and were got into Inner Temple Lane, when all at once I heard a voice like thunder. This was occasioned by Johnson, who, it seems, upon a little reflection, had taken it into his head that he ought to have done the honours of his literary residence to a foreign lady of quality, and, eager to show himself a man of gallantry, was hurrying down the staircase in violent agitation. He overtook us before we reached the Temple Gate, and, brushing in between me and Madame de Boufflers, seized her hand and conducted her to her coach. His dress was a rusty-brown morning suit, a pair of old shoes by way of slippers, &c. A considerable crowd of people gathered round, and were not a little struck by his singular appearance."

It was in the year 1763, while Johnson was living in the Temple, that the Literary Club was founded ; and it was in the following year that this wise and good man was seized with one of those fits of hypochondria that occasionally weighed upon that great intellect. Boswell had chambers, not far from the god of his idolatry, at what were once called " Farrar's Buildings," at the bottom of Inner Temple Lane.

Charles Lamb came to 4, Inner Temple Lane, in 1809. Writing to Coleridge, the delightful humorist says :—" I have been turned out of my chambers in the Temple by a landlord who wanted them for himself; but I have got others at No. 4, Inner Temple Lane, far more commodious and roomy. I have two rooms on the third floor, and five rooms above, with an inner staircase to myself, and all new

best room commands a court, in which there are trees and a pump, the water of which is excellent, cold—with brandy; and not very insipid without." He sends Manning some of his little books, to give him "some idea of European literature." It is in this letter that he speaks of Braham and his singing, and jokes "on titles of honour," exemplifying the eleven gradations, by which Mr. C.

OLIVER GOLDSMITH (*see page* 169).

painted, &c., for £30 a year. The rooms are delicious, and the best look backwards into Hare Court, where there is a pump always going; just now it is dry. Hare Court's trees come in at the window, so that it's like living in a garden." In 1810 he says :—" The household gods are slow to come; but here I mean to live and die." From this place (since pulled down and rebuilt) he writes to Manning, who is in China :—" Come, and bring any of your friends the mandarins with you. My

Lamb rose in succession to be Baron, Marquis, Duke, Emperor Lamb, and finally Pope Innocent; and other lively matters fit to solace an English mathematician self-banished to China. The same year Mary Lamb describes her brother taking to water like a hungry otter—abstaining from all spirituous liquors, but with the most indifferent result, as he became full of cramps and rheumatism, and so cold internally that fire could not warm him. It is but just to Lamb to mention that this ascetic period was brief. This same year Lamb wrote his fine essays on Hogarth and on the tragedies of Shakespeare. He was already getting weary of the dull routine of official work at the India House.

Goldsmith came to the Temple, early in 1764, from Wine Office Court. It was a hard year with him, though he published "The Traveller," and some say, to write secretly the erudite history of "Goody Two-Shoes" for Newbery. In 1765 various publications, or perhaps the money for "The Vicar," enabled the author to move to larger chambers in Garden Court, close to his first set, and one of the most agreeable localities in the Temple. He now carried out his threat to Johnson—started a man-servant, and ran into debt with

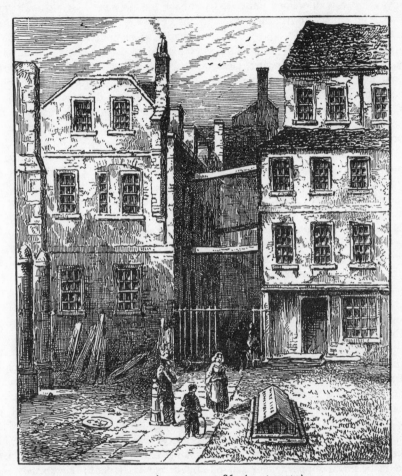

GOLDSMITH'S TOMB IN 1860 (*see page* 171).

opened sundry negotiations with Dodsley and Tonson. "He took," says Mr. Forster, "rooms on the then library-staircase of the Temple. They were a humble set of chambers enough (one Jeffs, the butler of the society, shared them with him), and on Johnson's prying and peering about in them, after his short-sighted fashion flattening his face against every object he looked at, Goldsmith's uneasy sense of their deficiencies broke out. 'I shall soon be in better chambers, sir, than these,' he said. 'Nay, sir,' answered Johnson, 'never mind that—*nec te quæsiveris extra.*'" He soon hurried off to the quiet of Islington, as his usual gay and thoughtless vanity to Mr. Filby, the tailor, ot Water Lane, for coats of divers colours. Goldsmith began to feel his importance, and determined to show it. In 1766 "The Vicar of Wakefield" (price five shillings, sewed) secured his fame, but he still remained in difficulties. In 1767 he wrote *The Good-Natured Man*, knocked off an English Grammar for five guineas, and was only saved from extreme want by Davies employing him to write a "History of Rome" for 250 guineas. In 1767 Parson Scott (Lord Sandwich's chaplain), busily going about to negotiate for writers, describes himself as applying to Goldsmith, among others, to induce him to write in favour of the Administration. "I found him," he said, "in a miserable set of chambers in the Temple. I told him my authority; I told him that I was empowered to pay most liberally for his exertions; and—would you believe it!—he was so absurd as to say, 'I can earn as much as will supply my wants without writing for any party; the assistance you offer is therefore unnecessary to me.' And so I left him," added the Rev. Dr. Scott, indignantly, "in his garret."

On the partial success of *The Good-Natured Man* (January, 1768), Goldsmith, having cleared £500, broke out like a successful gambler. He purchased a set of chambers (No. 2, up two pairs of stairs, in Brick Court) for £400, squandered the remaining £100, ran in debt to his tailor, and borrowed of Mr. Bolt, a man on the same floor. He purchased Wilton carpets, blue merino curtains, chimney-glasses, book-cases, and card-tables, and, by the aid of Filby, enrobed him in a suit of Tyrian bloom, satin grain, with darker blue silk breeches, price £8 2s. 7d., and he even ventured at a more costly suit, lined with silk and ornamented with gilt buttons. Below him lived that learned lawyer, Mr. Blackstone, then poring over the fourth volume of his precious "Commentaries," and the noise and dancing overhead nearly drove him mad, as it also did a Mr. Children, who succeeded him. The cause of these noises Mr. John Forster relates in his delightful biography of the poet. An Irish merchant named Seguin "remembered dinners at which Johnson, Percy, Bickerstaff, Kelly, 'and a variety of authors of minor note,' were guests. They talked of supper-parties with younger people, as well in the London chambers as in suburban lodgings; preceded by blind-man's buff, forfeits, or games of cards; and where Goldsmith, festively entertaining them all, would make frugal supper for himself off boiled milk. They related how he would sing all kinds of Irish songs; with what special enjoyment he gave the Scotch ballad of 'Johnny Armstrong' (his old nurse's favourite); how cheerfully he would put the front of his wig behind, or contribute in any other way to the general amusement; and to what accompaniment of uncontrolled laughter he once 'danced a minuet with Mrs. Seguin.'"

In 1768 appeared "The Deserted Village." It was about this time that one of Goldy's Grub Street acquaintances called upon him, whilst he was conversing with Topham Beauclerk and General Oglethorpe; and the fellow, telling Goldsmith that he was sorry he could not pay the two guineas he owed him, offered him a quarter of a pound of tea

and half a pound of sugar as an acknowledgment. "1769. Goldsmith fell in love with Mary Horneck, known as the 'Jessamy Bride.' Unfortunately he obtained an advance of £500 for his 'Natural History,' and wholly expended it when only six chapters were written." In 1771 he published his "History of England." It was in this year that Reynolds, coming one day to Brick Court, perhaps about the portrait of Goldsmith he had painted the year before, found the mercurial poet kicking a bundle, which contained a masquerade dress, about the room, in disgust at his folly in wasting money in so foolish a way. In 1772, Mr. Forster mentions a very characteristic story of Goldsmith's warmth of heart. He one day found a poor Irish student (afterwards Dr. M'Veagh M'Donnell, a well-known physician) sitting and moping in despair on a bench in the Temple Gardens. Goldsmith soon talked and laughed him into hope and spirits, then taking him off to his chambers, employed him to translate some chapters of Buffon. In 1773 *She Stoops to Conquer* made a great hit; but Noll was still writing at hack-work, and was deeper in debt than ever. In 1774, when Goldsmith was still grinding on at his hopeless drudge-work, as far from the goal of fortune as ever, and even resolving to abandon London life, with all its temptations, Mr. Forster relates that Johnson, dining with the poet, Reynolds, and some one else, silently reproved the extravagance of so expensive a dinner by sending away the whole second course untouched.

In March, 1774, Goldsmith returned from Edgware to his Temple chambers, which he was trying to sell, suffering from a low nervous fever, partly the result of vexation at his pecuniary embarrassments. Mr. Hawes, an apothecary in the Strand (and one of the first founders of the Humane Society), was called in; but Goldsmith insisted on taking James's fever-powders, a valuable medicine, but dangerous under the circumstances. This was on Friday, the 25th. He told the doctor then his mind was not at ease, and he died on Monday, April 4th, in his forty-fifth year. His debts amounted to over £2,000. "Was ever poet so trusted before?" writes Johnson to Boswell. The staircase of Brick Court was filled with poor outcasts, to whom Goldsmith had been kind and charitable. His coffin was opened by Miss Horneck, that a lock might be cut from his hair. Burke and Reynolds superintended the funeral, Reynolds' nephew, Palmer, afterwards Dean of Cashel, being chief mourner. Hugh Kelly, who had so often lampooned the poet, was present. At five o'clock on Saturday, the 9th of April, Goldsmith was buried in the Temple churchyard. In 1837, a slab of white marble, to the kindly poet's memory, was placed in the Temple Church, and afterwards transferred to a recess of the vestry chamber. Of the poet, Mr. Forster says, " no memorial indicates the grave to the pilgrim or the stranger, nor is it possible any longer to identify the spot which received all that was mortal of the delightful writer." The present site is entirely conjectural; but it appears from the following note, communicated to us by T. C. Noble, the well-known City antiquary, that the real site was remembered as late as 1830. Mr. Noble says :—

" In 1842, after some consideration, the benchers of the Temple deciding that no more burials should take place in the churchyard, resolved to pave it over. For about fifteen years the burial-place of Dr. Goldsmith continued in obscurity; for while some would have it that the interment took place to the east of the choir, others clung to an opinion, handed down by Mr. Broome, the gardener, who stated that when he commenced his duties, about 1830, a Mr. Collett, sexton, a very old man, and a penurious one, too, employed him to prune an elder-tree which, he stated, he venerated, because

it marked the site of Goldsmith's grave. The stone which has been placed in the yard, 'to mark the spot' where the poet was buried, is not the site of this tree. The tomb was erected in 1860, but the exact position of the grave has never been discovered." The engraving on page 169 shows the spot as it appeared in the autumn of that year. The old houses at the back were pulled down soon after.

Mr. Forster, alluding to Goldsmith's love for the rooks, the former denizens of the Temple Gardens, says : "He saw the rookery (in the winter deserted, or guarded only by some five or six, 'like old soldiers in a garrison') resume its activity and bustle in the spring; and he moralised, like a great reformer, on the legal constitution established, the social laws enforced, and the particular castigations endured for the good of the community, by those black-dressed and black-eyed chatterers. 'I have often amused myself,' Goldsmith remarks, 'with observing their plans of policy from my window in the Temple, that looks upon a grove where they have made a colony, in the midst of the city.'"

CHAPTER XVI.

THE TEMPLE (*continued*).

LIVES there a man with soul so dead as to write about the Temple without mentioning the little fountain in Fountain Court ?—that pet and play-thing of the Temple, that, like a little fairy, sings to beguile the cares of men oppressed with legal duties. It used to look like a wagoner's silver whip—now a modern writer cruelly calls it " a pert squirt." In Queen Anne's time Hatton describes it as forcing its stream "to a vast and almost incredible altitude"—it is now only ten feet high, no higher than a giant lord chancellor. Then it was fenced with palisades—now it is caged in iron ; then it stood in a square—now it is in a round. But it still sparkles and glitters, and sprinkles and play-fully splashes the jaunty sparrows that come to wash off the London dust in its variegated spray. It is quite careless now, however, of notice, for has it not been immortalised by the pen of Dickens, who has made it the centre of one of his most

charming love scenes? It was in Fountain Court, our readers will like to remember, that Ruth Pinch —gentle, loving Ruth—met her lover, by the merest accident of course.

"There was," says Mr. Dickens, "a little plot between them that Tom should always come out of the Temple by one way, and that was past the fountain. Coming through Fountain Court, he was just to glance down the steps leading into Garden Court, and to look once all round him ; and if Ruth had come to meet him, there he would see her—not sauntering, you understand (on account of the clerks), but coming briskly up, with the best little laugh upon her face that ever played in opposition to the fountain and beat it all to nothing. For, fifty to one, Tom had been looking for her in the wrong direction, and had quite given her up, while she had been tripping towards him from the first, jingling that little reticule of hers (with all the keys in it) to attract his wondering observation.

"Whether there was life enough left in the slow vegetation of Fountain Court for the smoky shrubs to have any consciousness of the brightest and purest-hearted little woman in the world, is a question for gardeners and those who are learned in the loves of plants. But that it was a good thing for that same paved yard to have such a delicate little figure flitting through it, that it passed like a smile from the grimy old houses and the worn flagstones, and left them duller, darker, sterner than before, there is no sort of doubt. The Temple fountain might have leaped up twenty feet to greet the spring of hopeful maidenhood that in her person stole on, sparkling, through the dry and dusty channels of the law ; the chirping sparrows, bred in Temple chinks and crannies, might have held their peace to listen to imaginary skylarks as so fresh a little creature passed ; the dingy boughs, unused to droop, otherwise than in their puny growth, might have bent down in a kindred gracefulness to shed their benedictions on her graceful head ; old love-letters, shut up in iron boxes in the neighbouring offices, and made of no account among the heaps of family papers into which they had strayed, and of which in their degeneracy they formed a part, might have stirred and fluttered with a moment's recollection of their ancient tenderness, as she went lightly by. Anything might have happened that did not happen, and never will, for the love of Ruth. . . .

"Merrily the tiny fountain played, and merrily the dimples sparkled on its sunny face. John Westlock hurried after her. Softly the whispering water broke and fell, and roguishly the dimples twinkled as he stole upon her footsteps.

" Oh, foolish, panting, timid little heart ! why did she feign to be unconscious of his coming ? . . .

"Merrily the fountain leaped and danced, and merrily the smiling dimples twinkled and expanded more and more, until they broke into a laugh against the basin's rim and vanished."

"L. E. L." (Miss Landon) has left a graceful poem on this much-petted fountain, which begins,—

" The fountain's low singing is heard on the wind,
    Like a melody, bringing sweet fancies to mind—
    Some to grieve, some to gladden ; around them
        they cast
    The hopes of the morrow, the dreams of the past.
    Away in the distance is heard the vast sound
    From the streets of the city that compass it round,
    Like the echo of fountains or ocean's deep call ;
    Yet that fountain's low singing is heard over all.'

Fig-tree Court derived its name from obvious

sources. Next to the plane, that has the strange power of sloughing off its sooty bark, the fig seems the tree that best endures London's corrupted atmosphere. Thomas Fairchild, a Hoxton gardener, who wrote in 1722 (quoted by Mr. Peter Cunningham), alludes to figs ripening well in the Rolls Gardens, Chancery Lane, and to the tree thriving in close places about Bridewell. Who can say that some Templar pilgrim did not bring from the banks of " Abana or Pharpar, rivers of Damascus," the first leafy inhabitant of inky and dusty Fig-tree Court ? Lord Thurlow was living here in 1758, the year he was called to the bar, and when, it was said, he had not money enough even to hire a horse to attend the circuit.

The Inner Temple Library stands on the terrace facing the river. The Parliament Chambers and Hall, in the Tudor style, were the work of Sidney Smirke, R.A., in 1835. The library, designed by Mr. Abrahams, is 96 feet long, 42 feet wide, and 63 feet high ; it has a hammer-beam roof. One of the stained glass windows is blazoned with the arms of the Templars. Below the library are chambers. The cost of the whole was about £13,000. The north window is thought to too much resemble the great window at Westminster Hall.

Paper Buildings, a name more suitable for the offices of some City companies, were first built in the reign of James I., by a Mr. Edward Hayward and others ; and the learned Dugdale describes them as eighty-eight feet long, twenty feet broad, and four storeys high. This Hayward was Selden's chamber-fellow, and to him Selden dedicated his " Titles of Honour." Selden, according to Aubrey, had chambers in these pleasant riverside buildings, looking towards the gardens, and in the uppermost storey he had a little gallery, to pace in and meditate. The Great Fire swept away Selden's chambers, and their successors were destroyed by the fire which broke out in Mr. Maule's chambers. Coming home at night from a dinner-party, Maule, afterwards a judge, put a lighted candle under his bed by mistake. The stately new buildings were designed by Mr. Sidney Smirke, A.R.A., in 1848. The red brick and stone harmonise pleasantly. In 1878-9 Hare Court Buildings were extended towards the river, to answer to them.

The entrance to the Middle Temple from Fleet Street is a gatehouse of red brick pointed with stone, and is the work of Wren. It was erected in 1684, after the Great Fire, and is in the style of Inigo Jones—"not inelegant," says Ralph. It probably occupies the site of the gatehouse erected by order of Wolsey, at the expense of his prisoner,

Sir Amyas Paulet. The frightened man covered the front with the cardinal's hat and arms, hoping to appease Wolsey's anger by gratifying his pride. The Inner Temple gateway was built in the fifth year of James I.

Elm Court was built in the sixth year of Charles I. Up one pair of stairs that successful courtier, Guildford North, whom Jeffreys so tormented, commenced the practice that soon won him such high honours. Elm Court was demolished in the autumn of 1879.

In 1752 the poet Cowper, on leaving a solicitor's office, had chambers in the Middle Temple, and in that solitude the horror of his future malady began to darken over him. He gave up the classics, which had been his previous delight, and read George Herbert's poems all day long. In 1759, after his father's death, he purchased another set of rooms for £250, in an airy situation in the Inner Temple. He belonged, at this time, to the "Nonsense Club," of which Bonnell Thornton, Colman junior, and Lloyd were members. Thurlow also was his friend. In 1763 his despondency deepened into insanity. An approaching appointment to the clerkship of the Journals of the House of Lords overwhelmed him with nervous fears. Dreading to appear in public, he resolved to destroy himself. He purchased laudanum, then threw it away. He packed up his portmanteau to go to France and enter a monastery. He went down to the Custom House Quay, to throw himself into the river. He tried to stab himself. At last the poor fellow actually hung himself, and was only saved by an accident. The following is his own relation :—

"Not one hesitating thought now remained, but I fell greedily to the execution of my purpose. My garter was made of a broad piece of scarlet binding, with a sliding buckle, being sewn together at the ends. By the help of the buckle I formed a noose, and fixed it about my neck, straining it so tight that I hardly left a passage for my breath, or for the blood to circulate. The tongue of the buckle held it fast. At each corner of the bed was placed a wreath of carved work fastened by an iron pin, which passed up through the midst of it; the other part of the garter, which made a loop, I slipped over one of them, and hung by it some seconds, drawing up my feet under me, that they might not touch the floor; but the iron bent, and the carved work slipped off, and the garter with it. I then fastened it to the frame of the tester, winding it round and tying it in a strong knot. The frame broke short, and let me down again.

"The third effort was more likely to succeed.

I set the door open, which reached to within a foot of the ceiling. By the help of a chair I could command the top of it, and the loop being large enough to admit a large angle of the door, was easily fixed, so as not to slip off again. I pushed away the chair with my feet, and hung at my whole length. While I hung there I distinctly heard a voice say three times, 'Tis over!' Though I am sure of the fact, and was so at the time, yet it did not at all alarm me or affect my resolution. I hung so long that I lost all sense, all consciousness of existence.

"When I came to myself again I thought I was in hell; the sound of my own dreadful groans was all that I heard, and a feeling like that produced by a flash of lightning just beginning to seize upon me, passed over my whole body. In a few seconds I found myself fallen on my face to the floor. In about half a minute I recovered my feet, and reeling and struggling, stumbled into bed again.

"By the blessed providence of God, the garter which had held me till the bitterness of temporal death was past broke just before eternal death had taken place upon me. The stagnation of the blood under one eye in a broad crimson spot, and a red circle round my neck, showed plainly that I had been on the brink of eternity. The latter, indeed, might have been occasioned by the pressure of the garter, but the former was certainly the effect of strangulation, for it was not attended with the sensation of a bruise, as it must have been had I in my fall received one in so tender a part; and I rather think the circle round my neck was owing to the same cause, for the part was not excoriated, nor at all in pain.

"Soon after I got into bed I was surprised to hear a voice in the dining-room, where the laundress was lighting a fire. She had found the door unbolted, notwithstanding my design to fasten it, and must have passed the bed-chamber door while I was hanging on it, and yet never perceived me. She heard me fall, and presently came to ask me if I was well, adding, she feared I had been in a fit.

"I sent her to a friend, to whom I related the whole affair, and dispatched him to my kinsman at the coffee-house. As soon as the latter arrived I pointed to the broken garter which lay in the middle of the room, and apprised him also of the attempt I had been making. His words were, 'My dear Mr. Cowper, you terrify me! To be sure you cannot hold the office at this rate. Where is the deputation?' I gave him the key of the drawer where it was deposited, and his business requiring his immediate attendance, he took it away with him; and thus ended all my connection with the Parliament office."

In February, 1732, Tanfield Court, a quiet, dull nook on the east side of the Temple, to the south of that sombre Grecian temple where the Master resides, was the scene of a very horrible crime. Sarah Malcolm, a laundress, aged twenty-two, employed by a young barrister named Kerrol in the same court, gaining access to the rooms of an old lady named Duncomb, whom she knew

Malcolm went to execution neatly dressed in a crape gown, held up her head in the cart with an air, and seemed to be painted. A copy of her confession was sold for twenty guineas. Two days before her execution she dressed in scarlet, and sat to Hogarth for a sketch, which Horace Walpole bought for £5. The portrait represents a cruel, thin-lipped woman, not uncomely, sitting at a table. The Duke of Roxburghe purchased a perfect impression of this print, Mr. Timbs says, for £8 5s.

THE TEMPLE FOUNTAIN, FROM AN OLD PRINT (*see page* 171).

to have money, strangled her and an old servant, and cut the throat of a young girl, whose bed she had probably shared. Some of her blood-stained linen, and a silver tankard of Mrs. Duncomb, stained with blood, were found by Mr. Kerrol concealed in his chambers. Fifty-three pounds of the money were discovered at Newgate hidden in the prisoner's hair. She confessed to a share in the robbery, but laid the murder to two lads with whom she was acquainted. She was, however, found guilty, and hung opposite Mitre Court, Fleet Street. The crowd was so great that one woman crossed from near Serjeants' Inn to the other side of the way on the shoulders of the mob. Sarah

Its original price was sixpence. After her execution the corpse was taken to an undertaker's on Snow Hill, and there exhibited for money. Among the rest, a gentleman in deep mourning—perhaps her late master, Mr. Kerrol—stooped and kissed it, and gave the attendant half-a-crown. She was, by special favour (for superiority even in wickedness has its admirers), buried in St. Sepulchre's Churchyard, from which criminals had been excluded for a century and a half. The corpse of the murderess was disinterred, and her skeleton, in a glass case, is still to be seen at the Botanic Garden, Cambridge.

Not many recorded crimes have taken place in

PART OF INNER TEMPLE, 1800. (From a Drawing in Mr. Crace's Collection.)

the Temple, for youth, however poor, is hopeful. It takes time to make a man despair, and when he despairs, the devil is soon at his elbow. Nevertheless, greed and madness have upset some Templars' brains. In October, 1573, a crazed, fanatical man of the Middle Temple, named Peter Burchet, mistaking John Hawkins (afterwards the naval hero) for Sir Christopher Hatton, flew at him in the Strand, and dangerously wounded him with a dagger. The queen was so furious that at first she wanted Burchet tried by camp law; but, being found to hold heretical opinions, he was committed to the Lollards' Tower (south front of St. Paul's), and afterwards sent to the Tower. Growing still madder there, Burchet slew one of his keepers with a billet from his fire, and was then condemned to death and hung in the Strand, close by where he had stabbed Hawkins, his right hand being first stricken off and nailed to the gibbet.

In 1685 John Ayloff, a barrister of the Inner Temple, was hung for high treason opposite the Temple Gate.

In 1738 Thomas Carr, an attorney, of Elm Court, and Elizabeth Adams, his accomplice, were executed for robbing a Mr. Quarrington in Shire Lane (see page 74); and in 1752 Henry Justice, of the Middle Temple, in spite of his well-omened name, was cruelly sentenced to death for stealing books from the library of Trinity College, Cambridge, but eventually he was only transported for life.

The celebrated Earl of Mansfield, when Mr. Murray, had chambers at No. 5, King's Bench Walk, apropos of which Pope wrote—

"To Number Five direct your doves,
  There spread round Murray all your blooming loves."
                    (Pope "to Venus," from "Horace.")

A second compliment by Pope to this great man occasioned a famous parody:—

"Graced as thou art by all the power of words,
  So known, so honoured at the House of Lords"
                    (Pope, of Lord Mansfield);

which was thus cleverly parodied by Colley Cibber:

"Persuasion tips his tongue whene'er he talks,
  And he has chambers in the King's Bench Walks."

One of Mansfield's biographers tells us that "once he was surprised by a gentleman of Lincoln's Inn (who took the liberty of entering his room in the Temple without the ceremonious introduction of a servant), in the act of practising the graces of a speaker at a glass, while Pope sat by in the character of a friendly preceptor." Of the friendship of Pope and Murray, Warburton has said: "Mr. Pope had all the warmth of affection for this great lawyer; and, indeed, no man ever more deserved

to have a poet for his friend, in the obtaining of which, as neither vanity, party, nor fear had a share, so he supported his title to it by all the offices of a generous and true friendship."

"A good story," says Mr. Jeaffreson, "is told of certain visits paid to William Murray's chambers at No. 5, King's Bench Walk, Temple, in the year 1738. Born in 1705, Murray was still a young man when, in 1738, he made his brilliant speech on behalf of Colonel Sloper, against whom Colley Cibber's rascally son had brought an action for immorality with his wife, the lovely actress, who on the stage was the rival of Mrs. Clive, and in private life was remarkable for immorality and fascinating manners. Amongst the many clients who were drawn to Murray by that speech, Sarah, Duchess of Marlborough, was neither the least powerful nor the least distinguished. Her grace began by sending the rising advocate a general retainer, with a fee of a thousand guineas, of which sum he accepted only the two-hundredth part, explaining to the astonished duchess that 'the professional fee, with a general retainer, could not be less nor more than five guineas.' If Murray had accepted the whole sum he would not have been overpaid for his trouble, for her grace persecuted him with calls at most unseasonable hours. On one occasion, returning to his chambers after 'drinking champagne with the wits,' he found the duchess's carriage and attendants on King's Bench Walk. A numerous crowd of footmen and link-bearers surrounded the coach, and when the barrister entered his chambers he encountered the mistress of that army of lackeys. 'Young man,' exclaimed the grand lady, eyeing the future Lord Mansfield with a look of displeasure, 'if you mean to rise in the world, you must not sup out.' On a subsequent night Sarah of Marlborough called without appointment at the chambers, and waited till past midnight in the hope that she would see the lawyer ere she went to bed. But Murray, being at an unusually late supper-party, did not return till her grace had departed in an overpowering rage. 'I could not make out, sir, who she was,' said Murray's clerk, describing her grace's appearance and manner, 'for she would not tell me her name; but she swore so dreadfully that I am sure she must be a lady of quality.'"

Charles Lamb, who was born in Crown Office Row, in his exquisite way has sketched the benchers of the Temple whom he had seen pacing the terrace in his youth. Jekyll, with the roguish eye, and Thomas Coventry, of the elephantine step, the scarecrow of inferiors, the browbeater of equals, who made a solitude of children wherever he came, who took snuff by palmfuls, diving for it under the mighty flap of his old-fashioned red waistcoat. In the gentle Samuel Salt we discover a portrait of the employer of Lamb's father. Salt was a shy indolent, absent man, who never dressed for a dinner party but he forgot his sword. The day of Miss Blandy's execution he went to dine with a relative of the murderess, first carefully schooled by his clerk to avoid the disagreeable subject. However, during the pause for dinner, Salt went to the window, looked out, pulled down his ruffles, and observed, "It's a gloomy day; Miss Blandy must be hanged by this time, I suppose." Salt never laughed. He was a well-known toast with the ladies, having a fine figure and person. Coventry, on the other hand, was a man worth four or five hundred thousand, and lived in a gloomy house, like a strong-box, opposite the pump in Serjeants' Inn, Fleet Street. Fond of money as he was, he gave away £30,000 at once to a charity for the blind, and kept a hospitable house. Salt was indolent and careless of money, and but for Lovel, his clerk, would have been universally robbed. This Lovel was a clever little fellow, with a face like Garrick, who could mould heads in clay, turn cribbage-boards, take a hand at a quadrille or bowls, and brew punch with any man of his degree in Europe. With Coventry and Salt, Peter Pierson often perambulated the terrace, with hands folded behind him. Contemporary with these was Daines Barrington, a burly, square man. Lamb also mentions Burton, "a jolly negation," who drew up the bills of fare for the parliament chamber, where the benchers dined; thin, fragile Wharry, who used to spitefully pinch his cat's ears when anything offended him; and Jackson, the musician, to whom the cook once applied for instructions how to write down "edge-bone of beef" in a bill of commons. Then there was Blustering Mingay, who had a grappling-hook in substitute for a hand he had lost, which Lamb, when a child, used to take for an emblem of power; and Baron Mascres, who retained the costume of the reign of George II.

In his "Essays" Lamb writes :—"I was born and passed the first seven years of my life in the Temple. Its church, its halls, its gardens, its fountain, its river I had almost said—for in those young years what was the king of rivers to me but a stream that watered our pleasant places?—these are of my oldest recollections. I repeat, to this day, no verses to myself more frequently or with kindlier emotion than those of Spenser where he speaks of this spot. Indeed, it is the most elegant spot in the metropolis. What a transition for a country-man visiting London for the first time—the passing

from the crowded Strand or Fleet Street, by unexpected avenues, into its magnificent, ample squares, its classic green recesses ! What a cheerful, liberal look hath that portion of it which, from three sides, overlooks the greater garden, that goodly pile

'Of buildings strong, albeit of paper hight,'

confronting with massy contrast, the lighter, older, more fantastically shrouded one named of Harcourt, with the cheerful Crown Office Row (place of my kindly engendure), right opposite the stately stream, which washes the garden foot with her yet scarcely trade-polluted waters, and seems but just weaned from Twickenham Naïades ! A man would give something to have been born in such places. What a collegiate aspect has that fine Elizabethan hall, where the fountain plays, which I have made to rise and fall, how many times ! to the astonishment of the young urchins, my contemporaries, who, not being able to guess at its recondite machinery, were almost tempted to hail the wondrous work as magic. . . . .

"So may the winged horse, your ancient badge and cognisance, still flourish ! So may future Hookers and Seldens illustrate your church and chambers ! So may the sparrows, in default of more melodious quiristers, imprisoned hop about your walks ! So may the fresh-coloured and cleanly nursery-maid, who by leave airs her playful charge in your stately gardens, drop her prettiest blushing curtsey as ye pass, reductive of juvenescent emotion ! So may the younkers of this generation eye you, pacing your stately terrace, with the same superstitious veneration with which the child Elia gazed on the old worthies that solemnised the parade before ye ! "

Charles Lamb, in his "Essay" on the old benchers, speaks of many changes he had witnessed in the Temple—i.e., the Gothicising the entrance to the Inner Temple Hall and the Library front, to assimilate them to the hall, which they did not resemble; and the removal of the winged horse over the Temple Hall, and the frescoes of the Virtues which once Italianised it. He praises, too, the antique air of the "now almost effaced sun-dials," with their moral inscriptions, seeming almost coeval with the time which they measured, and taking their revelations immediately from heaven, holding correspondence with the fountain of light. Of these dials there still remain—one in Temple Lane, with the motto, " Pereunt et imputantur ;" one in Essex Court, " Vestigia nulla retrorsum ;" and one in Brick Court on which Goldsmith must often have gazed — its motto, "Time and tide tarry for no man." In

Pump Court and Garden Court are two dials without mottoes; and in each Temple garden is a pillar dial—"the natural garden god of Christian gardens." On an old brick house at the east end of Inner Temple Terrace, removed in 1828, was a dial with the odd inscription, "Begone about your business," words with which an old bencher is said to have once dismissed a troublesome lad who had come from the dial-maker's for a motto, and who mistook his meaning. The one we have engraved at page 180 is in Pump Court. The date and the initials are renewed every time it is fresh painted.

There are many old Temple anecdotes relating to that learned disciple of Bacchus, Porson. Many a time, says Mr. Timbs, at early morn, did Porson stagger from his old haunt, the "Cider Cellars" in Maiden Lane, where he scarcely ever failed to pass some hours, after spending the evening elsewhere. It is related of him, upon better authority than most of the stories told to his discredit, that one night, or rather morning, Gurney (the Baron), who had chambers in Essex Court under Porson, was awakened by a tremendous thump in the chamber above. Porson had just come home dead drunk, and had fallen on the floor. Having extinguished the candle in the fall, he presently staggered downstairs to re-light it, and Gurney heard him dodging and poking with the candle at the staircase lamp for about five minutes, and all the time very lustily cursing the nature of things.

We read also of Porson shutting himself up in these chambers for three or four days together, admitting no visitor. One morning his friend Rogers went to call, having ascertained from the barber's hard by that Porson was at home, but had not been seen by any one for two days. Rogers proceeded to his chambers, and knocked at the door more than once; he would not open it, and Rogers came downstairs, but as he was crossing the court Porson opened the window and stopped him. He was then busy about the Grenville "Homer," for which he collated the Harleian MS. of the "Odyssey," and received for his labour but £50 and a large-paper copy. His chambers must have presented a strange scene, for he used books most cruelly, whether they were his own or belonged to others. He said that he possessed more *bad* copies of *good* books than any private gentleman in England.

Rogers, when a Templar, occasionally had some visitors who absorbed more of his time than was always agreeable; an instance of which he thus relates: "When I lived in the Temple, Mackintosh and Richard Sharp used to come to my chambers and stay there for hours, talking metaphysics. One

day they were so intent on their 'first cause,' 'spirit,' and 'matter,' that they were unconscious of my having left them, paid a visit, and returned. I was a little angry at this; and to show my indifference about them, I sat down and wrote letters, without taking any notice of them. I never met a man with a fuller mind than Mackintosh—such readiness on all subjects, such a talker."

Before any person can be admitted a member of the Temple, he must furnish a statement in writing, describing his age, residence, and condition in life, and adding a certificate of his respectability and fitness, signed by himself and a bencher of the society, or two barristers. The *Middle* Temple requires the signatures of two barristers of that Inn and of a bencher, but in each of the three other Inns the signatures of barristers of any of the four Inns will suffice.

The educational year is divided into three terms, namely, from the 1st of November to the 22nd of December, from the 11th of January to the 30th of March, and from the 15th of April to the 31st of July; and instruction is given to students by means of lectures, but the attendance of the students at such lectures is not compulsory.

Professors of jurisprudence, of common law, of equity, and of the law of real and personal property, are duly appointed by the council, for the purpose of giving instruction to the students, such professors being at liberty to receive, in addition to their salaries, fees from the students who attend the classes.

Legal students worked hard in the old times; Coke's career is an example. In 1572 he rose every morning at five o'clock, lighting his own fire; and then read Bracton, Littleton, and the ponderous folio abridgments of the law till the court met, at eight o'clock. He then took boat for Westminster, and heard cases argued till twelve o'clock, when the pleas ceased for dinner. After a meal in the Inner Temple Hall, he attended "readings" or lectures in the afternoon, and then resumed his private studies till supper-time at five. Next came the moots, after which he slammed his chamber-door, and set to work with his commonplace book to index all the law he had amassed during the day. At nine, the steady student went to bed, securing three good hours of sleep before midnight. It is said Coke never saw a play or read a play in his life—and that was Shakespeare's time! In the reign of James I. the Temple was often called "my Lord Coke's shop." He had become a great lawyer then, and lived to become Lord Chief Justice. Pity 'tis that we have to remember that he reviled Essex and insulted Raleigh. King James once said of Coke in misfortune that he was like a cat, he always fell on his feet.

History does not record many riots in the Temple, full of wild life as that quiet precinct has been. In different reigns, however, two outbreaks occurred. In both cases the Templars, though rather hot and prompt, seem to have been right. At the dinner of John Prideaux, reader of the Inner Temple, in 1553, the students took offence at Sir John Lyon, the Lord Mayor, coming in state, with his sword up, and the sword was dragged down as he passed through the cloisters. The same sort of affray took place again in 1669, when Lord Mayor Peake came to Sir Christopher Goodfellow's feast, and the Lord Mayor had to be hidden in a bencher's chambers till, as Pepys relates, the fiery young sparks were decoyed away to dinner. The case was tried before Charles II., and Heneage Finch pleaded for the Temple, claiming immemorial exemption from City jurisdiction. The case was never decided. From that day to this (says Mr. Noble) a settlement appears never to have been made; hence it is that the Temples claim to be " extra parochial," closing nightly all their gates as the clock strikes ten, and keeping extra watch and ward when the parochial authorities " beat the bounds " upon Ascension Day. Many struggles have taken place to make the property rateable, and of late the question has more than once arisen; and it is hardly to be wondered at, for it would be a nice bit of business to assess the Templars upon the £32,866 which they have returned as the annual rental of their estates.

A third riot was with those ceaseless enemies of the Templars, the Alsatians, or lawless inhabitants of disreputable Whitefriars. In July, 1691, weary of their riotous and thievish neighbours, the benchers of the Inner Temple bricked up the gate (still existing in King's Bench Walk) leading into the high street of Whitefriars; but the Alsatians, swarming out, pulled down as fast as the bricklayers built up. The Templars hurried together, swords flew out, the Alsatians plied pokers and shovels, and many heads were broken. Ultimately, two men were killed, several wounded, and many hurried off to prison. Eventually, the ringleader of the Alsatians, Captain Francis White—a " copper captain," no doubt—was convicted of murder, in April, 1693. This riot eventually did good, for it led to the abolition of London sanctuaries, those dens of bullies, low gamblers, thieves, and courtesans.

At the Middle Temple time has proved a great worker of change, and many curious customs of the old banquets have died out. The ante-prandial horn is sounded, it is true, and the loving cup goes round, but oysters are no longer brought in every Friday in term before dinner; nor, when one bencher dines, does he, on leaving the hall, invite the senior bar man to come and take wine with him in the parliament chamber, answering to the " Common Room " of Oxford colleges. Yet the rich and epicurean Inner Temple still cherishes many worthy customs, affects *recherché* French dishes, and is curious in *entremets;* while the Middle Temple has to content itself with plainer fare, that some hungry wit has compared to " eating a gravel-walk, and meeting an occasional weed." A writer in *Blackwood*, quoting the old proverb, " The Inner Temple for the rich, the Middle for the poor," says few great men have come from the Middle Temple; and the statement is partly true, even in the present day. At a dinner in 1865, Mr. Timbs tells us, there were present only three benchers, seven barristers, and six students.

An Inner Temple banquet is a very grand affair. At five, or half-past five, the barristers and students in their gowns follow the benchers to the hall; then the head porter strikes the table solemnly three times, grace is said by the treasurer, or senior bencher present, and the men of law fall to. In former times it was the custom to blow a horn in every court to announce the meal, but how long this ancient Templar practice has been discontinued we do not know. The benchers observe somewhat more style at their table than the other members do at theirs. The general repast is a tureen of soup, a joint of meat, a tart, and cheese, to each mess, consisting of four persons, and to each mess is allowed a bottle of wine. Dinner is served daily to the members of the Inn during term time; the masters of the Bench dining on the state, or dais, and the barristers and students at long tables. On grand days some of the judges often are present; they used to dine in succession with each of the four Inns of Court. To the parliament chamber, adjoining the hall, the benchers repair after dinner. The loving cups used on certain grand occasions are huge silver goblets, which are passed down the table, filled with a delicious composition, immemorially termed " sack," consisting of sweetened and exquisitely-flavoured white wine. The butler attends the progress of the cup, to replenish it; and each student is by rule restricted to a *sip;* yet it is recorded that once, though the number present fell short of seventy, thirty-six quarts of the liquid were sipped away. At the Inner Temple, on May 29th, a gold cup of sack is handed to each member, who drinks to the happy Restoration of Charles II.

The writer in *Blackwood* before referred to alludes to the strict silence enjoined at the Inner Temple dinners, the only intercourse between the several members of the mess being the usual social scowl vouchsafed by your true-born Englishman to per-

ings or discussions on points of law. The mere student sat farthest from the bar.

When these " mootings " were discontinued deponent sayeth not. In Coke's time (1543), that great lawyer, after supper at five o'clock, used to join the moots, when questions of law were proposed and discussed, when fine on the garden

SUN-DIAL IN THE TEMPLE (*see page* 177).

sons who have not the honour of his acquaintance. You may, indeed, on an emergency, ask your neighbour for the salt; but then it is also perfectly understood that he is not obliged to notice your request.

The old term of "calling to the bar" seems to have originated in the custom of summoning students, that had attained a certain standing, to the bar that separated the benchers' dais from the hall, to take part in certain probationary moot-

terrace, in rainy weather in the Temple cloisters. The dinner alone now remains; dining is now the only legal study of Temple students.

In the *Middle Temple* a three years' standing and twelve commons kept suffices to entitle a gentleman to be called to the bar, provided he is above twenty-three years of age. No person can be called to the bar at any of the Inns of Court before he is twenty-one years of age; and a standing of five years is understood to be required of every member before being called. The members of the several universities, &c., may, however, be called after three years' standing.

The Inner Temple Garden, three acres in extent, has probably been a garden from the time when the white-mantled Templars first came from Holborn and settled by the river-side. This little paradise of nurserymaids and London children is entered from the terrace by an iron gate (date, 1730); and the winged horse that surmounts the portal has looked

present; and when Paper Buildings were erected, part of this wall was dug up. The view given on this page, and taken from an old view in the Temple, shows a portion of the old wall, with the doorway opening upon the Temple Stairs.

The Temple Garden, half a century since, was famous for its white and red roses, the Old Provence, the Cabbage, and the Maiden's Blush; and the lime trees were delightful in the time of bloom. There were only two steamboats on the river then;

THE TEMPLE STAIRS, 1680.

down on many a distinguished visitor. In the centre of the grass is such a sun-dial as Charles Lamb loved, with the date 1770. A little to the east of this stands an old sycamore, which, fifteen years since, was railed in as the august mummy of that umbrageous tree under whose shade, as tradition says, Johnson and Goldsmith used to sit and converse. According to an engraving of 1671 there were formerly three trees; so that Shakespeare himself may have sat under them and meditated on the Wars of the Roses. The print shows a brick terrace faced with stone, with a flight of steps at the north. The old river wall of 1670 stood fifty or sixty yards farther north than the

but the steamers and factory smoke soon spoiled everything but the hardy chrysanthemums. However, since the Smoke Consuming Act has been enforced, the roses, stocks, and hawthorns have again taken heart, and blossom with grateful luxuriance. In 1864 Mr. Broome, the zealous gardener of the Inner Temple, exhibited at the Central Horticultural Society twenty-four trusses of roses grown under his care. In the flower-beds next the main walk he managed to secure four successive crops of flowers—the pompones were especially gaudy and beautiful; but his chief triumphs were the chrysanthemums of the northern border. The trees, however, seem delicate, and suffering from the cold winds, dwindle as they approach the Embankment, which separates the garden from the river. The Temple rooks—the wise birds that Goldsmith delighted to watch—were originally brought by Sir William Northcote from Woodcote Green, Epsom, but they left in disgust many years since. Mr. Timbs says that 200 families enjoy these gardens throughout the year; and about 10,000 of the outer world, chiefly children, who are always in search of the lost Eden, come here on summer evenings. The flowers and trees are rarely injured.

In the secluded Middle Temple Garden is an old catalpa tree, supposed to have been planted by that grave and just judge, Sir Matthew Hale. On the lawn is a large table sun-dial, elaborately gilt and embellished. A magnificent new library was opened here in 1868. From the library oriel the Thames and its bridges, Somerset House and the Houses of Parliament, form a grand *coup d'œil*.

The revenue of the Middle Temple alone is said to be £13,000 a year. Of the savings the outside world is entirely ignorant. The students' dinners are half paid for by themselves, the library is kept up on very little fodder, and altogether the system of auditing the Inns of Court accounts is as incomprehensible as the Sybilline oracles; but there can be no doubt it is all right, and very well managed.

In the seventeenth century (says Mr. Noble) a benevolent member of the Middle Temple conveyed to the benchers in fee several houses in the City, out of the rents of which to pay a stated salary to each of two referees, who were to meet on two days weekly, in term, from two to five, in the hall or other convenient place, and without fee on either side, to settle as best they could all disputes submitted to them. From that time the referees have been appointed, but there is no record of a single case being tried by them. The two gentlemen, finding their office a sinecure, have devoted their salaries to making periodical additions to the library. May we be allowed to ask, was this benevolent object ever made known to the public generally? We cannot but think, if it had been, that the two respected arbitrators would not have had to complain of the office as a sinecure.

He who can enumerate the wise and great men who have been educated in the Temple can count off the stars on his finger and measure the sands of the sea-shore by teacupsful. To cull a few, we may mention that the Inner Temple boasts among its eminent members — Audley, Chancellor to Henry VIII.; Nicholas Hare, of Hare Court celebrity; the great lawyer, Littleton (1481), and Coke, his commentator; Sir Christopher Hatton, the dancing Chancellor; Lord Buckhurst; Selden; Judge Jeffries; Beaumont, the poet; William Browne, the author of "Britannia's Pastorals" (so much praised by the Lamb and Hazlitt school); Cowper, the poet; and Sir William Follett.

From the Middle Temple have also sprung swarms of great lawyers. We may mention specially Plowden, the jurist, Sir Walter Raleigh, Sir Thomas Overbury (who was poisoned in the Tower), John Ford (one of the latest of the great dramatists), Sir Edward Bramston (chamber-fellow to Mr. Hyde, afterwards Lord Clarendon), Bulstrode Whitelocke (one of Cromwell's Ministers), Lord-Keeper Guildford (Charles II.), Lord Chancellor Somers, Wycherley and Congreve (the dramatists), Shadwell and Southern (comedy writers), Sir William Blackstone, Edmund Burke, Sheridan, Dunning, (Lord Ashburton), Lord Chancellor Eldon, Lord Stowell, as a few among a multitude.